Linguistic ecology

In *Linguistic Ecology*, Peter Mühlhäusler examines the transformation of the Pacific language region under the impact of colonization, Westernization and modernization. By focusing on the linguistic and sociohistorical changes of the past 200 years, he brings a new dimension to the study of Pacific linguistics, which up until now has been dominated by questions of historical reconstruction and language typology.

In contrast to the traditional portrayal of linguistic change as a natural process, Mühlhäusler focuses on the cultural and historical forces which drive language change. Using the metaphor of language ecology to explain and describe the complex interplay between languages, speakers and social practice, Mühlhäusler looks at how language ecologies have functioned in the past to sustain language diversity, and at what happens when those ecologies are disrupted.

Whilst most of the examples used in the book are taken from the Pacific and Australian region, the insights derived from this area are shown to have global applications.

Peter Mühlhäusler is Foundation Professor of Linguistics at the University of Adelaide and Supernumerary Fellow of Linacre College, Oxford.

The politics of language

Series editors:
Tony Crowley, *University of Manchester*,
Talbot J. Taylor, *College of William and Mary, Williamsburg,
Virginia*

'In the lives of individuals and societies, language is a factor of greater importance than any other. For the study of language to remain solely the business of a handful of specialists would be a quite unacceptable state of affairs.'

Saussure

The Politics of Language Series covers the field of language and cultural theory and will publish radical and innovative texts in this area. In recent years the developments and advances in the study of language and cultural criticism have brought to the fore a new set of questions. The shift from purely formal, analytical approaches has created an interest in the role of language in the social, political and ideological realms and the series will seek to address these problems with a clear and informed approach. The intention is to gain recognition for the central role of language in individual and public life.

Linguistic ecology

Language change and linguistic
imperialism in the Pacific region

Peter Mühlhäusler

London and New York

First published 1996
by Routledge
11 New Fetter Lane, London EC4P 4EE

Simultaneously published in the USA and Canada
by Routledge
29 West 35th Street, New York, NY 10001

Typeset in Times by
Datix International Limited, Bungay, Suffolk
Printed and bound in Great Britain by
Redwood Books, Trowbridge, Wiltshire

British Library Cataloguing in Publication Data
A catalogue record for this book is available from the British
Library

Library of Congress Cataloguing in Publication Data
A catalogue record for this book has been requested

ISBN 0-415-05635-7
0-415-05636-5 (pbk)

The outcome of this process is that in the course of the past century, a few cases of linguistically imperialist peoples, who had established relatively monolingual but powerful states, have been promulgated as a model for the World.

(Guy 1989: 47)

To Jackie, Beverly and Tim

Contents

Illustrations

FIGURES

TABLES

Acknowledgements

I would like to acknowledge the generous help I received from the Australian Research Council in 1994 and 1995, which enabled me to complete this project.

Thanks are due to my wife, Jackie, for her editorial help with the book, and to the many friends and colleagues who have discussed the issue of linguistic imperialism with me: in particular, Stephen Wurm, George Grace, René Dirven, Martin Pütz, Tove Skutnabb-Kangas, Robert Phillipson, Rob Amery and the fellows of Linacre College, Oxford. I am particularly grateful for the many references and documents they have fed me over the years and the good advice they have given me.

1 The changing linguistic ecology of the Pacific region

> Ecology shows that a variety of forms is a prerequisite for biological survival. Monocultures are vulnerable and easily destroyed. Plurality in human ecology functions in the same way. One language in one nation does not bring about equity or harmony for the members or groups of that nation.
>
> (Pattanayak 1988: 380)

INTRODUCTION

This book is about linguistic heterogeneity, its decline and the costs of such decline and loss. It is also a book about the study of human languages and the inability of most practising linguists to understand what is happening around them, that their very object of study is disappearing at an alarming rate, that the transition from polylingualism to monolingualism is accelerating, and that the prospects of survival of traditional languages and forms of communication are very slim indeed. To be sure, there is a growing body of literature on topics such as language death, minority languages, language maintenance and standardization. However, in most instances documentation is available for the disappearance of European languages and dialects in Western Europe and North America rather than the loss of traditional non-European languages. Moreover, the approach in most studies is particularistic rather than ecological. The main thrust of this book is that an understanding of language death and ecological matters go hand in hand.

According to Haugen (1985), the ecology of language can be defined as 'interactions between any given language and its language ecology may be defined as the study of environment'. The term 'language ecology', like 'language family', is a metaphor derived from the study of living beings. The view that one can study languages as one studies the interrelationship of organisms with and within their environments presupposes a number of subsidiary metaphors and assumptions, most notably that languages can be regarded as entities, that they can be located in time and space and that the ecology of languages is at least in part different from that of their speakers. None of these assumptions is without problems and I shall deal with these in the course of this book. However, in the absence of my having immaculate perception or divine insights, my explanations of a new subject matter will of necessity involve use of metaphor. I have found that the ecological metaphor is particularly productive and a great deal more appealing than a systems metaphor. The latter suggests that we can hope for mechanical, albeit complex explanations or that it is indeed legitimate to study a self-contained system or language as part of a larger system. An ecological view, on the other hand, suggests that we can at best achieve partial and local explanations but that we can hope for understanding and empathy.[1]

The ecological metaphor in my view is action oriented. It shifts the attention from linguists being players of academic language games to becoming shop stewards for linguistic diversity, and to addressing moral economic and other 'non-linguistic' issues.[2] The area I shall be concerned with in this book is the Pacific, including Australia and, to a lesser extent, the Pacific rim. This choice is motivated by a number of considerations:

1   the availability of a number of studies on Africa, in particular, that of Calvet (1974) on 'glottophagie' and Phillipson's (1992) study on the impact of English teaching
2   my familiarity, through fieldwork and readings, with the area, its linguistic literature and the linguists practising in it
3   the concentration, in this area, of a very large number of small to very small languages
4   the diversity of ecological changes that have taken place there
5   the neglect of the Pacific languages in most internationally available treatments of language decline.

I trust that many of my findings for the Pacific region will have relevance elsewhere.

ARGUMENTS FOR AN ECOLOGICAL PERSPECTIVE

To understand the linguistic picture of the Pacific means to abandon attempts to view the many languages spoken on geographically isolated islands or inaccessible areas as test cases for language divergence in a family tree model or as an opportunity for linguists to be able to describe 'their' language. Rather, I would like to argue that the consideration of ecological factors is a prerequisite to any account of either the history or the grammatical structures of languages of an area. It is ecological factors which bring languages into being, define their boundaries and decide on their growth and survival.

The history of the term 'ecology of language' is a recent one. The paper bearing this title was read by Haugen in 1970, and subsequently published in a number of places, including a collection of his papers bearing the same title (Haugen 1972). Haugen rejects the narrow view that 'the referential world to which language provides an index' constitutes this environment; he states that 'the true environment of a language is the society that uses it as one of its codes' (Haugen 1972: 325). His subsequent discussions of 'environment' make it clear that Haugen sees more in the ecology of language than just sociology of language or the study of speech situations or contexts. The study of language ecology is a complex job which involves the collaboration of a number of disciplines, as is made explicit in the following catalogue of questions that Haugen lists as relevant to forming a picture of the ecology of a given language.

For any given 'language', then, we should want to have answers to the following ecological questions:

(1) What is its *classification* in relation to other languages?
(2) Who are its *users*? This is a question of *linguistic demography*, locating its users with respect to locale, class, religion or any other relevant grouping;
(3) What are its *domains* of use? This is a question of *sociolinguistics*, discovering whether its use is unrestricted or limited in specific ways;
(4) What *concurrent languages* are employed by its users? We may call this a problem of *dialinguistics, to identify the degree* of bilingualism present and the degree of overlap among the languages;
(5) What *internal varieties* does the language show? This is the task of a *dialectology* that will recognize not only regional, but also social and contactual dialects;
(6) What is the nature of its *written traditions*? This is the province of *philology*, the study of written texts and their relationship to speech;
(7) To what degree has its written form been *standardized*, i.e. unified and codified? This is the province of prescriptive linguistics, the traditional grammarians and lexicographers;
(8) What kind of *institutional support* has it won, either in government, education, or private organizations, either to

regulate its form or propagate it? We may call this study *glottopolitics*;

(9) What are the *attitudes* of its users towards the language, in terms of intimacy and status, leading to personal identification? We may call this the file of *ethnolinguistics*;

(10) Finally, we may wish to sum up its status in a *typology* of *ecological* classification, which will tell us something about where the language stands and where it is going in comparison with the other languages of the world.

(Haugen 1972: 336)

A small number of writers, such as Mackay (1980), or those in a collection edited by Enninger and Haynes (1984), have addressed such questions. Arguably, what work has been done has tended to be regarded as part of sociolinguistics and of quite marginal importance to the concern of linguistic theoreticians. The reasons for the failure of the 'ecology of language' to make a greater impact would seem to lie in Haugen's acceptance of a number of key notions held by the linguistic establishment which can be used as arguments to marginalize his varied proposals. Of particular importance would seem to be

1 his view that there can be such a thing as 'a given language'
2 his view that description, history, internal evolution, and so forth, are separate issues to be investigated by different groups of specialists.

These two points are of course interrelated, as it is precisely the reification of 'a language' that enables it to be studied in isolation, outside time, and allows one to distinguish between structure and use. Happily, Haugen avoids another problem which could have occurred with the greatest of ease given his metaphor of an ecology, that is, the problem of regarding languages as natural objects that inhabit the mixed human-made and natural ecology. For Haugen, the family tree metaphor of language can accommodate both the view of natural growth, and 'the development of standard languages' that are 'artefacts that result from either pruning or grafting the tree' by 'a special priesthood of taste and learning' (1972: 266). The possibility that many languages are indeed 'cultural artefacts' is thus acknowledged by Haugen. Let me return to my criticism of the term 'given language' now, which is rendered problematic on two accounts:

1 the lack of linguistic criteria for deciding in all instances on a determinate number of languages in a postulated ecology
2 the problem of separating languages from other forms of communication.

A small body of literature exists on aspects of the former problem in the Pacific area. That it got recognized at all is due mainly to the fact that comparative linguistics, in order to compare languages, need to know what these languages are. Grace (1993a; 1993b) has re-examined the notion of 'languages' as employed by mainstream linguists and demonstrated its insufficiency in cases other than a few mainstream standard national languages. The problem that language and dialect chains posed to their enterprise is discussed by Wurm and Laycock (1962) and Tryon (1979). The criteria appealed to by these investigators are, by and large, cognate counts and similar established procedures of historical linguistics. It is assumed that it is possible to identify languages (though this may in some cases involve additional criteria such as intelligibility or typological similarity). Languages, if not given, are seen to be at least discoverable. Thus, after discussing the problem of dialect and language chains, Tryon (1979: 13) identifies 105 languages for the New Hebrides (Vanuatu).

What most observers fail to realize is that the identification of languages and their subsequent naming is far from being an act of objective description, and it can constitute a very serious trespass on the linguistic ecology of an area. The very view that languages can be counted and named may be part of the disease that has affected the linguistic ecology of the Pacific and, as I shall show in subsequent chapters, an obstacle to attempts to reconstruct the linguistic past. Let me labour this point in more detail.

In many parts of the Pacific, including the New Guinea Highlands (Wurm and Laycock 1962), Micronesia (Bender 1971) and Vanuatu (Tryon 1979) we find long chains of interrelated dialects and languages with no clear internal boundaries. Thus, with regard to Micronesia, a group of very closely related languages are spoken all the way from Truk in the east to Tobi in the west. As observed by Bender (1971) 'there are some indications that it is possible to establish a chain of dialectal connections from one end to the other with all contiguous dialects being mutually intelligible'. However, the question as to how many distinct languages can be counted in the group remains difficult to answer, for those who regard it as a sensible question. Bender (1982: 46) concludes that 'altogether there has between 10 and 20 languages indigenous to the cultural-geographic area of Micronesia. The indeterminacy in numbers reflects the indeterminacy as to languages limit among certain of the nuclear languages.'

In spite of these difficulties, professional linguists have identified such languages as Sonsoralese, Ulithian, Satawalese, Puluwat, Namonuiti and Trukese, the latter having become the language *par excellence* in this chain, as it is the best described variety and spoken at the centre of economic and communicational activities. A similar situation is found in many other areas; the place where missionaries, administrators or linguists settle becomes the focus of development of linguistic systems of 'language' status. Arbitrary points on a linguistic continuum are made into discrete abstract entities called 'languages' whereas all other reference points on the same continuum, unless of course some important outsider settles there, become marginalized, dialectal deviations from the standard.

Thus brought into being, the languages identified are labelled and classified. On these processes Laycock and Voorhoeve (1971: 509) write, using Papuan languages to illustrate their point:

> A word must be said on nomenclature. Names of languages are cited in the form considered by the authors to be most appropriate, or – in some cases – in the form used in the literature cited; but it must not be assumed that these names have any more validity than as convenient labelling devices. It is rare for speakers of Papuan languages to have a name for themselves, in their own language, as a linguistic unit; rather, they will use a word which simply means 'the people' in an ethnocentric sense, and this term may frequently be much narrower in its extent than the linguistic group. This deficiency of nomenclature has been overcome by European observers in a number of ways:
>
> (1) by using a locality name, which may be the indigenous name of a village, island, mountain valley, or other geographical feature; or it may be an introduced topographical name ('Western Highlands language', 'Big Sepik language', etc.);
> (2) by using a group name given to the people by another tribal group;
> (3) by using a group name: clan, totem, dialect designation;
> (4) by using an arbitrary name based on the language's form for some common word. Those that have been frequently chosen are words for 'man' (Tuo, Moando, Nor, Pondo); 'water' (Ok); 'language' (Kam, Pay, Pila); 'no' (Olo, Elkei, Au); 'what' (gaing); and 'my child' (Natik, Barok).

The same type of naming is used for linguistic groupings. The introduction of such 'convenient labelling devices' has a couple of major side-effects, however. First, it upsets the pre-colonial equilibrium by assigning differential status to different forms of language, thus paving the way for social and economic differentials. Secondly, the misfit between the expatriate tree model of language relationships and observed linguistic reality becomes attenuated or disappears: reality has been made to conform to the model. The challenge that linguistically complex areas such as Melanesia or North America pose to comparative linguistics has yet to be successfully met. Finally, the existence of separate languages also reduces the significance of fusion and mixture with that of gradience. It enables Pacific linguists such as Biggs (1972) to state that:

> It will be agreed, I think, that anyone who speaks a language A, knows that he is speaking A, and not a different language B. Moreover, a bilingual can always distinguish between the two languages in which he is competent. . . . At any one time a speaker knows what language he is speaking. He can never claim to be speaking two languages at once, or a fusion of two languages.
>
> (Biggs 1972: 144)

One is led to conclude that the notion of 'a language' is one whose applicability to the Pacific region, and in fact most situations outside those found within modern European type nation-states, is extremely limited. No ecological study can afford to take languages as given. Nor can one expect that linguists will ever be in a position to provide determinate answers as to the number of languages found in any area. A second objection against the notion of 'a given language' is that it constitutes the acceptance of Chomsky's 'independency hypothesis'. This is not the place to go into details as to why such a view is to be discarded, as is the associated sociolinguistic view that a neat separation can be drawn between rules of a language and rules for the use of a language. Arguments in favour of an integrationist view to replace the 'western language myth' have been given by Harris in a number of places (e.g. 1979, 1980, 1990). Arguments in favour of an integrational position include the following.

> Whatever name we choose to give it, this is the principle that as human beings, whose humanity depends on social interaction, we do not inhabit a communicational space that Nature has already divided for us between language and the non-linguistic. Or, to put it another way, language is not an autonomous mode of communication, and languages are not autonomous systems of signs. Integration, in short, is not to be construed on the model of a jigsaw puzzle or construction kit, where we start with separate pieces, some linguistic, others non-linguistic and then fit them together. On the contrary, the jigsaw puzzle is a typically segregationalist model of how a language works.
>
> (Harris 1990: 203)

A thoroughgoing integrationalism would mean taking seriously the consequences of Sapir's observation that communication is based on structural correspondences between certain forms of behaviour in a situational context. It would mean recognizing that passing the salt when asked to do so is no less a linguistic act than uttering the words *Pass the salt, please* in order to get it. Both are complementary manifestations of linguistic knowledge, of proficiency in a language-game, and we unhesitatingly treat them so in the communication situations of everyday life. Only a blind acceptance of the theoretical dogma which equates language with spoken language and thus induces the mistake of identifying vocalization as the mark of the linguistic act *par excellence* will prevent us from recognizing that truth. To make that mistake is on a par with believing that you are not running except during the seconds when your feet touch the ground and only playing tennis at the moments when your racquet hits the ball.

(Harris 1990: 207–8)

For the purposes of an ecological approach to language, the integrationist point is a particularly suitable one, as it is capable of highlighting the complex interdependence between forms of human communication and the multitude of environmental factors. In doing this it leads to understanding of a very complex phenomenon, rather than descriptions of alleged models of arbitrarily isolated aspects of it. A less radical notion of integration, one which leaves open the possibility of 'given languages', is that associated with the work of C. J. N. Bailey. One of Bailey's principal contributions to linguistic theory is that social, stylistic and geographical variation are in fact reflexes of change over time and that a linguistic theory constructed around the notion of change over time can account for the facts of historical linguistics, sociolinguistics, descriptive linguistics, dialectology and stylistics in a uniform manner. His theory thus allows us to integrate the recognized branches of diachronic and synchronic or a-temporal theory, but at the same time further integration with pragmatics, situational or environmental factors is not encouraged. However, the notion that variation and change is ordered and that time needs to be integrated into explanations of human linguistic behaviour is consonant with the general thrust of my arguments.

LINGUISTIC DIVERSITY

In adopting an integrationist and ecological perspective, our focus will shift from the consideration of countable languages to that of human communication and from the question of what is happening to languages to what processes bring languages into being and how the nature of these processes affect a linguistic ecology. Leaving aside technical considerations of dialect, language chaining, communalect, boundaries and overlap, it remains clear that the number of ways that the inhabitants of the Pacific have communicated with each other is a very large one. Available accounts speak of up to 4,000 languages, though human awareness as to the number of and interest in these different languages of the Pacific or indeed the world is surprisingly recent. We are looking at a tradition of barely 300 years, a tradition which significantly coincides with the colonial expansion of modern European nation-states. Forerunners were, as pointed out by Max Müller (1875: 143ff.), 'Christian missionaries who heeded the command "go into all the world and preach the gospel to every creature".'

Theseo Ambrosia, in 1539, contains the Lord's Prayer in fourteen languages whilst Perion (1554) lists seventy-two languages, a number which allegedly sprang from the Tower of Babel (see Müller 1875). Mageserius gives the Lord's Prayer in fifty languages in 1593. The view that Hebrew was the beginning of all human speech, including that of the New World, continued to be widely held, a view which prevented scholars from considering the possibility of greater diversity and in some instances prompted them to give rather unhelpful advice, such as advising Columbus to take a Hebrew interpreter into the New World.

The first serious collection of a large number of the world's languages is said to have been undertaken by Leibniz who, in his dissertation on the origins of nations (1710), advocates the systematic collection of 'the modern languages which are within our reach' (Leibniz 1713; see also Aarsleff 1982: 99). He was helped in this enterprise by missionaries, ambassadors, and the Czar, Peter the Great.

Leibniz was not to complete his enterprise. Another major attempt at listing the world's languages is that of the Spanish Jesuit Hervas (1735–1809) who had worked in South America and whose catalogue of languages was published in 1800 in six volumes containing, among other things, forty sketch grammars by the author. Meanwhile, in Russia, Katarina the Great devoted herself to the project of an inventory of the world's languages, many from the newly conquered areas of Siberia, others sent to her by ambassadors, monarchs and politicians from around the globe. Müller reports that (1875: 160) the first volume of the Imperial Dictionary appeared in 1787, containing a list of 285 words translated into 51 European and 149 Asiatic languages.

Knowledge of the linguistic diversity of the Pacific area was similarly slow to emerge. It is only since the 1960s that it has become known that up to 4,000 languages are spoken in the region, most of them in Melanesia where 2 million people speak one-quarter of the world's languages, according to Laycock (1969). Attempted explanations and value judgements regarding the linguistic diversity of the area are numerous. The explanations wholly fall into two main categories:

1 evolutionary
2 psychological/ethnographic.

As regards evolutionary arguments, I share Steiner's (1975) scepticism of evolutionary arguments.

> Few modern linguists, with the exception of Swadesh and Pei, have shown the curiosity which this situation ought to arouse. Where an answer is given at all, it is put in casually evolutionary terms: there are many different tongues because, over long stretches of time, societies and cultures split apart and, through accretion of particular experience, evolved their own local speech habits. The facile nature of such an explanation is worrying: it fails to engage precisely those central and philosophical and logical dilemmas which spring from the admitted uniformities of human mental structures and from the economically and historically negative, often drastically damaging role of linguistic isolation. Turn the argument around: let reasons be given why the adoption by the human race of a single language or a small number of related languages would have been natural and beneficial. It appears at once that post hoc justifications for the facts as we know them are wholly unconvincing. The problem lies deeper.
>
> (Steiner 1975: 56)

The insufficiency of evolutionary explanations, particularly when combined with the view that the evolutionary process was a divergent one, and that the formulae provided by glottochronology for the time depths of splits, is not difficult to demonstrate.[3] The exclusion of qualitative considerations further detracts from the evolutionary perspective. No writer on this topic has suggested that the languages of the Pacific have multiplied because of structural improvements or functional adaptive considerations or died out because of their absence. On the contrary, most present-day Pacific linguists are insistent that there are no qualitative differences between the languages of the region.

The concept of evolution can be analysed as involving two major but independent components. The first of these, the notion of transformation of kinds, is valid but was well established in linguistics prior to Darwin. The second component, that of progress or advance, is not valid in the instance of language and its application whether under the flag of Darwinism or under other influence has led to no positive results.

The views of the latter-day evolutionists were not shared in days past. The Reverend Farrar (1899) provides the following list containing remarks on languages spoken outside Europe. Farrar asks:

> What shall we say, for instance, of the tallow-coloured Bosjesman, who lives for the most part on beetles, worms, and pismires, and is glad enough to squabble with the hyena for the putrid carcass of the buffalo or the antelope? Of the leather-skinned Hottentot, 'whose hair grows in short tufts, like a worn-down shoe brush, with spaces of bare scalp between' and who is described as a creature 'with passions, feelings, and appetites as the only principles of his constitution'? Of the Yamparico, 'who speaks a sort of gibberish like the growling of a dog', and who 'lives on roots, crickets and several but-like insects of different species'? Of the aborigines of Victoria, among whom newborn babes are killed and eaten by their parents and brothers and who have no numerals beyond three? Of the Puris of Brazil, who have to eke out their scanty language by a large use of signs, and who have no words for even such simple conceptions as 'tomorrow', and 'yesterday'? Of the naked, houseless, mischievous, vindictive Andamaner, with a skull hung ornamentally round his neck? Of the Fuegians, 'whose language is an inarticulate clucking', and who kill and eat their old women before their dogs, because, as a Fuegian boy naively and candidly expressed it, 'Doggies catch otters, old women no'? Of the Banaks, who wear lumps of fat meat, artistically suspended in the cartilage of the nose? Of the negroes of New Guinea, who were seen springing from branch to branch of the trees like monkeys, gesticulating, screaming and laughing? Of the Alforese of Ceram, who live in trees, 'each family in a state of perpetual hostility with all around'? Of the forest tribes of Malacca, who lisp their words, 'whose sound is like the noise of birds'? Of the wild people of Borneo, whom the Dyaks hunt as if they were monkeys?

> (Farrar 1899: 36)

Writing around the same time, Max Müller (1875: 11) feels inclined to take seriously theories 'which would make Polynesian the primitive language of mankind'. Similar sentiments were rife among the white administrators, missionaries and residents of the area, as will be shown in later chapters. Since the mid-1970s, evolutionary arguments have been revived somewhat, no doubt under the impact of sophisticated, typological language studies, for as Greenberg (1971: 16) rightly points out, 'any attempt to show the evolutionary advance in language development must rest on a typological basis'. Some of the more interesting efforts are those by Bichakjian (1988) and Markey (1987).

One of the principal problems of evolutionary argumentation has been, at least in the view of some commentators, that the outcome of evolution has been a seemingly dysfunctional proliferation of species, 'destructive prodigality' in Steiner's words (1975: 56). Steiner indeed denies that this diversification can be linked to the adaptive process of making human languages suited to an increasingly larger number of ecological niches.

> The Darwinian parallel also breaks down on the crucial point of large numbers. The multiplicity of fauna and flora does not represent randomness or waste. It is an immediate factor of the dynamics of evolutionary breeding, cross-fertilization, and competitive selection which Darwin set out. Given the range of ecological possibilities, the multiplication of species is, quite conceivably, economical. No language is demonstrably adaptive in this sense. None is concordant with any particular geophysical environment. With the simple addition of neologisms and borrowed words, any language can be used fairly efficiently anywhere; Eskimo syntax is appropriate to the Sahara. Far from being economic and demonstrably advantageous, the immense number and variety of human idioms, together with the fact of mutual incomprehensibility, is a powerful obstacle to the material and social progress of the species.
>
> (Steiner 1975: 56)

Steiner's views are echoed in numerous writings about linguistic diversity in the Pacific given throughout this book. Similarly Schuchardt (1928: 370) calls the multitude of human languages 'ein Übel' – a curse. That diversity was a relic of a more primitive way of thinking and thus could not, even in principle, be of any interest to Westerners, is a frequently encountered claim.

None of the languages of the Pacific area was held in greater contempt than those of Tasmania. Consider the following comment by Milligan (1859) addressing the general theme of language as an index of evolution or cultural progress.

> The language of a people, whether it be possessed of a copious or sparse vocabulary – whether it consist of a plain collocation of a few simple and arbitrary sounds, or be characterised by elaborate inflexions and a complex arrangement of words of analogical

import – ought to be accepted, one would say, as the index of the degree of mental culture and social and intellectual progress attained by those who make use of it, and find it sufficient for the expression of their various thoughts, feelings, and desires. A glance at the vocabulary of aboriginal dialects of Tasmania, and at the condition of aborigines themselves, will perhaps be thought to lend confirmation to the opinion.

The habit of gesticulation and the use of signs to eke out the meaning of monosyllabic expressions, and to give force, precision, and character to vocal sounds, exerted a further modifying effect, producing, as it did, carelessness and laxity of articulation, and in the application and pronunciation of words.

(Milligan 1859: 278–9)

Thus, few visitors to the area of New Guinea failed to comment adversely on the linguistic diversity of this island. Representative quotations are the following.

New Guinea is the country of many languages. Its linguistic diversity is a consequence of its ethnic disunion. . . . As these small isolated tribal languages can have no future in either church or state, our mission has worked for decades to unite them into a larger entity.

(Pilhofer 1933: 13, my translation)

Interpretation is among one of the greatest bugbears of the district officer. New Guinea is notoriously a Babel, and to combat this appalling multiplicity of tongues – I have found three distinct languages within a two-mile radius of a station – the Administration has wisely encouraged the use of English among the natives. . .

(Beaver 1920: 38)

The language difficulty is one of the most serious obstacles to our work. Roughly speaking, there are two distinct languages on the north-east coast of New Guinea: a Melanesian language . . . and a Papuan language. . . . Of both of these, but especially the Melanesian, there are many dialects. The structure of the language remains firmly fixed, but the vocabulary alters every few miles along the coast and pronunciation varies with it, so that he who knows one dialect will find that spoken a few miles from home unintelligible, nor will he be understood.

(Revd H. Newton, Bishop of New Guinea, in White 1929: 48)

The assessment of the situation varies from a punishment to that of a self-inflicted injury, a view expressed by Höltker (1945).

The natives of New Guinea have not been able to make any of their native idioms a *lingua franca* of importance. A primitive feeling of superiority, self-sufficiency, a predilection for tribal separatism, lack of community spirit, tribal warfare and so on prevented the development of a means of intercommunication.

(Höltker 1945: 44, my translation)

The metaphor of Babel continues to haunt our profession. Chapter 12 of Fromkin and Rodman's widely used *Introduction to Language* (1988) significantly bears the title 'The Tower of Babel: Languages of the World'. It is only in the 1990s that it began to be realized that the 'language problem of the region' was in fact an imported one, the problem of outsiders of adapting to the complex linguistic ecology of the area, and that the great diversity of languages was an asset rather than a liability. A turning point in the history of value judgements on the Pacific area are the writings of Sankoff (1977), Grace (1975) and Laycock (1981). The last-named author pointed out that diversity may be a deliberate choice. Speaking of the linguistic situation in Melanesia he observed:

The causes of this linguistic differentiation lie in the Melanesian attitudes to language. It would not be good if we all talked the same; we like to know where people came from. In other words, linguistic diversity is perpetuated as a badge of identification. Language is used to maintain social groupings at a small and meaningful level.

(Laycock 1981: 34)

Laycock's observations match those of LePage and Tabouret-Keller (1985) who focus on the acts of identity that bring social contracts called 'languages' into being. There is no reason that such social constructs need to cater for a certain standard number of speakers. In an egalitarian situation, such as that prevailing in the South-West Pacific, the size of communication communities needs to be small, as pointed out by Laycock:

Language in Melanesia is, in its very diversity, being used constructively, to maintain social groupings at a small and manageable level – and, conversely, to keep other groups at a distance. Someone who speaks exactly as you do may or may not be a friend; but someone who speaks differently is always automatically an outsider, no matter how close the degree of contact.

(Laycock 1981: 35)

The insufficiency of traditional views of linguistic diversity is further demonstrated when one differentiates between languages as instruments of social identification and intra-group communication on the one hand, and instruments for communication with outsiders on the other. What distinguishes, say, the Melanesian language situation from that found in modern European nation-states is not just the number and size of individual languages, but the very large extent of bilingualism and multilingualism, a factor largely ignored by linguists as this phenomenon was of only slight interest to missionaries and administrators, and as linguists concentrated on the grammar of individual languages rather than on the aspects of communication. Reliable information dating back to earlier times is very hard to come by. For New Guinea, in parts of which multilingualism was probably endemic, only a few systematic studies of multilingualism or code switching had been made by 1960 and the few that did exist are concerned primarily with the status of Tok Pisin, a variety of Melanesian Pidgin English, versus English and/or local vernaculars (e.g. Bateson 1944; Reed 1943). Salisbury (1962) expresses surprise at the fact that the presence of bi- and multilingualism has gone virtually unnoted:

> Not being a linguist I assumed that such observations were common in the linguistic literature, as many anthropologists have described similar situations to me in conversation. . . . Recent conversations with linguists have indicated that such situations have, in fact, been rarely described.
>
> (Salisbury 1962: 1)

Laycock (1969: 1) points out that phenomena such as subcodes had received very little attention and that, furthermore, 'reports of such phenomena by anthropologists and missionaries are often linguistically naive'.

The first proposal for a systematic study of sociolinguistic phenomena, and in particular code switching, comes from Taylor (1968). His arguments are aimed at the role of sociolinguistic knowledge in providing a practical means of solving certain educational and literacy matters. Taking the position of certain missions as an example, Taylor remarks:

> They face decisions not only about which languages to do such work in, but also which dialect to prefer, a choice to be based on social as well as purely linguistic factors. Thus the dialect with the greatest number of speakers may not have the prestige of the dialect spoken around the patrol post or mission station.
>
> (Taylor 1968: 45)

Taylor illustrates his point with a concise study of multilingualism and code switching in the village of Tubuseria, situated about twenty miles east of Port Moresby. His exploratory study clearly illustrates that the choice of the main available codes of Motu, Hiri Motu and English is determined by social factors, and that the choice of a certain code for a certain context, in his example the use of English as a medium of instruction, can in turn have repercussions on the society.

Switching from one system of semantactic rules to another is often preceded by a period of intensive lexical switching and lexical borrowing. This phenomenon has been described by several authors, including Laycock (1966), who deals with Tok Pisin borrowings in Abelam, and Hans Fischer (1962), who deals with the same question in north-east New Guinea. Though lacking in theoretical sophistication, Fischer's article presents a wealth of data and observations on vocabulary borrowing.

Few studies have been made about special subcodes. However, both Aufinger (1948–9) and Laycock (1969) have made a substantive contribution to this topic. While Aufinger concentrates on secret registers of vernaculars and Tok Pisin on some islands in the Madang areas, Laycock investigates the linguistic structures of various subcodes of Buin, in particular play and avoidance sublanguages.

A problem with these studies is that, in most instances, they refer to a post-contract situation where Tok Pisin, Hiri Motu and other intrusive languages have already changed the traditional, more stable multilingualism towards a transitional form of bilingualism. The experts are not agreed as to the extent of bi- and multilingualism in pre-colonial times. Thus whereas Laycock (1966: 44) argues that multilingualism is a recent phenomenon, Sankoff (1977) postulates extensive multilingualism in pre-European times. We shall return to this issue at a later stage.

An important new consideration was introduced into the debate by Thurston (1982, 1987) in his investigations into the language situation in North Western New Britain. Thurston distinguishes between exoteric and esoteric languages (Thurston 1987: 96–7).[4] Speakers of complex and small esoteric languages had in their communicative repertoire one or more exoteric languages, and their ability to communicate with outsiders was not affected. Whether or not the linguistic situation was one that provided adequate possibilities for intercommunication or not was of course of little interest to the first Europeans that arrived on the scene. Neither esoteric or exoteric languages were intelligible to them. In many cases their subsequent task was not made easier by their insisting on penetrating into the perceived true (esoteric) languages rather than being content with acquiring a more widely used exoteric one.

The opinion that linguistic diversity may be a very positive phenomenon did not automatically coincide with the decline of such diversity
and even now is not a widely accepted view. Labov (1972), however,
remarked on the desirability of variability in the big towns of North
America:

> Most linguists who work with small, diverse groups must recognize
> in themselves a natural prejudice in favour of the survival of their
> subjects. The anthropological or comparative linguist will in-
> tuitively fight for the existence of his group, and he resists the
> notion that the cost of bilingualism is too great to be borne. He
> refuses to weigh the value of a language or a dialect in terms of its
> attractiveness to printers, the size of its literary output, or how well
> it prepares children to fit into a European school system. Linguists
> must recognize that they are interested parties in this argument.
>
> With this precaution, I am inclined to believe that the develop-
> ment of linguistic differences has positive value in human cultural
> evolution – and that cultural pluralism may even be a necessary
> element in the human extension of biological evolution.
>
> (Labov 1972: 324)

An even stronger plea was made by Bechert (1990) to a group of
distinguished linguists:

> That the world-wide disappearance of animal and plant species is a
> topic for both the public and specialist biologists, is a major reason
> why things are done. Why isn't the disappearance of languages a
> topic for a similar public debate!
>
> (Bechert 1990: 2350; my translation)

Much of what is now regarded with concern is little different from the
warning given by American linguists such as Boas, Sapir and their
followers around the turn of the century, and what numerous philosophers, historians and others have remarked on the effects of Westernization (e.g. Heidegger 1986: 103).

Some while ago I explored the effects of Pacific languages in two
articles (Mühlhäusler 1987a, 1992) and the numerous responses I have
received prompt me to elaborate my arguments in this book. I repeat,
my concern is with the ever-increasing changes in the ecology of the
languages of the Pacific. In my view these changes are very different
in quality and order of magnitude from those which occurred in the
area prior to European penetration and colonization. The loss of
structural and semantic diversity is only one of the less desirable
outcomes of this process. Equally disturbing is the loss of traditional
modes of intercultural communication and the increasing concentration

of linguistic, economic and political power in the hands of a few. By approaching the issue from an ecological perspective, a deliberate link has been established with arguments concerning the loss of biological diversity and environmental issues. At the same time an ecological metaphor will draw attention to the similarities of the moral issues involved in bio-engineering and language engineering, nature protection and culture protection, and so forth. Perhaps the most important aspect of this argument is that we are now facing a situation in both nature and language which requires tough decisions and actions. Ignorance and *laissez-faire* policies will do little to stem the tide let loose by linguistic imperialism.

The concept of linguistic imperialism is introduced in an attempt to dispel the myth that the loss of linguistic diversity is a natural process (a view found throughout the relevant literature). In its place, I would like to propose that we are dealing with a historical 'accident' brought about by deliberate human agency.

LINGUISTIC IMPERIALISM

That the consequences of such agency were not necessarily intended but that, rather, the large scale collapse of linguistic ecology has involved many invisible hand processes does not diminish the extent of the tragedy (see Keller (1990) for the applicability of this notion to language change and Kulick (1993) for a highly informative micro-study from the New Guinea region). We are far from understanding linguistic diversity and, though I hope to provide glimpses of insights throughout this book, my main theme is not diversity in itself, but the processes which have eroded it over the last 200 years or so under the impact of the large European empires. Imperialism in its most general meaning is the imposition of a single set of economic, political or cultural norms by a powerful outside group. It is most clearly linked to European colonial expansion, but there are numerous other examples, such as the Inca Empire (Hardman de Bautista 1985), the Chinese Empire and the Mongolian Expansion under Genghis Khan. This last case is of particular importance as it illustrates the complete circle from rise to fall of an empire and its language (see Brosnahan 1963), in particular the rapid disappearance of the Turkish language as soon as the instrumental reason to use it was gone.

The original meaning of imperialism as 'a political system in which colonies are governed from an imperial centre' (R. Williams 1983: 159) has experienced a number of re-definitions and refinements and the generic term imperialism has been supplemented by subordinate terms such as economic imperialism,[5] and more recently ecological imperialism (Crosby 1986) and linguistic imperialism (the first book bearing this title being Phillipson 1992).

Crosby's account of the displacement and replacement of native peoples in many parts of the world (particularly Neo-Europes such as the USA, Australia, New Zealand) supplements accounts of imperialist policies and military conquest with a biological argument. As summarized on the inside front cover of his book:

> By focusing on the ecological side of European expansion, Crosby shows how the Europeans were able to take over temperate lands because of the rapid and almost automatic triumph of the plants, animals, and germs they brought with them. European organisms had certain decisive advantages over their New World and Australasian counterparts; Europeans and their descendants shared in these advantages. As a result, in the centuries after Columbus's voyages, the proportion of Europeans and their descendants to the rest of the human species increased, and these imperialists became proprietors of perhaps the most important agricultural lands in the world.
>
> (Crosby 1986)

The effect of such biological imperialism is habitat destruction. As I shall demonstrate in my discussion of linguistic diversity, habitat destruction is the main cause of its decline as well. In a survey on the survival changes of Micronesian languages (Bender and Rehg 1991), for instance, the language most likely to disappear was identified as Chamorro which currently has by far the largest number of speakers of any Micronesian language and, moreover, at present 'enjoys' the status of an official language. A detailed account of the fall of Chamorro is given below. Of the various accounts of linguistic imperialism, Gilliam's (1986: 4) characterization of the present-day patterns of communication in the Pacific, as 'a situation in which virtually all communication – spoken, written, heard and seen – is controlled by external power' supplements Phillipson's (1992) main general definition:

> A working definition of *English linguistic imperialism* is that *the dominance of English is asserted and maintained by the establishment and continuous reconstitution of structural and cultural inequalities between English and other languages.* Here *structural* refers broadly to material properties (for example, institutions, financial allocations) and *cultural* to immaterial or ideological properties (for example, attitudes, pedagogic principles). English linguistic imperialism is one example of *linguicism*, which is defined as 'ideologies, structures, and practices which are used to legitimate, effectuate,

and reproduce an unequal division of power and resources (both material and immaterial) between groups which are defined on the basis of language.

(Phillipson 1992: 47)

This definition needs to be widened to include imperial languages other than English, in particular, 'killer languages', a term invented by Anne Pakir (1991), such as Mandarin, Spanish, French and Indonesian. The definition also lacks the historical dimension which explains how the present-day situation came into being. The origin of such killer languages can be traced back to the development of European public schools, in particular in France, where the idea of central government was shaped by the insistence on having one language spoken by everyone in the nation. It is this idea, which was strongly supported by the European enlightenment and the French revolution and their imitators, which has dominated the social history of the world's languages ever since. The justifications for the dominance by these languages are variably given as political (how else could a nation be held together), economic (the cost of diversity) and moral (people need languages free from superstition and local antagonisms), but can all be accommodated under the common denominator of 'development'.

What distinguishes the languages mentioned from the vast majority of other languages is their being developed and modernized. This means, in the technical sense, empowered by language planners to be capable of expressing

1 up-to-date concepts in all areas of technology and society
2 being fully intertranslatable with a functional language such as English or French.

The formal diversity that distinguishes French and English from Indonesian or Tagalog thus turns out to conceal almost total conceptual overlap.

Imperialism, like many abstract norms, under-emphasizes activity, temporality and situatedness and other contextual factors. In this book, I shall try and unpack this reified expression by commenting on the development of 'imperializing' in the Pacific region.

Linguistic imperialism, like other ideologies, has its own language. The discourses that support it, as already pointed out, are economic, moral, political and scientific (an example of the latter being the case, the discourse of 'scientific' linguistics). Linguists, for a long time, have argued for the ideological neutrality of their own position, a strategy which has neither benefited their profession nor the speakers of the numerous languages that have been their subject matter. A principal aim of this book is to expose the unsoundness of such an attitude and to make future generations of Pacific and Australian linguists aware of their responsibility to the linguistic ecology of the region.

2 Language ecology in pre-European days

> Nothing ... authorizes us to project the picture which emerges very far back into the Melanesian past.
>
> (Lyons 1986: 13)

INTRODUCTION

Let me begin with a disclaimer. I cannot hope to offer an exhaustive empirical study of the very complex topic of this chapter. Instead, I shall try to make sense of a rather motley, often unreliable or patchy butterfly collection of evidence. My attempts to make sense will take place against the background of ecological questions such as:

1 What were salient properties of the linguistic ecologies of Australia and the Pacific area?
2 What factors promoted the well-being of traditional language ecologies?
3 What properties made traditional language ecologies vulnerable?
4 What were the advantages and drawbacks of the characteristic linguistic diversity of the area?

Not only will the answers to such questions help reconstruct the sociolinguistic past of the area, thereby providing urgently needed constraints or reconstructions of the past based solely on structural linguistic evidence, but also such knowledge is an indispensable part of any attempt to preserve and strengthen or reconstitute the remaining traditional languages.

Before attempting to isolate the salient properties of the 'prehistorical' linguistic picture, it would seem useful to comment on past attempts to learn about the language and culture of the Pacific region. Knowing how reliable past information might be is important in the absence of the applicability of the uniformitarian method and the scarcity of in-depth accounts of languages that have been minimally affected by recent developments. Studies such as those of the previously uncontacted Eipos (Heeschen and Schievenhövel 1987) are rare exceptions and are not necessarily easy to reconstruct from.

The history of European contacts with the Pacific can be divided very roughly into the following phases:

1500–1750	Spanish trade and exploitation
1750–1830	Scientific and anthropological discovery
1830–1880	Modern economic exploitation (whaling, sandalwood, bêche-de-mer, blackbirding)
1880–1975	Colonial contact.

Such idealized dates hide the fact that the time depth for contact was considerably shorter in areas such as Melanesia and that metropolitan involvement in the area was governed by a complex array of economic, religious and political facts throughout this period. Nevertheless, there would seem to be some relevance of our classification to the job of ascertaining conditions in pre-colonial days.

The period from 1500 to 1750 was characterized by the almost complete lack of scholarly interest in the area. Its people and natural resources were of interest only in as much as they lent themselves to direct economic exploitation.

The period 1750–1830, on the other hand, is one of very intense European interest in almost any aspect of life, including customs and language. Influenced by the ideas of the European enlightenment, anthropologists, philosophers and scientists attempted to study the principles of the development of human reason and cultures. Interest in the social life of the Pacific (particularly Polynesia) dominated this period. Numerous documents giving information about the linguistic ecology of the time are in existence. A common theme in these is the vulnerability and the rapid changes following European contacts.

Thus, with regard to the Tahitian language, the missionary John M. Orsmond of the London Missionary Society remarked in 1837 that

> the content of the aboriginal language had changed in the twenty years he had resided in Tahiti, largely because of the increased influence of English-speaking foreigners. Orsmond also believed that a standardized reference was needed before the aboriginal character of Tahitian was lost.
>
> (Tagupa 1979: 145)

Rensch (1991) provides a detailed account of the intense interest in the language of the noble savages of Tahiti during this period, an interest that was followed by an almost equally pronounced neglect of matters linguistic and cultural.

The period between 1830 and 1880 was one of extensive economic exploitation and large-scale destruction of the natural resources of the area. These resources were mined rather than harvested. The first through whaling (particularly 1820–60), then sandalwood followed by bêche-de-mer and, more locally, pearling.

The rate of exploitation of these resources was such that natural replacement did not occur. Sandalwood was logged to such an extent, first in Hawaii then in Fiji, that the native forests simply disappeared. The void created by upsetting the indigenous ecology was soon filled by introduced weeds and cultivated plants. For example, Crosby (1986: 162) reports that by 1803 the Europeans had brought 100 species of plants to New South Wales intentionally and many more unintentionally. As a consequence, traditional modes of living could no longer be sustained. Consider, for instance, the case of New Caledonia: here, in addition to sugar plantations erected on land formerly occupied and cultivated by Kanaks, the expatriate cattle industry had the greatest impact on the indigenous ecology. The first herd of cattle (1,000) was put out to grazing in 1859. 'By 1878, there were 80,000 head in New Caledonia and they did untold damage to native plantations' (Lyons 1986: 49). The animals roamed at will in unfenced pastures, and their destructive impact was followed by substantial land grants to whites (up to 40,000 hectares) and the creation of tribal reserves. The Kanaks, having been pushed into the interior hills, became dependent on handouts from the Europeans.[1] The example of New Caledonia illustrates the role of habitat destruction in the changing language ecology of the Pacific.

Next to the setting up of pastoral properties and plantations (particularly in the larger islands of the Pacific), the period 1830 to 1880 featured two additional activities that were to have a dramatic effect on the linguistic ecology of the area:

1 the establishment of the missions
2 the growth of permanent expatriate and mixed communities.

As regards the linguistic documentation of this area, we find that the dominance of economic considerations together with the fact that many settlers, sailors and traders were near illiterate made for a patchy and rather unreliable record. Much better information can be gleaned from mission documents. However, in contrast to the earlier period where attempts were made to learn from the cultures indigenous to the area, mission efforts were often geared at obliterating or changing them. Reliable, objective information can thus not be expected.

The last period to be considered here, the colonial period from about 1880 to 1975, is one that can be dealt with only in very rough outlines and only for selected areas, though its effects have been more far reaching and permanent than those of the previous periods. The colonial carving up and penetration began with the white settlement colonies (Hawaii, New Zealand, Australia and New Caledonia), the smaller islands of Polynesia and the coastal areas of Melanesia, to reach the interior of the larger islands of Melanesia only a few years ago. Documentation of the linguistic ecology of this area is generally extensive although of very mixed quality. Of particular importance for the purposes of this book are the many explicit statements, policies, acts of planning and interferences that have occurred. Of particular relevance for the question addressed in this chapter is the linguistic and anthropological research carried out in the 1960s and 1970s in opened up areas of Melanesia. A constant problem with such linguistic and anthropological studies is that the tools employed by Western researchers often prejudge the outcome of their research and that the range of research questions asked was highly restricted and typically not geared towards wider questions of language ecology.

ON RECONSTRUCTING THE PAST

Typically, the reconstruction of the linguistic prehistory of the Pacific and Australia has tended to be dominated by the historical-comparative approach developed for the Indo-European languages in the nineteenth century. For some of the more problematic areas (e.g. Melanesia) explanations which favoured pidginization and convergence over the establishment divergence model have, at times, been proposed. On the whole, however, the family tree model has remained central to most arguments about linguistic prehistory. Sapir (1966) argued, from the point of view of American Indian languages:

The methods developed by the Indo-Europeanists have been applied with marked success to other groups of languages. It is abundantly clear that they apply just as rigorously to the unwritten primitive languages of Africa and America as to the better known forms of speech of the more sophisticated peoples. It is probably in the languages of these more cultured peoples that the fundamental regularity of linguistic processes has been most often crossed by the operation of such conflicting tendencies as borrowing from other languages, dialectic blending, and social differentiations of speech.

The more we devote ourselves to the comparative study of the languages of a primitive linguistic stock, the more clearly we realize that phonetic law and analogical leveling are the only satisfactory key to the unravelling of the development of dialects and languages from a common base.

(Sapir 1966: 66–7)

This has also tended to be accepted for those of Australia and the Pacific. As I shall address Pacific linguistics as a discipline in the appendix to this book, I shall mention here only a few of the implications of this process:

1 Questions of phonology and sentence-grammar have dominated the field to the virtual exclusion of language use.
2 Linguistic description has centred on those aspects of grammar that appeared most suited to the job of linguistic comparison (pronoun systems, word order over morphology).
3 Monostylism, rather than polystylism or multilingualism, has been the dominant theme.
4 'All or none' phenomena have been preferred over gradient ones.

Further characterizations of such practices and problems they have caused are highlighted in Thurston (1987: 35ff.). As a consequence, existing findings are not of great relevance to an ecological view of language.

Additional difficulties in reconstructing the linguistic past include the great time depth (up to 50,000 years for Papua New Guinea and Australia), incomplete and uneven coverage of the area and the virtual absence of certain information.[2] Ecological reconstruction thus cannot hope to achieve the same neat results that have been presented to us by the adherents of the family tree model. To be true, we have eye-witness accounts of early explorers and observers, but these in most instances are incomplete, superficial and unreliable and, moreover, need to be interpreted. As regards concrete evidence, we are thus forced to extrapolate from a small body of incomplete observations.

Our best bet would seem to be to develop methods of reconstructing those aspects of language structure and language use that conventional historical grammarians have not been able to reconstruct, in particular language contacts, pidginization, convergent processes of all sorts and, with the help of disciplines other than linguistics, aspects of past cultural ecologies (Mühlhäusler 1987c). I share Sutton's view (1980: 89–90) that 'it is unlikely that any reasonable model of linguistic change can be developed for Australia without detailed studies of the traditional role of language in Aboriginal social structuring and the functioning of communication networks'. Indeed, this would seem to be applicable to linguistic reconstruction anywhere.

In addition, while not wishing to subscribe to the view that Pacific linguistics and its concern for the origin of the languages of the area is a logical problem (however much the funding bodies would like it to be precisely that), I nevertheless feel that some aspects of our problem are best served by logical analysis.

Finally, making progress in exploring the unknown in all disciplines involves the appeal to new heuristic metaphors. This, it would seem, is suggested by Grace (1981) in his discussion of the 'aberrant' (from the point of view of comparative linguistics) Melanesian languages of New Caledonia:

> There, then, is the explanation which I propose for the aberrancy so often encountered in Melanesia. Where does it leave us? First, it is obvious that the picture which I have drawn is a very tentative one. I hope it will attract discussion from those who are in a position to judge where it is valid and where mistaken and that they will lead us to a more accurate conception. Second, to the extent that it is valid, it suggests that we might attempt to develop a second, complementary, model of linguistic diachrony – one in which a community of languages is seen as the entity undergoing change. Finally, it suggests that for the long run we should be looking for a new metaphor – one which does not require us to see diachrony in terms of internal changes in structured entities which maintain their identity over time. But that may take time.
>
> (Grace 1981: 267)

My own suggestions for such new metaphors are twofold: a less radical revision which continues to utilize the idea of both family trees and families, and a more radical one which emphasizes the interrelations between languages and the process of communication and de-emphasizes the role of individual linguistic systems. Regarding the former, family trees need to be extended to cater for convergent development and interbreeding between members of different as well as the same generations. Relatedness between different languages of a family can be captured best by using a Wittgensteinian notion of 'family resemblances' rather than conceiving of languages as similar because of a shared set of constant properties. Such a view would also allow for a distinction between prototypical and more marginal members of a family of languages. Diagrammatically, the new family tree would look somewhat like the one I suggested for a group of English-

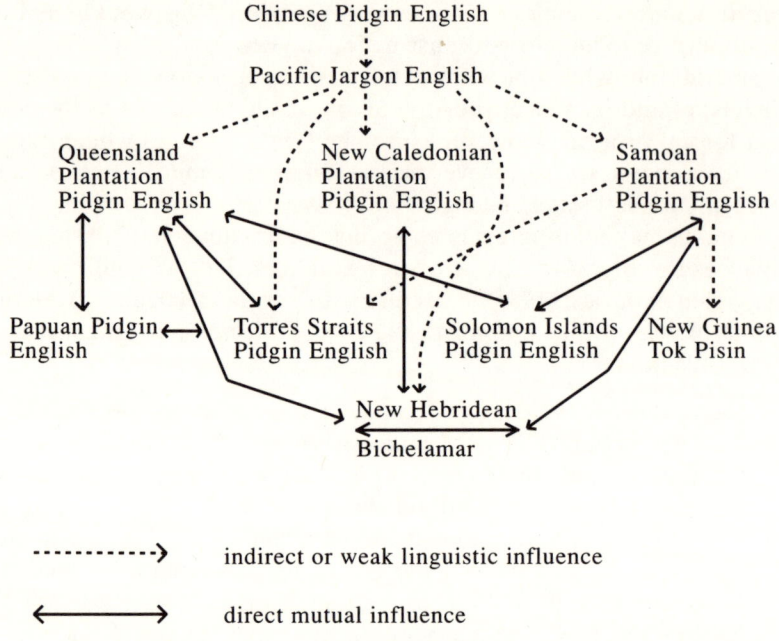

```
-----------> 	 indirect or weak linguistic influence

<------------> 	 direct mutual influence
```

Figure 2.1   Pacific Pidgin English around 1880

derived Pacific Pidgin languages many years ago (which explains why some of the details seem somewhat out of date).

The development of stable pidgins on the Pacific plantations and in the principal recruiting areas around 1880, as well as their linguistic relationship to one another and earlier forms of pidginized English, can be represented, tentatively, as shown in Figure 2.1. The principal parameter that distinguishes this suggestion from the more radical alternative is the absence of gradience. Languages, including contact pidgins, are regarded as separate entities with determinate boundaries.

Whilst the modified family metaphor could solve some of Grace's problems of accounting for simultaneous similarities and diversity, it is not appropriate for language and dialect chains such as are common throughout Australia and Melanesia. I suggest we approach this situation through a restaurant metaphor or, more precisely, by regarding the area as covered by different chains of restaurants, McDonald's, Chicken World, Kentucky Fried Chicken, Big Rooster and so forth. The members of each chain, whilst exhibiting certain idiosyncrasies derived from those who operate individual franchises, are related by numerous financial, social and human ties. Moreover, their relationship with other restaurant chains is defined by the rules of business competition, the wish both to imitate and improve on the competitors' performance and by numerous contacts between both customers and personnel. I am not going to develop this metaphor at any length, nor do I wish to claim that it is without shortcomings; rather, my point is that, in order to break out of the established comparative paradigm, it is necessary to combine new findings with new lateral ways of accounting for them.

Such a modified 'family' metaphor would seem capable of accommodating some of the complexities of language chains or communities. However, it still maintains some problematic features, such as refined linguistic systems independent of other parameters, and it is very difficult to apply to larger areas.

In my view, the main obstacle to obtaining more explanatorily powerful models of language change in the Pacific has been that European and European-trained linguists have approached the problem through unsuitable metaphors such as the reification metaphor which portrays languages as entities, or the container metaphor which provides places in time and space for them. Common to such visions is that languages are seen to be more or less self-contained and amenable to study in isolation from other languages and other factors.

What then, I would like to ask, can we ascertain about past language ecology in the Australian and Pacific region?

Reconstructing the past of any phenomenon needs to rely on memories. Climatologists and oceanographers have such a memory in the layers of ice which have accumulated over tens of thousands of years around the two poles and in high altitudes. Fossils provide important clues to past fauna and flora and genetics can reveal a great deal about past population movements. The memories that linguists have at their disposal would seem to pertain almost exclusively to the grammatical structures and parts of the lexicons of languages rather than the wider questions of language ecology. Methods such as comparative linguistics, internal reconstruction, glottochronology and lexicostatistics, in spite of some spectacular success, all presuppose the existence of relatively abstract, self-contained languages, a presupposition which may be far too indelicate for the task addressed in this chapter. The ontological status of the reconstructed word shapes, grammar and language groupings found in the Pacific area remains quite shaky and, even if it could be shown to be more solid, would still tell us little about the interrelationships between languages, their speakers and other environmental factors. A paradigm which regards as its legitimate domain the nature of the grammar of the languages ancestral to the ones spoken in the present, principles of grammatical change and structural relationship between languages is hardly suited to wider ecological questions.

Sociohistorical linguists since Labov (1972) have frequently appealed to the uniformitarian principle, arguing that the kind and order of magnitude of the factors governing language change in the past was not different from that obtaining in the present. Uniformitarianism, however, can work only in an environment of continuity of transmission. A principal theme of this book is that the effects of imperialism over the last 200 years have been largely catastrophic in nature, leading both to significant qualitative changes and a destruction of memories of the past. The numerous population movements triggered by the arrival of imperialistic powers, for instance, have led to types of multilingualism which are in all likelihood very different from those prior to this event and many attempts to argue from the present to prehistory consequently remain highly problematic. A more promising version of uniformitarianism is one which combines temporal and spatial considerations by arguing that present-day processes in peripheral locations recapitulate those of more central locations in the past. An investigation of relatively isolated groups in the interior of Papua New Guinea, for instance, can provide useful insights into what must have been the case in other groups in the more distant past. My own use of this method to reconstruct the contact history which gave rise to Tok Pisin (Mühlhäusler 1979) illustrates the usefulness (and some of the dangers) of such an approach.

Finally, it would seem quite outrageous to attempt to reconstruct the linguistic (or sociolinguistic) prehistory of the entire Australian and Pacific area. What one can realistically hope to do is to highlight some salient themes.

SALIENT PROPERTIES

Saliency is a concept which presupposes an observer for whom certain properties stand out from a whole. To the putative naive author of the *Papalagi* (Scheurmann 1921), a range of behaviours and objects found in Western urban centres gained such saliency whilst they had no saliency for the inhabitants of the same centres, as they were so habituated to these phenomena. This section then is concerned with what strikes me as a representative of a Western academic tradition, as notable to the language ecology of the Pacific. I have tried to transcend the resulting tendency merely to collect a cabinet of oddities by concentrating on phenomena which appear to constitute a particularly powerful challenge to conventional Western ideas of languages, ideas to which we have grown accustomed such as the above mentioned metaphors. These ideas which drive many of our activities need to be challenged.

From the point of view of an increasingly monocultural/monolingual perspective, the most salient property of the Pacific language ecology is its enormous diversity. Linguistic ecologies, like many others, are examples of structural diversity. In the case of the Pacific and Australia this diversity happened to be greater than in almost any other part of the world. The reader has already been alerted to the problem of counting languages and the following figures (quoted from Dixon 1991: 229) are to be taken as a very rough approximation only.

	Population	*Languages*
Philippines	60m	160
Indonesia, excluding Irian Jaya	180m	350
Irian Jaya	1.6m	200
Papua New Guinea	3.6m	760
Pacific Islands	*c*. 2m	260
Aboriginal Australia (pre-European)	1–2m	250

Many commentators have drawn attention to the very small size of many of the languages of the Pacific. Thus, in the Solomons, Tryon's (1979) data for the seventy-five-plus Austronesian languages give the average number of speakers as around 1,600 and for New Guinea, Sankoff (1980c: 95–132) gives an average of about 3,000 speakers per language. Such statistics hide the fact that the distribution of speakers appears to have been rather uneven even in prehistoric times. Thus, of the seventy-five Solomon languages, about half had fewer than 1,000 speakers and at least a dozen had fewer than 200 speakers. Similarly, in New Guinea, more than 500 languages have fewer than 1,000 speakers. In both territories, some languages have a particularly large number of speakers (100,000 for Enga in the New Guinea Highlands and Kwdra'ac ae in Malaita with 12,400).

Such fluctuation is probably best interpreted as reflecting historical changes and shifts in power relations and population patterns. The dynamic diachronic flux of pre-colonial days appears to have been arrested within a very short timespan through 'pacification', introduced diseases and other ecological factors (to be discussed on pp.

73–8) and to have been converted into a deceptively stable syn-chronic picture.

The example of Australia, which had around 200 languages for up to 300,000 inhabitants, illustrates that it is difficult to generalize about the pre-colonial linguistic situation. Certainly, the first groups con-tacted were in all likelihood not typical of the majority of speakers of Australian languages. The area of present-day Sydney was divided between the subgroups of the Iora, the Cameragal and the Kadigal who 'spoke two distinct languages. For them, the harbour formed a linguistic chasm as wide as the English Channel' (Hughes 1987: 10).

Employing the somewhat questionable concept of tribe, Hughes comments:

> The Daruk, the Iora and the Tarawal (whose territory began on the south shore of Botany Bay) were the three tribes with whom the white settlers of Australia first had to deal.
>
> Watkin Tench (1758–1833), a young officer of marines on the transport Charlotte, was struck by the ease with which the tribes understood one another. He supposed that the Daruk language was only a dialect of Iora, 'though each in speaking preferred its own [tongue]'. In fact, the variety of aboriginal language arose from the tight social structure of the tribes, their specified restricted territories, and their more-or-less fixed patterns of movement in relation to other tribal boundaries. These factors encouraged each tribe to keep its own language intact, while nomadism forced them to learn others.
>
> (Hughes 1987: 10)

The eradication of nomadism, of course, was very often one of the first acts of colonial administrators: the Tok Pisin term *sindaunim* 'to settle down, civilize' aptly describes this. The Europeans' image of traditional people living in villages of thatched huts very often is not an accurate account of forms of settlement in prehistoric time and the study of language within such non-traditional villages is unlikely to inform us about the much more complex communicative networks of the more nomadic distant past.

Linguistic diversity was at its most prolific in Melanesia where fewer than 2 million people are said to speak about one-quarter of the world's languages (Laycock 1979b). This enormous number of linguis-tic forms is probably the most widely commented on and documented property. The second aspect of diversity, the structural relations between the multitude of forms, is much less well accounted for. In spite of anecdotal accounts to the contrary, and genuine problems in some instances, my own conclusion is that, by and large, no communication problems were experienced by the inhabitants of this ecology and that, moreover, diversity provided some significant benefits.

The explanations of linguistic diversity in the past have tended to be given in a rather simplistic and mechanistic fashion. The received view has been that linguistic diversity is simply a function of the fact that language communities from time to time split up and develop in isolation from one another. There are some fairly pedestrian ways of calculating all this, called glottochronology: once separated it takes a language about 1,000 years to develop into two which, if applied to 50,000 or more years of human occupation of Australia should have yielded 250 languages about 42,000 years ago and several billion languages by 1788, for which date the estimate of 250 holds. Ignoring some of the problems of the mechanical diversification view as outcome, present-day diversity is something of relatively minor theoretical importance, particularly if it is assumed, as do the majority of practising linguists, that there is such a thing as total effability: anything can be said in any language and all languages consequently are intertranslatable (see Schnitzer 1982). Thus, diversity is superficial variation of a universal theme. Moreover, diversity in this view manifests itself as an unstructured collection, a phenomenon where the whole equals or is less than the sum of its parts; many commentators, inspired no doubt by the story of the Tower of Babel, have indeed pronounced on the dysfunctionality of diversity.

Similarly, one of the most sophisticated attempts to reconstruct the linguistic past of the Pacific (Terrell 1986) states that

> Contrary to what Dyan and others have argued, it may only be Inland Melanesia and in the more remote parts of remote Oceania that isolation has been complete enough to let us draw direct correlations between language diversity and the passage of time.
>
> (Terrell 1986: 61)

That diversity may not simply be a process passively endured by its human victims, but rather a deliberate choice, has been argued convincingly by Laycock (1981) and more recently Grace (1996).

According to Laycock, diversity is favoured both because of close association of linguistic and group identity and because mastery of a variety of languages enhances an individual's status. Taken together these two properties have interesting social consequences. The fact that there are very many small language communities, each of them regarding their own variety as the best, inhibits the spread of single powerful languages and thus promotes the egalitarian status of different groups. Empire building and colonization are absent in areas such as Melanesia or Aboriginal Australia. In addition, the association of language skills with power within communities promotes a more open access to such power whilst hereditary power is relatively rare in the most highly multilingual areas such as Melanesia (see also Sankoff 1980c).

The function of multilingual skills as an index of social status can be very clearly seen from the widespread phenomenon of 'gratuitous translation'. Salisbury's observations in the Highlands of Papua New Guinea (1972: 54ff.) are an example of a much more widely encountered phenomenon:

> More striking than the speech adjustments made in informal conversation were those made on formal occasions when ceremonies involved a clan of Komunku speakers and a clan of another speech community. In such situations each formal speech would be followed immediately by a translation of it into the other language.
>
> The distinction between informal conversations and formal speech-making that I have used to contrast the environments in which different patterns of bilingualism occur is somewhat imprecise, as the following anomalous examples will show. One Emenyo man, Kaumfa, of which more details will be given below, spoke Dene on almost all occasions within his own village. He was an important man and when speaking publicly in Emenyo village he used Dene and was not translated; when speaking publicly in any other Komunku-speaking village he used Dene and was translated; when speaking privately with me when no one else was about he used Siane, but when groups were present he used Dene and it was translated to me.
>
> (Salisbury 1972: 54)

Salisbury emphasizes that translation is not needed to ensure better understanding of a message but that:

> We must interpret repetition and the translation of speeches as a linguistic means of emphasizing the importance and public nature of the discourse. The mechanism is deliberately used by speakers to distinguish the two linguistic environments, rather than its use being unconsciously determined by the speaker's finding himself in a particular social situation. Bilingualism is thus a useful accomplishment for anyone who is likely to make public speeches and who wishes to be able to attract attention to the importance of what he says.
>
> The prevalence of bilingualism also opens up the possibility of other manipulations of the language spoken on any one occasion. In any one locality there is a 'home' language where translation

is not called for, and a 'foreign' one which calls for translation. The language a speaker chooses to use may thus symbolically indicate that he is 'at home' in a foreign area, that he wishes visitors to feel 'at home' in this area (or to feel they are 'foreigners'), that he wishes to flatter his hosts (or his guests) by assuming that they are well-travelled men who need no translation. Which particular symbolic meaning is intended in any one instance cannot be definitively determined however, since the use of language in Siane is one of the many ploys used in the competitive one-upmanship involved in most spheres of social relationship.

(Salisbury 1972: 55)

Interestingly, being a monolingual speaker of a numerically more important language is not regarded as a sign of power, unlike for instance in the case of many monolingual Anglo Saxons. Salisbury notes that:

> The fact that there are more Emenyo bilingual in Dene, than Dene-speakers who are bilingual in Komunku is not associated with any feeling among the Emenyo that they are politically less important or that their language is inferior to Dene. Bilingualism is treated as a desirable accomplishment and their command of Dene makes them, if anything, superior to the Dene.

(Salisbury 1972: 56)

Such a view of diversity would seem to be a major reason why even very small languages could survive in Melanesia over long periods of time. It is radically different from that taken for granted by most practising linguists (with exceptions such as LePage and Tabouret-Keller (1985), Grace (1996), Joseph (1987) or Harris (1979)). It should be noted that the concept of a 'language', together with the metalinguistic labels for 'language', 'dialect' and similar entities are conspicuous by their absence.[3] Language was not a self-contained object of inspection. The practice of naming languages was far from universal and when it occurred it rarely corresponded to the entities that present-day linguists set up on the basis of criteria such as shared lexicon, mutual intelligibility, geographic or political boundaries or separate literacy tradition. The difficulties of distinguishing between languages, dialects, communalects and such phenomena encountered by present-day linguists (e.g. Abel 1977; Grace 1981; Wurm and Laycock 1962) do not so much reflect their inability to find these 'objects' as their non-existence.

That the existence of 'languages' depends on perspectives that bring them into being is asserted by Thurston (1987) in his study of special varieties in North-West New Britain:

> Distinguishing different languages from dialects of the same language is problematic both linguistically and socially for reasons that are well covered in the literature. From the point of view of native speakers, it also depends on where the information originates. For example, linguistically, Tourai and Aria are clearly dialects of a single language. In New Britain, however, Tourai is considered to be a separate language from Aria by all speakers of Tourai, Lamogai and Aria (except those of Bolo); but it is not distinguished from Aria by any others. In fact, the name Tourai was unknown in the Lusi village of Kandoka until 1981, when the data for this survey were being collected. Aria, as spoken on the bank of the Aria river, has a mixture of Tourai vocabulary; the Aria of Denga overlaps in vocabulary with the Kove; and the Aria of Bolo is disowned as true Aria by other Aria speakers who say that the people of Bolo, as a result of proximity to Salkei, really speak Mouk. Meanwhile the people of Salkei say that the people of Bolo really speak Aria. The people of Bolo, on the other hand, claim to be speakers of Anêm – traditionally, this was true. Now, however, only a handful of very old people speak the Bolo dialect of Anêm with anything approaching fluency. Everyone in Bolo recognizes that Aria has become the functional language and that Anêm has really been lost here. The coastal Anêm villages know of the traditional relationship between their language and that of Bolo, but say the people of Bolo no longer speak acceptable Anêm. Thus, Bolo, which is said to speak Anêm, Aria, and/or Mouk, speaks no language that is accepted as valid by other speakers of those languages.
>
> (Thurston 1987: 28–9)

The situation is clearly very different from that stated by another Pacific linguist, Biggs (1972):

> It will be agreed, I think, that anyone who speaks language A, knows that he is speaking A, and not a different language B. Moreover, a bilingual can always distinguish between the two languages in which he is competent. . . . At any one time a speaker knows what language he is speaking. He can never claim to be speaking two languages at once, or a fusion of two languages.
>
> (Biggs 1972: 144)

That the criteria for what counts as the same and what counts as different vary from community to community is a widely accepted fact (with textbook examples such as names for colours, kin or plants).[4] It is difficult to understand why the very linguists that use such examples should assume that there is a culture-neutral unitary phenomenon 'language'. In those instances where bounded entities labelled 'language' exist, the locus of social conventions for communicative practices can be extremely complex, involving such parameters as knowledge of the right to use certain forms, place in which a speech event takes place, age, gender or social standing of participant, taboo considerations, or purpose of speaking. An account of some of the complexities in an Australian context is given by Sutton (1991).

The difficulty of identifying language boundaries is further compounded by the prevailing integrationist view of human communication in traditional societies. Javanese *basa*, for instance, as pointed out by Ben Anderson (1990), included in its broad semantic field the notions of civility, rationality and truth:

> Basa, just like bahasa in Classical Malay, meant 'language'; but it always included in its broad semantic field the notions of civility, rationality, and truth. This conception of 'true' language meant that in the profoundest sense Javanese (or in their local habitats, Sundanese, Balinese and Buginese) was isomorphic with the world, as it were glued to it. It was this isomorphism, this inherence, that made for the efficacy of mantra. Because words, or particular combinations of them, contained Power, like kings, krisses, banyan-trees and sacred images, their utterance could unleash that Power directly on, and in, the world.
>
> (Anderson 1990: 28)

The absence of a clear boundary between linguistic and other cultural practices is also documented for numerous other groups as well (Malinowski's 1935 account of the Trobriand islands being an early example) and the prevalence of this phenomenon raises some interesting challenges to notions of a self-contained discipline of linguistics or the concept of the arbitrariness of linguistic signs.

This belief in the isomorphism between linguistic forms and the world is encountered again and again, and in many societies was seen as the reason for careful language instruction and language monitoring. The case of Miriam Mer (Torres Straits Islands) is one of the few well-documented examples. In this language 'mis-speech is virtually never allowed to pass uncorrected. And the corrections of vocabulary, or of tense, or of grammar, may be rendered by anyone present who notices the error' (Cromwell 1980: 27). That such corrections differ from European schoolteachers' correcting their pupils' grammar, however, is evident from the remainder of this quotation:

In noticing the error he is making an implicit claim to a more able command of the language, and in noticing and correcting it he makes his claims explicit. But in such acts of correction it is important to note that what is being corrected is the way of speaking. That is, the corrective utterance embodies the sense that the speaker who erred DID NOT SAY WHAT HE MEANT.

(Cromwell 1980: 27)

Next to sophisticated monitoring practices this belief also explains the widely found practice of word taboo. Word tabooing occurs when a group of users agrees to replace an entire word form with a new one (either coined or borrowed) in order to avoid bad luck, illness or disaster. Linguists have tended to concentrate on the problems that this process creates for those in the business of reconstructing languages by means of the comparative method rather than as a sociolinguistic phenomenon and whilst individual case studies exist 'the phenomenon, has received little comparative study' (Keesing and Fifi 1969: 154).

The practice of taboo presupposes a very considerable overlap in the knowledge of participants in speech events, particularly knowledge about kin relationships and ancestry. Such knowledge presupposes a fairly complex (multiplex) and dense communication network (see Milroy 1980) and a low-information society. As has been pointed out by Keenan and Keenan (1971) for the Austronesian language of Madagascar, new information is a scarce commodity in many traditional societies and consequently can have a high price. In the absence of private information, i.e. information not known to everybody in a settlement the cognitive referential/denotational function of language, a function which is associated with the 'transmission' of new information from 'sender' to 'receiver' cannot be central to communication in traditional societies.[5] In fact, the telegraphic model of communication which has dominated linguistic theorizing for well over 100 years (see Harris 1979; Reddy 1979) is ill suited to capturing the ways in which meaning is created in traditional societies.

In contrast to our Western societies, the gap between total available information and individual knowledge is small and the need to make choices among available information is much less pressing or altogether absent. This is an important reason for the invalidity of the standard missionary argument, forwarded for instance by an organization such as the Summer Institute of Linguistics (SIL). To argue that introducing literacy and Christianity simply increases the choices that people can make entirely misses the point that the notion of choice was imposed on a society where it was pretty well meaningless. What one can know, what one is allowed to know, and how new knowledge can be added is highly prescribed in most low-information societies. The chapters on literacy and the influence of missions will further develop this theme.

The differential rights to knowledge or information are one of the reasons for diversity as well as the tendency to have sublanguages specific to certain cultural purposes, such as sago gathering, hunting, fishing (see Pawley 1993), special groups (mothers-in-law, initiated men) or locality (sacred or dangerous areas). Some of these practices are summarized in Laycock (1972). An important distinction developed in Thurston's writings (e.g. 1982, 1987) is that between exoteric and esoteric languages, the former being freely available for intergroup communication, whilst the latter are restricted to a well-defined group who often contribute to its exclusiveness by making it difficult for outsiders to learn. To sustain an esoteric language requires considerable social effort, as it involves formal teaching, monitoring and correcting. The case of the Papuan language Anêm, and its relationship with surrounding Austronesian (AN) languages reported by Thurston (1982), is a good illustration:

> The Anêm are unusual in the area for their language-learning propensities. Aside from Lusi/Kove and Tok Pisin, some Anêm also know Kilenge, Mouk, Bariai, Amara, or Bali (a Kimbe (AN) language spoken in the Vitu Islands). All AN-speaking peoples in the area consider Anêm far too difficult to learn; phonologically and lexically, Anêm is perceived as very different from their own languages. It also has little value as a lingua franca. The Anêm, then, are in the envied position of being able to converse with most of their neighbours, while possessing what is virtually a secret language. The Anêm have elaborated on this advantage further by creating a set of secret code lexemes to talk about common things, the words for which might be recognised by some outsiders. For example, the normal Anêm word for 'pig' is /aba/ and many Lusi and Kove know this much, but would fail to recognise the secret term /tigî tanoi/, literally 'it has four legs'. Similarly, the normal /tabu/ 'cassowary' is rendered as 'tigî niak/' 'it has two legs', and /rais/ 'rice' (from Tok Pisin) becomes /nilkî ênîk/'tree ant pupae'.
>
> (Thurston 1982: 11)

As Markey, in discussing esoteric languages, observes (1987: 19) 'grammatical complexity is unnecessary for effective communication and the chances of their survival is low once cultural practices change'.

One reason why so many esoteric languages could survive in the past is that most communicative needs of their speakers, particularly that of communication across groups, were fulfilled by other solutions including:

1 language chains
2 silent barter
3 communication through interpreters
4 dual-, bi- or multilingualism
5 the use of another 'full' language known to both parties, i.e. lingua franca
6 the development of a pidgin language.

Historically, all of the above solutions have been documented in some areas of the Pacific. The choice as to what solution to adopt is determined by many outside (i.e. other than structural linguistic) considerations, including, for example:

1 the length and institutionalization of contacts
2 the number of groups involved
3 the degree of intimacy between the groups
4 patterns of dominance
5 the size of the groups concerned
6 the purpose of communication.

Thus, for infrequent exchange of a small range of commodities, silent barter is sufficient, whereas for regular marriages across two speech communities bilingualism is a more viable solution, as is communication through an interpreter for regular high-level institutionalized contacts. The development of pidgin languages, on the other hand, is favoured by the presence of a large number of different groups, by the wish to maintain relative non-intimacy and often, though not always, the dominant status of one of the groups in the contact situation.

Silent barter has begun to be investigated by Dutton (1987) and some aspects of communication through interpreters are discussed by Schlesier (1961). However, the study of translating practices in the Pacific remains rudimentary, though a particularly readable account of chain translation across several languages in Papua New Guinea (Voorhoeve 1979) suggests that there is considerable scope for research here. As regards bi- and multilingualism, Salisbury (1972) has remarked:

> During anthropological fieldwork in the New Guinea Highlands in 1952–3 I made numerous observations on the prevalence of bilingualism and multilingualism. Not being a linguist I assumed that such observations were common in the linguistic literature, as many anthropologists have described similar situations to me in

conversation. The scene in The African Queen of a multilingual church service is part of the folklore. Recent conversations with linguists have indicated that such situations have, in fact been rarely described.

(Salisbury 1972: 52)

Since then, considerable progress has been made in the understanding of bilingualism in the New Guinea area, summarized, for instance, by Sankoff (1980c) and Laycock (1979b). As regards the use of lingue franche (plural of lingua franca) and pidgins, widespread ignorance (both in the sense of 'not knowing' and of 'not wanting to know') continues.

A crucial turning point was Dutton's (1985) research on Hiri Motu which led to the discovery of two rare pidgins in the Gulf of Papua and, more recently, work by Foley (1986a) in the Sepik area which led to his discovery of Pidgin Yimas. It has now become clear that the small list of pidgins and lingue franche dating back to pre-colonial days given in Schlesier (1961) is only the tip of a large iceberg.

For the wider Pacific area, the research project for the *Atlas of Languages of Intercultural Communication in the Pacific Area* (Wurm, Mühlhäusler and Tryon 1996) has yielded new insights into the massive incidence of language contacts and contact languages through-out the Pacific area, suggesting that present accounts of isolation and separate development have little to recommend themselves. Rensch (1987) makes the important observation that the spatial isolation experienced in many parts of the Pacific in fact promoted contacts. Addressing this problem against the general background of the family tree metaphor of language relationships, he points out:

The contradictory analyses reflect methodological difficulties of applying the family tree model in Polynesia. Unlike a mathematical theorem the tree model is context dependent. It requires a specific setting in which certain geographical and sociocultural conditions are met. In Europe and Asia, for example, speech communities could break away from each other without ever getting into contact again. Natural boundaries, geographical distance and the emer-gence of political states would limit or prevent communication, lead to linguistic separation and result in the development of distinct languages. The Indo-European languages area is a case in point.

In the Pacific, however, the situation is quite different. Human existence is restricted to a few small islands. Although separated by wide stretches of water, these islands do not provide the same conditions for isolation and separation that large continents do.

For the skilled Pacific seafarers of old the ocean was a challenge never an obstacle. It provided the opportunity to sail to islands beyond the horizon. Taking into account not only the deliberate expeditions of exploration, but also the many cases in which islands were reached and settled through unintended drift voyages, one can assume that bidirectional contact with neighbouring archipelagoes and probably one-directional contact with islands further apart never ceased to exist in the Pacific.

In Polynesia the linguistic situation and relationship between languages is best described in terms of a network model, which unlike the tree model does not treat language contact as an interference phenomenon disturbing the neat growth of subbranches. On the contrary, a network model incorporates contact between its members as a basic tenet in its theory and adjusts its methodological approach in accordance with the extralinguistic facts.

(Rensch 1987: 565ff.)

What applies to Polynesia also goes for Melanesia, Micronesia and the Pacific rim and one is left wondering whether the diversification of the Indo-European languages constitutes a special rather canonical case of language development. A long time before the advent of the first European explorers there existed in the area a sophisticated trade network and the linguistic means to facilitate trade and contacts. The suspicious, shy and withdrawn tribesman has to be relegated to the status of a discursive category.

One of the most problematic areas for reconstruction is that of past dynamics. The history of the languages of the Pacific area is no less dynamic than the history of other regions of the world, though to what extent it was qualitatively different remains to be ascertained. Boretzky (1984), in a study concerned with smaller Melanesian and Australian languages, claims that the social life of these languages results in a pattern of sound change which differs dramatically from those found in Indo-European languages:

Though, in European languages families, sound change is for the most part governed by rules that can be precisely formulated, several exotic groups (as, for instance, the Arantic family of Australia and the Papuan Kâte group examined here) appear to behave differently. At least, this conclusion must be drawn from the sound shapes of semantically comparable items in each of the groups. The languages of each group differ etymologically to a greater extent than do interrelated European languages, whereas the etymologically related items (the cognates) display very few regular sound correspondences. It can be assumed that this state of affairs was produced by extralinguistic factors such as the smallness of the tribes and the lack of a central power, which led to a splitting up into many small languages, as well as the frequent practice of tabooing names and worlds related to them, which accounts for the etymological dissimilarity and / or non-systematic sound correspondences between related languages.

(Boretzky 1984: 50)

The relatively small size of language communities would seem to be a key factor in the development of traditional languages in the Pacific Hemisphere. Small communities are more susceptible to catastrophic disruptions such as diseases, natural disasters and warfare. For instance, the already mentioned Anêm were affected by a series of disasters just prior to the arrival of the first Europeans which nearly annihilated them. Thurston here (1982) reports:

The present Anêm territory used to be more densely populated. Three events are held responsible for the near extinction of the Anêm; judging from genealogical details, these events can be placed in the latter half of the nineteenth century. First, an unusually long period of drought dried up all but the largest rivers, destroying gardens and promoting extensive forest fire damage. The ensuing famine was associated with widespread murder to confiscate food, and with cannibalism. Before they could really recover from the drought, an epidemic of a lethal disease characterised by skin sores left so many dead that they could not be buried. This plague may be associated with the first European contacts in the area. Finally, many people were drowned by a tidal wave that extended quite a distance inland.

(Thurston 1982: 7)

The effects of such natural disasters on the selection of both linguistic features and languages, and the particular importance of such selection in the case of highly diverse language ecologies inhabited by small languages, have been studied in much detail by Stross (1975) whose conclusions deserve much greater attention than they have received. The same can be said for an article by Hockett (1950) in which he explores the consequences of different types of speech communities for linguistic continuity.

Whilst it has been maintained throughout this book that the arrival of the Europeans in the Pacific was causally connected to a dramatic decline in the numbers and viability of the languages in the area, it needs to be remembered that languages also disappeared before their arrival. The indications are that prehistoric obsolescence occurred at a much slower pace, however Terrell (1986: 91ff.) provides a long list of once inhabited Pacific Islands that had been abandoned by the time the first Europeans arrived, and traces of extinct peoples are found also in Australia (e.g. Bauer 1970) and throughout the entire region. One can say little about the language obsolescence that may have coincided with the abandonment of settlements and again very little can be ascertained about the Papuan languages that may have been lost following Austronesian excursions into the area of New Guinea. A careful study of contemporary language atlases (e.g. Wurm and Hattori 1982) can provide a valuable, albeit static picture of the changes in the language ecology which must have occurred in prehistoric times and sophisticated modelling such as employed by Terrell (1986) is suggestive of interesting scenarios of the past.

There are also a number of areas where a uniformitarian approach can be employed. Prominent among these is South East Papua. The suitability of this area was first suggested by Dutton (1978):

> South-Eastern Papua New Guinea is a particularly good place to look for cases of language change and disappearance that might provide insight into linguistic change in the past for it is here that we find a relatively large number of AN languages in contact with NAN ones, and where it is still possible to probe into the interplay between social, geographical and other factors involved in language change that were at work when Europeans arrived and froze the situation with the imposition of their law and order.[6]
>
> (Dutton 1978: 3)

The languages Dutton singled out for study were

1 the Motu around Port Moresby
2 the Magori and associated languages of Ouma, Yoba and Bina around Table and Amazon Bays on the south coast
3 the Maisin around Cape Nelson on the north-east coast.

His reasons for this selection were that

> In each case we have an AN language speaking population that is presently (or was in the recent past) surrounded by, or included in, other populations speaking genetically unrelated languages, and whose languages show in varying degrees the effects of contact with these and/or other populations – from almost nil in Motu, to heavy borrowing of basic vocabulary in Magori, to a complex mixing or heavy borrowing at all levels in Maisin.
>
> (Dutton 1978: 3)

Four years later Dutton (1982) presented the interim results of his Magori studies, including (p. 159) the observations that there was a reversal in the direction of borrowing between AN and NAN language systems after a change of power relations between the different speaker groups. A sourcing analysis of sixty of the clearest cases of borrowings showed that

(a) these languages have borrowed from one another in a closed system (that is, there is negligible external borrowing);

(b) Ouma and Magori have borrowed from different languages – Ouma from those presently located around and inland of Cloudy Bay and Magori from Magi now spoken along the whole coast and its offshore islands;

(c) the borrowing between these AN and NAN languages was intense and ranged over the whole vocabulary including basic vocabulary;

(d) there was a complete reversal in the borrowing pattern: firstly borrowing was from AN to NAN and then from NAN to AN.

Thus although much still remains to be done before the borrowing and loaning pattern in this and neighbouring areas can be said to have been well studied these were quite startling and unexpected results based as they are on the restricted data presently available. What is more they have profound implications for the prehistory of the area. In particular when taken together with other information that is presently available they suggest that there has been a complex and interesting interaction between the speakers of the two different types of languages presently found there. Thus it is clear from what has been said that after the arrival of ANs in the area NANs entered into a close relationship with them apparently attracted by their knowledge of sailing and trading. Some time later something happened to this relationship and the ANs were attacked and driven into the interior. Although it is not yet proven it would appear that the stimulus for this reversal in relations, if not a manifestation of it, was the rise to power of one group of NANs, notably the Mailu Islanders. They presumably learned the skills of the ANs in situ and somehow took over a system that the ANs had introduced to them and they developed it to the point of monopoly. As a result they could colonise areas left vacant by the now fugitive ANs and could expand their trade into new areas.

(Dutton 1982: 159)

Relatively little has been added to the study of NAN–AN contacts since, an exception being a number of important papers by Malcolm Ross. Ross (1987) deals with the situation among the Bel languages. This work profits from the author's use of up-to-date theoretical studies on language contacts and, in particular, addresses the question of the convergence of grammatical structure rather than the lexicon. The most widely encountered view of the process of borrowing, a view derived from what can be observed in contemporary European languages, is that there is a hierarchy of susceptibility to borrowing, with lexical material at the top of this hierarchy and morphosyntax at its lower end. Cases such as the well-known convergence at the grammatical but non-convergence at the lexical level in Kupwar village, India (Gumperz and Wilson 1971) are regarded as peripheral (and for this reason are relegated to creolistics). Ross, however, provides an explanation of why borrowing in Melanesia did not operate like this:

> The reason why borrowing did not begin with lexicon is that it is precisely the words of the language which are perceived by its speakers as its substance and therefore as the emblem of identity. Adaptive changes in morphosyntax, on the other hand, occur unconsciously and hence have no emblematic significance.
>
> (Ross 1987: 597)

Ross's concept of emblematic significance yet again underlines two important characteristics of the traditional languages of the area:

1 There is a perceived non-arbitrary link between words and the external world and control over the external world depends on correct word choice.

2 Word forms are indexical of user groups.

This latter point was studied in some detail by Thurston (1988). This study suggests that next to instances where unrelated languages become structurally but not lexically more similar (as in the cases studied by Gumperz and Wilson 1971, and Ross 1987) there is a converse phenomenon of closely related varieties of the same language becoming less similar as a consequence of deliberate attempts to reduce these similarities. Prominent among such attempts is borrowing from different external sources:

> A much more common and effective way of establishing a language barrier is to copy words from a neighbouring language that is different from the source language used by opponents. Lusi, Kove and Kasbana, for instance, are superficially very similar, but each

has copied a large number of words from different languages. Lusi has copied from Anêm, Aria from Mouk; Kabana from Maleu (Lolo and Kileŋe); and Kove from Kakovi and probably from Bali-Yitu. Similarly, to distinguish themselves from the Aria, the Mouk copy from Anêm, while the Tourai copy from Lamogai. According to some informants, this is a deliberate policy. Clearly, lexicon is the single most important feature distinguishing one language from another.

(Thurston 1988: 6)

All of these cases seriously undermine the standard view that differentiation is due to isolation and non-communication. Rather, to speak with LePage and Tabouret-Keller (1985) such differences reflect deliberate acts of identity, in the form of deliberate boundary marking and suggest that the much neglected indexical functions of language are a great deal more important than the exchange of information which linguists have tended to regard as the central purpose of human communication. The notion of 'natural language' is hardly appropriate for such cases.

LANGUAGES AND THEIR PHYSICAL ENVIRONMENT

Much of the evidence discussed in this chapter suggests that in the traditional language ecology of the Pacific there was none of the separation between an external reality or environment on the one hand and the description of this reality or environment on the other. In fact, many studies of traditional cultures (e.g. Ong 1982 and Olson 1988) bear out that this separation is a consequence of literacy. Olson (1988), after examining several aspects of this problem, concludes:

The distinction between the given and the interpreted, then, invented for reading and interpreting texts, was simply borrowed for 'reading' the book of nature. The product of the distinction was modern science, science built on the notion of a discontinuity between observation and inference, facts and theory, claims and evidence. Furthermore, when scientific epistemology succeeded in exorcising interpretations from the world, the source of such interpretations came to be recognized as products of the mind. This new awareness of mind and of the autonomy of ideas was the basis for Cartesian mentalism and the beginning of modern notions of subjectivity. Modern scientific epistemology, like modern notions of subjectivity, was, therefore, a by-product of the hermeneutics of written texts.

(Olson 1988: 136–7)

Instead of the simplistic view that languages simply map an external territory, there are numerous links between language practices and all sorts of aspects of life. These links tend to be necessary or indexical in the technical sense. Any semantic analysis of traditional languages which simply suggests that there is a single reality of which all languages are descriptive and which subscribes to the principle of total effability (intertranslatability) will fail to do justice to the very complex ways in which meaning can be created, negotiated and maintained in traditional societies. There is, not unexpectedly, a great shortage of adequate semantic accounts of the languages of the region. To fill this gap goes far beyond the scope of this book. I would like to note, however, that much can be learnt from the many different ways in which different groups have created their own linguistic perspectives of the world. Traditional languages should be regarded as repositories of accumulated knowledge and learning from such knowledge could prove very beneficial to speakers of Standard Average European (SAE) languages. I have given an illustration of what could be learnt in the domain of environmental discourse from the traditional Pacific languages (Mühlhäusler 1995).

CONCLUSIONS

As I indicated at the outset, the questions asked in this chapter are too complex to be answered satisfactorily within the confines of a book such as this. But the recognition that there remain many unstated questions in the linguistic prehistory of the Pacific is in itself a first step to finding answers. Much of the ignorance and misinterpretation found in earlier work was caused by the absence of adequate questions, promoted by a tendency to see similarities with SAE languages or supposed universals.

Most of the labels employed by Western linguists stand in need of revision, including key concepts such as language, meaning or communication. The prospects of finding comprehensive answers are not good. Much of the evidence has been irretrievably lost and access to existing evidence is very difficult indeed. However, I have identified a number of promising new departures and it is possible that such new insights as are beginning to emerge will bring about the long overdue revision of the practices currently used in reconstructing linguistic prehistory.

3 Disruptions in the linguistic ecology

> The dynamics of this process of language shift are exceedingly subtle and complex.
>
> (Kulick 1993: 177)

INTRODUCTION

One of the principal differences between an ecological and an earlier mechanistic approach to languages is that the former subscribes to the interdependency between linguistic and numerous other ecological factors. It sees the well-being of individual languages or communication networks as dependent on a range of language-external factors as well as the presence of other languages and thus not as something which can be meaningfully studied in its own right, though it is possible to focus on certain symptoms of language death and decline, as will be been done in Chapter 11. The arguments put forward here have their analogies in studies concerned with the disappearance of natural species. The change of a single link in a ecological network can precipitate very considerable overall changes, the disappearance of one species typically leading to that of a dozen of others.

The term 'ecology' is derived from the Greek word for house or home. We can employ this house metaphor by pointing at the removal of only small, but important, parts of a building which can lead to its collapse or vastly reduce its fitness for habitation. Few approaches of linguistics cater for such a concept of language. The one which I have found most suited is the ethnography of communication approach developed by Hymes (1974), which focuses on a wide range of components of speech situations and speech events occurring within a language ecology.

I shall examine the use of Hymes' scheme for the study of the language decline shortly. Before doing this, however, let me contrast the ecological approach with another, atomistic approach influenced by the independency hypothesis of language. Its characteristics are as follows:

1 Languages are seen as self-contained entities which can be studied in isolation from other languages.
2 Linguistic structure is regarded as independent of non-linguistic parameters.
3 Individual causes of language attrition can be identified and added up.

The typical question asked within this approach is: What factors cause the decline of language X? Thus, in discussing the decline of the Boumaa Dialect of Fijian, Schmidt (1991b: 114–15) lists six factors conducive to dialect levelling in Fijian:

1 intermarriage
2 compulsory education in Standard Fijian
3 the Church
4 the media
5 increased communication with other dialect areas
6 centralization and urbanization in Fiji.

It is true that all the factors are involved somehow, but more is needed than a simple listing.

A second problem with these and similar accounts is that they are based on common-sense speculation rather than empirical study. It is by no means certain, for instance, that there is clear support for the notion that the media promote dialect levelling; data from Britain and Germany in fact appear to contradict this claim, nor is it clear what causal role intermarriage, which after all is a traditional institution, may be playing. The very few empirical studies of language decline in the Pacific have suggested that a complex array of factors, some of them quite unexpected, are involved (see Kulick 1993).

This leads me to the next important distinction, that between macro and micro studies. There is a growing number of macrostudies of language decline phenomena (Dixon 1991; Mühlhäusler 1987a; Schmidt 1991a) but very few studies of the important microprocesses that lead to radical changes in the larger linguistic picture of the Pacific area. The arguments in this chapter are no exception. Whilst drawing on the insights of the few available microstudies and the more numerous macrostudies, it is in itself an attempt to provide a macroview. However, it differs from most other studies in asking what factors sustain and change the overall language ecology rather than individual languages, and is stressing the interrelatedness of the various parameters involved.

TOWARDS AN ETHNOGRAPHY OF LANGUAGE CHANGE

The Hymesian approach, which I shall adopt here, is concerned with isolating individual parameters rather than interdependencies. The features of speech events at one time were very much regarded, as were the features of phonetics or semantics, as primitive atoms which could be combined in many ways to form larger, meaningful structures. This way of analysing communicative events has the great advantage of directing researchers to ask a wide range of questions, and surveys, such as that of Malcolm (1982) for Australian Aboriginal languages, have demonstrated the usefulness of an 'etic' framework, such as the ethnography of speaking, for comparative purposes. The status of the following pages then is that of a butterfly collection, a research stage following the recognition that we are dealing with a problem whose causes are many and which come in different packages in different parts of the Pacific. What I cannot aim at here is an exhaustive treatment.

Hymes' approach distinguishes three ranks or levels for analysis: speech acts, speech events and speech situations. In conformity with the top-down approach I have applied throughout this book I shall concentrate on the two latter levels, isolating each of the parameters that would appear to have a bearing on language change.

CHANGES AT THE LEVEL OF SPEECH SITUATION

By situation, in its broadest sense, we understand the material and human setting of communication. In both respects, the Pacific has been drastically changed, since European colonization. Here I can give only a very brief summary of the kind of changes portrayed by Clerk (1984), Crosby (1986) and Moorehead (1966).

1 The introduction of new plants, animals and diseases caused a very rapid change in the physical world. The disappearance of indigenous flora and fauna was accelerated by indiscriminate exploitation of natural resources by consecutive groups of whalers, sandalwood collectors, bêche-de-mer fishers, and others. In areas such as Australia, land that had previously been used for indigenous crops (e.g. yam plantations in Western Australia) was seized by the colonial agriculturalists. In other areas, tropical plantations were established, thus putting an end to pre-existing 'coral gardens and their magic'.

2 Introduced human diseases, drink and drugs rapidly decimated the population of most islands. The loss of life was accelerated by

genocide, deportation and labour recruiting, which led to the total destruction of many traditional societies.

3 European colonization promoted the influx of large groups of outsiders which either replaced (as in Australia) or severely affected the previous indigenous population (as in Fiji, New Caledonia or Guam).

4 The pre-existing material culture was replaced rapidly by a heavily Westernized culture, iron tools replacing stone and bone tools, firearms, traditional weapons, and European forms of transport replacing indigenous ones. The Westernization of the material culture has accelerated greatly since the 1970s and has led to the disappearance or displacement of pre-existing forms in many areas.

5 Existing communication networks were destroyed by not only the imposition of arbitrary colonial boundaries but also the reorientation of the communication from a horizontal (inter-indigenous) to a vertical (master-dominated group) process, thus bringing groups into contact that had not communicated previously.

6 Much of the spiritual culture was destroyed (deliberately or accidentally) by intensive missionization, education programmes, and other forms of colonial social control. In the process, many domains of traditional discourse simply disappeared.

7 An aspect which is often overlooked is that the social and residential groups encountered in the 1990s are not a continuation of pre-contact patterns in many cases. In the area of New Guinea, for instance, successive governments have discouraged semi-nomadic groups and group living in small hamlets and vigorously promoted larger villages in order to facilitate the administrative process. Very much the same goes for residence groups in Australia and elsewhere. Consequently, the notion of speech community or communication community has a very different meaning from that which it had 200 years ago.

Most of these changes were triggered off by European colonial penetration from about 1800 but the effects of the development of strong indigenous states with policies of internal colonization (such as China or Indonesia) or external (such as Japan in the first half of the twentieth century) were very similar. So-called political independence in many instances has not changed the lot of small language groups, rather it may have accelerated their decline. Present-day policies of Islamic missionization and imposition of Malay in parts of Borneo would seem to be little different in nature or order of magnitude from earlier Christian mission policies in the same area.

8 The factors of overpopulation and urbanization which have led to

renewed large-scale regional mobility and the further erosion of traditional forms of settlement are found throughout the Pacific.

Schmidt (1991a) has commented on the strong link between language decline and urbanization in Aboriginal Australia:

> For many Aboriginal language speakers, however, an urban life-style often appears incongruous with and inappropriate for the use of an Aboriginal language. The pressures to switch to English and to adopt associated Western identities, role models and aspirations are immense. Moreover, there are many fewer opportunities to speak an Aboriginal language, in terms of both availability of speakers and suitable contexts of use.
>
> Consequently, a common pattern which emerges across the continent is for a given Aboriginal language to remain relatively strong in more isolated settlements away from urban centres, while in cities and towns the same language weakens in favour of English.
>
> (Schmidt 1991a: 14)

9 The change from low-information to high-information societies has led to events distant in time and space becoming increasingly important to all inhabitants of the area. This does not mean, however, that one is dealing with the development of a global village as there are few multiplex communication networks. Information flow is from a few centres mainly overseas and small groups remain at the receiving end of information.

10 The development of national identity and its consequent adoption of new national languages as expression with traditional vernaculars of social identity and the competition between such languages with traditional vernaculars. This contrasts with traditional bilingualism of the endo–exo type where dealing with outgroups did not require a shift of identity.

Much more could be said about macrochanges at the level of situation. Let us instead consider some of the major results of the changes outlined:

1 The formerly egalitarian status of the languages of the region has been changed to a hierarchical one with the metropolitan expatriate languages occupying top position, followed by a smaller number of languages which were lucky enough to be singled out for mission and government purposes, followed by the pidgins derived from the metropolitan languages, with a large number of local languages and language varieties at the bottom of the hierarchy. Status changes in areas with changing colonial administrations complicate the picture, as pointed out by Solenberger (1962) for Micronesia. Note that the concept of 'a language' is brought into existence by this process, as

are those of 'minority language' and 'dialect'. Structured entities which maintain their identity over time begin to exist with the setting up of administrative and mission centres and the description of the variety of speech used there.

Indigenous conceptions of language thus have given way to European concepts such as that of modern 'bahasa' in Bahasa Indonesia. The relative status of such countable languages can be measured in terms of such factors as size of a political entity, availability of lexicons and grammars, teaching materials and radio programmes.

2 The usefulness of many local languages to their speakers is greatly reduced as former communication partners become inaccessible. Small local trade languages, for instance, give way to large cross-regional pidgins that give access to imported Western goods. The structural dependency of the pidgins on outside languages mirrors the economic dependency of their users on outside providers, as does the large-scale influx of loan words from 'modern' languages into the traditional ones.

3 The indexical function of the numerous small languages of the area as markers of local group membership becomes attenuated as geographic mobility, life in non-traditional settlements and marriages outside the traditional exchange patterns become common. Very often, being a speaker of a small local language carries negative indexicality, marking users as underdeveloped, country-bumpkins.

4 Pre-existing multilingualism is changed in character. Instead of being proficient in several local languages and trade languages, bilingualism typically involves the local vernacular, a metropolitan language (English, French, Thai, Bahasa Indonesia) and, sometimes, a Pidgin derived from the metropolitan language.

Thus, the first part of my argument regarding the causes of changes in the linguistic ecology in the Pacific area is that, over the last 200 years, the speech situation in which these languages and their speakers are embedded has changed very dramatically; speakers now find themselves in a radically changed physical and cultural environment and have to adapt their linguistic resources to numerous new requirements.

In terms of our ecological metaphor, the life support system for the traditional languages has changed dramatically, and whilst some of them may have either thrived or found a secure niche for their survival, a very large number of others are under increasing threat of disappearance. In Australia, certain plants and certain species of marsupials have thrived following increased irrigation by farmers or selected cultivation for commercial purposes (e.g. macadamia nuts or grevilleas) but the overall amount of diversity has been very rapidly reduced and the situational support for complex indigenous systems is diminishing.

CHANGES IN SPEECH EVENTS

The Hymesian model is most developed in the area of speech events and their constituent components. It is argued that – analogous to phonetic and semantic features – the features that contribute to make up speech events are universal but that the packages (or molecules made up of event patterns) differ widely across cultures. As we have opted to employ Hymes' categories as a heuristic tool rather than a description of reality, we shall postpone judgement of the matter of the universality of the components, leaving open the possibility that at least some of these are highly culture-specific. Events that are found in the Pacific area such as the Samoan Fono (Duranti 1981) or the Hiri trade encounter are dependent on the sustainability of a range of factors. Again, no exhaustive survey can be given here. However, such evidence as I shall produce should suffice to demonstrate that the maintenance of traditional speech events is becoming increasingly difficult in the region. Of the many events provided for in Hymes' model and in the somewhat smaller collection of events I have presented for the Pacific, I shall single out the following:

1 message form
2 message content
3 scene
4 sender
5 addresser
6 hearers and addressees
7 purposes
8 key
9 forms of speech.

Message form

This category is concerned with the means of expression in a community for the performance of speech events such as greetings, addressing, thanking, conveying new information, joking and so forth. It should first be noted that different cultures attach different values to such forms (verbal means for thanking may be highly developed in one culture and absent in another) and that, furthermore, situational factors govern some aspects of this component. One of the most striking aspects of many traditional language communities is the relative lack of new information (i.e. information that is not available or known to every member of the community) and thus forms for conveying this. With limited communication with the outside world and with closed (homodynamic) communication networks within small self-contained communities, the function of language which modern Western linguistics has taken to be the primary one, namely the cognitive or informative one, plays a relatively subordinate role. This fact was initially commented on by Malinowski (1930) and, more recently, illustrated for Malagasy by Keenan and Keenan (1979).

The creation of new communication networks with the outside, the introduction of new media, and the process of religious and educational/political conversion have greatly enhanced the role of the cognitive function of language and the need for message forms appropriate for it.

Let us briefly consider some other forms. Several observers have remarked on the absence of verbal forms for thanking (which, of course, is not to be confused with the absence of gratitude) and on European efforts to introduce local equivalents to English 'thank you'.

Naming and calling someone by their name in the languages of the Pacific (for the language of Manus see Nevermann 1934: 305ff.) used to be associated with giving power and/or having power over the named person. Both the practice of missionaries in giving people Christian names (even adults after baptism) and that of governments of taking down the names for census purposes drastically altered existing practices of naming. Most people in the area now have – like their Standard Average European (SAE) model – a Christian name and a surname rather than a name derived from the often extremely complex traditional naming practices (as described for instance by Wassmann 1982).

A major social effect of introduced naming practices has been observed by Senft (1992: 74) in the Kilivila language of the Trobriands. When the first high school was set up in the late 1970s it was decided that the school fees had to be paid by the schoolchildren's fathers.

> The Trobriand Islands' society is matrilineal, however, and therefore the children's fathers have no kin relationship with, and thus no direct control at all upon, their children. If they 'invest' in their children, they actually invest in their children's mother's matrilineal line. Already in 1983 we had noticed that some schoolchildren claimed that their father's given names were their surnames. This phenomenon developed as far as we know independently of the

school policy found in some other provinces of Papua New Guinea where the fathers' given names were assigned to schoolchildren as their surnames.

(Senft 1972: 74)

Senft continues:

Any Trobriand Islander hearing the given name of another Trobriand Islander can immediately identify the clan membership of the respective individual. If the members of the younger generation with school education now give their proper name (the name they inherit from their mother's matrilineal line) together with a surname which is actually their father's name (and thus the property of their father's mother's matrilineal line) this may cause some confusion with respect to the identification of kin membership in the Massim area. Now suddenly the father's matrilineal line is mentioned and thus obviously obtains an equal status with the mother's, the 'real' kinfolks', matrilineal line. We are very much inclined to interpret this observation as a first step towards a fundamental change in the complex system of Trobriand Islands' kin relationships and roles, and we suspect that the Trobriand Islands' society is in the process of changing from a matrilineal to a patrilineal one – for changing economic reasons. That such a change will have fundamental consequences for the Trobriand Islands' sophisticated construction of social reality, if it continues, is evident.

(Senft 1972: 74)

Introduced views of kinship, parental control and the role of children have taken over in many other parts of the Pacific as well and have led to very dramatic changes in many verbal practices. Naming in many Polynesian societies is not for life: children in Samoa and elsewhere can be given quite outrageous and seemingly insulting names which are replaced by more serious adult names in later life. This practice is giving way to that of giving a child his or her name for life at baptism.

Methods of counting is another area where practices radically different from SAE ones are found. The most comprehensive general discussion is that of Laycock (1975a) who analyses a large number of non-decimal counting and tallying systems in Melanesia. With the latter, parts of the body are used as reference points such that, for larger numbers, more than one person is needed for the counting process. Even those languages employing a decimal system may differ in detail from European counting practices. An interesting example is provided by some of the languages of Micronesia, where different

Table 3.1 Cardinal number sets in languages of Micronesia

number	humans	taro
1 tang	tang	tëluóng
2 orúng	tërúng	ëruóng
3 odei	tëdei	ëdeiuóng
4 oáng	tëoáng	ëuáiuóng
5 oím	tëím	ëímuóng
6 malóng	tëlólom	a lolom uóng
7 uíd	tëuid	ëuíd uóng
8 iái	tëái	ëáiuóng
9 ítiu	tëtíu	ëtiuuóng
10 mágod	tërúiug	ëtrúiug

fish	coconuts	trees, leaves
1 tang	geimóng	tegetóng
2 gërúng	tëblóng	gëregetóng
3 gëdei	kedei	gëdeiegetóng
4 gëoáng	klaoáng	gëodiegetóng
5 gëím	kleím	gëimegetóng
6 gëlólom	klólom	gelólomegetóng
7 gëuíd	kleuíd	
8 gëái	kleai	
9 gëtíu	kltíu	
10 telbúdok	tágar	

cardinal number sets are chosen for counting different entities, as in the Palauan data (shown in Table 3.1) adapted from Krämer (1919: 331).

The changeover from traditional counting and tallying systems to European imperial or decimal systems is often the first change subsequent to contact with the colonizers. Even in those languages where indigenous literacy was initially promoted (as for instance, in the Loyalties) the indigenous counting system was rapidly replaced.

Closely related to counting are the processes by which the day, the growing season of the yam or the solar year are subdivided into small sections. In most instances the solar calendar of SAE speakers has replaced indigenous methods, an example of which is that of Micronesian Kusaiean (Kee-dong Lee 1975).

It is also true that many words become obsolete. In Kusaiean there are the following words which refer to different phases of the moon:

maspang 'full moon'	luhlti
mesalem	kowala met
alwat	kowala tyok
mesohn	sropahsr aphnak
mesait	sropahsr
	srohsluhn
me saul	suhan kusahf
lohlohtoh	kusahf suhnak
sriafong	srohmpahr
arfohkoh	arip
seken par	li 'moonless night'
sohfsen	sripuhp
aohlwen	linguli
fahkfong	lingalang
mesr '14th phase'	
el '15th phase'	

Except for the four words meaning 'full moon', '14th phase', '15th phase', and 'moonless night', most Kusaiean speakers cannot associate the words with particular phases of the moon. Before the solar calendar was introduced to Kusaiean culture, the lunar calendar must have been closely related to Kusaiean culture, especially as it related to fishing. But since the introduction of the solar calendar, the lunar calendar was less frequently used. As a result, some of the words are becoming obsolete.

(Kee-dong Lee 1975: 393)

Finally, the message form of 'joke' was widely absent in the Pacific area in 'prehistoric' times, though the culture was rich in humour and funny tales. However, jokes of a Western type, together with cartoons and comic strips, are becoming widespread among the indigenous speakers of the area.

Message content

The principal effect of contacts between the Pacific area and the Europeans has been a large-scale change in the range of topics featuring in conversations. On the one hand, numerous new topics have been added to the traditional inventory. Malcolm (1982), for instance, reports motor cars, pushbikes and motor bikes, and the future as topics in Australian Aboriginal languages in addition to old established ones such as witch doctors, spirits of deceased persons, strife in camp and hunting. With the spread of a cash economy, money, betting and gambling have also become important topics. With increasing urbanization some of the traditional topics have declined, with traditional myths and oral history dying out at an ever faster rate. Perhaps even more drastic than the changes in the inventory of message content are changes in its patterns of access and use. In many traditional societies knowledge of and talk about topics were restricted to subgroups according to sex, age or other social parameters. Thus, talk about menstruation, birth and pregnancy in many Aboriginal societies tended to be reserved for women. With governments promoting birth control programmes, missionaries instructing males about the birth of Jesus, and, most recently, government-sponsored campaigns against sexually transmitted diseases, these topics are now open to men as well.

Senft (1992) provides a detailed study of the various domains of Kilivila discourse that are in the process of disappearing, including that of traditional dressmaking.

> First of all we have to note that with the decline of the importance and appreciation of craftsmen's work, with a repression of various personal concepts of aesthetics expressed in ornaments of manufactured objects of everyday use, and with the changing dress style on the Trobriand Islands a loss of certain areas of vocabulary is to be observed. Thus, the vocabulary of the wickerworker, of the net maker, of the manufacturer of adornments, and of the master carver is in great danger of being lost, so much so that it is likely that in a few years it will be rather difficult to find a Trobriand Islander who will be able to name all the various parts of a basket or fish trap, all the various names of special ornaments and designs to be found on traditional objects of everyday use, old canoes and canoe boards, or who is able to describe the manufacturing of a shell adornment or of a sail or of the various net types and who can still enumerate all the materials to make such objects.
>
> That this danger is indeed critical is emphasised by the results of my research on processes of language change in progress that are affecting the system of Kilivila classifiers. Here the data show that classifiers associated with technical language are among those formatives that are extremely rare or almost obsolete.
>
> Another linguistic change is observed in connection with the manufacturing of so-called 'grass skirts'; it affects Kilivila colour terms which undergo important processes of language change. As noted elsewhere Western chemical dyes were prepared from certain plants. This has resulted in the loss of the traditional knowledge of folk-botany with respect to the dyeing of skirts. In consequence,

the folk-botany terms that were used to refer to the respective
colours of these natural dyes are dying out now.

(Senft 1992: 72)

Scene

By scene we understand the psychological context of speech events,
such as the human context (e.g. are children and adults part of the
same scene?), or degree of formality, comfort or discomfort. For
much of the colonial period, of great importance has been the question
of whether indigenes and expatriates are regarded as being factually
or potentially members of the same scene or not. Thus, one can
expect quite diverse linguistic consequences from the Dutch policy up
to about 1860 of preventing indigenes from learning and using Dutch,
French assimilation policies in New Caledonia or Tahiti, and a
sequence of different policies ranging from separation to assimilation
with regard to Australian Aborigines as well as differences between
different administrators in different localities of a traditional communication area. The conflicting signals received by the local population
are reflected, for instance, in the ambivalent status of pidgin and
creole varieties that resulted from such contacts. An introduced pidgin
language such as Tok Pisin was referred to at different times and
different places as the language of the white man, or the language of
the indigenous male in European service and in the north of Australia
even now there is considerable variation in views on whether English
and the local English creole varieties are one language or two. As
regards the place of children, European presence has in many instances
led to a separation of age groups. Thus, boarding schools, mission
reserves, special centres for children of the indigenous workforce and
so on have left few of the pre-existing traditional patterns of language
transmission between the generations intact (see Hockett 1950).

The effects of boarding schools in Aboriginal Australia have been
characterized by Schmidt (1991a):

In more isolated communities, post-primary education presents a
serious threat to Aboriginal language vitality. In many communities, the local school caters only for primary grades. In order to
gain further secondary education or continue schooling until the
compulsory age of 15 years, it is necessary for Aboriginal students
to leave their community to attend all-English white majority
schools in other areas. This removal of teenagers from their language community is detrimental in various ways. Firstly, there is
often no recognition of the Aboriginal language or identity in the

secondary school curriculum. Indeed, if a second language is taught, it is usually Japanese, French or a migrant language. Secondly, the student is plunged into an alien social situation and experiences intense assimilatory pressure to switch to English and white values and aspirations.

(Schmidt 1991a: 18)

The disruption of traditional ways of language learning is not restricted to teenagers' physical absence. Language socializers such as fathers and members of secret men's clubs, who acted as primary linguistic sources for the 'high' varieties of speech in traditional societies, lost this role as men were absorbed in the workforce, recruited to workplaces far away, or stripped of their authority in favour of government appointed officials. The setting up of larger settlements made it possible for larger viable groups of children to become involved in their own linguistic socialization. To what extent adult norms can disappear in the process is illustrated by Schmidt (1985).

As long as most indigenes found themselves at the bottom of the colonial hierarchy, many aspects of traditional scenes were not under direct threat. However, with increasing social mobility, new differences between groups are created, changes in status initiated, and new definitions of formality and deference needed. Victims in such circumstances are the very widely distributed respect languages of the area. Whereas in some instances (e.g. Japan) the old honorific system has been adapted successfully to changed social circumstances, in most other areas surveyed respect language is either lost or restricted to traditional contexts. Thus, Javanese people faced with new social distinctions will adopt the neutral language of Bahasa Indonesia rather than mapping former distinctions on to the new situation.

Sender

By sender we mean the actual source of information which may but need not be identical with the addresser. Thus ambassadors speak on behalf of their governments, solicitors on behalf of their clients and so on. A brief survey of the literature of the area suggests a number of dramatic changes in the wake of European penetration. First and foremost, a number of new distant senders are added including the Christian God, the Queen, the Kaiser, the French Emperor, followed by directors of trading companies, big bosses, and many other senders far away in the metropolis. They all write letters and send messages through their various representatives in the Pacific area.

A direct consequence is that the principal source of knowledge is located outside the area: knowledge about language in British and American publishing houses or universities, knowledge about agriculture at the United Nations or World Bank headquarters and knowledge about education in psychology departments or administrative headquarters abroad and so on.

At the same time, the role of at least some local senders decreases; thus traditional chiefs, spirits, gods and ancestors and the special forms of speech they may have employed (Sankoff 1976) diminish in importance. The colonial governments also institute new rules for who can speak for a group, often bypassing traditional solutions. The role of intermediaries between members of different groups is changed by both the development of pidgin languages and the mixing of members from many different backgrounds on ships, plantations and in camps.

Cumulatively this has resulted in the silencing of the indigenous voice and the drying up of indigenous sources of knowledge.

Addresser

Addressers are speakers who communicate their own message. Neither in traditional nor in Western societies is it possible to address whoever one likes, though the restrictions in different societies can vary greatly. A widespread feature among the languages of the area is ownership of words and expression, that is, the utterance (but not understanding) of forms is restricted to members of a particular social group. This in some instances, particularly in Aboriginal Australia, extends to language ownership. The teaching of such languages by non-owners can create considerable confusion and anger. The rules regulating this phenomenon depend on the viability of those groups and with a rapid breakdown in social structures the rules of linguistic use also disappear.

In many documented instances, even such basic rights as the right of the parents to address their children were interfered with by the colonizing powers, principally by a number of mission organizations who took children away from their parents to educate them in Christian doctrine. As late as 1973 I participated in a church service in New Guinea where the converted members of the church were warned against talking to their non-converted relatives. Some of the political boundaries established in the Pacific (e.g. that between the western and eastern halves of New Guinea) also restricted the right of individuals to address former addressees.

As already indicated in my discussion of 'sender', there appears to be a continued weakening of indigenous peoples as a source of knowledge. Senft (1992) comments on this fact and some of its linguistic consequences:

> fewer young Trobriand Islanders experience specific conversation situations which are characterised by status differences between the participants, namely prestigious experts and their young apprentices. The interaction between these persons was characterised by the use of elaborate strategies subsumable under the label 'politeness phenomena'. In the course of his/her apprenticeship a Trobriand Islander not only acquired the respective expert skill and knowledge; he/she also received excellent and highly elaborate training in the culturally appropriate use of linguistic 'politeness' strategies. Thus the changes in the Trobriand Islanders' concept of aesthetics also imply for the young generation a loss in the range of language-use strategies. This loss itself most probably will cause further changes with respect to the Trobriand Islanders' construction of social reality, for up till now a person who mastered the whole range of Trobriand Islanders' rhetoric, versatility and erudition could exercise much political influence in Trobriand Islands society. A loss of such linguistic means of influencing political decision-making processes necessarily implies shifts in the sophisticated balance of political power in this society.
>
> (Senft 1992: 73)

Many traditional societies were characterized by taboo practices which prevented direct talk between groups and subgroups such as different kinds of relations. Missionization and government regulations have removed many such restrictions.

Hearers and addressees

The distinction between hearer and addressee parallels that between speaker and addresser. One particularly important effect of European colonization is the establishment of a hierarchical society with numerous mediaries between the source and destination of a message. Thus, the appointment of government translators is an important stage in the spread of both the message and the code of the external seat of power, often by complex chains of translation, such as those discussed by Voorhoeve (1979).

Equally important has been the introduction of mass media such as radio (which is now universal in the area) and television (which is becoming so), by means of which the number of hearers as well as addressees has multiplied. One effect has been the rapid decrease in restricted information, i.e. information accessible only to a certain class of hearers or addressees. Michaels (1986) illustrates some of the potential consequences of this with the following scenario, following the introduction of Aboriginal television in Central Australia:

> This report has presented alarming evidence in relation to this question. For example, the probability of national broadcast of Aboriginal material without Aboriginal control by agencies such as the ABC, assures disaster for the Aboriginal tradition. The single most certain act of culturecide that I could imagine would be the public airing of a secret ceremony. If the ABC's archives (or the Institute's) were transmitted on AUSSAT, it seems likely that no tribal elder would be left standing within a week. This scenario seems entirely plausible, encouraged by an Aboriginal Affairs media policy which will 'embed' Aborigines in the mass media in ways that are intended to make them more attractive to Europeans, rather than to assure their own cultural survival. 'We use media to destroy cultures, but first we use media to create a false record of what we are about to destroy.'
>
> (Michaels 1986: 153)

The invasion of previously taboo areas is not restricted to the media, however. The right not to reply or respond, a widespread feature in the languages of the area, is being diminished by the growing power of government agencies that have the right to expect a reply or justification.

The range of addressees appears to have shifted gradually from the traditional ones which may have included animals, objects, spirits or natural forces to that prevailing in European societies. Thus, Franklin and Stefaniw (1992) report that the special language use during pandanus gathering in remote 'dangerous' areas in the Kewa territory is under threat of extinction.

> Although the language is still used the people think that it will die out (as well as Imbongu). Some people consider that pandanus language is already dead and claim they do not need to use it because they are no longer afraid when they go to the forest areas where the bush spirits reside.
>
> (Franklin and Stefaniw 1992: 4)

Purposes

The example of the pandanus language and comments later in this book on the uses of literacy demonstrate that events can have a number of purposes. It has already been mentioned that the transmission of new information is a rare occurrence; a second reason for this lies in differences between culture-derived learning practices. Learning by explicit verbalization was not common in the traditional past where learning in informal situations was the preferred type. Formal schooling modelled along Western lines has changed this process greatly.

The use of language for social control is probably a sociolinguistic universal, though the types of control that can be exercised differ from society to society. In traditional Melanesian societies, for instance, political power at village and regional level was associated with multilingual skills. The traditional big men, as described by Sankoff (1976: 290ff.), were skilful rhetoricians. However, their linguistic skills were drastically reduced in value with the introduction of government-appointed village leaders whose main linguistic asset was typically a knowledge of an English-derived pidgin, and with the realization of the villagers that access to political power meant playing a game defined by outside government, and that even this gave only very limited power. With decolonization and increasing social mobility the metropolitan languages have increasingly become the tool for social advancement and participation in modern society. Such patterns of multi-and bilingualism that have existed in the past are rapidly disappearing.

Significantly different from European emphasis on social control are indigenous objectives such as creating or maintaining social harmony. Malcolm (1982: 77ff.) elaborates on such purposes of Aboriginal speech events as 'relaxing in company', 'desensitising to unpleasant fact' and 'evasion', events geared towards minimization of social friction. Liberman (1982) gives a detailed account of the role of language in achieving consensus in Australian Western Desert Aboriginal decision-making:

> The seemingly endless circulation of summary accounts occupies a great deal of time; indeed, it is not absolutely certain that a given assembly will come to a decision. If the decision cannot be a consensual one, it is likely that no decision will be made.
>
> (Liberman 1982: 52)

The main difference with European modes of decision-making is that

> Aboriginal deliberation involves an interactional praxis which differs greatly from that of Europeans. As with other aspects of Aboriginal life, it is essentially a passive affair – the decisions are received and the authorship is either unknown or unimportant. Such an interactional system is highly respectful of the wishes of

the participants, preserves the egalitarian character of Aboriginal political life, and provides a foundation for congenial relations.

(Liberman 1982: 53)

The spread of mission activities throughout the Pacific was one of the factors involved in changing local views on purposes of talking, particularly in the area of decision-making. Many missionaries regarded indigenes as children, incapable of making their own decision. Making decisions for them often involved deliberate changes in the lexicon and grammars of vernaculars. Whilst there are many isolated studies of how this was done for individual languages (e.g. Mosel 1980 for Tolai; Renck 1978 for Yagaria; Schütz 1976 for Hawaiian), only a few writers discuss the wider implications (e.g. Lynch 1979).

Missionization often also implies the obsolescence of pre-existing functions. Thus, in the case of the Ilongot of the Philippines, traditional oratorical skills used for negotiating personal, economic and political advantages were given up from one generation to the next in a deliberate break with the past.

Rosaldo (1984) describes this process as follows:

> Thus, Christianity, opposed to headhunting, came to be seen as incompatible with a style of verbal art that construed persons in ways alien to the national legal system. Young men, knowledgeable in national speech and ways, could then invoke their newfound faith in the defense of their desires for law or power. And persons who defined their claims in terms of goods (and threatened the supportive intervention of police) could understand and argue for their style and stance with reference to an opposition between things made by men (betar) – the customary ways of 'anger' – and Catholic Filipino norms of 'order', understood, ironically enough, as those dictated by a Protestant God.
>
> In brief, for Ilongots a set of verbal skills that once were used to balance and display the 'passion' held by would-be equal men came to be seen as fundamentally disruptive because the sociocultural world that they portrayed and shaped had lost its sense.
>
> (Rosaldo 1984: 159)

A last goal to be considered here is that of marking identity. As has been illustrated by a number of writers (e.g. Laycock 1981), the multiplicity of languages and sublanguages in the Pacific often served the primary purpose of marking speakers as belonging to different social groups. In many languages, this is no longer possible for one or more of the following reasons:

1 Standardization and graphicization of languages have led to a significant decline in non-prestige varieties. Speakers prefer language forms indexical of status to those indexical of location.
2 Traditional settlement and marriage patterns have broken down.
3 The linguistic socialization of new generations of speakers is only partial: indexical aspects are no longer transmitted.

A comparative study by Thurston (1992) on linguistic changes in north-western New Britain identifies considerable variation in the extent to which languages remain markers of social identity. Interestingly, the worst survival chance is given by Thurston to indigenous exoteric languages (lingue franche):

> Initially, the lingua franca function probably helped to promote languages of the Bariai group to the extent that, without external European interference, they might have replaced the other languages of north-western New Britain completely. With the introduction of Tok Pisin, which functions as a lingua franca over a much wider range, however, the shift to Bariai languages was interrupted before completion, and the Bariai languages were forced into an intermediate position – as lingua francas, they are not as useful as Tok Pisin; and as markers of ethnic identity, they are not as good as interior languages. With both these functions impaired, there is now little impetus to cherish them and keep them distinct from other languages.
>
> (Thurston 1992: 137)

Thurston's remarks would seem to contradict Markey's (1987: 3ff.) observation that esoteric languages are the ones that are particularly vulnerable in times of rapid social change. Of course, the fact that the esoteric languages of north-western New Britain are seemingly healthy in the 1990s does not say much about their future, as is readily acknowledged by Thurston himself. The links between the purposes of language use, the strength of languages and the wider situational context in which such languages are found are extremely complex.

Key

This parameter is concerned with the tone, manner and style of speech events. For the Pacific area, we have only scattered observations, in addition to a number of shorter summaries such as that by Fischer (1971). Some aspects of key are closely bound to the medium of speech and it is here that some of the greatest changes have taken place. The literary revolution of the Polynesian languages in the nineteenth century (Parsonson 1967) was followed by similar literary revolutions in Micronesia and Melanesia in the twentieth century, mainly as a consequence of missionary efforts to provide Bible translations. New standardized written forms of the language, often exhibiting structural influence from the languages of expatriate translators, exist for a substantial proportion of the languages of the area.

Missionary concern for improving the morality of their flock, in a number of places, has led to the decline of 'rough' types of speech and swearing, e.g. in the case of Kilivila, as observed by Senft (1992):

> Moreover, the *misinari* try to suppress and to put an end to a number of games, play, accompanying verses, and dances that topicalise the breaking of certain taboos and that 'play' with obscene language varieties. It is not taken into account at all that these games and the playful use of a certain vocabulary allow the – verbal – breaking of taboos in a clearly defined situation only. This situation serves as the forum that permits a specially marked way of communication about something 'one does not talk about' otherwise and thus serves the function of so-called 'safety valve customs'. These customs can be found in every society because they actually help to secure the observance of important taboos within a society.
>
> (Senft 1992: 90)

A similar effect of missionization can be sometimes seen in the area of traditional metaphor, related to the belief, widely found among missionized and Westernized indigenes, that talk should be 'straight'. For the Ilongots, Rosaldo (1984) reports:

> But what is clear is that from at least the mid-1960's the art of traditional oratory was increasingly called into question. Ilongots argued about whether to conduct debate in the elaborate oratorical style or, instead, in the manner of lowland authorities. They criticized metaphorical turns of phrase in the name of a Christian god who desires 'straight speaking'. And, in response to my disappointment at the lack of artful speech in a bridewealth meeting recorded, men told me that talk in the 'old style' would have bred conflict. Concerned to display their 'new knowledge', they all had, as Christians, submitted to the dictates of a pistol-waving young 'captain', who directed participants to eschew 'curvy speech', 'name' their objects, and follow the way of 'the law'.
>
> (Rosaldo 1984: 132)

A phenomenon deserving particular attention is the use of post-pidgin and post-creole continua in a number of English-related varieties in

Australia and Melanesia. This phenomenon is relatively recent (post-1970) and coincides with two conflicting patterns:

1 the possibility of upward social mobility
2 the need to have indices of group identity.

Whilst the former force is likely to lead to the eventual merger of pidgins and creoles with the acrolect, the latter continues to hold the language from this process. The study of variation exhibited by users of post-creole continua can provide some interesting insights into their social position and aspirations. Influence from the acrolect has had an important impact on the key of many other languages. Generally speaking, next to more traditional forms of language, varieties reflecting the influence from European languages are used, and such varieties are likely to become dominant after a couple of generations. Malcolm (1982: 79) refers to some recent developments in Aboriginal Australia, developments which go hand in hand with the development of new urban Koines (talking in a 'light' non-traditional fashion):

> 'Talking light' is using careless, casual speech. It may be used to refer to the talk which accompanies drinking activities, or it may be used deprecatingly by Aborigines of one group to refer to the language use of another group. Frank Wordick, a linguist working in Roebourne (Pilbara), found the term used there to refer to a form of Yindjibarndi exhibiting a good deal of other language interference and grammatical simplification (pers. comm.). At Fitzroy Crossing (E. Richards, pers. comm.) it refers to Walmatjari with phonological interference. According to Sharpe and Sandefur (1976: 63–4), at Roper River a less pronounced form of pidgin is 'light' pidgin. Presumably, 'strong' and 'weak' may have similar referents in the Northern Territory: at Umbakumba (Leeding 1976: 3) 'strong' Anindilyakwa was that which was not mixed with Nunggubuyu. In Watjari (Douglas, pers. comm.) 'light' and 'heavy' speech were associated with the use of interdentals and palatals respectively.
>
> (Malcolm 1982: 79)

Finally, with massive changes in society, styles expressing respect, including the use of honorifics, special voice adaptation or pronominals are changing fast. In some instances, the presence of a socially neutral lingua franca has led to the diminishing use of respect register, e.g. in the case of Javanese, where a much less diversified Bahasa Indonesia is now used, but previously many levels of Javanese had to be distinguished (Geertz 1972: 178–9). However, my Indonesian students confirm, as has been already pointed out, that new conventions signalling hierarchies in the Malay-speaking modern nation-states have emerged, diminishing the role of the national languages as promoters of greater equality.

Forms of speech

By forms of speech we understand varieties indexical either of the language used to address certain groups (e.g. baby talk, mother-in-law languages) or varieties associated with certain social groups (e.g. hunters, females, initiated persons, old people). Few comprehensive inventories of the speech forms of the languages of the area exist, and there remains a dearth of information about the metalinguistic labels used to describe them. One of the exceptions is an account of the speech forms of Kewa, a non-Melanesian language of Papua New Guinea. Among the numerous named forms, discussed in Franklin (1977b), we find:

tata ne agaa	'baby talk, the first words a baby may use'
ona rumaa pe agaa	'marriage talk, referring to the specific bartering exchange of fathers or brothers of prospective couples'
yaini pi agaa	'bespelling talk or ritual speech used to cure sicknesses or warding off an unwanted situation'.

It would seem that the last form is particularly sensitive to change, as it depends on a situation which is threatened by the introduction of new cultivated plants and a cash economy or medical services consisting of aid posts and hospitals staffed by outsiders.

Senft (1992) comments on the actual loss of a number of speech forms in Kilivila, including the following:

> But the changes in the evaluation of the concepts 'magic' and 'religion' do not only affect a whole text category. They are also responsible for the loss of a complete 'situational-intentional' variety of Kilivila, the speech 'register' the Trobriand Islanders call *biga tommwaya* (old people's language) or *biga baloma* (language of the spirits of the dead). In 1983 this archaic language variety was very rarely used as a kind of sociolinguistic variable indicating high social status in everyday discourse and conversation. In 1989 we could no longer observe or document any such utterance in the *biga baloma* variety in everyday language use. This situational-intentional variety is also used in magical formulae. We just stated

that this text category will most probably be lost in the not too distant future. Moreover, songs that are sung during the harvest festival (*milamala*) and during a certain period of mourning are also sung in the *biga baloma* variety. These songs have been passed on from generation to generation. Already in 1983 the majority of the people singing these songs no longer understood their meaning. In 1989 I found only four informants who could sing a variety of these songs and who could also translate the *biga baloma* variety into 'ordinary' everyday Kilivila.

(Senft 1992: 81)

Under particular threat of disappearance are languages that rely for their perpetuated use on stable kinship patterns, e.g. the relationship languages of Aboriginal Australia, such as the various mother-in-law languages, brother and sister languages or the ritual insults between harmonic relatives of different generations. As residence and marriage patterns change, these speech forms become more difficult to apply. Moreover, the lexical and structural sources, typically languages spoken in the vicinity or languages from marriage exchange communities, can become unavailable.

The above sketch of processes at the level of speech event is by no means complete, but what has been represented is indicative of a wider realignment of indigenous forms of speech events in favour of more European ones. The effects of this realignment, as can be expected, are again felt at the level of speech act. As Kreckel (1981) has demonstrated, the expectations of earlier writers on speech and theory that such acts and the associated set of felicity conditions reflected universal properties of human languages has proved not to obtain.

An instance is in the well-known and much commented on examples of replying to questions (e.g. Eades 1982) in Aboriginal languages of Australia and many other Pacific languages. The act of answering in most European languages, however, is subject to felicitating conditions such as supplying information requested by interlocutor with speakers having little option but to respond to the seemingly meaningless questions, Aboriginal answers, as pointed out by Malcolm (1982), are characterized by:

Optional responding. It is not incumbent on the addressee of a question in Aboriginal society to respond to it. . . .

Resistance to answering obvious questions. Grey and Harris have noted that Aboriginal interlocutors will resist answering obvious questions. Seeing no obvious call for the question, they may not know how to handle it.

(Malcolm 1982: 88)

Many of these conventions for answers are greatly discouraged by the dominant school and legal systems and may well be replaced by more European speech act conditions within the next generation. The speech acts of questioning and answering are only two of the many examples that illustrate the effects of changing power relations on discourse.

CONCLUSIONS

The factors discussed here represent only a fraction of those that can be encountered in actual situations of language decline and research in this field supports the claim that factors not provided for in the present ethnography of communication approach need to be added. Kulick's (1993) microstudy of child socialization in Taiap highlights the importance of developmental factors, whilst a study by Coulmas (1994) demonstrates the pervasive influence of economic change. To consider the full gamut of parameters is clearly way beyond the scope of this book. For this reason, the most realistic strategy would appear to be combining detailed case studies with an in-depth analysis of a small number of particularly salient parameters such as literacy and education.

To start with, however, I would like to comment on a class of languages which have been both the effect and the cause of much disruption: pidgins and creoles, and I shall turn to these in the following chapter.

4 Pidgins and creoles

We shall equally have to bear in mind that there is a great difference in the attitude of the civilized man and that of the savage, and that, with his assumption of the right to rule the barbarian through white franchise and with his advantage in the possession of the tawdry wares which to the islander seem such treasures, the white man must be the directive force in this creation of a speech which shall become common.

(Churchill 1911: 11)

INTRODUCTION

Much has been written about the social role of pidgin languages of individual territories and we have numerous comments on the close association between pidgins and imperialist policies. However, the standard view has remained more or less that of Reinecke (1937a: 537), of a 'supplementary tongue for special forms of intercourse', that is, pidgins are languages supplementary to existing languages. Their main function is seen as being to enable communication between insiders and outsiders (for instance 'visiting' Europeans and indigenous populations) or between indigenous groups brought into closer contact by a colonial administration, contact described as the result of 'pax germanica, pax britannica' and so forth.

One can understand this view in the light of the history of pidgin and creole studies, the first large sociological analyses of pidgins and creoles being carried out by Reinecke (1937b) and Schultze (1933). At that time, the main function of pidgins was indeed supplementary. However, it was already becoming clear in the 1930s that pidgins were very much a transitional phenomenon (for instance in Reinecke 1937b):

In short, the trade jargons are the product of frontier trade conditions, and as the frontier disappears and is replaced by closer association of the groups concerned, a more adequate linguistic accommodation is made. And the present Western régime, with its rapid transportation and its schools, is rapidly restricting frontier conditions.

(Reinecke 1937b: 124)

This chapter is concerned primarily with this transition process. Like other aspects of linguistic imperialism in the Pacific, it can best be understood through the ecological metaphor, and, in particular, specific secondary metaphors that highlight the process of transition.

In addressing the topic of how pidgins and creoles have affected the overall linguistic ecology in the Pacific one can appeal to the metaphor of a weed.[1] A weed in the technical sense is

any plant that spreads rapidly and outcompetes others in disturbed soil.

(Crosby 1986: 140)

Analogous to this definition, we can regard pidgins as languages that spread rapidly and outcompete others in a disturbed language ecology. This view of pidgins really shifts the focus from their being supplementary, auxiliary interlanguages to their being both consequences and agents of linguistic change. It focuses our attention upon the rarely mentioned weakening of the indigenous language ecology before their spread and provides reasons for their dynamic character.

The second characteristic of weeds is their being transitional between indigenous species and imported cultural species. They occupy the interim period during which the old equilibrium has not as yet been replaced by a new one. They are both transitional and indices of larger transitions.

A third characteristic of weeds concerns their spread. They spread together with introduced feral animals and introduced diseases which move much faster than the boundaries of European colonization. Thus, there are many reports of pidgins having spread to areas not yet contacted by Europeans, reports that parallel the spread of introduced germs and weeds.

The weed metaphor may also be useful in the context of the history of value judgements. More or less right from their inception pidgins were held in very low esteem by the speakers of their related metropolitan source languages and their eradication and replacement by the standard languages was at times compared to 'weeding out'. When going back to the original definition of weeds, we note that 'weed' is a subjective cultural definition; attitudes to them and their economic usefulness may shift and it has also to be borne in mind that many weeds have at some time become valued cultivated plants.

Applying this metaphor to the domain of languages, we find that the pidgins and creoles that developed in response to introduced new languages and their disturbance of the traditional linguistic ecology by acts of Western imperialism have given rise to numerous transitional pidgins as well as a handful of cultivated creoles such as Bislama in Vanuatu and possibly Northern Australia Kriol. Of course, seen from the perspective of the indigenous vernaculars, the outcome is the same. Thus, both pidgin and creole development, either as the outcome or as the intermediate stage, has led to the weakening of their role and their eventual regression. There is a further interesting parallel between the introduction of weeds into the neo-Europes and European colonies and the introduction of pidgins. Both processes were unintentional and in both instances entities that had developed in other environments were transplanted into a new one.

When Western powers first began to establish themselves in the Pacific they had neither clear language policies nor an overall cultural and economic development plan. Moreover, they had a very rudimentary understanding of local conditions. Their understanding of the linguistic ecology of the Pacific was as rudimentary as that of its natural ecology. Generally speaking, instead of getting to know the unknown, the strategy was to convert it into the known, by introducing European plants and animals. With this introduction of cultivated species came the introduction of weeds. Within a short period, introduced animals and the cleaning of land had stripped large areas of their indigenous vegetation. Weeds had been introduced unwittingly through fodder and soon began to spread in the disturbed soil.

> The imported weeds must have taken over large areas in the West Indies, Mexico, and other places, because the Iberian conquest created enormous areas of disturbed ground. Forests were razed for timber and fuel and to make way for new enterprises; burgeoning herds of Old World animals grazed and overgrazed the grasslands and invaded the woodlands; and the cultivated fields of the declining Amerindian populations reverted to nature, a nature whose most aggressive plants are now exotic immigrants. Friar Bartolomé de las Casas told of large herds of cattle and other European animals in the West Indies eating native plants down to the roots in the first half of the sixteenth century, followed by the spread of ferns, thistles, plantain, nettles, nightshade, sedge, and so forth.
>
> (Crosby 1986: 151)

The examples quoted show that the weeds of the New World had their origin in two sources:

1 plants that had specialized as weeds in the old world were imported by accident
2 cultivated plants developed into weeds in the conditions offered in the new world, for example of the decorative lantana in Queensland or the gorse bush in New Zealand.

Analogously, some of the pidgins and creoles of the Pacific area were introduced from elsewhere. For instance, New South Wales Aboriginal Pidgin may have been influenced by the forms of speech used in communication between speakers of Gaelic and English in Ireland. Some Creole Spanishes of the Philippines may be traced back to the Portuguese Creole of Ternate and perhaps ultimately the Portuguese Pidgin that had developed in Portugal itself in the context of Arab Muslim–Portuguese encounters or the employment of black domestic workers. In other instances, such as on isolated mission stations (Tayo in St Louis, New Caledonia or Unserdeutsch in Vunapope, Papua New Guinea), the development of creoles is a local phenomenon.

THE DISTURBED LINGUISTIC ECOLOGY

The principal condition under which introduced weeds can assert themselves is that of a disturbed ecology. Analogously, we can consider the disturbed linguistic ecology in attempting to explain aspects of the spread of pidgins and creoles.

The best way of characterizing the traditional linguistic ecology of the area is one of structured diversity. Depending on a number of external conditions, such diversity can range from a stylistically highly diversified single language on some Polynesian Islands to complex multilingualism in Australia and Melanesia. Typically, communication across linguistic boundaries posed few problems and could be attained by means of indigenous solutions.

The first manifestation of European linguistic imperialism is not the reduction of the quantity of indigenous languages but the destruction of the region's linguistic ecology, a fact often overlooked by those who write about language decline. As a matter of fact, for the first decade or so of colonization, the absolute number of languages spoken in both the area as a whole and in individual regions probably increased as the result of the influx of foreigners from many parts of the old world. Thus, with the first fleet in Australia came speakers of Gaelic and other languages as well as English, and a considerable amount of multilingualism could be found in the early days of places such as Sydney. The economic activities begun by the Germans in Samoa in the 1860s brought together speakers of English, German, Gilbertese, Fijian and many Melanesian languages on this once monolingual group of islands. Some of the new settlements that grew up around the exploitation of commodities such as pearl shell, copra, sandalwood or gold were described by contemporary observers as veritable Babels. Hanlon (1995, quoted as forthcoming in Keesing 1988: 17), for instance, describes the multilingual population in Pohnpei:

> Other Pacific Islanders also found themselves carried by circumstance to Pohnpei. Some deserted from whaling ships while others, brought to collect bêche-de-mer, . . . were abandoned by their white employers. In the middle decades of the nineteenth century, men from the East Indies, the Loyalty Islands, Belau (Palau), the Gilberts, Hawaii, Rotuma and Mangareva all struggled for survival on the island. . . . Exiles from the harsh life aboard a whaling ship, five Maoris . . . had established themselves at Rohnkiti, [where they had taken] Pohnpeian wives . . .
>
> By 1850, deserters from whaleships had raised the number of foreign residents on Pohnpei to approximately 150. Americans replaced Englishmen as the dominant nationality among the beachcomber community. Fishermen from the Azores and Cape Verde Islands . . . also reached the island aboard American whaling ships.
>
> (Hanlon 1995, quoted as forthcoming in Keesing 1988: 17)

Dutton (1985: 48ff.) provides a highly detailed documentation of the early inhabitants of Port Moresby which included (in the 1880s) Chinese, Malays, South Sea Islanders, Ceylonese, Indians, Germans, Swedes, French and Americans as well as numerous British Australians.

Similar accounts have been given for many other beach communities. However, what characterizes many of these new settlements is that they were plural societies rather than integrated, multicultural ones. It is for this reason that I would like to distinguish between plurilingual and multilingual communities. The former term characterizes situations where many languages are spoken in a politically or economically defined community with no established traditional forms of intercultural communication. Such a situation requires linguistic solutions which are compatible with the preservation of social distance and/or dominance by a powerful group. The development of pidgins is one of the most likely outcomes. Genuine multilingual societies are characterized by mutual dependencies and the use, active or passive, of a number of languages by most members of such a community.

The effect of the first wave of European penetration, then, was twofold.[2]

1 the creation of a number of new plurilingual communities
2 the weakening of existing, traditional, multilingual societies.

Plurilingualism (many languages being spoken but not used in intercultural communication) was promoted by deliberate policies as well as indirectly. Among such policies were the predilection for recruiting the indigenous workforce from many different parts of the Pacific, the resettlement of nomadic populations in villages, the dispersal of groups which forced them into new contacts or, as in the case of Tasmania (see Chapter 5), brought them together in a supervised Government station.

Unintended new plurilingualism was created by factors such as introduced diseases which promoted large-scale population movements and new mergers of groups which had escaped the scourges, the setting up of isolated hospitals (lock hospitals in Western Australia or leprosaria in Hawaii), the prison system and mission stations. Cumulatively such measures affected large proportions of the indigenous population and created new pressures for intercommunication. Typically, the only viable languages left to serve as a model for such intercommunication were the invaders' languages;[3] everywhere where the indigenous linguistic equality had been upset pidgin varieties of the invaders' language sprung up.[4] Thus, there was Pidgin English in the whaling and sandalwood industries, the big plantations employing Melanesian labour (Samoa, New Caledonia, Queensland) and the government stations of the Solomons; Pidgin Spanish in the Spanish garrisons of the Philippines; Pidgin French in the French plantation of New Caledonia and Pidgin German on the major mission stations of German New Guinea. The development of such individual pidgins has been extensively documented (for an exhaustive survey see Wurm, Mühlhäusler and Tryon 1996).

It is one of the principal insights of ecology that the loss of a single species is a very rare event indeed. Typically, losing one species affects a whole series of other species which are dependent on it for food or shelter. The loss of languages appears to be governed by a similar principle. Traditional languages are often dependent for their growth and development on borrowing from and close contacts with surrounding languages. Once the complex network of linguistic interrelationships in the traditional settings had collapsed, the pidgins came to fulfil two functions:

1 they served as the principal and sometimes the only lingua franca
2 they became the main source of lexical borrowing. [5]

An important aspect of the weed metaphor is the nature and order of magnitude of their spread. Let us consider the example of Tok Pisin in Papua New Guinea, since we are in a fortunate position to have extensive data on the spread of this language. Around 1870, the first reports suggest that there were probably not more than a few hundred Papuan New Guineans who had any knowledge of a pidginized type of English. However, with the commercial exploitation of New Britain and the Duke of York Islands from 1873 onwards, a dramatic change appears to have taken place. Hernsheim, a trader at Matupit observed that whilst in 1873

> No native understood any European languages. Now everybody and particularly children spoke that English in question. [6] I had often heard natives using this jargon in talking about the white men and their matters!
>
> (quoted in Schuchardt 1979: 20)

By 1890 the number of speakers of Pidgin English in New Guinea was probably around 1,000, located mainly around Rabaul. From there the languages gradually spread to the new Government, mission and plantation settlements on the New Guinea mainland coast. The number of Tok Pisin speakers during German times grew from a few hundred to about 15,000, more than a third of whom had acquired the language in German Samoa. Assuming that the population of German New Guinea was around half a million, this accounts for 3 per cent of the total population.

After the First World War, under Australian administration, the plantation labour system was greatly expanded and new industries, in particular gold mining, were added to the existing ones. Between 1930 and 1938 the number of black contract labourers rose from around 25,000 to 40,000. Basing his estimates on labour contracts made between 1921 and 1936, Reed (1943: 284) comes to the conclusion that around 85,000 additional workers had acquired Tok Pisin, bringing the total number of speakers to about 100,000, or one-fifth of the population. Because of the disruption during the Second World War, this number probably did not increase significantly, although after 1945 another spectacular rise in the number of speakers occurred. By 1966 when the first census was carried out, 530,000, or 36 per cent of the population of Papua New Guinea, spoke Tok Pisin. By the time of the next census in 1971 this had risen to 700,000, or 44 per cent of the population. As the census questions have since been changed, no comparable data are available for the 1980 census, though it is estimated that in excess of 50 per cent of the entire population of Papua New Guinea, including that of Papua, which was formerly not a Tok Pisin speaking part of the new nation, now speaks Tok Pisin. If one was to represent this development in graphic form, it would take on the well-known S-curve shape.

The effects of this rapid spread of Tok Pisin appears to have taken place in a number of stages. In the first stage, following the collapse of traditional means of intercultural communication, Tok Pisin takes over as the principal language for intergroup communication. For instance, in the Sepik area of New Guinea, there were dozens of small, inter-village pidgins of the type described by Foley (1986a) and J. P. Williams (1990), whereas, in other parts of Papua New Guinea, there were interregional trade languages such as Dobu and the Motu trade language, described by Dutton (1985: 20–40).

Similar observations have been made for other areas, for instance, Thurston (1987: 6–27), in speaking about multilingualism in Western Britain, remarks:

> As stated earlier, because Tok Pisin is so useful as a lingua franca, it has supplanted the former high degree of multilingualism that was characteristic of the area. Though this trend is cause for concern among some of the elders, most young people, particularly in the coastal villages which speak a language of the Siasi group, are content to speak only their own vernacular and Tok Pisin.
>
> (Thurston 1987: 27)

Virtually all the inter-village pidgins have been replaced by Tok Pisin within a couple of generations. Indigenous pidgins that were functional in the 1930s are now functionally dead.

We can appeal to our ecological metaphor for an explanation. Traditional forms of multilingualism were destroyed by a number of factors introduced by the colonial administration, including:

1 the replacement of local trade contacts by missions and private traders
2 resettlement of populations
3 the non-use of local languages by the powerful representatives of the missions and governments
4 new contacts between language groups that had not been in contact previously.

Thus, the ground was cleared for the introduction of a new form of interlanguage contact, namely Pidgin English, a process which severely affected the local pidgins and lingue franche. Greenberg (1965: 52) remarked, on the spread of lingue franche, that 'the only thing that is likely to arrest its spread is a rival lingua franca'.

What seems particularly important, and typically is ignored by those linguists who concentrate on the description of individual languages, is that extended contacts with other languages appear to have provided the life support system for many smaller languages.

Most traditional multilingualism, pidgins and other forms of intercultural communication appear to have served the function of preserving diversity rather than changing languages, culture or relationships between them. Once this life support system had been removed, nontraditional pidgins could take over and spread almost unimpeded.

During its subsequent expansion, the domains and functions in which traditional languages were used are gradually being taken over by Tok Pisin, leaving only small niches such as traditional myth or private family talk and so on. Within a couple of generations Tok Pisin tends to change from an additional language, used to communicate with outsiders or on non-traditional topics, to a language catering for almost all aspects of life. We have a growing body of evidence demonstrating the new universality of this phenomenon in rural New Guinea, that is, an environment which in common belief was regarded as an intact linguistic ecology.

An interesting study by a native speaker of Abu, a language in the Sepik area of Papua New Guinea, is that of Neketeli (1984). Neketeli documents the very rapid change from the traditional situation where all villages spoke Abu and were competent in one or more nearby languages, to one where Tok Pisin has become the primary language of the village. A similar situation has been reported for the more remote village of Gapun by Kulick and Stroud (1989). Other cases are reported in Dutton and Mühlhäusler (1989) and in Romaine (1992: 95ff.). The total replacement of small languages by Tok Pisin appears to be an ever-growing trend. Larger, more viable languages, on the other hand, tend to borrow extensively from Tok Pisin, both lexically and grammatically, and are being replaced more gradually. What is remarkable about this process is its very recent nature. Vernaculars that seemed viable in the mid-1970s are now in danger of disappearing. The functional roles of vernaculars and Tok Pisin have been reversed. Use of Tok Pisin is normal in most contexts, whilst that of the traditional languages is supplementary, for specially marked circumstances.

It is important to note that this is not necessarily an outcome intended by the speakers of traditional languages and thus in many instances not explicable by deliberate choices or human structures. Rather, as has been demonstrated in much detail by Kulick (1991), rational local communication and child-rearing strategies may lead, like other invisible hand processes, to a weakening of the traditional language. This is often perceived only once it is too late.

From the perspective adopted in this book it is the lack of attention paid to ecological factors needed to sustain a traditional language over long periods of time to which much of their loss is due.

It would be simplistic to assume that pidgins always thrive in situations where there is a new kind of pressure for intergroup communication. Rather, the reasons for their spread are much more complex and typically indicative of considerations of social indexicality. Thus, as traditional multilingualism was no longer valued as a source of power in colonial societies, the colonial pidgin became the new index of status and social mobility. Young men who had worked in the white men's towns and plantations and acquired a knowledge of such a pidgin could rise to powerful positions in their home villages without traditional linguistic skills.

Tok Pisin and other Pacific Pidgins were also thought to be means of gaining access to Western cargo – goods and commodities. The vast majority of Melanesian cargo movements employed Pidgin English as the language through which they attempted to manipulate reality in their favour (see Mühlhäusler 1979 for secret cargo varieties of Tok Pisin and their use). Other motives promoting the use of pidgins can be found in a number of articles on attitudes towards pidgins (e.g. in Wurm and Mühlhäusler 1985).

Having taken over most of an ecology does not mean that a weed is permanently established. Rather, it can subsequently be pushed aside or replaced by cultivated species. The linguistic parallelism is the replacement of many varieties of Pidgin English by a more standard 'cultivated' form of English. This process is more or less completed in many parts of Aboriginal Australia, in Hawaii, the Chinese Coast, Singapore and Micronesia and it is in full swing in parts of Melanesia where Pidgin English was until the mid-1980s numerically dominant. Let us now consider this second phase of language shift in Papua New Guinea, the gradual replacement of Tok Pisin with English.

This process is best understood against the background of the socioeconomic changes occurring in the area. In the early 1990s, Litteral (nd) drew attention to the role of Tok Pisin in the transition from local development to Westernization.[7] Literal locates Tok Pisin in the area in between these two:

Between the two extremes is modernization. In this change process there is a willingness to pay the cost of moderate amounts of sociocultural change in order to obtain some Western technology, be it coffee, trees or basic education. Tok Pisin is the instrument that enables this for much of PNG whether it be acquired informally or as the by product of formal education in English. For ever increasing numbers it provides access to the national economy and culture. It permits horizontal transethnic mobility and limited vertical class mobility, e.g. knowledge of Tok Pisin is necessary if one is to overcome the social stigma of 'bus kanaka', 'unsophisticated rural person'.

(Litteral nd: 2)

He then points to the gradual change in government policies: up to the Second World War developmental change was predominant. Between the Second World War and the early 1960s a transitional period of modernization was found, whilst from pre-independence days onwards Westernization, particularly in the educational field, began to take over. Litteral (nd: 12) concludes that Tok Pisin has the advantage over English that it can provide many benefits to a large proportion of the population at a low cost, a sentiment which echoes that of Dutton's (1975a) inaugural lecture where again the cost efficiency of Tok Pisin modernization over English Westernization was pointed out. The reality, both as regards official policies and the behaviour of the population, appears to be different, however. A knowledge of English is perceived as the precondition of all types of progress.

When we look at the spread of English, the picture is similar to the that of Tok Pisin but occurs much later. Again, we seem to be dealing with an S curve beginning with a very slow increase in English speakers between 1920 and 1945, a more significant increase up to 1970, and a rather more accelerated one ever since. The statistical information is revealing (see Table 4.1).

Between 1966 and 1971 the percentage of the total population 10 years and older who could speak English rose from 13.3 to 20.4 per cent. The increase of English is most significant in areas that have been under colonial control longest, such as East New Britain (40 per cent), Central District of Papua (45 per cent) or Manus (46 per cent). On the other hand, in the Southern Highlands (opened up in the 1960s), only 7.1 per cent of the population claimed to be able to speak English. In one district, the Milne Bay district, more speakers use English as their lingua franca than either Tok Pisin or Hiri Motu.

When we look at the increase in those who speak English only, we can observe a very moderate change from 2.67 to 3.13 per cent of the population between 1966 and 1971. If we consider those who had acquired English in addition to skills in other languages then the

Table 4.1 Language distribution in the seven largest towns of Papua New Guinea

Major towns of Papua New New Guinea	% of Tok Pisin speakers		% of English speakers		% of Hiru Motu speakers		Total population (expatriates excluded)	
	1966	1971	1966	1971	1966	1971	1966	1971
Port Moresby (Central)	5.49	61.0	64.4	64.6	77.8	71.1	31,983	59,563
Lae (Morobe)	94.2	95.1	36.1	43.8	14.8	12.9	13,341	32,076
Rabaul (East New Britain)	97.1	94.0	37.4	51.4	11.9	7.3	6,925	22,292
Madang (Madang)	96.2	97.4	30.8	47.4	8.0	7.2	7,398	14,696
Wewak (East Sepik)	96.2	97.0	27.8	52.8	5.2	6.9	7,967	13,837
Goroka (E. Highlands)	89.6	85.9	31.6	41.4	14.3	9.1	3,890	10,509
Mt Hagen (W. Highlands)	82.7	76.8	27.0	37.3	13.5	7.1	2,764	9,257
Total							74,268	162,230

Source: Adapted from Sankoff (1980a: 126)
Note: Percentages are calculated on the population over 10 years old, whereas the total population includes all age groups.

picture looks very different. There is a spectacular increase of 7.1 per cent in only five years, which is more spectacular if we contrast the total of 193,000 in 1966 with that of 323,000 in 1971, i.e. 66 per cent more speakers in five years. In 1971 the percentage of those who knew English had reached 20 per cent. It is interesting to compare such data with the knowledge of Tok Pisin. There seems to be some correlation between an increase in English and a decrease in Tok Pisin skills, though it is not a very clear one (see Romaine 1992: 95ff.). Laycock's (1985) prognosis that English (and possibly a few regional languages) will take over from Tok Pisin may turn out to be correct.

At the beginning of this chapter I drew attention to the fact that the term 'weed' is a strictly synchronic term and that over time weeds can become cultivated plants, and vice versa. In this connection one can draw attention to a number of pidgins and creoles which have become cultural languages, such as Bislama, the official language of Vanuatu, Torres Straits Broken, Northern Territory Kriol as well as the Malay-based pidgins which have developed into the national languages Bahasa Indonesia and Bahasa Malaysia. Of these, the former four continue to be in a relationship of semi-dependency on English as the number of monolingual Creole speakers remains low and English is becoming many speakers' dominant language. It has been pointed out by a number of observers that languages such as Broken and Kriol were stronger as long as they were suppressed and persecuted by the speakers of the dominant languages and that their fate is now in doubt following their official recognition and use in the education system.

I shall leave the weed metaphor here and now turn to another aspect of pidgins and creoles in the Pacific – attitudes and policies towards them.

ATTITUDES AND POLICIES TOWARDS PIDGINS

The following list of expatriate opinions of Tok Pisin was given by Höltker in 1945:

> 'a strange universal language', 'a screamingly funny way of speaking', a 'comical', 'amusing', 'ingenious', 'terrible', 'arbitrarily pruned language', 'a wondrous mishmash', 'a hotchpotch', 'hideous jargon', 'the most difficult language to learn in the world', 'a dreadful parody of the Anglo-Saxon language', 'ghastly mutilated English', 'very apt caricature of English', 'a peculiar, cross-bred physiognomy', 'incredibly primitive with amazing simplicity', 'of cannibalistic primitiveness', 'the most dreadful language of all', etc.
>
> (Höltker 1945: 44, my translation)

This list can easily be enlarged. Kale (1990b) has culled the following examples from her readings of Pidgin English around the world:

> Among the pejorative epithets bestowed on them historically were: 'argot', 'primitive', 'bastard jargon', 'compromise', 'contact', 'makeshift' or 'hybrid' language, 'broken English', 'mongrel lingo', 'grammarless', 'gibberish' to name a few (Adler, 1977: 4). A number of Australian researchers in the 1960s evaluated Australian pidgins and creoles thus: 'A collection of disjointed elements of corrupt English and native words' (Turner, 1966: 202); 'English perverted and mangled ... ridiculous gibberish ... childish babbling' (Strehlow, 1966: 80); 'lingual bastardization' (Baker, 1966: 316).
>
> (Kale 1990b: 110)

Rickford and Traugott (nd) and Rickford (1983) provide a principled analysis of this phenomenon by pointing out that years of 'rubbishing' and stigmatizing of pidgins and creoles have resulted in highly ambivalent attitudes of their users (see also Reinecke 1987; Spitzer 1966).

Having created the conditions that brought pidgins into being and strengthened their continued use, the white colonizers then blamed indigenous idleness, mental inferiority and similar factors for their speakers' inability or willingness to speak proper European standard languages. More recent developments, such as the national independence of a number of pidgin speaking countries, have redressed the balance somewhat, but even in Vanuatu, where Bislama has been a national language, much of the earlier ambivalence continues. Thomas (1990) remarks that such negative attitudes, of course, have their historical roots.

It is hoped, then, that the negative attitudes and inherited prejudices which have so far proved insurmountable obstacles to a reappraisal of language policy in Vanuatu are being dispelled. Doubts about the viability of Bislama and the vernacular languages as media of instruction have, hitherto, led to feelings of language insecurity. In the post-colonial period, there is likely to be less pressure on parents to regard English or French as the sole key to wealth and economic progress. Some would go so far as to claim that in present-day Vanuatu knowledge of English or French is almost totally irrelevant for many school leavers.

(Thomas 1990: 256)

When Captain Cook landed in Hawaii in 1786, it was a monolingual country. From about 1800 on a large number of whites jumped their ships and settled in Hawaii and Hawaiians began to serve on whaling and trading vessels belonging to Britain and the United States. For the first twenty-five years of contact it looked as if Hawaiian would develop as the dominant language, strengthened by having been given a writing system and also by the fact that the Hawaiian-based Pidgin language Hapa Haole had become an important means for Hawaiian dealings with outsiders. In actual fact, even these initial, small-scale contacts constituted a severe disruption of the pre-contact linguistic ecology, as observed by Reinecke (1969: 30–1).

The linguistic ecology of Hawaii was further changed by the rapid influx of foreign plantation labourers, mainly after 1880, comprising speakers of Portuguese, Japanese, Korean and many languages from the Philippines and mainland China. The dealings most of these temporary or permanent migrants had were with English-speaking haoles or mixed race Hawaiians rather than the remaining pure Hawaiians. Under pressure of finding a means of communication on the plantation, Pidgin English emerged and became the principal lingua franca of the entire Island group.

The history of this can be found in Reinecke (1969) with an update and reassessment by Bickerton and Odo (1976–7) and Roberts (1991). Because of the gap between the 'imported' plantation workers on the one hand and middle-class white Americans on the other and because of the need of the children born within the plantation society to have a means of identification, Hawaiian Pidgin soon became creolized (whilst continuing to be called Pidgin). Reinecke (1969: 190) observes that it became 'creolized chiefly in school ground surroundings among a very youthful population, and has been perpetuated as elder children have passed it on to younger children, whose parents could not speak standard English and who, in my view, did not pass on their own language'.

It is not surprising that Hawaiian Creoles became seen by education-alists and politicians as parasitic, possessing all the negative attributes that in the common view distinguish parasites from useful plants or animals. An example of this biological metaphor applied to Hawaiian Pidgin in Robinson (1943):

> In the family of languages, we also find parasitic, degenerate relatives. The 'pidgin' so commonly used in Hawaii is one of many such unlovely 'poor relations'. It is degenerate because it violates the basic principles of good language – precision, clarity and exactness. It is parasitic because it throws its weight upon reputable efforts at communication, smothering good English, good Hawai-ian, good Spanish and all other good speech at the source. Precise utterance in Hawaii is all too frequently throttled in a network of 'No can', 'No got', and 'No make'.
>
> (Robinson 1943: 180)

The term 'parasitic', incidentally, is also used by Chomsky (1966: 21) to characterize the lingua franca.[8] Educationalists' attempts to stamp out Hawaiian Pidgin remained unsuccessful as new immigrant groups arrived and as the economic rift between rich haoles and other groups persisted. However, there has been considerable rethinking among some educators and policy makers about the role of Pidgin in educa-tion and society. As observed by Nunes (1965) Hawaiian Pidgin, like other forms of non-standard speech in the USA, is different but not inferior:

> The linguist thus avoids value judgements about language forms. To him pidgin is not 'the lazy man's language'. It is inherently neither 'good' nor 'bad', 'right' nor 'wrong', but right in certain social situations, linguistically poor manners in others. He concedes that pidgin may not be, as is commonly thought, a corruption of standard English, but an independent system with a logic and

structure of its own – like many English-based creoles, a language in its own right and thus worthy of investigation. Moreover, the linguist does not presume to impose or prescribe a standard. Rather than 'correct' or 'remedy' or 'replace' non-standard forms, he speaks of adding the standard patterns to the student's language repertoire as an alternative mode of communication advantageous for him to master. His aim is a bi-dialectalism which will enable the speaker to move freely back and forth between dialects as changing situations demand.

(Nunes 1965: 6)

The change of emphasis away from standard language only to bilingualism and bi-dialecticism means that Pidgin is now used both as a means of social enrichment and as an aid for adding standard English to a speaker's repertoire.

Nunes appears to subscribe to the view that Pidgin remains less than a full language and he appeals to the authority of Labov and other sociolinguists who

have pointed out the relationship between the impoverished dialect spoken by underprivileged minorities and the impoverished, lowered self-image of members of these groups. The social implications of this relationship are profound and frightening. These concerns of serious students of dialect have relevance for Hawaii, and educators have the responsibility of drawing upon the systematic knowledge already available for application in the classroom. But language is not the responsibility of schools alone. It is a collective responsibility in which the entire community – home, school, university, business – must share.

(Nunes 1965: 7)

The last sentence suggests that we are dealing with a matter of language ecology rather than simple education policies. The home for Pidgin in Nunes' perception for a long time has been a disturbed and debased linguistic ecology. What is needed is a rehabilitation of this ecology, not simply the addition of skills in a second language whose relevance to the inhabitants of this ecology is minimal if unemployment and social inequality continue.

The case of the Solomons again illustrates that the new multilingualism of a transformed language ecology rather than endemic multilingualism is the principal cause for the development of a pidgin language. Pidgin English was introduced to the Solomon Islands in about 1870 onwards by Solomon Islanders who had served a term of indenture on one of the large Pacific plantations. Subsequently, it became the language of the internal plantation system and the unofficial language of the administration and of modernization in general.

As pointed out by a number of writers, including Keesing (1990), there was

> the ideology that views Pidgin as a debased form of English and an impediment to modernity: an ideology primarily a product of decades of British colonial rule.

> (Keesing 1990: 149)

Jourdan (1990) characterizes this ideology as follows:

1 they considered it as a debased and bastardized English language that had no structure;
2 they never thought it necessary to learn it in a serious way, as they would have with other foreign languages, in order to speak it properly; and
3 they never considered it as a real language but rather as a bad variety of English that was in competition with standard English, and thus had to disappear.

> (Jourdan 1990: 167)

While holding the language (and its users) in contempt, the British colonizers created the very ecological conditions in which pidgins could grow and spread, including:

1 They vastly increased regional mobility through the creation of new infrastructure and various labour schemes.
2 They set up temporary (plantations) or quasi-permanent (government stations) localities where Pidgin was the only language shared.
3 Pidgin was the de facto language in which the colonial administrators dealt with most Solomon Islanders.

Since the late 1970s, permanent shift to the urban centres has become an important phenomenon and one that has left a deep impact on the traditional language ecology.

> Whereas Pijin used to be for the Solomon Islanders a second and secondary language, contextually bound to work places, commerce or intercourse with speakers of other languages, it is now becoming the predominant language of a growing urban population. It used to be a male prerogative, learned in young adulthood in sociolinguistic contexts to which women and children had no access. It is now being used in town and other multilingual centres as the main medium of communication, irrespective of age, gender, activities and social status. Pijin permeates the life of the town. If it is

possible for Solomon Islanders to arrive in town without any knowledge of Pijin, it is virtually impossible for them to leave the town, even after a short stay, without any knowledge of it. As soon as urbanities leave the family circle and the 'wantok system', they enter a Pijin-speaking world: Pijin at the clinic with the nurse from Isabel; Pijin at the Co-op shop with the salesman from Choiseul; in the bus with the driver from To'abaita; at the pharmacy with the cashier from Santa Cruz; with the neighbours; at church; at work, etc. . . .

Not only has Pijin become the main language of the urban adult population, but it is becoming the mother tongue, solely or in conjunction with a vernacular, of an expanding generation of children raised in town.

(Jourdan 1990: 180)

The use of Pijin as the principal language of urban communities has removed, in Jourdan's view, one of the remaining obstacles denying Pijin its legitimacy.[9]

At last Pijin has acquired not only native speakers through creolization, but a natural and permanent culture of which it is the medium. As Honiara is in the process of becoming the cultural core of the country, Pijin's cultural legitimacy is being established. The growing generation of urban children having Pijin as a mother tongue might very well contribute to Pijin acquiring this legitimacy.

(Jourdan 1990: 180)

All this has had little effect, to date, and apart from a few nationalist and populist grassroots movements, support for the elevation of Pijin's status remains diminutive. As Keesing observes (1990):

The dominant ideology continues to denigrate Pidgin as a bastardized form of English, created by Europeans as a form of domination and to be replaced as soon and as efficiently as possible by a language less demeaning and vulgar with which it is in direct competition for the minds and habits of the young – 'proper' English.

(Keesing 1990: 164)

The continuation of the colonial ideology among the indigenous elite is also evident, though to a lesser extend in Papua New Guinea and Vanuatu. Romaine (1992: 87ff.) presents detailed information about the preference of the Papua New Guinea elite for English medium education and in a comment on Vanuatu where the Pidgin English, Bislama, has acquired official status, she writes:

Vanuatu is unique among all the territories, colonies, and independent countries of the Pacific in having a non-European language with a constitutional status higher than either of the existing metropolitan languages, English or French. Paradoxically, the current Minister of Education has banned the use of Bislama in the high schools (even outside the classroom) and in the Ministry offices (Siegel 1989 [b]: 2). This may be the only example where a country forbids the use of its national language.

(Romaine 1992: 339)

Whilst it may suit politicians to express their support for the Melanesian Pidgins, their own acts would seem to provide evidence that their belief in the superiority of English continues.

THE FATE OF INDIGENOUS PIDGINS

The term 'indigenous pidgin', as used by most linguists, fails to draw a proper distinction between those languages that predated European penetration and those that were triggered off by it. As already noted, the fate of the former, in the vast majority of instances, was to be replaced either by a European initiated pidgin or by introduced metropolitan languages. Examples of such languages triggered off by colonial activities are Hiri Motu, Pidgin Fijian and Bahasa Malay along with a number of shortlived, extinct mission and industrial pidgins. It is significant that the colonial origin of these languages is typically played down or even outright denied when they become symbols of nationalism. Thus, the supporters of the Papuan Separatist Movement in the 1970s renamed Police Motu, Hiri Motu and portrayed it as the continuation of a Hiri Motu trade language.[10] However, its true origins were that of a colonial lingua franca (Dutton 1985).

The Australian administration of Papua used it as a language of pacification and control, and one result is that it maintains its parochialism at the national level.

(Kale 1990a: 186)

However, this act of linguistic identity was rather weak and it now appears that Hiri Motu has been pushed into the background by English and Tok Pisin.

Pidgin Fijian, like Police Motu, vaguely cognate to a pre-existing pidgin (used between Fijian and visiting Tongans), was developed mainly to control the multilingual workforce on the Fijian plantations (Siegel 1987) and to extend Britain's control over the south-east

Pacific (including the Solomon Islands and Samoa for a short period). Its demise was due to changes in the workforce, in particular the indenture of Indian workers, and to the fact that the missions had developed a prestige variety of Fijian as the lingua franca of the territory. As a lingua franca, it was also replaced in the Solomons and Samoa by Pidgin English.

PIDGIN AND SOCIAL CONTROL

Yule (1988), at the time a newcomer to pidgin studies, suspected that

> it is possible that in colonial days in some places it may have been thought desirable to keep natives in their place by communicating with them in a low-status dialect that could not help them gain social mobility.
>
> (Yule 1988: 30)

I suspect that, in the interim, he will have discovered that this is an almost universal motif in imperialist relationships between colonizer and colonized. It is true that this is not overtly stated at all times, but we have sufficient documentary evidence. The role of pidgin languages in this process is a particularly interesting one, as one can document a whole range of historical changes in their use for purposes of social control.

By social control through language I mean those acts and policies aimed at controlling the social position and activities of individuals and groups by linguistic means. This may range from rather crude acts, such as excluding members of certain groups from using a language (the use of Dutch by indigenes of the Dutch East Indies was forbidden until the middle of the nineteenth century), to much more subtle activities based on evaluative criteria (excluding speakers with a Creole accent from becoming radio announcers in Hawaii for instance). Underlying this is the belief that certain social roles, functions and domains are correlated with the use of particular language variants.

For most of the colonial period, the various colonizers had aims such as

1 the creation of a cheap, non-European labour force
2 the prevention of political dissent among the colonized people
3 cheap but effective administrative structures
4 mobilization of indigenous groups for special economic and war efforts
5 preventing indigenes from migrating to the mother country.

In discussing these and other factors one has to distinguish between

1 the role of social control in the build up and spread of pidgins
2 the use of pidgins to achieve certain social goals.

Since in real life situations one encounters a complex array of factors, it might be best to begin the discussion with reference to a planned pidgin language, *Kolonialdeutsch* (Schwoerer 1916) invented during the First World War as language of a consolidated German colonial empire. The German Military expected a victory which, among other things, would lead to a considerable expansion of Germany's Pacific empire. Areas such as Papua, Samoa, the Solomons, Guam and the Philippines as well as the vast hinterland for Germany's Chinese possession Kiautschou, were projected additions. A simple colonial German had been demanded by a number of lobbies in the mother country before 1914 but concrete steps were taken only during the war. Schwoerer's (1916) proposal for a radically simplified colonial German was meant to meet the following purposes:

1 to provide a unified lingua franca to be used both between Germans and 'natives' and among 'natives' from different language groups
2 to increase the geographical mobility of native workers and thus reinforce a divide et imperia policy: 'natives can be transferred from one colony to another . . . thus increasing their reliability' (1916: 13)
3 to provide a symbol of German authority
4 to provide a 'working language for the German masters and colonizers'.

It was not intended as a means of communication between native speakers of German living in the German colonies and one can easily see the desire for social control as the overwhelming motif in the creation of such a colonial pidgin. Similar motifs, albeit in a somewhat less pure form, are encountered again and again in the history of the Pacific. In actual fact, such control measures typically predate the linguistic emergence of a pidgin and its use for social control.

Let us consider the German Pacific before the First World War. One of the main obstacles of efficient control was the fact that numerous languages were spoken: hundreds of languages in Kaiser Wilhelmland, dozens in Micronesia and one in Samoa.

In New Guinea (see Mühlhäusler 1979) there was an early German attempt to make (Bazaar) Malay the colonial lingua franca. This seemed attractive for a while as the New Guinea Company sought to emulate the Dutch plantation economy of Java by importing workers from the Dutch East Indies. It also appealed to those administrators and politicians who were anticipating a merger of the German and Dutch colonial empires. However, the fact that the language gained little acceptance outside a few government stations and plantations combined with some objections from the Missions against Islamic Languages, led to the abandonment of this plan. An attempt to elevate an indigenous language, Tolai, to one of colonial control remained similarly unsuccessful. Instead, Pidgin English was found to be best suited for the day-to-day needs of administration and in the face of all official opposition the rank and file of the administration promoted the use of this language. The prison in Rabaul became the unofficial school where New Guineans were sent to acquire a knowledge of Pidgin (Nolde 1966).

> We often encountered some of the wild men who had arrived with us on the steamer. . . . The purpose of their forced stay in Rabaul was to gradually acquire means of communication, be it gestures, the customary 'Pidgin English' or German concepts and words. Once this had been achieved after many months, they were returned to their home villages taking with them all sorts of cheap finery. The returned men had to serve as interpreters when agents of the planters tried to recruit men for work on the plantation.
>
> (Nolde 1966: 65, my translation)

Social control and the spread of pidgin languages went hand in hand in numerous other contexts as well. Thus, the setting up of a black police force in Queensland (see Rosser 1990) helped spread Aboriginal Pidgin English inland, and the same process promoted the penetration of Police Motu in Papua. The crucial role of the police force and army in the shaping of the linguistic nature and spread of pidgins is also documented for other parts of the world, e.g. Africa (see W. J. Samarin 1982). Once trained in Pidgin English, the indigenous speakers of the language often became important intermediaries between the administration and the local population.

The practice of recruiting workers from many different language groups for the same plantation is another well-known cause of the development of pidgins. Once developed, plantation pidgins such as Kanaka Pidgin in Queensland could be used for social control in a number of ways:

1 by the Melanesian missions to convert islanders to Christianity
2 by the white overseers to issue orders and control movement
3 by excluding the Kanakas who did not speak proper English from the rights that proper English speakers enjoyed.

Let us focus in a bit more detail on such control in the plantation economy. The fact that the working language of the plantation differed from that of the surrounding regions made it easier to enforce the prohibition against fraternizing with the local population and to keep the plantations as controllable ghettos. Thus, Pidgin English was the language of the German plantations in Samoa and contacts between imported Melanesian workers and indigenous Samoans were forbidden and consequently quite rare. An even more extreme example is cited by Herzfeld for the Costa Rican plantation of the United Fruit Company (referred to as Mamita Yunai by the Spanish speakers), which employed Creole speaking West Indian workers:

> The defacto control of the lowlands exercised by foreign investors (1870–1948) caused the West Indian Negro – especially the Jamaican peasants – to settle down in Costa Rica transitorily (first to work on the railroad and later on the banana plantations, but always thinking of returning 'home'). The 'indisputably monopolistic, totalitarian, and imperialistic' . . . government established by Protestant, English-speaking United Fruit Company officials, fostered the existence of a politically powerless group – coerced by the Company to avoid all Costa Rican government interference. The acculturation and assimilation process to Costa Rican culture and society was considerably slowed down. Obviously encouraged by Mamita Yunai, workers found it easy to comply with the managers' request to maintain both their own language and religion.

and

> If we consider that the Company was from its inception (1899) until it folded on the Atlantic coast (1942) responsible for the ecological, agricultural, economic, cultural, and social peculiarities of the province, it is not surprising that English had a prominent position in the life of the region. More than merely as the language of instruction, English was used as its official language and modus operandi for all transactions. During this time, Jamaican Creole was the communicative medium in family and communal life for the greater part of Limon's population. This gave rise to a local continuum of variation: Limon Creole.
>
> (Herzfeld 1980: 83)

In the Solomons where most of the plantation workers were recruited from within the colony, native languages were not employed on the plantations. Instead, as Keesing (1990) points out:

> As an internal plantation system expanded, through the first three decades of this century, the planters became a dominant voice in the Protectorate. The planters learned Pijin, often relatively well, and used it as the medium of command. The dominant tone

toward Pijin was of smug superiority: Pidgin English was a simple and childlike form of English of which they, the planters, were fluent speakers; it was a low register appropriate to command, and to the mental simplicity of 'the natives'. In the slick propaganda magazine *Planter's Gazette*, published by Solomon Islands Planter's Association to put political pressure on the colonial government, a regular column (Cannibals and Coconuts) reported what were supposed to be howlingly funny examples of linguistic misunderstandings and Pidgin absurdities on the part of unsophisticated 'natives'. Pidgin was a simple and droll medium for communicating about a superior culture and technology to savages, whose linguistic ineptitude was the mirror of their cultural backwardness and lower mental powers.

> (Keesing 1990: 153)

What this meant, in concrete terms, is that the Pidgin English of agriculture, like *Kolonialdeutsch* or Orwell's language of *1984* (Newspeak), was not suited for its speakers to discuss or reflect on many aspects of their new lifestyle and work. This is illustrated in a detailed critique of the Tok Pisin used for agricultural purposes by Scott (1977).

The language of agriculture thus grew around the needs of the foreigners as he saw them, and around the felt needs of the natives whose horizons were limited by what the foreigners wished to teach them – and this was very little.

> (Scott 1977: 724)

The native farmer needed little pidgin to fulfil his limited role in the commerce of the country: a role limited by his own ignorance and the dominance of the foreigners.

> (Scott 1977: 724)

Scott notes that, instead of providing an adequate terminology to enable the native farmers to take part in decision-making and to cope with new technologies,

as techniques became more complex . . . the farmer became even less involved in decision making for he did not have the knowledge to make the decisions, nor the words to convey his decisions to the didiman.

> (Scott 1977: 727)

This appears to indicate that the growth of the lexicon was kept at an artificially low level through the patronizing attitudes of the colonial power and its agencies. The predominant use of Tok Pisin in the directive function can also be seen in many other domains. Perhaps its most blatant use was that of controlling the population during the Second World War. Following the temporary retreat of the Australian administration during the Japanese occupation, the Australians mounted a vigorous leaflet-dropping campaign of millions of leaflets, telling New Guineans how to behave towards the Japanese. Such was the success of this type of war propaganda that the Japanese tried to copy it and/or spread misinformation to undo the Australian propaganda effort. Once New Guinea was recaptured the reinstated Australian administration kept up the momentum of such control through Tok Pisin by sponsoring a number of local newspapers. The use of Tok Pisin literature and attempts to implement strict censorship have been discussed by Laycock (1977).

To what extent Tok Pisin had been entrenched as a language of order giving can be seen in studies of code switching carried out by Sankoff (1980a). She reaches some interesting conclusions for the Buang community she studied:

> The regimented character of the contacts between villagers and visiting whites in the early colonial period, added to the highly disciplinary tone of contacts between master and servant (the primary work relationship known to Buang workers up to and including the present, though the style of most current masters probably differs considerably from the earlier ones we are discussing here), made for a strong association between Tok Pisin and authoritarian behavior. Tok Pisin was demonstrably a language in which one could give orders and expect to be obeyed, even if the persons to whom the orders were given displayed little comprehension (as was the case for most workers during the early phases of their indenture). Though as we shall see below, Tok Pisin is now a common denominator, even a language of equality, among urban New Guineans from diverse linguistic groups, it has retained its associations with and connotations of power and authority at the village level, learned by each new generation in the context of giving orders and shouting at people, as well as in playful imitation of such contexts.

(Sankoff 1980a: 21f)

Analogous observations can be made for Solomons Pidgins, Vanuatu Bislama and the Northern Australian Pidgins. The predominance of social control in the 1940s and 1950s does not have to mean that this same picture continues in the 1990s. For many of the young users of these languages in the Pacific they have become means of self-assertion, group identification and control of their own destiny. But then, the expanded or creolized pidgins of today are structurally and lexically a far cry from the restricted and regimented colonial control languages of earlier days.

The process of transition, it could be argued, has not been without cost. Speakers of languages such as Tok Pisin have lost much of their knowledge of the traditional vernaculars, a process which may be slowed down but hardly reversed by recent attempts to help vernacular education. At the same time, the loss of power of such pidgins is also due to the decrease in status of their speakers and the increasing importance of English. It is perhaps not accidental that the language of advertising in Papua New Guinea's principal Tok Pisin newspaper *Wantok* appears to have become predominantly English and that politicians who wish to control their audiences mix Pidgin English with standard acrolectal English.

PIDGINS AS REPOSITORIES OF INDIGENOUS CULTURES

Professional linguists have characterized Pidgin English variably as simplified forms of English lexicon with indigenous grammar, naturally developed new systems and so forth. These characterizations have had considerable educational and political consequences. D. S. Walsh (1984) is of the opinion that the label 'English-based' has

> also reinforced lay opinion among some ni-Vanuatu, in particular the influential English or French language educated minority, as to the alien nature of Bislama, an alien nature which is associated with relative undesirability, and as to the low status of the language as a mere sub-standard/impoverished/distorted version of English. The development of these negative attitudes concerning a language without which in its role as lingua franca, the Vanuatu polity would not have come into being and could not continue to exist is unnecessarily counter productive.
>
> In the present state of our knowledge as to just how pidgins in general come into being, as to how Bislama in particular came into being, the describing of Bislama as 'English based' is, to say the least of it, injudicious.
>
> (Walsh 1984: 5)

That a label such as 'English-based' has, for a number of reasons, undesirable connotations has also been argued by Baker (1990) and many years ago I offered a critique of the notion of the English 'origin' of Pidgin lexical items (Mühlhäusler 1979).

Before commenting on some prevailing linguistic views let me make a few more general observations:

1 Pidgins are not static systems but dynamic and changing, changing faster than either their substrata or superstrata languages. Similarities with other languages thus may become dissimilarities at a later point in time. As pointed out by Baker and Mühlhäusler (1990), for instance, some significant changes took place in the course of the life of Chinese Pidgin English.

2 There are probably a number of universal constraints that all languages are subject to. In as much as these are found in pidgins, they do not reflect any genetic relationship.

It would, however, be much too simplistic to conclude, as Reesink (1990: 303) does, that 'If universal features are truly universal, or at least typological for certain groups of languages, they would be present as well in the substrata languages as in the developing Pidgin.' Such a view ignores the important differences between natural and abnatural developments. The latter are maintained over time only with cost, such as deliberate cultural teaching, or language monitoring. The transfer of abnatural developments, however statistically 'normal' among substratum speakers, would seem to be an unlikely feature to be transferred to a pidgin.

3 The Western notion of languages with fixed grammars and lexicons is at best a useful cultural metaphor but not a model of any reality. It would seem quite illegitimate to derive the shape of any given Pidgin utterance from a finite closed grammar or the meaning of a Pidgin lexical item from a finite, well-defined lexicon. *Linguists* make grammars and produce lexicons; such products do not directly reflect spoken contextualized discourse. Even if grammars were closed systems, the notion of 'substratum grammar' would be in strife, for it is not the entire system of oppositions and rules that gets 'transferred', not the form of a postulated, traditional grammar, but bits of substance. Most substratists operate with an atomistic pre-structualist concept of grammar or ill-defined concepts such as 'Oceanic grammar'. Given such vague notions, together with the lack of criteria for disconfirming a particular construction as substratum, the substratist point remains to be proven.

4 Pidgins, particularly in the first stages, are subject to very considerable, individual fluctuations. At this stage they do not have a social grammar in any interesting sense. These individual strategies are not just production strategies, and production-centred models of grammatical description such as are customary in creolistics may not be the best point of departure for their study. Hockett (1987) has demonstrated the need for linguists to pay proper attention to the job of listening to utterances, more precisely, situated utterances.

Note also that the interlocutors, of whose speech pidgin speakers had to make sense, differed from time to time and place to place.

5 One should take seriously contemporary accounts, often illustrated with extensive data, that indigenous culture could not be properly dealt with by means of Pacific Pidgins. One of the main reasons why missions, in the early years, used indigenous vernaculars was precisely that these vernaculars, unlike pidgins, enabled them to find out about the workings of the indigenous people's culture and minds.

6 Pidgins abound with conceptual structures that are not of indigenous origin, e.g. the organization of time into years, days, weeks and hours, or the widespread reification of adjectives and verbs (qualitative processes) as in the *sindan* 'behaviour', *bilip* 'belief' or *edukesin* 'education'.

7 That successful communication depends on a shared grammatical and lexical code is a Western assumption, not a fact. Pidgin communication involves the construction of situated meaning through accommodation and other communicative acts, not looking meanings up in a dictionary. Communication in a pidgin involves making sense of the utterances one hears and producing utterances likely to make sense to one's interlocutors.

8 Very much the same also goes for all spoken discourse in other languages particularly in non-formal, so-called 'natural' settings. The notion of 'a language', which applies to written European standard languages, is infelicitously applied to communication in the Pacific.

Such considerations lead me to the conclusion that any question of the type, 'Is Pidgin grammar or Pidgin lexicon Oceanic?', rarely makes sense. [11] A more fruitful way of looking at Pidgins is to address the question: What is the totality of the forces that change their development and lead to either their expansion or their contraction?

It would also seem useful to consider the findings of research into second language learning. Above all, one needs to ask: Do Pidgins impose any constraints on what can be transferred from another language? In all those studies of substratum influence that I have perused it is quite obvious that at best a selection of substrata features but not an entire substratum grammar or lexicon can be carried over. This also goes very much for semantic features. Thus, features such as the use of 'cold' also to mean 'wet', 'disinterested', 'impotent' or 'hear' to mean 'smell', 'perceive', or 'grass' to mean 'feathers' and 'hair', can be encountered in significant numbers and constitute a good reason for dismissing the notion of 'lexical base language'. However, as I have tried to show in my longitudinal study of my Tok Pisin semantics (Mühlhäusler 1979), it can be observed that the meaning commonly assigned to lexical items at one stage in their history can change over time (e.g. *Pisin* first meant 'any animal' and later 'bird') over time. This is not the place for a full technical linguistic discussion. However, I would like to emphasize again that pidgins and creoles in Australia and the Pacific abound with discontinuities in their history, show numerous signs of structural and semantic colonization from SAE languages, have never absorbed much of the finer grammatical and cultural distinctions of most of the local languages and, finally, have changed and adapted to new circumstances.

The fact that pidgins have been shaped increasingly by local people in the business of making sense of introduced change and of creating a new modern culture makes them something very different from both their substratum and their superstratum languages. Pidgins and creoles reflect their speakers' construction of new communication systems, not continuity with the past. Those who have sought to play down the replacive, discontinuous nature of pidgins and creoles will need to rethink their arguments.

CONCLUSIONS

Metonymy is a powerful force in human affairs and phenomena that become associated with developments perceived as undesirable rarely escape from assuming undesirable connotations themselves. Pidgins, without doubt, are strongly associated with many undesirable events including forced labour, forced cultural change, displacement, racism and colonial exploitation. At the same time, they have also had many positive associations, including:

1 offering a linguistic solution to potentially difficult problems of intercultural communication
2 helping their users adapt to externally introduced culture and change
3 becoming languages of travel, excitement and opportunities
4 becoming languages of solidarity and self-identification.

The ambivalence associated with pidgins derived from such antagonistic associations continues and their detractors and defenders continue to argue their case in highly emotional terms (see, for instance, the debate triggered off by Dutton's inaugural speech: McDonald 1976).

In this chapter I have tried to explore some of the positive and negative forces in more depth and, in particular, to show that pidgins are more than by-products or indices of change, they are promoters of change, from traditional to modern ways of communication. Having fulfilled this role they tend themselves to become victims of change and be replaced by more powerful and more highly regarded metropolitan languages.

5 Case studies

The rape of Oceania began with Guam.

(Oliver 1951: 234)

INTRODUCTION

Linguistics for many years has been a battlefield between generalizers seeking all-embracing explanations and others who have pointed to singularities that do not fit general theories. It is in the nature of a book such as the present one to favour the former approach. One reason why I regard the notion of a linguistic ecosystem as theoretically fruitful is that it has generated a number of promising research questions which non-ecological activity, which regards languages as self-contained entities, has not been able to ask. My work on the *Atlas of Languages of Intercultural Communication in the Pacific Hemisphere* (Wurm, Mühlhäusler and Tryon 1996) supports the view that there has been a very significant extent of interrelationship between the languages of the region. At the same time, a growing body of sociolinguistic and anthropological studies confirms the interrelatedness between such communication networks and speakers' cultural practices. It therefore seems reasonable to seek explanations in non-local causes and, in particular, in the massive change in interlinguistic relations over the last 200 years.

Kulick (1992), in commenting on some of my earlier writings (Mühlhäusler 1987a, 1991a), takes the view that it might be more productive to concentrate on single languages, and carry out miscrostudies of local change.

> While there are valid theoretical reasons for treating this entire area as a linguistic ecosystem, many of the generalizations made about the area . . . or about the reasons for language shift, are not well founded and are generated in the absence of detailed knowl-

edge about how people in Pacific societies, in fact, think about and use language in their day-to-day lives.

(Kulick 1992: 23)

His own studies of changes in Taiap (Kulick 1991, 1993) are full of valuable observations and, in particular, many details about the ways in which the unique value system of this community interacts with outside developments. Together with Schmidt's (1985) study of the decline of traditional Dyirbal, it stands as an impressive, in-depth study of language shift in the Pacific.

This chapter cannot hope to achieve the same level of depth and explanatory power. However, it will give the reader a more coherent account of the fate of individual languages than has been given in the discussion of the various 'themes' in my characterization of the changing linguistic ecology of the area.

The choice of languages was dictated largely by the availability of data, that is, the studies involve the impact of European colonization, rather than the equally important input of the Chinese colonization of Formosa on the local Austronesian languages or the fate of small languages in the new nation-states of South East Asia. Three of the case studies deal with pre-existing traditional languages – Chamorro, Maori and Tasmanian – whilst in the fourth study, Papuan Pidgin English was added to illustrate the extent to which external forces have controlled even the pidgin languages that developed spontaneously in response to colonization.

CASE STUDY ONE: CHAMORRO

Oliver's statement at the head of this chapter would seem to provide an excellent reason for beginning with an examination of the language of this island. Commenting on this quotation, Alkire (1977) writes:

he was referring to a predominant theme in Oceanic–European relations, one that has surfaced time and again since Magellan first burned forty houses and killed seven men while recovering a stolen skiff. The people of the Marianas suffered from the severity of seventeenth-century colonialism not because there was much of economic value in the Marianas, but rather because the islands were strategically located on the Spanish galleon route between Acapulco and Manila, and because the Spanish world view of the time thought it essential that Pagans be missionized and converted.

(Alkire 1977: 19)

The original Chamorro language is said to have been most closely related to the languages of the Philippines, but its traditional area of currency has been the Mariana Islands. Chamorro is most closely related to Palauan within Micronesia, though Lewis (1972: 32) reminds us that there were also many ancient trade links with the Caroline Islands to the south.

According to Topping (1973: 2), available archaeological evidence suggests that the Marianas were settled first around 1600 BC, that is, the Chamorro language had been around for about 3,500 years before first contacts with the Spanish. During much of this period trade with the Philippines continued, as probably did linguistic contacts.

The colonization of the Marianas began in the mid-seventeenth century:

> In 1668 a Jesuit mission was established on Guam, but within two years the Chamorro began to resist forced conversions and efforts by the missionaries to disband community clubhouses. Consequently a prolonged period of warfare between the Chamorro and the Spanish began, a war which regretfully became one of extermination. Spanish massacres, introduced diseases, and two devastating typhoons within 30 years reduced an estimated Chamorro population of 50,000 to fewer than 4,000 by the early 1700s.
>
> (Alkire 1977: 19)

Spanish atrocities were not restricted to Guam but covered the entire archipelago. By 1680 the island group had been conquered and depopulated. A large number of Mariana islanders fled to the Carolines and sought refuge among their trade partners. The remaining population of the Northern Marianas was resettled by force on Guam.

From the early eighteenth century onward the cultural transformation and Hispanicization was intensified. Day (1985) describes the process where,

> After a ruthless and successful campaign of genocide, the surviving Chamorros intermarried with Spanish, Mexicans, Filipinos, and other Pacific Islanders (Manchester 1980). The Spanish developed a new class system based on both birth and merit which resulted in a new Chamorro elite. This new elite justified itself on Spanish lineage, which affects life on Guam today. Those Chamorros who successfully claimed Spanish lineage have come to occupy high positions in the political and socioeconomic fabric of the island.
>
> (Day 1985: 172)

As a consequence we find:

There are no 'pure' Chamorro. The population that has survived is thoroughly mixed with the Spanish, Filipino, American, and Japanese who at various times resided on the islands. Furthermore, there are no communities in the Marianas that are following or possess a 'traditional' culture. What we know about traditional Chamorro culture is sketchy and often biased, since it is based on early reports of travellers, missionaries, and government agents.

(Alkire 1977: 20)

Some of the linguistic and sociolinguistic aspects of this process are as follows:

1 Traditional trade routes were replaced by new Spanish-introduced ones, bringing into existence new linguistic contacts.
2 The traditional settlements were replaced by more regulated villages with a Spanish-inspired hierarchical village administration.
3 Large numbers of Filipinos, Spaniards and Mexicans settled and mixed with the indigenous population.
4 The matrilineal clan system disappeared and was replaced by a patrilineal one: 'Family names have been adopted and are transmitted in the patriline' (Alkire 1977: 23).
5 Traditional agriculture was replaced by plantations.
6 European concepts of time were introduced and replaced earlier Micronesian ones (see Spoehr 1952).
7 Most importantly, a new Chamorro elite and a class consciousness developed, an elite that believed that all educated people should speak Spanish. Day (1985) comments on the consequences of this last development:

Since educated people controlled the government, in the 1790s and the nineteenth century, one of the requirements for government employment was knowledge of Spanish. It is not too difficult to imagine the effect this thinking had on the Chamorro language. It aided in the development of a negative attitude by Chamorros towards their language. Not only was it not the language of the Church, but it was not even fit to be used in the governing of the island.

(Day 1985: 173)

In spite of the large number of lexical borrowings from Spanish and other subsequent contact languages (German, Japanese and English), linguists working on the languages have maintained that the Chamorro language remained essentially a Micronesian language. Topping (1973) observes:

One very remarkable thing about the history of the Chamorro language is its ability to survive. In spite of the drastic reduction in population during Spanish times to an estimated 3,678 speakers the language survived. In spite of intensive efforts by Spanish and American administrative authorities to 'stamp out' Chamorro, the language survived. In spite of the current 'Americanization' of the Marianas, complete with mass communications and education in English, the language is still surviving. I, for one, hope that it will continue to survive.

(Topping 1973: 3–4)

Of course, the identity of a language over time and the essential Micronesian nature of Chamorro can be measured in a number of ways. In my view, Topping and others have given undue prominence to a selection of grammatical structures, whilst ignoring the very considerable semantic and pragmatic changes that have occurred. However, what many years of active persecution have not achieved may well result from more benevolent policies adopted by subsequent colonizers.

Germany and the USA took over Spain's Micronesian possessions after the Spanish–American war in 1899. After this date the language and communication area of the Marianas was split up into politically separate entities, that is, an American colony (Guam) and the remainder, which was first controlled by the Germans, then the Japanese, then, under a UN mandate administered by the United States and finally became independent. The result is that Chamorro, which was spoken in both political spheres, came under different external influences in the two areas, was given different writing systems and exposed to different language policies. The end point of these developments was characterized by Bender and Rehg (1991):

We consider two languages to be especially endangered – ironically, those with the most and the fewest living speakers. On Guam, where most Chamorros live, the language has been largely supplanted by English (comparable to the status of the Hawaiian language of Hawai'i); only the fact that there are still some 10,000 speakers in the other Mariana islands to the north (Saipan and Rota especially) gives the language some hope for survival on a par roughly with the other official Micronesian languages.

(Bender and Rehg 1991: 3)

Let us now examine the effects that the American colonization of Guam had, as Guam historically was the focal point of the Chamorro language community and it was here that 'the Spanish laid an excellent foundation for the death of Chamorro on which the Americans were to build' (Day 1985: 174). Benton (1981) sums up the first seventy-five years of American control:

> Although the Chamorro language survived the Spanish invasion and two hundred years of Spanish rule, it did not prosper under the succeeding American administration. For a while, the language was used in the first grade to help children adjust to an otherwise all-English curriculum, but even this concession ceased in 1922, when the language was completely banned from the schools and all Chamorro dictionaries were gathered and burned. Chamorro was widely used in sermons and prayers in Catholic churches, occasionally on radio and television (especially during elections) and even in the legislation, after the Second World War, but government employees were forbidden by law to speak any language other than English during working hours.
>
> (Benton 1981: 122)

Still, Topping (1973), in his *Chamorro Reference Grammar* was optimistic that the language could survive in face of all these developments and that the many borrowings from English were just as superficial as those left by a hundred years of Spanish occupation.

We are in the fortunate position of having a reasonably complete account of the developments subsequent to 1974, when Chamorro was made an official language in Guam. By that time a cultural and demographic revolution had already been experienced in Guam, undermining the related efforts to make Chamorro a fully functioning language in the modern Guam language ecology. Riley (1977) characterized this as follows:

> Until 1960, communication between Guam and the outside world was effectively curtailed by the simple expedient of the United States Navy's deciding that the strategic position of Guam was of such great importance that anyone wishing to visit the island had to undergo the scrutiny of a naval investigation and be eligible for a security clearance. The difficulty and inconvenience this caused effectively precluded any significant outside influence on the traditional social and cultural instructions of Guam. During the years which followed, however, immigration to the island began to increase rapidly, the immigrants being both foreigners, Filipinos for the most part, and Americans born in the continental United States. The census of 1970 (U.S. Bureau of the Census, 1972) showed the foreign population to be 13,484 and that of Americans born in the United States about 2,000 excluding the military.

Between 1960, the year the security clearance requirement was removed, and 1964, the total number of immigrants was 1,081. Between 1965 and 1966, the number was 2,950. Between 1967 and 1968 (the last year for which figures are available), the number of immigrants had soared to 5,672. The vast majority of these individuals settled in the more populous, urbanized areas of the island, where the influence for social and cultural change would be most strongly felt for, as we shall see, it is in these urbanized areas that indigenous cultural awareness first develops as it comes into contact with alternate value systems.

(Riley 1977: 113)

Riley further mentions the effects of the natural disaster, Typhoon Karen of 1962, which led to a total rebuilding of housing and roads:

New concrete housing developments, very similar to the common American tract development, replaced the traditional cluster-style of housing and, most significantly, many new, modern schools were built.

(Riley 1977: 113)

The next factor was the influence of massive foreign investment and the setting up of a tourist industry. Finally modern media, such as television and video, accelerated the modernization and Westernization of the Chamorro community. Unfortunately, their role remains insufficiently understood, as Day (1985) reminds us.

There is one major difference between the linguistic genocide of Hawaiian in the nineteenth century and the possible death of Chamorro in the twentieth century: the mass media. The use of English most of the time in the major newspaper and magazine, on radio, and on television on Guam must be taken into account. Although I am aware of no research on this topic it is reasonable to assume that the mass media have played a crucial role in the shift from Chamorro to English. We might expect to find, when this matter is investigated, that the use of English in the mass media has helped to undermine the Chamorros' confidence in their own language and has helped them to learn English. Given the lack of empirical evidence on this topic, we can do no more than mention it here, and point out the urgent need for research not only on Guam but in other areas of cultural contact as well.

(Day 1985: 176)

In 1973, just a year before official recognition was given to Chamorro,

Riley carried out his first survey of the sociolinguistics of Guam, where he found:

> The number of monolingual Chamorro speakers is minimal, consisting almost exclusively of some of the most aged members of the community who now live in areas that in the not too distant past were quite remote.
>
> (Riley 1977: 119)

At least three-quarters of the Chamorro speakers were bilinguals. Also noted was that about 50 per cent of the population were non-Chamorro, American residents, American troops, Taiwanese, Koreans, Vietnamese, Filipinos and other islanders who had no competence in Chamorro at all (Riley 1977). Foreign migration continues unabated.

The introduction of Chamorro in Guam schools, as pointed out by Benton (1981)

> met with considerable resistance from parents, many of whom had ceased to use Chamorro language with their children. Chamorro was also introduced as a subject for teacher training and university courses in the mid-1970s in conditions which seem to parallel those obtaining in New Zealand at this time – the value of the indigenous language is being recognized by an educated elite after the masses have decided to abandon its use in their daily lives. One Guamanian commentator summed up the prevailing feeling in Guam by saying that the tourist slogan, 'Guam is where America's day begins', applies also to the contemporary cultural attitudes of the Chamorro people.
>
> (Benton 1981: 122)

The introduction of Chamorro into the schools took place at a time when there was a major shift away from Chamorro to English in large sections of the population, as observed by Riley (1977).

> English, on the other hand, is a language of world communication and, as such, is worthy of the prestige it carries. It would appear that the vast majority of Chamorro/English speakers today recognize this linguistic fact and, as the growth and development of a civic awareness prevails, especially in formal societal situations, the shift towards English will accelerate.
>
> (Riley 1977: 123)

As Chamorro survives in some intimate speech situations among some speakers, use in public discourse and by younger people is fast declining. A second survey carried out by Riley in 1980, after the inception of the official Chamorro programmes, concludes that the official language policies have been incoherent and ineffective and that,

> comparing the data of the 1973 study with those of the current study, one is immediately struck by the similarities in the reported ethnocentric knowledge and usage means of the subjects. This would seem to suggest that in spite of the emphasis given to ethnocentric awareness and the importance of the use of the indigenous language over the past seven years by the educational systems in the Territory, these students seem not to have been strongly impressed. As was pointed out in the earlier study, these students are still in the process of undergoing a cultural change, wherein their value system is slowly changing from a communal, traditional state to that of a civic, post-traditional state at least in the formal societal domains.
>
> (Riley 1980: 332)

About half the Chamorro speakers maintained that loyalty to the language alone, and not its actual use, was sufficient for identification with the culture, and whilst support for making Chamorro co-official with English increased, actual use of the language declined over the same period (Riley 1980: 333).

By 1991 Bender and Rehg regarded the chances for a survival of a rival Chamorro as remote, although official 'chemotherapy' may keep it alive for a while. This does not mean, of course, that the language will survive in anything resembling the traditional form, as Western concepts and Western rules of language use, among bilinguals, are beginning to turn the language into a standard average European one.

In a discussion on the role of English in Guam, Underwood (1987: 78ff.) suggests an explanation for the loss of Chamorro which is criticized by Nayar (1991) as follows:

> Underwood's conclusions that the loss of Chamorro as a language is the unintended result of the Chamorro people's own reinterpretation of the ideology of their daily lives (81) seems unfair and inconsistent with his own earlier analysis (e.g., 78) of the etiology of the language loss. One wonders if the conclusion would have been the same if the author had been a Chamorro.
>
> (Nayar 1991: 325)

The case of Chamorro illustrates a number of frequently occurring motifs in the disappearance of Pacific languages:

1 fluctuation between official suppression and official support

2 apparent persistence of a language over long periods of time, followed by a rapid language shift
3 the inability of last-minute rescue programmes to reverse the course of history
4 the portrayal of the consequences of brutal historical events as a natural process.

It also illustrates the almost total dependence of the islanders on outside decisions by politicians, educators and language planners and casts doubt on the notion that the size of the speech community is a guarantee for the survival of the language.

CASE STUDY TWO: MAORI

The case of Maori is probably better known to linguists than any of the others discussed in this chapter and a number of writers have commented on the model status of this language in the context of recent attempts to reverse its decline. Weber (1990: 8) has grouped Maori together with Welsh, Navaho, Romani and Araucan under the label of 'languages on the edge', that is, languages whose fate remains undecided.

The history of Maori has, until about 1975, followed the well-known path of attrition, after the establishment of the white communities and mission posts and subsequently a settlers' colony in New Zealand. New Zealand was one of the largest Polynesian communities and about 200,000 speakers of a relatively homogeneous language lived there by the time of European discovery in 1642. Abel Tasman never set foot on New Zealand soil but had a violent encounter with Maoris at sea. The history of language contacts between Maori and Europeans began with Captain Cook's three visits between 1769 and 1777 and of some French visitors during the same period. Maori in this first period of contact was the dominant language and had to be learnt by European visitors. Clark (1991: 101) reports the existence of a foreigner talk version of Maori in widespread use.

More important than linguistic influence is that Cook's visits initiated a transformation which, in the first instance, manifested itself in the spread of European plants and weapons and later numerous diseases. Cook was followed by other European explorers and whalers and by 1814 the first pakeha white settlers arrived in the Bay of Islands. They were Church of England missionaries who offered protection in exchange for European goods and power. Around the mission station a community of whalers and beachcombers grew up and intensive trade relations developed between the Maori and pakeha, the most desired European commodity being firearms.

During this period Pidgin Maori remained the main language of intercultural contacts but English gained currency, and above all status, in a number of domains. Clark (1991) reports that

> The lexically mixed nature of the language described here is illustrated in the speech of 'Toogee', as given by King: etiketica no eteka 'a chief never deceives'. . . . The first and last words can be explained as Maori tiketike 'high, important' and teka 'lie, deceive', with agglutinated particles; but the negative can only be English. As with other short utterances in the literature, we are unsure here whether to classify this as pidgin English or pidgin Maori.
>
> (Clark 1991: 103)

Gradually the contact language became mixed with more and more words of English origin.

The main transformation of New Zealand began with the treaty of Waitangi in 1840 (R. M. Ross 1972) which opened the way for New Zealand to become a settlers' colony, a Neo-Europe. Clark comments:

> Within a decade or two the population balance had radically shifted so that Maoris were a minority in their own country. Geographically and socially separate European communities grew up, within which it was possible for Pakehas to live out the course of their lives without any significant contact with the native people. Thus whereas all early writings contain some mention of meetings and dealings with Maoris, in the later nineteenth century many New Zealand journals, biographies, letters and the like refer to a completely European world.
>
> (Clark 1991: 109)

From now on Maori developed in social segregation and in a situation of rapidly diminishing economic and political power of the indigenous population. Coinciding with this segregation is the development of Maori as a language of missionization and literacy.

Mission influence was initially very slow and its eventual success is seen by some not as the result of their teachings but of the realization that missions were a way of becoming literate. Parsonson (1967) writes:

> The Pacific Islanders had long grasped the fact that the real difference between their culture and the European was that theirs was non-literate, the other literate. The key to the New World with

all its evident power was the written word. Indeed, the missionaries had often told them so and every fresh contact with the foreigner emphasized the point.

The sheer magic of the written word in primitive eyes needs to stressed. Quiros [see Markhan 1904: 228] notes how the Taumakoans 'were much astonished at seeing one reading a paper, and taking it in their hands, they looked at it in front and behind'. Henry Williams [see Rogers 1961: 222–3], speaking of the Maori, mentions how on one occasion he spent some time in reading, writing and drawing: 'This last greatly astonished the natives, to see the effect of a few pencil marks on paper.'

(Parsonson 1967: 44)

Crosby (1986) offers the following picture of the rapid spread of literacy among the Maori:

The missionaries, all but a few of them Protestants who viewed literacy as a major virtue, flung themselves at the problem of Maori illiteracy as if it were the boulder to be rolled away from Christ's tomb. They learned the Maori tongue, devised an alphabet for it, and in 1837 published the entire New Testament in Maori. By 1845 there was at least one copy of that publication for every two Maori in the country.

The missionaries offered the Maori a new religion, new skills, new tools, and the magic of the alphabet, but it was the Maori themselves who accepted (no, seized) the opportunities offered. The most effective transmitters of Christianity and literacy were the prisoners taken by the Ngapuhi and allies – the lowest of the low, the slaves – who embraced the new religion with the greatest fervor, and then, as the wars waned and they were freed, returned home bearing the Word with them. When the missionaries penetrated the southern central districts of the North Island, they found the Maori there already clamouring for instruction and books, and often village schools under Maori teachers already in operation.

There were no Maori conversions up to 1825, and only a few usually of the moribund – between 1825 and 1830. Ten years later, the Anglicans alone claimed 2,000 communicants and thousands more, adult and child, under instruction in Christianity and the basic skills of literacy.

(Crosby 1986: 246)

Similarly vigorous illustrations of the spread of literacy are given by Parr (1963). According to Hohepa (1984: 1), by 1856 'some 90%

of the Maori population were able to read and write in their own language; in that year, the numbers of white settlers equalled the total Maori population'.

As was the case with other Pacific languages (Chamorro, Hawaiian), literacy did little to strengthen the Maori language and the realization that this was so soon led to widespread dissatisfaction with literacy among Maori speakers. In a very perceptive study of early Maori literacy, McKenzie (1987: 179) draws attention to its less desirable side-effects: 'printing had helped fix the Maori language – albeit in one dialect and with some dangerous neologisms'.

Next to the weakening of the dialectal diversity of Maori, literacy failed to strengthen the Maori cause when it was most needed. It 'had failed lamentably to equip the Maori to negotiate their rights with the Pakeha in the one area that really mattered to them – land' (McKenzie 1987: 178). Far from empowering the Maori, literacy, and above all the spatial extension promoted by letterwriting, at times became 'politically potent in gathering the tribes and planning a war a decade or more later' (McKenzie 1987: 170). As Maori turned against Maori the white settlers became more powerful and numerically dominant and they actively discouraged the use of the Maori language in all public settings, in particular in education. Hohepa (1984) describes this process as follows:

> As white settler governments took control of education from mis-
> sions, and white settler children began attending schools formerly
> totally Maori from 1858 onwards, English based curriculum became
> dominant – English language and English literature and customs
> became the main medium and message.
>
> (Hohepa 1984: 1)

The Native Schools Act (1867) saw the formal replacement of mission schools based on the English village day-schools where teaching was in English, and the curriculum was that of primary schools. English was taught at first as a second language, using Maori as the medium in junior classes. Some bilingual education was thus in vogue, however this too was obliterated at the beginning of the twentieth century. At the same time teachers were ordered to encourage Maori children not to speak Maori in the school and its immediate locale. This 'encourage-ment' was then translated by teachers into harsh physical and mental punishment of any child speaking Maori. Low esteem for the language was a consequence. A sociolinguistic survey carried out in the early 1970s (see Benton 1981: 46) found that more than half of the adult informants interviewed reported having been punished at school for speaking Maori.

Apart from the systematic processes generating negative attitudes towards Maori, other processes began to undermine the vitality of the language, in particular a dramatic population decline from about 200,000 speakers in 1856 to 42,000 in 1895, by which date the number of white settlers had increased to 2 million. The first half of the twentieth century saw a continuation of an English-only policy and systematic assimilation of the Maori into mainstream society, a policy which was mellowed only from about 1930 onwards by the fact that some educationalists began to pay lip-service to Maori cultural contact in school syllabuses (Benton 1981: 25).

The decline of Maori continued until the 1970s by which time only one-quarter of the Maori population were native speakers, and more importantly, virtually all of them were bilingual in English. Positive changes in the official and private attitudes towards Maori became important only in the 1970s and it is too early to say whether these changes came too late to arrest or reverse the decline of the language. In 1977, under the Labour government, the Minister for Education noted that it was 'important to recognise the importance of the Maori language to the Maori people and to the wider community' (Benton 1981: 31) and enrolment in Maori language classes and regular attention to Maori culture became part of many school syllabuses. By 1984, 55,000 pupils at primary and 25,000 at secondary level attended Maori classes.

The most important change was the development of the Te Kohanga Reo or Language Learning Nest movement which got under way in 1982. This scheme has been defined as:

> a bilingual programme in Maori and English for under five-year olds, with a home-like environment where Maori language is spoken naturally as one of the two native tongues – the other being English, which is largely used at home.
>
> (Ryan 1987: 7)

> The basic principles for the child care system will be the best operating in the greater society, with the difference that Maori language will be the only means of verbal communication in the centre which will operate Monday to Friday. Children are not admitted without full counselling being undertaken with parents and their total agreement to participating in the programme for at least three years.
>
> (Ryan 1987: 7)

The number of Language Learning Nests has grown to about 400 for about 4,000–5,000 or one-seventh of all preschool Maori children. A further boost was given to Maori first by the announcement in 1974 that

> official recognition is hereby given to the Maori Language of New Zealand in its various dialects and idioms as the ancestral tongue of that portion of the population of New Zealand of Maori descent.
>
> (The Maori Affairs Amendment Act 1974, Section 51)

In 1982 legislation was passed that made Maori an official language of New Zealand in 1987.

Around the time that such official recognition occurred, the trend towards monolingualism in English was very powerful and the decline of Maori continues, as empirical studies confirm. Benton's (1980) sociolinguistic study of the Ruatoki District in the Central Bay of Plenty, one that has been noted for the vitality of its Maori culture, found that, in 1963, the vast majority of children were native speakers of Maori and Maori was the main language used in schools and playgrounds, in all communities (Benton 1980: 457).

In 1977

> children aged 11 years and older were probably functionally bilingual, some marginally more comfortable speaking Maori in casual conversation, others happier when speaking English. In the younger age groups a majority of children appeared to be passively bilingual – that is, they had a fair to excellent understanding of Maori but normally spoke English even when addressed in Maori by friends and relatives.
>
> (Benton 1980: 457)

In 1978, following the setting up of the first two bilingual schools (Ruatoki and Tawera), some important changes occurred.

> The amazing thing about the 1978 data is that, on first inspection, the linguistic situation in Ruatoki and Tawera seems to have undergone a profound revolution. While in Tawera code-switching seems to be a common phenomenon, there is noticeably less mixing of Maori and English in the same phrase in the recorded speech of children at each school. Taking the 17 most extensively recorded Ruatoki children as the basis for comparison with the two earlier groups, the use of English elements by fluent speakers of Maori seems remarkably restrained. A total of only 19 unassimilated major morphemes appears in this body of data, in the same kinds of categories as previously:- a few kin terms: 'aunty', 'uncle'; words connected with sport: 'longball', 'frisbee', 'football field'; television:

'TV', 'on' (meaning 'what's on' – i.e., 'programme'), 'turn off';
food: 'fish and chips', 'barbecue'; etc.

(Benton 1980: 461)

It was also noted that these changes affected boys and girls differen-
tially, a phenomenon well documented for language shift elsewhere:

> One possible reason for Maori having become an in-group language
> among boys would be their realization that they are likely to need
> to be able to speak Maori well if they are to take a leader-ship role
> on the marae when they are adults. In a community like Ruatoki
> where the traditional culture is still strong and visible, this could
> act as a powerful motivation to boys to become competent speakers
> of Maori. There are no parallel advantages in the traditional
> culture to motivate girls to retain a high level of competence in
> Maori. Independent confirmation of this difference in behaviour
> between boys and girls was obtained from teachers, who reported
> some months after the interviews with the children (unaware of the
> comments that were made on this topic) that on 'Maori Language
> Days' at the school they had a very hard job to get the older girls
> to co-operate in speaking only Maori.

(Benton 1980: 467)

In assessing his research findings, Benton notes disturbing trends,
among them the loss of grammatical complexity:

> This has also meant that certain complex structures, where English
> elements had been employed in 1977, were in 1978 often avoided
> altogether. As a long-term development, this could mean that
> Maori, when it is used, may have much less overtly English content,
> but will relate to a reduced universe of discourse. Alternatively,
> and this would seem to be more likely trend, it is possible that a
> 'school Maori' register is being developed in Ruatoki, and the real
> language spoken by children will be a blend of Maori and English
> like that revealed in the 1977 tapes for some children, English for
> others, with a few remaining speakers competent in both languages
> and able to separate them functionally with a minimum of
> difficulty.

(Benton 1980: 476)

A second trend is the increase of linguistic monitoring:

> Another side effect of the new consciousness of the importance of
> Maori in the school system has been to increase the difficulty of
> securing useful data on the ways in which children use the Maori

language in everyday life. Most of the speech samples collected in 1963 and 1977 were quite relaxed and natural. In those periods, an invitation to speak Maori was an invitation to chat informally. The 1978 material, however, has a more contrived character, and as is clear from some of the examples quoted, speaking Maori was perceived by many children as a task. Much of what was recorded, therefore, although by no means all, represents what children think they ought to say in a formal situation in a school setting; a taping session has become a kind of Maori language examination. (Ironically, the publication of this paper is likely to make it even more so.)

(Benton 1980: 477)

A more recent study by Boyce (1991) examines the use of Maori in the less traditional community of Porirua, twenty-five kilometres from Wellington. She encountered a steady decline in the number of young people speaking Maori with any degree of efficiency. Boyce also found that the strong presence of Language Nests does not appear to have made a significant difference yet:

The information presented above makes it very clear that there has been a shift towards English in Porirua over the past fifteen years. Fewer people in the community are first language speakers of Maori. Those that are, are older people. The introduction of kohanga reo in the community does not appear to be making a significant difference yet in the amount of Maori used, or in proficiency in Maori in the adult population. However, if a similar study was to be conducted in another fifteen years it may well find a more proficient population of young adults, graduates of the kohanga reo and the increasing number of bilingual and other Maori programmes in local schools.

(Boyce 1991: 16)

Fishman's (1991) examination of the kohanga reo identifies a number of disturbing trends:

Not all of them, by any means, are pedagogically effective, nor is their nearly total reliance on an untrained, volunteer staff a completely unmixed blessing, neither in the educative connection nor even in connection with childcare per se. While a large proportion of Maori pre-schoolers now attend these centers, there are probably even more who still do not do so. Finally, the growing dependence of these centers on funding by the Department of Maori Affairs may ultimately turn out to be a fatal flaw, not only because government priorities are subject to change.

(Fishman 1991: 238)

The Kohanga reos are not used to help render Maori-speaking the children's overwhelmingly English-speaking parents and older siblings, parents and siblings who are often Maori-positive in a passive way (sufficiently so to send their youngest family members to the Kohanga reos), but who have not yet, by and large, become even minimally Maori-speaking themselves.

(Fishman 1991: 239)

The thrust of Fishman's arguments is that insufficient consideration has been given to large questions of language ecology. Whilst there is a good support system for preschool children inside their language nests, there is no proper 'home, family and neighbourhood niche' to sustain Maori in later life.

Thus, the increasingly favourable attitudes towards Maori language and Maori culture are not matched by increasing linguistic competence. Though many aspects of the future of Maori remain unclear, the following predictions seem to be fairly uncontroversial:

1 There will be no monolingual speakers of Maori.
2 There will be no place for monolingual Maoris in New Zealand society.
3 Official support for Maori will not necessarily guarantee language survival. On the contrary, many speakers will see the involvement of schools and government in language preservation as an excuse for doing less about their language at home.
4 The language will be much altered and reduced lexically and structurally, and semantically dominated by English.
5 News media such as video, TV and computers will accelerate a shift towards English.
6 Maori will continue to enjoy a symbolic value.

The best one can hope for is the stabilization of a bilingual situation for the Maori population of New Zealand, a bilingualism that is no longer transitional, but what has been done thus far appears to be too little and too late even for that to happen.

CASE STUDY THREE: LINGUISTIC GENOCIDE IN TASMANIA

Day (1985: 179) has characterized linguistic genocide as 'a type of language death which occurs when two unequal societies come into lasting contact'. The examples that Day discusses, Hawaiian and Chamorro, both illustrate a subtype where part of the original indigenous population continues to survive, albeit much missionized, made literate and otherwise acculturated. An even more extreme situation obtains when entire language communities are killed off, an occurrence which is not infrequent in Australia and the Pacific area. Among these, the case of Tasmania stands out as a particularly brutal example of linguistic imperialism.

Most observers are agreed that Tasmania was populated by a number of separate Aboriginal groups, possibly four or more, each of them using their own linguistic conventions. The notion of separate languages would seem to make very little sense in describing the situation. A more realistic picture might be a chain of related varieties with intelligibility between adjacent varieties. As all records of Tasmania were made at a time when the Aborigines had already been displaced and resettled, we can at best guess how the indigenous language ecology functioned. The diversity (dialectal or otherwise) was generally commented on negatively by white observers. Milligan (1859) comments:

> The circumstance of the aboriginal inhabitants of Van Diemen's Land being divided into many tribes and subtribes, in a state of perpetual antagonism and open hostility to each other, materially added to the number and augmented the energy of the elements and agents of mutation ordinarily operating on the language of an unlettered people: to this was superadded the effect of certain superstitious customs everywhere prevalent, which led from time to time to the absolute rejection and disuse of words previously employed to express objects familiar and indispensable to all – thus imperiously modifying nomenclature and the substantive parts of speech, and tending arbitrarily to diversify the dialects of the several tribes.
>
> (Milligan 1859: 279)

Similarly, George Washington Walker, who visited the Aboriginal settlement on Flinders Island in 1832 and 1834, writes in his notes:

> It is extremely difficult to come at the idiom, as every tribe speaks a different dialect, it might also be said a different language, and even among the individuals of the same tribe a great difference is perceptible. The pronunciation is very arbitrary and indefinite.
>
> (Walker 1898: 172)

'Arbitrariness and indefiniteness' has also been commented on by other observers of these languages. Contemporary views on the linguistic nature of the Tasmanian languages were generally negative, the only concession made by some, but not all, observers being that it was melodious when sung. Plomley (1976) quotes a number of early observations:

> Marion du Fresne: Their language sounded to us very harsh: they seemed to draw their words from the bottom of the throat. 'Frederick Henry Bay', March 1772.
>
> James Cook: Their pronunciation is not disagreeable, but rather quick; though not more so than is that of other Indian nations of the South Sea. Dr William Anderson, Adventure Bay, 1777.
>
> William Bligh: Bligh speaks of voices 'like the cackling of geese', and tells of a party of natives who made 'a prodigious chattering in their speech', and also 'spoke so quick, that I could not catch one single word they uttered'. Adventure Bay, August–September 1788.
>
> (Plomley 1976: 27)

There is an almost general agreement on the lexical and syntactic properties of Tasmanian, i.e. that the language is totally deficient in those areas. This reflects the view prevailing at the time: that primitive people of necessity employ primitive languages. As Milligan (1859) states:

> The language of a people, whether it be possessed of a copious or spare vocabulary – whether it consist of a plain collocation of a few simple and arbitrary sounds, or be characterized by elaborate inflexions and a complex arrangement of words of analogical import – ought to be accepted, one would say, as the index of the degree of mental culture and social and intellectual progress attained by those who make use of it, and find it sufficient for the expression of their various thoughts, feelings, and desires. A glance at the vocabulary of aboriginal dialects of Tasmania, and at the condition of the aborigines themselves, will perhaps be thought to lend confirmation to the opinion.
>
> (Milligan 1859: 278)

Milligan comments on the perceived lexical and other deficiencies:

> The habit of gesticulation and the use of signs to eke out the meaning of monosyllabic expressions, and to give force, precision, and character to vocal sounds, exerted a further modifying effect, producing, as it did, carelessness and laxity of articulation, and in the application and pronunciation of words. The last named irregularity, namely, the distinctly different pronunciation of a word by the same person on different occasions to convey the same idea is very perplexing, until the radical or essential part of the word, apart from prefixes and suffixes, is caught hold of. The affixes,

which signify nothing, are la, lah, le, leh, leah, na, ne, neh, ba, be, beah, bo, ma, me, meah, pa, poo, ra, re, ta, te, ak, ik, &c. Some early voyagers appeared to have mistaken the terminals la, le &c, as distinctive of sex, when applied to men, women, and the lower animals. The language, when spoken by the natives, was rendered embarrassing by the frequent alliteration of vowels and other startling abbreviations, as well as by the apposition of the incidental increment indifferently before or after the radical or essential constituent of words.

(Milligan 1859: 279)

The lack of abstract terms, such as the absence of superordinate for 'tree', 'plant' or 'animal' is deplored in the next quotation, whose author a few lines later criticizes Tasmanian for having words which are very vague and very general (i.e. abstract):

Some of the aboriginal terms have a very indefinite and extended meaning, as in the words 'clackny' and 'pomleh'. The former means 'to be, to exist, to rest, sit down or lie down, to stop, remain, dwell, sleep', and I know not how many more significations. The latter is used in a variety of ways, but more particularly where art, or ingenuity, or an exertion of power is applied to the production of anything. Everything that has required any sort of manipulation has been 'pomleh', i.e., 'made, or put together, or called into existence'.

It is also remarkable that the aborigines have hardly any general terms. They have not even a term to represent 'trees' or 'animals' generally.

(Walker 1898: 171)

Such prejudices about the primitiveness of the language were subsequently translated into communicative practice by the small number of European settlers who bothered to communicate with the Tasmanians. Plomley (1976: 61) mentions the government agent Robinson, who is widely regarded as 'the best European speaker of Tasmanian'. Robinson in 1829, after eight weeks on Brunby Island, claimed to have preached to the Aborigines in their own language. An extract of this sermon is the following:

At 11am performed divine service in the natives' hut. Four of the prisoners attended. Preached to the aborigines in their own tongue. Part of the sermon – MOTTI (one) NYRAE (good) PARLERDI (God) MOTTI (one) NOVILLY (bad) RAEGEWROPPER (devil). PARLERDI (God) NYRAE (good). PARLERDI (God) MAG-

GERER (stop) WARRANGELLY (sky), RAEGEWROPPER (devil) MAGGERER (stop) TOOGENNER (below) UENEE (fire). NYRAE (good) PARLERWAR (native) LOGERNER (dead) TAGGERER (go) TEENY (road) LAWWAY (up) WAR-RANGELLY (sky) PARLERDI (God) NYRAE (good) RAEGE (whiteman) etc, etc. NOVILLY (bad) PARLEWAR (native) LOGGERNER (dead) TAGGERER (go) TEENNY (road) TOO-GENNER (below) RAEGEWROPPER (devil) UENEE (fire) MAGGERER (stop) UENEE (fire).

(Plomley 1976: 61)

Crowley (1990b) comments on the language in this text:

The text of his sermon contains words strung together in an order that is identical to English, but stripped of all grammatical markers (i.e. prefixes, suffixes, prepositions, articles and the like). What this text looks like, in fact, is a pidgin from which the English lexicon has been systematically replaced by vernacular words.

(Crowley 1990b: 8)

The primitiveness of Tasmanian, it would seem, was only such in the hand of the beholders.

By the time these observations were made the Tasmanian language had begun to disappear, as the remaining 300 Aborigines that were deported to Flinders Island in 1830 had dwindled to 150 by 1834 and 50 by 1842. The decline of the language appears to have followed the general picture postulated in Chapter 4 on pidgins. Following the destruction of the traditional ecology by about 1820 when the tradi-tional hunting ground and fertile parts of the island had been occupied by the Europeans, a pidgin language, first containing many words from Tasmanian, began to appear. An example of this mixed pidgin was recorded in 1837 on Flinders Island, and is quoted by Plomley (1976):

I said to Hector 'you are very sick?' Hector 'yes me plenty menaty' [sick]. You coethee God? Hector 'yes me coethee plenty'. You coethee Jesus Christ? 'Yes me coethee Jesus Christ the son of God'. Do you pray to him? 'Yes me pray to him plenty, me pray last night our Father which art in heaven pleny'. You very sick you krakabuka [die] by and bye? 'Yes me talbetee werthichkathe [?] to God, me coethee'.

(Plomley 1976: 39–40)

Subsequently, the language became increasingly lexically dependent on English. Flinders Island never developed into a viable linguistic ecology but gradually turned into 'the home of the miserable remnant of the native tribe of Tasmania, and for the greater part of them it was destined to become their grave' (Walker 1898: 146).

Preceding its final failure, the involuntary inhabitants of Flinders Island developed a number of short-lived solutions to their communication problems. For instance:

> Robert Clark, the catechist, states that on his arrival at the Flinders' Settlement in 1834, eight or ten different languages or dialects were spoken amongst the 200 natives then at the establishment, and that the blacks were 'instructing each other to speak their respective tongues.'
>
> (Walker 1898: 179)

This koine appears to have been gradually replaced by Pidgin English, a process described by Jorgenson (1842):

> It is difficult to imagine the rapid and ever-changing corruptions to which an oral language is subject in the mouths of a savage tribe; and in the present case many words, borrowed from the English, have added to the confusion produced by the irregular and careless pronunciation of the Aborigines. Thus Picanini, a child; Buckalow, or Bucala, bullocks; Tablety (corrupted from travel), to go, which again was contracted into Tablee, are all from the English. Lubra is a word introduced by the English from the Sydney natives (who do not at all understand the languages of our Aborigines), and it appears to have been substituted for Lurga, or Lolna, a woman.
>
> These remains of the Aboriginal dialects are recorded in their present unsatisfactory state, with the hope that some reader of these pages may be able to afford such corrections and additions as will possibly give a clue to the nature and origin of the language. The native tribes have no other memorial of the past, and even this is disappearing, as those who are not of the same tribe appear to converse in broken English.
>
> (Jorgenson 1842: 309)

The remaining forty-six Aborigines were moved from Flinders Island to the last Tasmanian Aboriginal settlement, Oyster Bay, in the remote south-east of the Island, where the last full-blooded Aboriginal in Tasmania died in 1876. Lennox (1984) reports that the linguistic practices of Flinders Island were continued in Oyster Bay.

> The Aboriginal dialects made it difficult for the members of one family to understand that of another; now however they all seem to have merged into one, and that is generally used by the natives

when talking to themselves. The men spoke English more frequently and better than the women; however both sexes invariably used English when quarrelling. Dandridge supposed that this was because it furnished 'more opprobrious epithets' than in their own language.

(Lennox 1984: 60)

Crowley (1990b) speculates that the last survivors used a Tasmanian type of Pidgin English and that

> if this community had been able to maintain itself for another generation, . . . these people would probably have ended up speaking English, just as we find among Aborigines in many parts of Victoria and New South Wales today.
>
> (Crowley 1990b: 13)

The replacement of Aboriginal ways with European ways and their language with English was the professed aim of successive administrators. There was very little interest in studying either, and much of the Aboriginal language is irretrievably lost, as observed by Plomley (1976):

> None of the exploring expeditions which visited Tasmania after 1803 paid any real attention to the aborigines, even after 1840, by which time it was realized that the race would become extinct. The same may be said of those living in Tasmania: they paid almost no attention to studying the aborigines as a people, and this included the recording of their language. Between 1803 and 1876 a few short vocabularies were recorded and one extensive one, that of Joseph Milligan, but no one studied the language and no one did more than record in a desultory way the Aboriginal words for common objects and activities . . .
>
> Although the Aboriginal settlement on Flinders Island was formed as early as 1832 and had several commandants and other officers, only Joseph Milligan recorded an extensive vocabulary. Even G. A. Robinson did not add significantly while he was there to what he had recorded during his expedition on the mainland, nor did he attempt to put his data into any order or to make any contribution to the study of the grammar of the language. The latter is at least understandable because his knowledge of English grammar was negligible. The cause of the failure by those at Flinders Island to record information about the Tasmanian language was that no one there was interested in the Tasmanian culture, only in the replacement of Tasmanian ways of life with

European ways and with the introduction of the English language as a means of doing this.

(Plomley 1976: 4)

The consequences are summed up in Capell's (1968) article entitled 'What do We Know of Tasmanian Languages?':

> The answer . . . is thus shown to be not quite 'nothing', but only 'very little', and that little contains many uncertainties, which it seems quite unlikely that time will resolve.
>
> (Capell 1968: 7)

There is a postscript to this story. Whereas full-blooded Tasmanians died out, about 4,000 mixed persons continue to claim to be Tasmanian Aborigines. They distinguish themselves from the mainstream white community by a number of conventions of language use, their accent and some lexical items (Crowley 1990b: 15–16). In the 1990s, the Tasmanian Aboriginal people have begun to organize the revival of their language. In view of the past history of Tasmania, it is not surprising that details of this revival are not given to white linguists and it is difficult to predict its outcome. It seems likely that Neo-Tasmanian will contain sufficient lexical and grammatical markers to serve as a means of group identification. However, it remains probably true that most traditional linguistic knowledge is lost and that the questions that historical linguists have in the 1990s about Tasmanian will never be answered.

CASE STUDY FOUR: PAPUAN PIDGIN ENGLISH (PPE)

Papuan Pidgin English illustrates the effects of a British Colonial ideology towards pidgin English which regards it as 'a "bastardized" form of English, a holdover from the days of plantation labour, to be progressively replaced by English' (Keesing 1990: 150 on Solomon Pijin).

These effects are twofold: a significant influence on the way the linguistic situation in Papua and later Papua New Guinea developed, and the adoption of an expatriate ideology as the dominant ideology of the indigenous population.

Tasmanian languages received scant attention from expatriate researchers; even less attention has been given to the phenomenon of PPE. One expert on the language situation even stated:[1]

> In Papua, as against the Territory of New Guinea . . . Pidgin had never been introduced. By early Government policy from the days

of the first government of British New Guinea right up to very recent times, one native language had been chosen as a means of general intercommunication.

(Capell 1969: 109)

This statement ignores the fact that, notwithstanding official policies of promoting Motu, Police Motu or Standard English, this did not necessarily prompt the average white trader, labour recruiter or administrator to employ these languages. Instead, they resorted to the practice of addressing the indigenous population in 'broken' English, as they were wont to do when communicating with Australian Aboriginal people or South Sea Islanders elsewhere. Thus, the earliest form of PPE spoken in Papua was a variety of the trade jargon universally used in the Pacific between visiting Europeans and indigenes. Unfortunately, only insufficient data about the early trade jargon have been located. John Moresby (1876) mentions that he found indigenes who could speak a little bit of English in various parts of the Torres Straits and D'Entrecasteaux Islands. Pearlers arrived in the former group of islands in the mid-1860s and some inhabitants of the adjacent Papuan mainland may have served as boat's crew and divers at that time. A knowledge of PPE resulting from the trepang trade is documented for the islands east of Papua from about 1885. However, much remains to be discovered about this early trading phase.

By the turn of the century, PPE was widely used by those Papuans who had contacts with the colonizers. King (1909) quotes the Administrator of the colony as having stated:

The great difficulty of language is becoming less. For the east end of the Possession the digger and the trader are propagating 'pidgin' English. The vocabulary is not always eclectic, but it is very useful.

(King 1909: 296)

Next to the trade in local commodities, the 'trade' in labourers relied almost entirely on Papuan Pidgin English. Recruitment of Papuans for the Queensland sugar plantations took place mainly in 1883 and 1884, after which time no further officially sanctioned recruitments occurred. According to Price and Baker (1976: 116) some 650 workers were recruited from Woodlark, D'Entrecasteaux and the Louisiades. Recruiting involved the use of Pidgin English, though at the time this medium of communication was by no means satisfactory. In fact, most recruits were simply misled and 'pulled' (taken by force), as can be seen from the Queensland Court Proceedings of 1885. However, after their return from Queensland many of them had a fair knowledge of Pidgin and thus helped to spread the language in the eastern islands.

The spread of PPE in one of the areas most affected by early colonial activities can be demonstrated by the example of Rossel Island, east of the mainland (see Mühlhäusler 1978b: 1382). The first indication that PPE was spoken on Rossel Island is found in a letter written by Captain Bridge in 1885:

> One or two of them knew the words 'tobacco' and 'pipe', to the use of which most of them were evidently accustomed; beyond this they were quite ignorant of English.

> (Bridge 1885: 41)

Sir William McGregor writes in the *Annual Report on British New Guinea* (1885):

> We found two men who could speak a little English which they had learnt when at work on the sugar plantations of Queensland.

Sir Hubert Murray, following a visit to Rossel Island in 1908, writes in the *Annual Report on British New Guinea* (1908):

> And the strangest trait of all in their somewhat complex character – they spend their spare time teaching one another English.

That we are dealing with a variety of Pidgin English is clearly seen from the language samples quoted by Murray, for instance: 'all the time he smell too much that fellow'. Later visits to Rossel by Murray led to more observations about the spread of PPE, for example several sentences quoted in the 1912 Annual Report. In the same year, Grimshaw (1912: 291) reports that 'the natives nearly all spoke English'.

Thus, during a brief period of twenty-five years, we find that PPE is adopted by almost the entire population of Rossel Island and that, moreover, it is beginning to replace the traditional vernacular. Whilst the reader is unlikely to agree with Grimshaw's explanation for the spread of PPE, it seems nevertheless worth quoting, as it illustrates the prejudices about Pacific languages prevailing at the time:

> To be addressed in reasonably good English of the 'pidgin' variety, by hideous savages who made murder a profession, and had never come into actual contact with civilization, is an experience perplexing enough to make the observer wonder if he is awake. Yet this is what happens on Rossel Island. English is the 'lingua franca' of the place, filling up the gaps – and there are many – in the hideous snapping, barking dialect that passes for speech along the coast,

and making communication possible among the tribes of the interior, who vary so much in language that many of them cannot understand one another. How did this come about? I fancy, through the unsatisfactory nature of the Rossel Dialects. Any that we heard were scarcely like human speech in sound, and were evidently very poor and restricted in expression. Noises like sneezes, snarls, and the preliminary stages of choking – impossible to reproduce on paper – represented the names of villages, people, and things.

(Grimshaw 1912: 191–2)

Note the progression of PPE from an additional language for communication with outsiders to a medium replacing indigenous languages, a theme which has been further developed in Chapter 4 on pidgins and creoles.

One of the reasons why PPE spread so quickly was via a string of plantations that had been set up along the coast. Because of the small size of the local languages and because of the practice of recruiting a mixed non-local workforce, PPE soon emerged as the lingua franca of a highly mobile multilingual workforce in this new linguistic ecology. The discovery of gold provided a further strong stimulus for the spread of PPE. For one of the centres of gold mining, Missima Island, we find the following report:

there is a native population of about 2,000 scattered along the coastline in about thirty villages. Most of them speak English.

(*Papuan Courier*, 14 November 1919)

The rest of the colony, with centres such as Daru, had in pre-colonial times been part of a communication network that included the Torres Strait Islands, which in 1885 had been declared part of Queensland. Whilst we have little knowledge of what languages were used in prehistorical contacts, there is ample evidence that Pidgin English rapidly became established as the language of the Torres Strait pearling industry and the language of intercommunication between Torres Strait Islanders and first coastal, and subsequently inland, Papuans. For instance, the use of PPE by VCs (village constables) in the remote Bensbach-Morehead-Wassi Kussi and Fly River area is documented for the years 1913 to 1933 in reports written by patrol officers from Daru who visited this area at regular intervals. This is confirmed in the writings of the Reverend King, who mentions the employment of Fly River men in the Papuan gold-mining industry:

Those boys have come from different parts of New Guinea, principally the Fly River and the islands. Of course they have learnt

English, and a very funny kind of English it is. The master will say to them: 'Work he finish now; you go catchee kaikai'.

(White 1929: 46–7)

Nevermann (personal communication 1977) confirms the use of PPE, intermingled with words of Malay and Motu origin, in this area in the late 1920s. Finally Bahnemann (1964) provides evidence that PPE was still used in the Dutch-Australian border area after the Second World War.

As is usually the case with pidgins, little information is available about indigenous attitudes and users in situations other than between expatriates and locals. However, from the linguistic rescue work I carried out on this language in 1975, I gather that PPE enjoyed considerable prestige, particularly among young males, as it was associated with travel, access to desirable commodities and sophistication. We note that in the neighbouring Trust Territory of New Guinea the very same motifs eventually led to the transformation of Pidgin English (Tok Pisin) into the language of political self-assertion and a new symbol of identity. Many observers point out that this linguistic stability and high social status derive from the fact that for a crucial period of forty years, when the territory was controlled by Germany, the language was not regarded as a debased form of the colonizers' standard language, but as a language in its own right.[2]

Dutton (1985: 133) points out that English was made the official language of Papua in 1895 which 'ensured that there was a corrective element injected into the scene' promoting the development of a continuum 'between "broken" English and standard English which made "broken" English appear even closer to standard English than otherwise' (Dutton 1985: 133). Evidence for such a situation is available for the Eastern Milne Bay Province. In an analysis of the 'English' spoken as the home language in more than 10 per cent of all households and as the most important intergroup language, Yarupawa (1986) observes that

> The English in the Milne Bay province ranges from at one extreme, a simplified variety of English, to a formal variety of English differing little in grammar and vocabulary from target English. There are however, substantial differences in phonology and intonation.

(Yarupawa 1986: 27)

It is interesting that this study, carried out by a linguist born in Milne Bay, attempts to reconstruct a history for Milne Bay English which does not take into consideration the well-documented use of Pidgin

English there (e.g. in Dutton 1985; Mühlhäusler 1978b) but seems to accept the official ideology that Pidgin English was never spoken in Papua and that 'Hiri Motu, because it was the lingua franca of the administration, was the regional language' (Yarupawa 1986: 27), a statement that is not supported by the evidence.

By ignoring that Pidgin English once was an important part of the linguistic ecology of Papua, its inhabitants not only have become cut off from their linguistic past, but also have come to accept an ideology which has had severe political and economic consequences in the independent nation of Papua New Guinea. Soon after its political independence in 1975, a debate on the future national language took place, during which many Papuans argued for a separate state in which Hiri Motu should be spoken and where Tok Pisin, which was identified with the former Trust Territory of New Guinea, should have no place. At the time, statements such as the following were made:

> Let it be known that I am a Papuan and that that ridiculous language Pidgin will never be spoken by my tongue, nor the tongues of my people (10 June 1976).
>
> (reproduced in McDonald 1976: 82)

What this writer overlooks, of course, is that the decline of Pidgin English is a consequence of a long campaign by the administration to promote a simplified form of Motu (known as Police Motu and after 1975 as Hiri Motu) as the lingua franca of the territory, and by the missions to promote a range of mission lingue franche. Reinecke (1937b) comments:

> There are no large language groups in the country. This has been to some extent altered during the last 40 or 50 years, mainly owing to mission activity. We now have such major languages as Kiwai, Toaripi, Motu, and Suau, all used by the L.M.S. [London Missionary Society] along the South Coast; Fuyuge in the R.C. [Roman Catholic] domain in the interior; Wedau used by the Anglican Mission on the N.E. coast; and Dobu and others by the M.M.S. [Methodist Mission Society] on the islands. These are languages deliberately chosen by the various missions for use in the areas where they are working. And it does not mean that they are native tongues of all the pupils who are taught in them.
>
> (Reinecke 1937b: 763)

This mission policy was adopted in part as a means of eradicating pidgin English rather than because of existing communication problems. Among the epithets given to PPE by missionaries, we find that the Rev. Bromilow (1929: 74) calls it a 'crude jargon of debased English', Cameron (1923: 103) 'very quaint', and that finally Newton (1914: 26) refers to it as 'that barbarous perversion of English'.

The instructions to the Methodist Missionaries operating on the Eastern Islands of Papua were

(a) teach the people to speak Dobu;
(b) teach the people to read and write Dobu;
(c) teach the people to sing Dobuan hymns;
(d) preach to the people in Dobu.

(Lithgow 1992: 30)

It appears that this policy initially made little impact on PPE but had a dramatic effect on the smaller indigenous languages of the region.

Dobu had, and is having, a profound effect on the languages of the D'Entrecasteaux Islands.

(Lithgow 1992: 47)

The choice of Motu by the government is largely due to the fact that the centre of the colony's administration was located in Motu-speaking Port Moresby and that the prejudices against Pidgin English of a few important administrators prompted them to adopt a form of Motu as the preferred language of day-to-day administration. It is not true (as present-day ideology has it) that this pidgin Motu is the continuation of an ancient indigenous trade language (Hiri Motu of the Hiri expeditions), nor is there much evidence for the administrator's view that one was dealing with a slightly simplified version of the local Motu language.

Among the practices the government adopted to spread Motu was the use of the prison system as a language school:

it was the practice to teach all new prisoners 'Motu' by placing them 'both at work and in the cell, with prisoners who use that dialect, and thus they soon pick it up' (AR, 1894/5: 28). In general, all prisoners who served a few months in Port Moresby spoke 'Motuan more or less' (ibid.).

(Dutton 1985: 77)

Whilst in neighbouring German New Guinea prisoners were taught Tok Pisin and employed as village interpreters after their release, in Papua

the prison system was a major source of recruitment for the Armed

Native Constabulary and Village Constable systems. Consequently, many policemen and village constables learned their 'Motu' in prison and took it back to their villages with them when they left prison or when they left the police force if they had joined it after leaving prison.

(Dutton 1985: 78)

The effects of such policies were rather slow to emerge. Reinecke (1937b: 727) comments on the competition between PPE and Police Motu: 'along the coasts of the Territory of Papua it is more extensively used than its competitor, the Pidginized Motu language'. And as late as 1943, little stability had developed in this language. The missionary Lock is reported by Dutton (1985) as having characterized the language in the following terms:

1 'there are very few rules' (p. 1);
2 'each [policeman] picked up more Motu words and added them to the Bastard [*sic*] language (p.1);
3 'nearly all different Tribes [*sic*] have their own formation of the Police Motu sentences' (p. 3).

(Dutton 1985: 80)

The second point suggests that the process that led to the eventual replacement of PPE by Police Motu might have been relexification, a hypothesis strengthened by examples of mixed language samples such as:

I been tink you like em pish, Taubada, belong supper. I been catch him this one along *pidi* (rifle).

(Humphries 1923: 78)

No good you drink em rano kava (plain water) all the time.

(Humphries 1923: 205)

The most interesting piece of evidence is the following conversation between a policeman and a cook:

Handing his fish to my cook, with whom he was always joking, he commanded, 'Clean him first time!' Whereupon the cook, with mock indignation, replied: 'You policeman; me cook, savee?' 'Yes, I savee.' 'Vadaieni, oi lau. Sedila oi diba pidi huria, oi diba lase huria pish!' (All right, clear out. You might know something about cleaning a rifle, but you know nothing about cleaning fish!)

(Humphries 1923: 78–9)

Of special interest is the word order in the Police Motu sentences:

   Police Motu reported by Humphries (1923)
      oi diba lase huria pish
   Present-day Miti Motu
      gwarume huria oi diba lasi

If one compares the first sentence with PPE 'yu no save kukim pis' one can see the close structural similarity of 1920s PPE and 1920s Police Motu.

The decisive factor in the demise of PPE in many parts of Papua was the Second World War, during which parts of the country were occupied by Japan and fierce battles were fought for several years. The war disrupted the established pattern for the transmission of PPE in the plantations and mines of coastal Papua. Instead, 10,000 young Papuan men were recruited for the Allied War effort with linguistic consequences characterized by Dutton (1985) as follows:

> The position of Police Motu is likely to have been considerably strengthened both socially and geographically. This follows from the fact that the Army recognized Police Motu as a language, had it written down, encouraged its use, taught it to its personnel, and used it for propaganda and morale purposes. At the same time, large numbers of labourers from outlying districts were working in the Port Moresby and surrounding areas where Police Motu was the recognized lingua franca before the war and even without the encouragement of the Army attitudes, these labourers are bound to have learned Police Motu if they did not already know it. Elsewhere, many worked with ANGAU officers and others who knew Police Motu and, because of the Army policy and attitudes, are likely to have used it and so encouraged outsiders to learn it. In the smaller specialist units of the Medical Service, Royal Papuan Constabulary and Papuan Infantry Battalion, Police Motu was the principal lingua franca until Pidgin English (now Tok Pisin) eventually took over in the latter two.
>
> (Dutton 1985: 122)

By 1945 Police Motu had gained sufficient status and use to develop into the language of administration of most parts of Papua, developments which have been written about in much detail by Dutton (1985: 124ff.).

The case of PPE illustrates the extent to which an external colonial power can suppress such linguistic practices as are not compatible with its ideologies and promote other forms of communication in order to create greater distance between colonizers and colonized and to exercise various forms of social control. In spite of the official declaration that made English the language of Papua in 1895, there are many signs that the colonial administration for a long time felt very unhappy about the thought of having a well-educated English-speaking population and virtually no resources were made available for this purpose. The campaign against PPE, interestingly, was not one of gradually turning it into standard English, but of replacing it with a local pidgin language whose linguistic adequacy at the time was quite reduced. This helped maintain the distance not only between colonizers and colonized but also between Australia and Papua. It eventually severed the many communication links between the Torres Strait Islands and Papua, thereby wrecking any further claims to these islands by an independent Papua New Guinea.

The cost, as has already been alluded to, were internal divisions, expensive translation and reduced regional mobility in the independent nation of Papua New Guinea. The spiritual cost is that the inhabitants of Papua have taken over the colonial ideology of the non-existence of PPE and the traditional indigenous origin of Hiri Motu. Commenting on Papuan objections to Pidgin English, Harry Bell (1971) observed:

> It is amusing that similar charges are not levelled at Police Motu. Yet it was the deliberate imposition of this minority tongue, by government enforcement, that obliterated Papua's Pidgin, the retention of which would have gone a long way to overcome present Papuan/New Guinean tensions.
>
> (Bell 1971: 34–5)

CONCLUSIONS

All four case studies illustrate the devastating impact of European colonization in the Pacific region which created discontinuities in transmission, severed the links that traditional languages had with the languages in a larger ecology and which led to the emergence of a number of *ad hoc* solutions to the problems created by the initial disruption.

Prominent in all four case studies are the conflicting and constantly changing measures imposed by outsiders. Persecution alternated with *laissez-faire* and maintenance policies and consecutive colonial administrators reinforced the arising discontinuities. The order of magnitude of these changes is considerably greater than that governing language change in the pre-colonial past. The effects of the rape of Oceania that began with Guam continue to be felt. The emergence of reconstructed histories from languages such as Tasmanian and Hiri Motu can be interpreted as an attempt to legitimize the role of neo-indigenous languages and of preserving the few fragments of linguistic heritage left unscathed by imperialism.

6 Mission languages and language policies

It is probable that some corruption of a native language is inevitable in Mission work.

(Codrington and Palmer 1896: VIII)

INTRODUCTION

To do justice to the complex issue of mission and language in a single chapter is almost impossible; impossible because of the enormous and often conflicting information, impossible because of the large number of different practices and time periods, and finally, impossible because of the ideologically charged and emotional nature of the topic.[1] Mission intrusion into the linguistic ecology of the Pacific is perhaps best characterized as an 'invisible hand' phenomenon of the type discussed by Keller (1990). Mission decisions regarding language matters tended to be *ad hoc* and local, aimed at achieving local goals such as facilitating preaching, education of the 'natives' or preparing Bible translations. Many of them were also shortlived. Of the 107 missions set up for Aboriginal people in Australia, for instance, most 'lasted less than ten years' (Fesl 1993: 76). It is true that from the outset the various Christian missions operating in Australia and the Pacific, and indeed elsewhere, were working towards the final goal of Christianizing the entire population. However, for most of the time there was little informed opinion on the part of the missions as to the role which language might play in this process. It is for this reason that one is justified regarding many of the dramatic consequences of mission language practices as unintended and uncontrolled.[2] It is only since the 1980s that missions have become involved in a more controlled use of language, aided by programmes in linguistics and computer technology.

LANGUAGES AS MISSION INSTRUMENTS

The metaphor of tool or instrument is employed frequently in the missionary debate about language. Whilst there was general agreement as to the task to be performed by the linguistic tool, one encounters considerable disagreement as to the suitability of the locally found 'tools' for this purpose. The literature abounds with debates on topics such as:

1 Are indigenous languages inherently suited to preaching the gospel?
2 Does the number of speakers justify the use of a particular language in mission work?
3 Should pidgins and creoles be used for religious purposes?
4 What changes are necessary to make indigenous languages adequate tools?
5 Is the use of indigenous languages a temporary or permanent solution?

The first question is one that was rarely discussed in an objective and informed manner and as a consequence a wide range of opinions can be found.

That the languages of the Pacific area were primitive was accepted as fact by virtually all missions throughout the nineteenth century. Thus Cargill in 1836, a year after his arrival in Fiji, noted that it was

> to the Wesleyan Mission Society that he had elucidated the structure of the 'basic' language and understood the derivations of the dialects, with the idea of the translation of the Bible ever before him. The often noted characteristic of 'primitive' languages – that of a wide and specialised vocabulary relating to objects of usefulness and importance – was observed.
>
> (Clammer 1976: 15)

Not only were these languages seen to be primitive, but also they were regarded as repositories of wickedness and moral degradation. In a report on missionary activities in Micronesia in *The Friend* (a Hawaiian newspaper) of 11 August 1859 the anonymous writer opines (p. 484):

> To study a people's language will be to study them, and to study them at best advantage, when they present themselves to us under fewest disguises, most nearly as they are.
>
> While the languages of Micronesia and other heathen nations or tribes are destitute of words and phrases to convey correct ideas of God and moral subjects generally, yet those same languages abound with words and terms respecting disgusting subjects and forbidden

thoughts. Their vocabularies are wonderfully prolific in unchaste and impure words and terms.

The same writer holds the view, widely subscribed to at the time, that this perceived imperfection of languages and their speakers reflects a fall from grace rather than imperfect creation:

> How painfully the mind of the missionary is tried, when he would translate the Bible into the language of the heathen. He finds that their languages are wanting in the words and terms required for translation. These languages may once have possessed those necessary sounds and terms, but alas, so far have the heathens wandered from the right way, and so grievously have they departed from God, that they have lost correct ideas of the Divine Being and his worship. Hence the missionary must spend toilsome days and sleepless nights, in his search after the proper terms, words and phrases to express religious truths.

A more comprehensive argument for this view can be found in Farrar (1899).

One encounters comments on the inadequacy of indigenous languages with an almost monotonous regularity. Here follow two more examples from my collection:

> The Tahitian language, as may justly be expected, is destitute of all such words, common among civilized nations, as relate to the arts and sciences, law proceedings, trade and commerce, and most of those made use of in Technology &c.
>
> (Reverend Davies, quoted in Newbury 1961: 85)

> Although the supposition that Satan had a special agency in the formation of the Chinese language cannot be proved, not with any strict propriety assumed to be a fact; yet we can hardly conceive of any tongue better adapted than this to promote his evil designs; and certain it is that no nation ever has been, for so long a time, completely given over to his sway as China.
>
> (Bridgman 1849: 53)

In connection with such quotations, it is worth pointing out that the Moravian Mission to the Aboriginal people in Australia was motivated by the desire to find 'the most degraded people on earth' (Fesl 1993: 219) and they regarded Aboriginal languages as incapable of expressing Christian doctrine. The West Australian missionary Smithies expressed the following views on Australian Aboriginal languages:

> An acquaintance with the Australian dialects here is of no value as to religious things, just because they have no religion, no .worship

of any kind, no sacrifices, no prayers, no fears or hopes with references to any other state. And therefore no terms to express anything of the kind, and hence any attempt at translation of a hymn or Scripture, or Lord's prayer shows at once the paucity thereof.... Now the translation of the Lord's prayer and parts of our catechism show a great paucity in the native dialect here on spiritual things yet after all a knowledge of the language as far as is known is of use to a Missionary for as much as it will enable him at least to know what the natives are conversing about and to detect many things which are wrong and to gain access to their hearts and feelings by this means.

(quoted in Fesl 1993: 90–1)

Whatever its origins, the missionaries' deficiency theory of indigenous languages was virtually universal and in a different form (modernizing traditional languages or adapting languages to the Christian message) continues to dominate mission thinking.

The deficiencies of traditional vernaculars from the missionary perspective lay in two areas:

1 their variability, which made them difficult to learn and employ for use as a printed medium
2 the lack of Christian concepts.

As I shall deal with the first question in Chapter 8 on literacy, let me add a few lines on the second topic.

The question of enriching the conceptual inventory of local languages is common to all missionary language planning, be it for vernaculars, mission lingue franche or pidgins. Mission objectives have been characterized by Fugmann (1976: 267): 'Our aim is to change the old ideas, replacing them by something new.' And this 'also involves introducing new concepts, because some older concepts are not sufficient to express the deeper meaning of the Christian message' (Fugmann 1977: 267).

Initial attempts to change and incorporate concepts were very much a haphazard business as they would not draw on much practical experience (see Wonderley and Nida 1963). Some missions, for instance, simply added words of Greek origin. John Williams (1865: 530, quoted in Schütz 1977: 86–7) wrote:

As the natives are never at a loss to express their thoughts or emotions, or to describe any of the qualities of matter with which they are acquainted, we have been obliged, in effecting our translations, to introduce but few new terms. These principally relate to the ordinances of the Christian religion, and to articles and ideas unknown prior to their intercourse with Europeans. Before admitting a new word, we have generally considered whether it could be Polynesianized: that is, whether vowels could be inserted between every two consonants without destroying its identity; and, secondly, whether any terms exist in the native tongue with which it was likely to be confounded. When we could adopt English words, we preferred doing so; but these cannot be accommodated to the South Seas dialects so easily as words from the Greek. Of this the term horse may afford an illustration. This, by the introduction of vowels, so entirely loses its identity, that horse would become horeti; but as the omission of one p and the s from the Greek word hippos gives us hipo, we adopt that word, because it harmonizes with the language, can be easily pronounced by the natives, and retains a sufficient resemblance to the original to preserve its identity. Arenio for lamb, and are to for bread, are examples of the same kind. In designating baptism, to avoid all disputes, we have adopted the original, baptizo. These phrases are soon understood by the people; for they are not only referred to in our discourses, and explained daily in our schools, but the natives themselves are constantly conveying such information from one to another.

(Williams 1865: 530, quoted in Schütz 1977: 86–7)

Another practice was to use non-verbal means of communication to supplement the meagre verbal resources available to the missionaries. Fesl (1993) provides the following account of how the Ten Commandments were taught to a baptism class in Queensland in 1930:

In teaching the First Commandment, I used an advertisement for Eno's Fruit Salts, representing an Easterner sitting by the roadside and holding a lemon in his hand. After blackening the face in the picture to make it appear more like that of an Aborigine, the cutting was shown to the class and introduced as the illustration of a medicine man – the lemon was misrepresented as a stone which the magician had just pretended to have extracted from the organs of a patient. (This, of course, is a common trick of the native witch doctor.) In association with this picture was learned by the class, 'Only one God – no more medicine.'
    . . . For the Seventh Commandment, a finger was dipped in dirt and used to dramatise, 'No think dirty, no speak dirty, no do dirty'; while the attractive properties of another digit smothered in glue were used to illustrate 'No steal'.

(Fesl 1993: 88)

A detailed survey of the relevant literature as well as an in-depth study of the Christianization of a New Guinea Highland Papuan language Yagaria is given by Renck (1990), whilst many more details on other mission languages can be found in Wurm (1979) for Melanesia, and Fesl (1993) for Australia.

Renck, like many of his predecessors and followers, ended up creating a non-traditional language, whilst employing the same label used to refer to the traditional one. As missionization has as yet not eroded the entire range of semantic differences among the languages of the Pacific on the one hand and between these languages and the European languages on the other, there is a strong tendency for most traditional languages that have come under the impact of mission language policies to move towards a Standard Average European typology, particularly in the semantic domains of time, being, causality, spatial organization, nature and nurture, human relationships and emotions. A number of examples are given in Chapter 8 on literacy.

The use of traditional vernaculars for mission work was practicable in some areas (e.g. the larger monolingual islands of Polynesia) but very labour intensive and costly in others, and there were numerous practical and ideological reasons why alternative strategies were employed by certain missions. Of these alternatives I shall comment on the following

1 mission lingue franche (mission languages)
2 mission attitudes towards pidgins and creoles
3 mission policies and metropolitan languages

but shall refrain from discussing the role of Latin, Hebrew and Greek in the Pacific.

MISSION LINGUE FRANCHE (MISSION LANGUAGES)

The task of Christianizing a language was a difficult and tedious one and, given the limited amount of time, personnel and money, it is understandable that most missions were not prepared to deal in this way with all the languages of the area. An apparent exception is the Summer Institute of Linguistics (SIL) whose members have set themselves the task of translating the Bible into all of the world's tongues regardless of the size of the speech community. The SIL approach can work, of course, only if there are indeed a determinate number of languages, say 710 in Papua New Guinea or 105 in Vanuatu. In actual fact, as has been pointed out many times in this book, the notion of 'language' is one that has not been important to the Pacific area and any decision as to how many languages are spoken here is of necessity arbitrary. Thus, one of the first tasks that has to be undertaken by SIL translators is that of bringing languages into being. A particularly well-documented case is that of the English-based creoles of Northern Australia which were turned by SIL missionaries into a language called Kriol, by creating a named entity, writing its grammar, a standard dictionary and providing Bible translation. Its creators, by and large, ignored

1 the metalinguistic intuitions of the speakers who distinguish a number of different (sometimes named) entities
2 linguistic differences which serve important social functions such as indexing group differences
3 the fact that questions of mutual intelligibility depend on factors other than having a common name.

A large number of speakers of the varieties of Creoles, particularly those in the western parts of Northern Australia, do not wish to be classified as speakers of Kriol and resent it as an explicit act of power, whilst others simply do not make sense of this notion (see Rhydwen 1993).

Similar practices were also brought to the traditional languages of the area. Verhaar (1989) relates, in connection with the problem of missionary prejudice:

> Or I remember reading about a report on a language by a missionary in the nineteenth century. The missionary described the language of the people, and distinguished five dialects in the language. He said more about what he called 'the principal dialect'. As I was reading, I wondered why that particular dialect was supposed to be the 'principal dialect', but soon it became clear from the context: it was the dialect of the area where the mission station was.
>
> (Verhaar 1989: 1)

In the late twentieth century, little has changed. Staalsen (1969) for instance, at the beginning of an article 'proving' that there are four dialects of Iatmul, states that:

> Direct questioning about dialect differences yields a few dozen separate dialects, each considered to be an aberrant form of the idiolect spoken by the individual being questioned. The members of each village believe that their speech form is central and all other are corrupted to varying degrees. Such subjective data is commonly misleading.
>
> (Staalsen 1969: 70)

Johnston (1980), after surveying the somewhat dubious practices of past researchers and missionaries in setting up a language called Nakanai in New Britain, accepts one variety of this continuum as the basis of his description (and presumably subsequent mission work and Bible translating):

> Bileki is the principal dialect of Nakanai. Firstly, it has the highest population, and is the most densely settled of the dialect areas. Secondly, it has the longest history of intense external contact and commercial development. Thirdly, it is the dialect closest to the large centres of Kimbe and Cape Hoskins, with their port and airstrip facilities, and a connecting road. Finally, whereas most of the speakers of all the other dialects can understand Bileki, and many can in fact speak it, the reverse is rarely the case.
>
> (Johnston 1980: 14)

What privileges this variety is its close association with non-indigenous economic activities and missionization, not any traditional role.

The way in which languages are first brought into being and subsequently demoted to dialects is also illustrated with the case of Kâte. When, in 1892, the Lutheran mission established a station at Sattelberg in the Finschafen Hinterland, they encountered people who spoke a Papuan form of speech. The missionaries identified five principal dialects, Bamota, Womara, Perec, Wemo and Wana, the largest of these being Womara. The dialects are believed to make up a language called Kâte which was one of several other Papuan languages spoken in the area, including Mape, Dedua, Sene and Migabac. The lexicon shared by these languages and Kâte appears to have been around 65 per cent of the basic lexicostatistical word list.

The dialectal diversification of Kâte caused the first missionaries considerable headaches for, as stated by Keysser (1929: 25), 'there were two highly divergent dialects in the vicinity of the (Sattelberg) station so that the missionary who had learned only one was scarcely able to understand a word of the other' (dialects referred to are Wemo and Wamora, my translation). In addition, the missionaries subscribed to the view that linguistic diversity promoted social friction. Flierl and Strauss (1977) comment:

> When the missionaries arrived, they found small mutually antagonistic groups of people. Before any progress could be hoped for, it was necessary for this antagonism and conflict to cease, and the imposition of a common language was regarded as one of the most promising methods for attaining unity.
>
> (Flierl and Strauss 1977: XII–XIII)

To overcome this problem the Wemo dialect was adopted as the basis of a mission standard language. The linguistic and sociolinguistic consequences of this decision were very considerable.

First, the selection of Wemo as the standard dialect has led to the virtual disappearance of all other varieties of Kâte. Hooley and McElhanon (1970) state that 'under the influence of the Lutheran mission the Wemo dialect has effectively supplanted the others and today only a few old people imperfectly remember the other dialects'.

Second, such was the influence of mission Kâte that the lexically related neighbour languages of Kâte are becoming either structurally or lexically more similar to it or are being replaced by it. Thus, Hooley and McElhanon (1970) report:

> on Mape: 'It appears that most speakers below the age of 40 mix a considerable amount of Kâte into their speech. Within another generation, Kâte will probably supplant Mape'.
>
> on Sene: 'The younger generation speaks only Kâte, which is 65 percent related to Sene'.
>
> on Momare: 'Although Kâte is well known it appears that Momare will persist for a number of years'.
>
> on Dedua: 'As is the case with Mape, the younger Dedua speakers freely mix Kâte vocabulary in their speech'.
>
> on Migabac: 'Limited success has been achieved by the Lutheran mission in supplanting Migabac with Kâte'.
>
> (Hooley and McElhanon 1970: 1,069)

The net result of these and similar mission-induced contacts is that formerly separate languages have become dialects of the mission language (i.e. dialects when applying lexicostatistical methods) within one or two generations. Having been reduced to this level, the future of languages such as Momare or Dedua looks bleak.

Third, McElhanon (1979: 285) points out that the mission description of Wemo is not a reflection of the traditional Wemo dialect but rather influenced by expatriate ideas about the nature of language and, more specifically, the idiolect of one particular missionary.[3] This idiolect also reflects the practice of the local speakers of Wemo of simplifying their speech when communicating with expatriates:

> In the case of Kâte the simplification led directly to the development of the MLF. This was accomplished through the Rev. G. Pilhofer assuming the major responsibility for preparing pedagogical materials both for the Kâte teacher training programs and schools, and for the incoming missionaries. The result was that new personnel,

whether local or expatriate, learned and used a kind of Kâte which reflected Pilhofer's idiolect. With a continuing reciprocal reinforcement through communication between these two groups, this idiolectal influence eventuated in the Mission Lingua Franca, ELCONG Kâte.

Noteworthy too, is the fact that the Kâte New Testament translation is primarily the work of Pilhofer, so that the common literature that brought together the missionaries and the locals in the greater proportion of their communication also bore the imprint of Pilhofer.

(McElhanon 1979: 285)

Because of the prestige of the missionaries, the mission form of Kâte is becoming more widespread. Thus, present Kâte only indirectly reflects the linguistic practices of former Wemo speakers, whilst access to other dialects and neighbouring languages has been gradually lost.

Finally, in pre-colonial days there appears to have been a relatively egalitarian attitude toward language. With the establishment of a prestige variety this has changed, as have other sociolinguistic attitudes.[4] McElhanon (1979) observes:

The expatriate influence upon Kâte was also conditioned by their attitudes toward language in general and the amount of control one might have in using it. This attitude may have developed from that associated with prescriptive grammars. In response to questions about syntax and semantics, one often gets the response, 'We use it like this'.

(McElhanon 1979: 285)

The German missionary Flierl is even reported to have stated:

It is a fact that many Lutheran Christians in New Guinea show a greater affection for their Church language than for their original mother tongue.

(Strauss 1971: 69, my translation)

I have shown elsewhere, in connection with attitudes towards Tok Pisin (Mühlhäusler 1985), that indigenous and expatriate views as to what constitutes good and bad language differ very widely. However, in Tok Pisin as in Kâte, it is the expatriate view of good language that seems to have prevailed. Less than a hundred years of contact history thus have produced a linguistic picture from which original historical relationships can no longer be reconstructed and which, moreover, includes structures that bear only a very indirect relationship to the structures encountered before contacts were established. Very much the same, one suspects, has also occurred in the areas of semantics and pragmatics and in the not too distant future we may have in Kâte a Standard Average European (SAE) language with Papuan lexical forms.

As missionary linguists 'clean up' the multilingual environment of the South East Asian islands and Melanesia, their role in bringing into being languages and language boundaries continues. Unlike the authors of 'scientific' descriptions whose writings less often have an influence on the speakers whose linguistic practices are studied, the Bible translator, literacy promoters and trainers of catechists by the same practices help reify an expatriate model of language.

The privileging of dialects is not the only way of reducing the Babylonian confusion identified by the missionaries. As the example of Kâte illustrated, promoting certain languages over others has been equally common. Different mission societies have adopted different strategies, and only a small selected range of examples can be discussed here. The Lutheran Church in Papua New Guinea initially was of the view (Osmers 1981: 84) that all local languages had to be studied, elementary literacy provided and Bible translation attempted. However, it became apparent, after forty years of very limited success with this strategy, that other solutions had to be considered. Thus, at a mission conference in 1920 two policies were debated:

1 Every people has to hear the Gospel in its own language, only smaller tribes with similar dialects are allowed to be integrated. The aim is the equality of all languages besides Kâte and Jabêm as ministerial and school languages.
2 The other opinion thrives for a unification of the multitude of tribes to one or two peoples: Melanesians and Papuans. This is to be achieved with the help of the introduction of Jabêm and Kâte as common church languages.

(Osmers 1981: 86)

The outcome was the adoption of the second policy, that is, the use of Jabêm in all Melanesian communities and the use of Kâte in all Papuan ones. It must be pointed out here that the term 'Melanesian' does not imply mutual intelligibility or even typological similarity and that the distinction Melanesian–Papuan is neither a traditional indigenous one nor one that necessarily correctly reflects linguistic prehistory (see Terrell 1986). Had linguistic and sociolinguistic criteria prevailed, another solution, that of adopting Azera as a mission language, a suggestion supported by a number of missionaries and missionary linguists, would have been adopted. Azera 'held a geographical and linguistic mid-position between the Melanesian and

Papuan tribes' (Terrell 1986: 90), but this suggestion was voted out and Jabêm accepted as a mission language by the Azera people themselves.

In the 1930s, with the rapid expansion to mission activities inland, speaking two separate mission languages was perceived to be undesirable and eventually Kâte became adopted as the sole mission lingua franca for speakers of all languages other than Jabêm.

The impact on the linguistic ecology of this was manyfold:

1 it promoted a language that had traditionally no dominant role
2 it created a hierarchy of languages replacing a situation where languages had been equal
3 it set in motion a gradual shift away from the local vernaculars to more powerful mission languages
4 it gradually silenced those who spoke up for the small languages.

The problem of setting up, developing and promoting mission lingue franche is shared by most missions. A list of such languages is given by McElhanon (1979) and individual accounts are given in Wurm (1977). The former gives the following general characterizations of the reasons and practice:

> When the missionaries were faced with the difficulty of trying to communicate their teachings to people speaking a multiplicity of apparently diverse and sometimes completely unrelated languages, it was not surprising that they turned to the available lingue franche. The immediate returns of such a policy were quite obvious. Not only would a common language aid communication at church councils and conferences and give a feeling of unity to the participants, it would also immensely simplify administration. Personnel could be freely transferred within the area, and nationals could be taught at a single secondary or tertiary school. Moreover, printing costs could be kept to a minimum since there would be no need for small production runs in many languages . . .
>
> In the situation where there was no established lingua franca these same reasons became the basis for introducing the Mission Lingua Franca policy. However, the choice of which language to promote as the Mission Lingua Franca depended upon a number of factors.
>
> In the case of Kâte and Yabem, it ultimately derived from the fact that Finschhafen provided an excellent harbor. The missionaries arrived in 1886 shortly after the Deutsch Neuguinea Kompanie began commercial operations there. Their choice of Simbang village as the site of the first work sealed Yabem's destiny as a

Mission Lingua Franca, as their decision to open a station at Sattelberg sealed the destiny of the Wemo dialect of Kâte. The choices of Motu and Kuanua were perhaps made along parallel lines.

'Historical accident' was also the reason for choosing Wedau and Gedaged, although in the latter case Gedaged only won out over Amele following many years of competition (Freyberg 1977: 860) . . .

Toaripi and Island Kiwai were used in related dialects or very small neighbouring languages so that one could say in these cases that there was no choice between competing languages. Gogodala, on the other hand, never reflected a policy decision. According to Neuendorf 'it just happened that way' (1977: 880). Yet, at times the difference between 'policy' and 'practice' can be simply a formal matter.

(McElhanon 1979: 280)

Historical accident, rather than rational planning processes, thus underlies the choice of most mission lingue franche, and it comes as no surprise that stories of failure abound.

It is sometimes argued that the elevation of local vernaculars to mission lingue franche helped strengthen their linguistic viability, but this claim ignores another effect of the choice of mission language, that is, their coming under the influence of expatriate and local second language speakers, with resulting dramatic structural and lexical reduction. Over time such reduction or even pidginization tends to become the basis of literacy and preaching and even the language of first language users is affected.

It is important to see such developments against the background of claims made by mission bodies (such as SIL) that

the vernacular languages reflect the heritage and identity of the people. It is rich in vocabulary which relates the people to each other, to geographical places and to the natural environment around them. The beliefs and myths of the people are reported through the cognitive framework expressed most adequately in the vernacular. It would be a simple matter to preserve cultural arte-facts so that they could be examined and in some sense remembered. However, in order to talk about the same objects, the vernacular alone supplies the richness and depth of emotions that are associ-ated with the customs surrounding mere objects. For this reason, if a vernacular is destroyed or allowed to be immersed by a larger cultural group the culture of the smaller group has also effectively been destroyed. We of SIL maintain that to bypass the vernacular in education is to bypass the basis of the very heart and soul of Papua New Guinea people.

(Franklin 1975: 140)

But vernacular, as we have seen often, is no more than a convenient label hiding the fact that linguistic practices before and after missionization may be quite different. The labels 'Kâte', 'Tolai' or 'Yagaria' currently stand for a language that no longer embodies the totality of the traditional culture. The large-scale destruction of 'undesirable' cultural artefacts is accompanied by the removal of the linguistic means of discussing them and it is the very removal of pre- and non-Christian practices and artefacts that deprives the vernaculars of their traditional anchoring. The creation of a body of non-traditional texts certainly is no compensation for the destruction of traditional discourse.

Mission lingue franche in many cases were also regarded as a means of 'keeping the natives in their place', that is, immunizing them against the influx of secular Western ideas and modes of behaviour, and it is this fact that led to their eventual decline. As pointed out by McElhanon (1979), far more important than the withdrawal of government funding for non-English schools

> was the fact that nationals recognized that education in Kâte represented a 'dead-end road', and that at the end there was no economic advantage. It is true that the positions of pastor, evangelist or teacher carried a certain amount of status among the villagers, but these paled in comparison to positions associated with English, which was commonly thought of as a potential key to wealth, and not infrequently associated with cargo-cult sentiments. An English education was so highly valued among the Selepet people that popular demand was that the first vernacular publication be a Selepet–English dictionary.
>
> (McElhanon 1979: 283)

The decline of the mission lingue franche does not mean that their effects on the traditional language ecology have disappeared. This can be illustrated with the example of Tuvalu (the language of Tuvalu, former Ellice Islands). For most of their mission history, the Tuvalu were Christianized not in their own (geographically relatively well-defined) language but in Samoan. This, it would appear, was a matter of expediency, as Samoan pastors were numerous and Bible translation and hymns in Samoan were already available when Tuvalu was first missionized. The status of Samoan (SAM) in the Tuvaluan diglossic situation is characterized by Besnier (1983) as follows:

Because of the close association between politics and religion in the early days of missionization, up to the middle of this century, all government matters were for a long time conducted in SAM, for the very reason that they were usually conducted by the Samoan pastors. Thus, examples of law codes and other government or official publications in SAM are many, some of them being bilingual in KIR and SAM if they were issued by the Gilbert and Ellice Islands Colony authorities.[5] All printed or written documents were for a long time in SAM. Schooling, as was mentioned above, was also a context in which the language used was exclusively SAM.

(Besnier 1983: 8)

The effects on the lexicon and grammar of Tuvaluan were far reaching and the language now is no longer like the traditional Tuvaluan language. Very much the same also happened to the Easter Island language, Rapanui, following the conversion of its population by means of the Tahitian language.

MISSION ATTITUDES TOWARDS PIDGINS AND CREOLES

As suggested elsewhere in this book, pidgin languages were one of the main consequences of outside disturbance of the Pacific language ecology. They developed in the wake of population displacement, blackbirding, new expatriate settlements and, not least, as a result of certain missionary practices. Mission stations and mission-run boarding schools were breeding grounds for pidgins and creoles, a fact rarely mentioned by pidgin and creole scholars, though arguably the effect of mission presence in the Pacific on pidgins and creoles may have been even more important than that of plantations. To name just a few examples:

1 The two principal Northern Australian Creoles (Kriol and Broken) both developed in mission boarding schools.
2 The only known German Creole (Unserdeutsch) developed in the boarding school for orphans in Vunapope/Rabaul.
3 The setting up of a mission for Melanesians on Norfolk Island brought into being a pidgin variety of the Mota language.
4 The stabilization and elevation of Tok Pisin, the most important Pidgin English of the Pacific area, was in large part due to mission policies.
5 A Creole French called Tayo developed at the St Louis Mission in French New Caledonia (Ehrhart 1993).

Nevertheless, the role of missions in the spread and growth of post-contact pidgins and creoles in the Pacific was highly ambivalent and even contradictory as, on the one hand, most missionaries shared the cultural prejudices against these languages and, on the other, pidgins and creoles were a cheaper and more effective mission medium than most other solutions.

Had the missionization of the Pacific begun in Melanesia rather than Polynesia, history would probably have been very different. As it happened the first experience that missionaries had were with the linguistically homogeneous island groups of Tahiti and Tonga. As missionary activity moved to Fiji it began to look for a while as if linguistic heterogeneity required new mission language policies, but by force and by a stroke of good luck a standard variety of Fijian could be forced upon the converts. Ironically, it is not altogether unlikely that the Mbauan variety of Fijian was a simplified and pidginized variety used in dealings between Fijians and Tongans, though the inadvertent elevation of a pidgin to mission language did not give rise to comments. The real problems began when missionaries were sent to Melanesia. Initially, the full extent of the linguistic diversity of the area was not realized and, as the range of mission influence in the early phase was not very extensive, the magnitude of the problem was not perceived. By the time most missions realized that the introduced mode of communication required linguistic solutions different from those indigenous to the area, the local population had already developed such solutions for themselves in the form of Pidgin English, Pidgin French or a pidgin derived from another metropolitan language.[6]

The reaction of the missions to these pidgin languages tended to be mainly negative, echoing the Edinburgh Christian Instructor's criticism of the use of the English Creole Sranan Tongo in Surinam, namely that Bible translation and preaching was 'putting the broken English of the negroes ... into a written and permanent form' being 'at pains to embody their barbarous, mixed, imperfect phrase in the pages of school books, and to perpetrate all its disadvantages and evil consequences by shutting them up to it as the vehicle of God's word' (quoted from Reinecke 1987: 24).

Thus, whilst initially the pidginized and koineized indigenous vernaculars were tacitly tolerated, the promotion of languages such as Papuan Pidgin English (PPE) was not. Newton (1914) appears to reflect the prevalent attitudes of the missionaries towards PPE when he deplores its use in religious services in Samarai prison:

It would approach blasphemy were one to put in print the form in which truths of religion appear in 'Pidgin' English, as for instance the way in which the Almighty is spoken of, or the relation of our Blessed Lord to the Eternal Father, even though the close connection of the sublime and the ridiculous has elements of humour. At least there is nothing blasphemous in the ways in which a South Sea Island teacher began his address one Sunday to the prisoners: 'My friends, I am glad to see so many of you here to-day.' For my own part, when I have taken the gaol service I could never bring myself to use 'Pidgin' English, and not simply because I am not familiar with it. Fortunately I have always been able to find an interpreter who knew Wedauan. He translated into 'Pidgin' English, and if at times I writhed at the form in which my teaching appeared, it was not always possible not to see the humour or to preserve one's gravity entire.

(Newton 1914: 26–7)

Whether or not God's word could be translated into pidgin was ultimately a matter of expediency and cost. There were a number of situations where any other solution was unrealistic, particularly in the context of transient multilingual plantations. Thus, in the 1850s on Kusaie in Micronesia a report in the Hawaiian newspaper *The Friend* states:

Before the missionaries landed upon the island, the natives had acquired a smattering of the English language. This was merely the result of their intercourse with foreigners, principally with seamen. They were able to employ intelligently a greater number of English words than those Hawaiians who have lived for years in foreign families in Honolulu. So great was their knowledge of English, that Mr. Snow endeavoured for nearly four years after commencing his mission to preach in broken English, or Anglo-Kusaien. He endeavoured to teach the English in school, but he finally abandoned the experiment, and fell back upon the vernacular of the native. He found it to be exceedingly difficult to communicate religious truths in this mixture of Kusaien, English, Spanish, Hawaiian and other languages.

Similarly, the South Seas Evangelical Mission (SSEM) that operated on the Queensland sugar plantation, according to Keesing (1990: 153), 'had a condescension towards the childlike "natives" (reborn into Christianity from wild savagery) for whom a childlike version of English was apt'.

Keesing notes that the use of pidgin, like the introduction of literacy discussed elsewhere in this volume, had an unexpected side-effect in the Solomon Islands:

Interestingly, one of the issues in the postwar anticolonial Maasina Rule movement was the way the SSEM had used Pijin as the vehicle for training catechists at the Bible School at Onepusu, hence withholding 'true' knowledge, education and literacy in English.

(Keesing 1990: 153)

Groups other than the SSEM have largely ignored Pidgin in spite of its wide currency and used local vernaculars or mission lingue franche. A similar situation is also encountered in Vanuatu, the former New Hebrides. Crowley (1989) comments:

while Bislama was relatively widely known from early on, it was regarded in the early years as a language unsuitable for evangelization. This was partly because many missionaries shared the typical attitudes of the time concerning the supposed inadequacies of the language as a means of effective religious communication, and partly because people in many parts of the country themselves viewed Bislama somewhat negatively, as it was considered to be the language of social misfits, who typically avoided village obligations by working on plantations.

(Crowley 1989: 120)

Ignoring a few local attempts by French-speaking missionaries to use Bislama for mission purposes, the mission support for this language began to appear only in the 1960s.

The third factor in the expansion and increased acceptability of Bislama was the impetus given it by the Church from the late 1960s. From its use for taking the minutes of the Presbyterian Church Assembly, Bislama advanced in strides to the publication in 1971 of a translation of the Four Gospels. Hitherto, local vernaculars had been widely used as the languages of evangelism, and extensive Scripture translations had been made. Certain languages had been elevated to the position of lingua franca, such as the Banks Island language of Mota by the Anglican Melanesian Mission. Other missions had adopted vernaculars for liturgical purposes outside their traditional speech communities. The volte-face on Bislama brought to a close the period in which the Church considered it a pariah among vernaculars, 'a plantation language, not fit for worship'. Psychologically, then, a major hurdle was negotiated with the publication of this translation, which was followed in 1980 by a translation of the New Testament, *Nyutesteman long Bislama*. Although not all linguists have viewed such translations as proof of the adequacy of Bislama as a medium of sophisticated communication, Ni-Vanuatu were more impressed. All concerned were, however, ready to concede that these translations were a step in the direction of a standardized form of Bislama.

(Thomas 1990: 237–8)

The area of former German New Guinea with its difficult terrain and a very large number of distinct language groups provided the greatest problems for the missions of Melanesia. These problems were compounded by large-scale internal population movements caused by the setting up of coastal plantations, resettlement of nomadic groups in villages and the absence of any coherent government language policy. Thus, some missions and government bodies for some time tried to make German the general lingua franca, the New Guinea Company promoted Bazaar Malay and Tok Pisin, whilst other official and semi-official bodies promoted local languages such as Tolai as regional lingue franche. In response to the destruction of the indigenous language ecology, the indigenous local population responded by using varieties of Pidgin English (the precursors of present-day Tok Pisin) both when dealing with outsiders and when communicating with each other on aspects of the new culture.

Mission activities in German times were carried out by four main groups, each of which had to find its own solution to the main problem of mission language policies in this period, namely their hostility towards Tok Pisin. The view expressed by the mission of the Divine Word in 1901 may be regarded as representative: 'This undesirable Pidgin English can neither serve as a real language in intercourse, nor as the bearer of culture. It might be most desirable and beneficial if it could be suppressed' (quoted in Gunther 1969: 48).

Like the Divine Word missionaries on the mainland, the Sacred Heart mission operating around Rabaul initially used local languages such as Tolai and Baining for mission purposes. The missionary Kleintitschen praises the efforts of the Catholic missions in the Gazelle Peninsula to replace Tok Pisin with the local language (Tolai) though he has to admit that these efforts had not as yet achieved the intended success.

There were, however, differences between the various stations established by the Divine Word missionaries. Thus Br Klarentius (1909–10: 110) remarks on 'the predominant use of the unbearable Pidgin English' (my translation) in Alexishafen and the widespread use of German on Tumleo and Ali Islands.

Reports concerning the success of the German language policy of the Divine Word missionaries are at variance. An anonymous article in the *Steyler Missionsbote* states that:

> The Catholic mission performs yet another cultural activity which cannot be overestimated because it only promotes German interests. They have adopted the principle of speaking only German with their 300 to 400 black pupils and workers, thereby pushing aside the ghastly Pidgin English. And they are doing it with total success.
>
> (*Steyler Missionsbote* 1910–11: 89, my translation)

Whilst pursuing policies directed against Tok Pisin, circumstances again and again occurred which forced the missionaries to avail themselves of this language. For instance, Kleintitschen reports from Manus:

> Unfortunately we could not communicate with the people in their language. But the conversation was not halted for that reason. It was conducted in the much abused Pidgin English. It may be regretted that this foreign language serves as a lingua franca in a German colony. But considering the conditions on the Archipelago this corrupted English is a necessary evil to which the individual must willy nilly adapt. It is spread over all islands of our South Seas Colony such that one can get by everywhere with kanaka English and communicate with totally foreign natives.
>
> (*Missionshefte* 1914, 31: 66, my translation)

Father P. J. Dick reports from the German Solomons:

> I made a long journey to the Solomon Islands. On this journey I land on an island and hear that a chief is near to death. I visit him and find him in a condition which leaves no doubt about his imminent death. The man understands Pidgin English and so I can, despite the fact that his language is completely unknown to me, give him rudimentary instruction and baptize him.
>
> (*Missionshefte* 1910, 27: 542, my translation)

As in Queensland and other plantation areas, the missionaries had to admit that the only way to reach the multilingual workforce was by means of Pidgin English. Thus, in the Gazelle Peninsula, regular services in Tok Pisin became institutionalized in the 1920s.

> In the year 1928 in Vunapope, a special Sunday service for the workers was established, which is attended by numerous workers from the entire surrounding area. Prayers and songs and, of course, the sermon are held in English (Tok Boi). This arrangement not only facilitates the Catholic workers' fulfilment of their religious

duties but it is also a means of spreading Catholic belief in areas where no missionary has hitherto been.

(Müller 1932: 133, my translation)

Necessity also led to its adoption as a mission language on Manus Island:

The most widely spread lingua franca at present is Pidgin English. The padres in Manus have used it successfully in teaching and in the catechism, since the numerous dialects rendered the use of a native language with the local population ineffective. Therefore they have made efforts to investigate Pidgin English more thoroughly, to set down its grammar and vocabulary and to use it in educational books. Apart from the linguistic interest, the great practical use justifies the effort made. All workers in the Archipelago speak this Pidgin English known as Tok Boi, moreover most natives, especially those of the smaller tribes, use it in conversation with whites and with black outsiders.

(Hüskes 1932: 191, my translation)

As a result, Tok Pisin was seriously studied in both Rabaul and Alexishafen. Höltker (1945) reports that the decision to use Tok Pisin for missionary work was the issue of a number of conferences. The most immediate aim of these conferences was to increase the efficiency of Tok Pisin for its new function. Thus, a number of grammars and dictionaries were prepared, the first being that of Brenninkmeyer (1924), followed by Borchardt's (1926) and a number of others, many of which were the result of teamwork and therefore do not bear the name of an author. These dictionaries and grammars were followed by the publication of catechisms, hymns, prayer books and literature of an entertaining kind such as *Frend Bilong Mi* and the comic *Piktel*. In about 1930 a meeting (convened at Marienberg) spent a whole month drafting publications in Tok Pisin (Father Ross, personal communication).

The adoption of Tok Pisin as a mission language by the Catholics was not, as has been pointed out by Höltker (1945: 44–63), an attempt to raise Tok Pisin to any official status. Rather, it was the result of practical considerations. Tok Pisin, it was argued, was the most widely spoken lingua franca in New Guinea and it therefore had to be used as a mission medium. It was hoped that Tok Pisin would eventually be replaced by other more suitable media.

The policy of the various Catholic mission societies was not followed by most Protestant mission; however, Osmers (1981) reports that by 1930, at a major conference by the Lutheran Mission, the missionaries gradually decided on a temporary truce as regards the use of Tok Pisin:

It was accepted that the use of Pidgin was justified to a certain degree because of its wide distribution, preferential treatment by the Government, neutrality within linguistic diversity and its easy acquisition. The knowledge of Pidgin was recommended for every missionary.

(Osmers 1981: 96–7)

But for mission work the Conference emphasized the severe disadvantages of the language:

1 Since Pidgin was not standardized and had been changing rapidly, the production of literature would cause insurmountable difficulties.
2 It promoted to a certain extent the negative influences of Western civilization on the people.
3 There is hardly any chance of creating a deep religious impact in the souls of the natives.

By the close of the Second World War, however, there had been a major reorientation in the stance of the missions towards Tok Pisin. This was largely due to

1 a general opposition to teaching vernaculars
2 the fact that Tok Pisin had increasingly over the years taken over the role of the most widely used lingua franca.

Osmers (1981) reports:

After 70 years of struggling for a common language to assist in building up and unifying an indigenous Lutheran Church, a tongue which had been neglected for such a long time, was recognized as a possibility in the very year of the foundation of the ELCONG [Evangelical Lutheran Church of New Guinea]. A few years later it was acknowledged as the lingua franca with the widest circulation and most speakers in the Church.

Although its value in spiritual matters was still disputed, its usefulness as communication medium at compounds and urban settlements and for inter-district conferences was unquestioned and antagonistic voices mainly among the missionaries had become less demanding.

Flierl still insisted on its inferiority concerning the proper expression of the deepest thoughts of the Christian faith and suspected Tok Pisin to favour shallowness in Christian life. However he pointed out that the language seemed acceptable for secular education. He considered that for the New Guineans Tok Pisin was

Table 6.1 Religious terms used by different missions

Alexishafen TP	Vunapope TP	Rabaul TP	Gloss
God	Deo	God	'God'
kilim	mekim dai	kilim	'to kill'
brukim pasin ⎫ bilong marit ⎭	pilai nogut	mekim trabel ⎫ long meri ⎭	'adultery'
lai	giaman	giaman	'to lie'

more suitable than English because of its Melanesian thought patterns and he stressed the need to increase the production of good literature.

(Osmers 1981: 104)

Up to this date each mission had pursued its own language policy, thereby complicating and further dividing an already complex linguistic ecology. Even in the efforts to make use of Tok Pisin (TP) for mission purposes, different missions have gone separate ways. It was probably hoped that by creating distinct varieties of Church Tok Pisin, contacts between the adherents of different confessions and consequent conversion could be minimized. As a result, one finds significant discrepancies between the various mission dialects (see Table 6.1).

In many cases it is difficult to locate the geographic origin of individual mission innovations. Table 6.2 illustrates the profusion of terms in use in one or another locality. The following abbreviations are used in referring to their linguistic origin: E = English; G = German; L = local languages; CP = compounding; Ex = extension of meaning; LA = Latin; PH = phrase formation.

Whilst the practice of indexing membership of a particular group by means of lexical differences is well-known Papuan New Guinean practice, a second type of mission language planning definitely is not. One of the main criticisms against Tok Pisin, it appears, was that it is full of crudities and obscenities. One expression in particular annoyed the missions: 'God dam', which according to a number of sources was a very frequent vocabulary item before 1930. Thus, in 1911, Friederici reported:

If a Melanesian exclaims: 'God dam! He savee too much!' when he refers to another Melanesian who is magnificently decorated as to look like a negro from Washington or Virginia, he will always

Table 6.2 Terms used by different Catholic missions

'acolyte'	ministran (G)	altoboi (CP)	kundar (L)
'incense'	wairau (G)	insens (E)	smelsmok (CP)
'church'	kirke (G)	sios (E)	haus lotu (PH)
'cross'	diwai kros (PH)	kruse (LA)	bolo (L)
'to believe'	bilip (E)	nurnur (L)	tok i tru (PH)
'heart'	bel (Ex)	hat (E)	liva (Ex)
'procession'	prosesio (LA)	varvaliu (L)	
'rosary'	roseri (E)	kurkurua (L)	corona (LA)
'holy'	holi (E)	santu (LA)	takondo (L)
'to pray'	pre (E)	beten (G)	raring (L)
'sin'	sin (E)	pekato (LA)	
'hell'	hel (E)	imperno (LA)	bikpaia (CP)
'to forgive'	pogivim (E)	larim (Ex)	lusim (Ex)
'virgin'	vetsin (E)	virgo (LA)	meri i stap tambu (PH)
'ascension'	goap bilong Jesus (PH)	asensio (LA)	

create amusement. But it made me really sad when I heard a man from Lamassa, while he was building a mon (Boat), muttering: 'God dam, work belong kanaka he no good!'

(translated by McDonald 1977: 22)

Mead (1931) comments on the initial effort of the missions to remove crude expressions from the language:

When the missionaries preach and translate the Bible into pidgin, they make some effort to smooth out the crudities of the language, but in the hands of the boys these all crop up again. Pidgin without continual 'goddams' and 'bloodys' is inconceivable to the boys.

(Mead 1931: 151)

Separate developments of mission varieties came to an end only in 1955, when the Catholic church

approached the Lutheran Church to study the type of Tok Pisin to be used in both missions with the intention of unifying terminology and spelling, the Lutherans agreed to cooperate. Later they asked the British and Foreign Bible Society about the possibility of translating the New Testament into Tok Pisin realising an urgent demand for its production.

(Osmers 1981: 104)

The agreed translation of the New Testament appeared in 1969 and, together with the establishment by the Catholic Church of the weekly newspaper *Wantok* and the setting up of the Protestant publishing house Kristen Pres in Madang, a period of concerted missionary support for Tok Pisin had begun.

The story of the missions and Tok Pisin in Papua New Guinea is one where local *ad hoc* solutions and ignorance of the overall linguistic situation prevailed for a long time. Most salient is that such policies that were adopted were driven by expatriate perceptions and in some instances were directly against the wishes of the local population. Whilst a very considerable amount of social control could be exercised this way, it would be wrong to portray the Papua New Guineans as passive recipients of expatriate language policies. Rather, as was observed in connection with literacy, missionary uses of Tok Pisin were changed by people to serve different purposes. Lawrence (1964) has illustrated the non-intended reinterpretation of messages in Tok Pisin by a number of cargo movements that sprang up in the wake of missionization and the introduction of literacy.

> When the doctrine was fully elaborated, it became, subject to local variations, part of the people's culture and had its own momentum. As such, it developed its own linguistic usages, expressed in both Pidgin English and the native vernaculars. Much of the phraseology was highly allusive or oblique (Pidgin English, tok bokis). Two of the most obvious phrases have already been presented: 'to root out evil' was translated into Pidgin English as 'rausim Satan', which was interpreted as 'to keep the local deities at bay'; and the Pidgin English 'opim/pasim rot bilong kako' (literally, 'to open/close the road of the cargo') was understood as 'to reveal/hide the ritual secrets which would ensure the cargo's arrival'. In Pidgin English, God was known as the '(bilong) kako' (the source of cargo). Again, among the Garia, for example, ordinary Christian phrases assumed new meanings. 'God blessed Noah' (Genesis ix. I) (Pidgin English: God i bigpela long Noa) came to mean 'God gave cargo to Noah' on the grounds that in Melanesian culture the concept of blessing could be given practical expression only by the presentation of wealth. The phrase 'the Mission wanted to help us' (Pidgin English: misin i laik halivim/litimapim yumi) came to mean 'the Mission wanted to give us cargo'. Such phrases as 'the period of ignorance' (Pidgin English: taim bilong tudak) and 'the understanding of God is with us' (Pidgin English: tingting bilong God istap) were understood as 'the time before the cargo secret was revealed to us' and 'we now have the ear of God (and the means of getting cargo)' respectively.

This oblique language increased the complexity of the situation. It could be used in conversations with European missionaries without their being aware of its hidden implications and – although some of them suspected what was going on in the natives' minds – the extent to which their teachings had been misrepresented. As a result, they unconsciously allowed the people to assume that they confirmed the truth of the new doctrines. Either they or the sincere and disinterested native mission helpers had only to fail to correct an equivocal sentence, or innocently make a statement capable of two meanings, to substantiate the Third Cargo Belief in its entirety. No stronger proof was necessary. In fact, during the 1920s, relations between natives and missionaries, although on the whole extremely amicable, were nevertheless based on complete mutual misunderstanding.

(Lawrence 1964: 84)

Pidgin languages, as has been pointed out, arise in a situation where the indigenous language ecology is disturbed. One of the most cataclysmic disturbances occurred where traditional people were driven off their land and picked out by missions and resettled on mission stations or where children were taken away from their families and educated in mission-controlled boarding schools. Both phenomena were very common in Australia until the 1960s.[7] In such situations children had to develop their own form of communication out of the imperfect and inconsistent input that was available to them (bits of the traditional language, bits of English, some Pidgin English) and the outcome tended to be a creole. Roper River Creole in Northern Australia, Broken in the Torres Straits and Unserdeutsch in Rabaul or Tayo in French New Caledonia are all creoles that developed in mission dormitories. They were the unintended outcome of mission policy designed to assimilate and transform traditional people.

MISSION POLICIES AND METROPOLITAN LANGUAGES

The missionary societies operating in the Pacific had many conflicting opinions regarding the correct way for encoding the Christian message. Moreover, the choice of a code was influenced by a number of factors that had little to do with missionary activity as such. I shall deal with the use of metropolitan languages by the missions in relatively little detail, as this topic still awaits better scrutiny.

Generally speaking, missions opted for languages such as Spanish, German, French or English for the following reasons.

1 It was felt that no other language was suited to expressing the message of the Bible; this view was particularly prevalent in the early days.

2 The missionaries themselves, as representatives of European nations, tended to see a strong link between national language and the processes of civilization and Christianization. Thus, Protestant missionaries in Vanuatu or the Loyalties tended to promote English in opposition to the Catholic promotion of French.

In many instances, external pressures were also important:

3 General policies in many colonies made grants towards education contingent on teaching the national language.
4 Economic pressures such as the availability of bibles, teaching materials and school primers in a national language made the choice of such a language attractive compared to the high cost of producing new materials in many indigenous languages.

Finally, one needs to mention:

5 The inability or unwillingness of many missionaries to speak foreign languages (for detailed comments see Deer 1975).

Many missionaries saw their role either as trying to bring about bilingualism in the local language and the metropolitan language or monolingualism in the latter. However, there are a number of documented studies of missions discouraging the use of European languages, the main motive being that these languages promoted the uncontrolled influx of secular Western ideas. As in other instances of mission language policy, a solution that had no undesirable side-effects was not available, however.

THE SUMMER INSTITUTE OF LINGUISTICS (SIL)

No discussion of missionary language policies could be complete without a mention of SIL, the Summer Institute of Linguistics, also known as Wycliffe Bible Translators. The former head of the Papua New Guinea branch, K. J. Franklin, characterized the historical background of this organization as follows (1977a):

The founder of the Summer Institute of Linguistics is Mr W. C. Townsend. A short biography of Mr Townsend and his work has been written by Eunice Pike and can be found in Elson and Comas, eds 1961, and a more detailed outline of the joint efforts of SIL and the Wycliffe Bible Translators in Hefley and Hefley 1974. Mr Townsend's motivation has always been to serve other groups through scientific, cultural, and spiritual efforts. Language is seen as a key to understanding people's aspirations, expressed through language, and without some understanding of the language of an ethnic group there cannot be a true identification with the people. Mr Townsend had always recommended a balanced programme with heavy practical emphasis on community and rural projects. The writing down of languages and providing descriptive grammars, dictionaries, literacy materials, and translation is one process of enhancing cultural pride and motivation. Without such an emphasis and interest, minority groups in any country may suffer complete cultural assimilation.

(Franklin 1977a: 1,228)

A self-characterization in one of its information pamphlets is:

A philanthropic, non-governmental organization committed to linguistic research, language development, literacy, and other projects of practical, social and spiritual value to the lesser known cultural communities of the world.

(quoted in Philpott 1993: 1)

A number of less optimistic and more critical accounts of SIL have appeared over the years, for instance Gilliam (1984: 309–12) and Crowley (1989).[8] Some of the themes recurring in the discussion of SIL's activities are summarized by Crowley:

In Papua New Guinea at least, one of the most visible missionary organisations towards the end of the colonial era, one which was also most conspicuously involved in the use of Melanesian languages for evangelization, was the Wycliffe Bible Translators cum Summer Institute of Linguistics (SIL). This dual-faced organisation came to be based in the township of Ukarumpa, and it began operations in 1956. Its membership since then has always tended towards being that of a religious fundamentalist, and socio-politically conservative nature, with a heavy predominance of American staff.

That work of SIL in promoting vernacular literacy in Melanesia has won educational awards from UNESCO. At the same time, the organisation has not been free from criticism however. It has been claimed that it, along with other western missionary organisations, promotes deculturalisation and western cultural imperialism, presenting God very much as embodying traditional American Republican virtues. Others have even gone so far as to suggest that the organisation has links with the American CIA. Such all-encompassing accusations seem naive, and even unfair, given the lack of direct evidence, especially in the Melanesian context.

Some countries in the Third World have actually expelled the organisation, or sharply reduced its activities, on the basis of the threats – whether real or only perceived – with which it was associated. It is true that those countries in South and Central America which appear to offer the organisation the greatest welcome are the more conservative and military governments of the region, while other governments – such as that of Nicaragua – have taken a more directly critical, or even hostile line. It is also true that the organisation had a very strong presence in the Melanesian Indonesian province of Irian Jaya, which is currently in the final stages of being politically, economically and culturally colonised by Asians from other parts of Indonesia.

Despite its reputation, and its sometimes unpleasant choice of bedmates elsewhere in the world, the organisation in Melanesia has done much valuable work in the area of linguistic description and analysis, and, as I have already pointed out, in the promotion of literacy.

(Crowley 1989: 120–1)

I am prepared to give SIL the benefit of the doubt and accept that most of its members are generally concerned with what they regard as bettering the lot of those they work with, and I take note of remarks made by Pike, the President of SIL (in a newspaper article which was sent to me without reference):

I would prefer to take the risk of trying to be helpful, while praying that God will make more good come from my good intentions and positive efforts than damage from my cultural insensitivities and ignorance.

My contention is that cultural as well as linguistic ignorance has tended to cause an enormous amount of damage and that the role of SIL in the preservation of traditional cultures has been much overrated.

An argument often adduced when I debate these matters with my SIL colleagues is that all they do is to provide the people they work with with a choice between traditional and Christian oral and literate ways of life. A representative statement to this effect was given by Hooley (1976):

What constitutes improvement will depend very much on the philosophical or other bias of the person judging. Therefore, the people concerned need knowledge of the various options open to them, and their implications, so that they can bring sound judgement to bear on their own culture and decide for themselves whether or not they want to change. . . .

To the extent that the people are denied the knowledge they need, to that extent they are open to exploitation in one way or another. To the extent that new information is available in a language and format primarily understandable only to the young people, the social life of the community will be damaged, even by changes which might otherwise be good.

(Hooley 1976: 2)

As observed by Lynch (1979), however, the range of choices offered is very restricted:

Rather, as I have tried to show, the use of the vernacular languages by religious organisations has been geared almost solely to the production of religious literature – *baibel, baibel, singsing nomo.*

(Lynch 1979: 15)

Attempts by SIL (described in Philpott 1993) to promote vernacular literacy by means of shell books and desktop publishing continue the tradition of dishing out a bland and culturally insensitive diet of vernacular literacy.[9]

My objections are that the very notion of choice is part of the conceptual garbage that twentieth-century big business in the USA is trying to push on to the rest of the world (fifty-seven varieties of Heinz, twenty-five McDonald's burgers, ninety-nine flavours of American ice-cream, etc.), that choice is culturally irrelevant in a Melanesian context and that, moreover, in this context of missioniza- tion the dice are very heavily loaded against the traditional culture. The aim of a mission society is to convert and not to provide free choices, as can be clearly seen from their attempts to exclude other choices (Marxism, hedonism, Islam, Buddhism, etc.) from the menu of options.

There is another aspect of choice that needs to be raised here – the choice between different brands of Christianity. Fox (1967), comment- ing on the Solomon Islands' experience of linguistic division, argues:

The other thing that has divided us is the divisions of the Churches. It is true that in the old days of mission schools, when a Melanesian language, not English, was used, some 30,000 of us became literate, that is, able to read and write our own languages. But the divisions between the churches were deep: there was hostility and suspicion between them. A Solomon Islander lately wrote 'At present, it is sad to say, but the truth is that the people in our islands are divided, not by the different islands, or languages, but by the different denominations of the Church'.

(Fox 1967: 69–70)

As regards the writing of 'scientific' grammars and dictionaries it must be remembered that neither concept is indigenous to the region. Traditionally, the meanings of lexical items were not established by looking them up in a finite dictionary, but by negotiating them in face-to-face communication. The dictionary, as an external authority regarding meanings, radically alters the way meanings are established in a society. Like dictionaries, 'objective' grammars also reinforce the myth of language being a fixed code. What is marketed as objective description in fact could become an agent of a radical conceptual and social change.

Very much the same goes for literacy, as I have argued elsewhere in this book, which is similarly a source of social practices and not just a technique. I would probably grossly insult the mental capacity of my SIL colleagues if I believed that they didn't realize some of the above considerations. The argument that SIL helps preserve the multitude of indigenous languages is also flawed if one is to accept that there is no determinate number of languages and that it is the descriptive process itself that brings such languages into being and determines their number. The activities of standardization and reducing language to writing thus reduce lectal variation, make inter-lectal borrowing difficult and, in turn, undermine the viability of small languages. By producing only a very small amount of literature (excluding traditional knowledge), SIL not only helped speed up the decline of the traditional patterns of life, but also encouraged the shift to larger languages. Turning now to the formal properties of vernacular literacy, the neo-Bloomfieldian theory (tagmemics) that has so much shaped SIL descriptive practices contains a number of other dangers. Its a-temporality desensitizes writers and users of linguistic descriptions to historical developments by forcibly suggesting that it is present-day patterns and not longitudinal developments that are the main source of meaning.

A final problem I have with the argument that SIL preserves linguistic heterogeneity is that the explicit goal of the organization is to bring about universal acceptance of a single conceptual framework: Christianity. In order to achieve this goal, the multitude of indigenous conceptual models as embodied in traditional languages has to be reduced to a single conceptual system. As the diversity of languages lies not so much in their surface structures but in their meanings it is the deeper diversity that is under threat.

Like most other mission linguistic policies, that of SIL is based on a range of culture-specific prejudices, but unlike some other organizations, it is based on a very considerable amount of financial and human resources making it powerful, respectable and confident.

CONCLUSIONS

In spite of the many contradictory and seemingly chaotic patterns of mission involvement with local vernaculars, there is one uniting element: virtually all such linguistic activity as was engaged in by the missions is directly derived from the conduit metaphor of communication (Reddy 1979), the view that the sending of messages involves converting them into signals which are then picked up and decoded by the receiver.[10] Implied in this metaphor is the fact that messages that are intended to bring about behavioural change in the receiver will do so if properly encoded. Under such an assumption the question of the correct code is a major issue as few missionaries ever have any doubt as to the validity of the message or the changes they wish to effect and it is only since the 1970s that one encounters a more critical approach, as, for example, in Whiteman (1974):

> Thus, even though the missionary is attempting to proclaim a message whose emphasis is upon a radical change for every follower, thus cutting across cultural distinctions, his inability to separate the essential principles of Christianity from their expression in his own cultural framework, causes him to disseminate a message that is very confusing at best, since it is expressed in the cultural tradition of the missionary rather than in the cultural idiom with which a New Guinean can identify. The result of this confusion is that, for the New Guinean, a 'new life in Christ' is perceived as a 'new life as a European'.
>
> (Whiteman 1974: 28)

With regard to the code, two options were open: either to equip the intended recipients with the knowledge of a code appropriate for the message or to change the recipients' existing code to make it suited to the job. There was little doubt that the large metropolitan languages (English, German, French) were indeed appropriate codes and the very considerable effort that has gone into teaching these languages to indigenes was regarded as a worthwhile investment.

Missionaries' resistance against pidgins and creoles on the other hand is typically based on their belief that these languages were inappropriate and deficient codes in principle and therefore should be disregarded or eliminated.

Opinions differed as to the suitability of the indigenous vernaculars, though there is almost universal agreement that they were not suitable media in their traditional shape. The repair needed involved the creation of doctrinal terminology, the purging of undesirable traditional knowledge and standardization necessary for writing literature.

A very strong, though by no means unusual, metaphor has been that of the Tower of Babel, the belief that the perceived linguistic compartmentalization of the Pacific area was a punishment or a curse. Reducing heterogeneity and replacing it with larger unified languages such as mission lingue franche was seen as bringing the recipients of missionary language planning closer to a state of Grace. As opined by Gunther (1958).

only Christianity can replace the myriad philosophies, legends, pagan practices and supernatural fears that 510 tongues have engendered. It is only by removal of these 510 tongues and the acceptance of a common language that the end of many unnatural behaviours can be achieved.

(Gunther 1958: 59)

The image of the Holy Spirit speaking in all human tongues is somehow in conflict with the Babel metaphor and may account for the efforts such as those of SIL to make all languages suited to the Christian message.

This concentration on the choice of code and Christianization of the code took place at the expense of many other activities which are incompatible with the conduit metaphor. The model of communication underlying most missionary thinking wrongly suggests a one-way process of learning, whereby the missionaries or teachers were teachers and the indigenous population pupils; it isolates language from other social practices and its cultural embedding and it plays down developmental considerations. Codes are chosen because of their potential for social control, not to enable people critically to reflect on their traditions and aspirations and to make them equal with expatriate colonizers, missionizers and their ideas.

Whereas missionary organizations used very considerable resources for their main objective, the conversion of large proportions of the population to Christianity, their impact on the wider linguistic ecology of the area appears to have been largely unintended and often self-defeating. Because most missionary linguistic planning was based on a mechanistic rather than a structural/systemic or ecological view, uncoordinated local tinkering abounded. Like other agencies, the missions were in the business of dismantling the traditional ways of life in the Pacific area and replacing them with a makeshift shelter in which some traditional languages could linger on for a while but most faced a very uncertain tenancy in the long run. Indirectly, many missions appear to have contributed to the ultimate decline in traditional languages, and if such languages survive it was probably more because of the lack of mission funds and time invested than deliberate mission policies to keep the linguistic ecology of the Pacific area intact.

The decline of the missionary lingue franche, and the decline of the moral system put in place by the missionaries, is paralleled by the ascent of a different type of missionization, that of Westernization, economic rationalism and spreading of English and French. The missionaries of this movement, economic advisers and modern educationists, as set out by Milner (1984):

> The old missionaries gave you education in your own languages, but what use are those in the modern world? Will they help you to repair a car or a marine engine, to market your crops and keep proper accounts? We on the other hand have a different plan. Now that we have the resources and the manpower, we shall teach your children English (or French) as early as possible and we shall also teach other subjects in English (or French). Our aim will be to phase out as soon as possible the vernacular as a medium of instruction in Government schools. Other languages can be left to the responsibility of parents and religious teachers. What is more, we shall also start to use English (or French) language textbooks. This will enable us to dovetail the new curriculum into that of overseas schools. Thus many more of your children will qualify for examinations recognised outside the Pacific Islands, including some which give entrance to a university. We shall also implement this policy with a much larger number of expatriate teachers seconded to island schools. At long last, your children will be able to compete with ours on a progressively wider and fairer basis.
>
> (Milner 1984: 15)

7 Official policies and language planning

A language policy which goes counter to existing sociocultural faces is not likely to be successful.

(Paulston 1992: 56)

INTRODUCTION

I have demonstrated in some detail that the linguistic ecology of the Pacific area has always been subject to deliberate acts of human interference. These range from traditional efforts to create esoteric and special languages and attempts by missionaries to create a suitable mission medium to more recent campaigns for literacy and language education. The term 'natural language' in referring to languages such as Kâte, Indonesian or Chamorro is therefore a totally unsuitable label, suggesting a spurious division between linguistic objects and human users, observers and planners.

This chapter takes cognizance of such past human activities. However, it will focus on a development from the mid-nineteenth century which coincides with the emergence of centrally controlled modern colonies and nation-states, namely the phenomenon of language planning. Traditionally, writers on this topic distinguish between status planning, that is, official policies enhancing the status of selected languages, and corpus planning, which constitutes activities directed at increasing the referential power, modernity or systematic adequacy of the languages thus selected. In the light of changes in the 1980s in this area, a second dichotomy is suggested, that between streamlining the information flow and maintenance of diversity.

All language planning requires certain ecological conditions. The planning activities described in this chapter presuppose:

1 control and power by government
2 clear goals
3 technical expertise.

For any planning activity to be successful, ways of implementing desired changes are also essential.

PRECONDITIONS FOR PLANNING

The development of the European nation-state and the accompanying system of colonial expansion (imperialism) in many people's view provided the catalyst for language planning in a modern sense. The political independence of former colonies provided a second powerful impetus to this idea. Central to the conception of a modern nation-state is the idea of a common language, a common form of administration and a common education system. The developments which gave rise to modern European national languages have been documented in much detail, for instance by Grillo (1989) for English and French, Kloss (1978) for the Germanic group of languages and Haugen (1972 and elsewhere) for the Scandinavian languages. As regards the languages of the Pacific area, much general information can be found in Sebeok (1971b) and Wurm (1979). The issues surrounding planning for South East Asian languages are summarized in Perez *et al.* (1978), for Australia and the South-West Pacific in Baldauf and Luke (1990) and for New Zealand and Oceania in Benton (1981). Tollefson (1991) contains a detailed critique of some of these activities as does Mühlhäusler (1987a, 1995). Baldauf and Luke (1990) provide a long annotated list of references to language planning in the Pacific area. The close link between the development of nation-states and language planning is borne out in the above studies.[1]

With a few exceptions the vast majority of the new states in the Pacific are highly multilingual, with more than 800 languages spoken in Papua New Guinea, more than 300 in Indonesia, more than 100 in Australia and Vanuatu. All those countries which were monolingual in traditional times (Samoa, Tahiti, Guam or Tonga) have become multilingual as a result of 200 years of contact with Europeans.

Effective control over large territories is a recent phenomenon (since the end of the eighteenth century) in most areas, though in some parts of the Pacific rim such as in China or Korea it dates back thousands of years. Early European colonization by the Portuguese and Spanish rarely extended beyond small fortified trade centres. It was only towards the end of the nineteenth century, when the Pacific was 'carved up', that meaningful control could be exercised by a central government over political units such as the Dutch East Indies, the American Philippines, German New Guinea, the British Solomons or French New Caledonia. In some instances this control was perpetuated by the influx of large numbers of settlers, leading to the creation of Neo-Europes such as Australia, New Zealand and Hawaii. In other areas the control by colonizing governments was more indirect or even absent. When Papua New Guinea gained independence from Australia in 1975, for instance, much of its populous interior had barely been under colonial control for twenty years and the concept of nationhood was hardly of great importance. None the less, in most instances, contact with European colonizers had created the conditions in which the ideas of nation-state and national language could take root. As the policies encountered today have tended to continue colonial practice it would seem useful briefly to examine the policies of the principal colonial powers.

COLONIAL LANGUAGE POLICIES

Portugal

Despite being the first on the scene, Portuguese control could rarely be maintained by the motherland and eventually was restricted to East Timor and Macau. The principal motif of Portuguese language policies was that literacy and a knowledge of Portuguese were the criteria for full citizenship. As very few resources were made available to promote the language through education, only a small elite ever learnt Portuguese, and after 410 years of Portuguese presence in Macau, everyday life is dominated by Cantonese and education by English (Harrison 1984). The Portuguese policy of encouraging mixed marriages to strengthen their control often had the unintended effect of creating new creole languages (Macanese in Macau or Papia Kristang in Malacca). In the case of Timor, this creole is based on a local language (Tetún). In sum, Portuguese assimilation policies were never given the resources needed to implement them on a significant scale.

The Dutch

Dutch language policies up to the mid-nineteenth century were very much an *ad hoc* affair. The administration of their vast East Indian colony relied heavily on indirect control via indigenous rulers who relied on established powerful languages such as Javanese or the spreading varieties of Bahasa Malay. Portuguese attempts to promulgate Christianity in Indonesia were continued by the Dutch. The language associated with this remained Creole Portuguese as there was a widespread perception that Dutch should not be spoken by the local population. In their desire to keep the indigenous population from the privileges associated with a mastery of Dutch, the colonial administrators, first a private company and subsequently the Dutch government, created their own medium of communication, Malay.

It is necessary to focus on the creation of this language in some detail as it illustrates a trend widely found in new nation-states, to rewrite their linguistic history and to justify policy decisions against the background of such reconstructed histories. The 'official' history of Bahasa Indonesia (as given, for instance, by Babib 1989) is that both its linguistic nature and spread as a lingua franca were local phenomena:

> Long before the arrival of the earliest European travellers in the archipelago there was evidence that Malay had been in use over a fairly large area of present-day Indonesia, stretching from South East Asia to the island of Tidore in the Moluccas. This meant that Malay had been used as early as the sixteenth century, but further evidence shows that Malay was used at least as early as the sixth century.
>
> (Babib 1989: 63)

> The attempt to introduce Dutch in its political and cultural sense did not take place until 1925 when the Director of Education expressed his belief that the only way to keep the East Indies close and loyal to the Netherlands was to use Dutch as a means of communication among the natives. The failure of the Dutch government to integrate the natives was due to the fact that the schools could not accommodate the pupils, and secondly the awakening of Indonesian nationalism which resulted in the Youth Pledge, declared in 1928.
>
> (Babib 1989: 64)

Against such a view Hoffman (1973) and several contributors to a special issue of *Prisma* (1989) argue that there is little continuity with older forms of Malay and that it is basically a Dutch creation.[2] Hoffman dismisses the view that the history of Malay is a continuous one culminating in a national language for an independent Indonesia:

> Yet explanations of the ultimate supremacy of the Malay Language as Bahasa Indonesia generally fall into the line of an 'inevitable' victory. Malay is called 'the' (not 'a') lingua franca – and this is usually assumed to comprehend all levels and variants of Malay. The Malay-based Srivijaya and Malacca Empires, with their maritime preponderance in the west of the Archipelago from the seventh

to the early sixteenth centuries, are cited. The general association of Islamic proselytising with much Malay literary and religious tradition is pointed to. And the supposed ease of pronouncing and of conveying one's meaning in Malay is declared – sometimes by those who have never tried to use the language correctly, if at all.

(Hoffman 1973: 20)

Such an account, Hoffman argues:

fails to reveal that the Malay language as the language of government – the language of unity – for the Archipelago was a careful fabrication extending over three hundred years of Dutch policy.

As to 'inevitability': at the end of the period we are considering today, that is, when the direction of government changed into the 'Ethical Course', there was no assurance that this Dutch-fabricated Malay was acceptable to any significant group apart from indigenous civil servants and members of the Netherlands Indies army in their working hours, and a small number of newspaper readers in the main coastal cities. Among the vast majority of the indigenous peoples, the nobility and the peasantry, Malay was neither nationally nor regionally the language of learning, culture or home life. Its success was in administration, and then in a downward, broadening sense, rather than as the language of an inspiring, liberating future. That, on the contrary, was the role then seen for Dutch.

Malay had been shaped to serve as the general language of government below the administrative deck trodden by Dutchmen. But that was a Dutch arrangement. There appears to be no indigenous tradition of government via Malay in the Java heartland of the Archipelago. Even in the Sundanese-speaking area of West Java, Javanese was the language of correspondence of the bupati or regent magisterial class until about the middle of the nineteenth century. Administrators' letters to these regents were drafted in Dutch or Malay for translation into High Javanese. Javanese was the language spoken in the regents' provincial courts even when, again, these were surrounded by Sundanese speakers.

And not only did the Dutch introduce Malay into areas of the Archipelago – particularly in the Great East, despite what may be deduced from the Pigafetta word-list that had been compiled in the Moluccas or through shipboard Malay interpreters. But the Dutch introduction of Malay as a language of government and religion caused resentment and 'passive resistance', according to the best cross-examination one can make of Dutch evidence of the seventeenth and early eighteenth centuries. The protests re-arose in the last half of the nineteenth century, this time among Dutch scholars and linguists who were also administrators, claiming that the Dutch-imported Malay was destroying or submerging local languages and dialects, or was reducing their standing or importance or capacity to edify. The protests were still heard in the Volksraad in 1923. The subject of complaint was only one among a range of actions taken by Batavia for administrative and economic co-ordination and expansion.

(Hoffman 1973: 21–2)

In making Malay an official language the Dutch carried out not only extensive status planning but also a great deal of corpus planning, including the purification from Islamic vocabulary and the introduction of a substantial administrative vocabulary.[3] Malay, or better a standardized high form referred to as Riau Malay, was developed deliberately as a language of unification and civilization but above all, as Heryanto (1988) points out, as a form of communication which was culture-neutral, intertranslatable with Dutch and other European languages and adapted to new conditions.

Hoffman quotes from an article on 'The Value of Malay as the Medium of Civilization', written by the high-ranking civil servant A. A. Fokker in 1891:

'People have for long not been made sufficiently conscious of the great importance of a universal language of civilization (beschavings-taal) especially with a dominated people. We believe decidedly that unity of language gives solidarity . . . . The government's task also becomes so much more easy when an identical idiom is understood and spoken everywhere. The small dialects must be lost; that is an unshakeable law: they may be used by importers of the Gospel as the key to the hearts of the inboorlingen, and even remain in existence as the language of more intimate life, but, as the thought-bearers of society, they must give way before the stronger and more developed. In Provence, the populace speaks an entirely different French from in Paris, but, just the same, everybody writes his letters in the generally customary French. In the Moluccas, every leader in the provinces where there is direct government knows good Riau Malay, although then each island also knows its own Alfoerese dialect. The language of Ambon is disappearing at an increasing rate: so strong is the influence of the more cultured Malay. It is sensible not to oppose such a gradual, natural process.'

Fokker believed that it was unrealistic to expect indigenous people of all classes to become fluent in Dutch. 'No language is so suitable for the inlander to acquire our concepts in, as Malay,' he wrote. 'It is astonishing that it can still be doubted.'

(Hoffman 1973: 34)

Very much the same arguments were put forward when the first generation of Indonesian nationalists emerged in the 1920s and, in a mildly modified form, continue to inspire present-day language planning in Indonesia.

Some of the misunderstanding surrounding the history of Malay in the Dutch East Indies results from the fact that there was a second, and probably secondary, trend in Dutch language policies, that is the promotion of the Dutch language as the medium of intercommunication. This promotion coincided with the influence of the European enlightenment and more liberal ideas reaching the colonial administration in the second half of the nineteenth century.

Alisjahbana (1971), in a detailed study of the varying official policies towards Malay, Javanese and Dutch, remarks:

> The Dutch colonial government's policy on the question of the language of instruction in elementary and secondary schools was repeatedly changed in the nineteenth century, mainly because opinions on the importance of the two languages for instruction purposes constantly altered. Whereas Governor General Rochussen, after his tour of Java in 1850, suggested that Malay be made the ordinary medium of instruction on the grounds that it was the lingua franca of the entire 'Indian' archipelago, and was used equally by all kinds of ethnic groups, Malays, Javanese, Chinese, Arabs, Buginese, Makassarese, Balinese and Dayakas in their ordinary social intercourse, the influence of Van der Chijs in the mid-nineteenth century was responsible for the progress made in disseminating knowledge of Dutch. He maintained that for this purpose it was not enough simply that Indonesians could attend European schools, but that special schools should be set up for the Indonesians alone where they could learn to speak Dutch. He also proposed to establish a system of secondary schools and of higher education, with this end in view.
>
> The turn of the century saw the rise of an ethical trend in colonial policy which tried to impart to the Indonesians some understanding of European culture by teaching them something of the knowledge and the methodology of Western civilization. When Mr. J. H. Abendanon became the Director of the Department of

Education in 1900, he made strenuous efforts to foster and spread the use of Dutch throughout Indonesia. He was convinced that a knowledge of Dutch would be the shortest way for the Indonesian people to absorb Western culture.

(Alisjahbana 1971: 1,092)

These pro-Dutch policies received considerable support from the educated and powerful Javanese, who tended to regard Malay as an inferior form of expression. An example of this view is given by Hoffman (1973):

> Contrast this with the prospects for the enlightenment of the Javanese then being entertained by the remarkable noblewoman Raden Adjeng Kartini, who wrote in 1900 of her brother having been taken to the Netherlands Language and Literary Congress at Gent. The young Javanese, expressing also the viewpoint of Kartini and her family, pleaded at the congress for Dutch to be made obligatory as the diensttaal, the official language for, as Kartini later put it, 'the vigorous spreading of the Netherlands culture among the Javanese people.' He had been taken to the conference by the eminent Indologist Professor J. H. C. Kern, who, at a similar congress at Dordrecht in 1897, had criticized the Netherlands Indies administration for having introduced a foreign language into the Minhahasa region of the Archipelago, the foreign language being not Dutch but Malay. Further, he condemned the Malay generally in use as a Low or gibberish Malay, in the well-established words of Van der Tuuk, what Kern also called a Volapük, that is, an artificial, international language.
>
> (Hoffman 1973: 33)

Official indigenous support for such a policy was expressed by the first gathering of 'culturally conscious, educated' Indonesians, held in Batavia in 1908.

> On that occasion the Congress demanded that standards for admission into Dutch schools be relaxed, and that special schools be set up for those Indonesian children who wanted to carry their study of Dutch further than the elementary level. People were no longer satisfied that Dutch was merely one subject among a number of others; they realized that the scanty knowledge of Dutch thus acquired barred their children from continuing their education beyond a certain point. When Hazeu became Director of the Department of Education, Dutch began to be taught in the primary schools from the 1st class upwards. But it was only in 1914

that the demands of Budi Utomo were recognized and carried out fully. As has been said, in that year the Dutch Government established the Dutch-Native Schools, which used Dutch over a seven-year period, so that children who had completed their studies there could carry on their education to the most advanced levels.

(Alisjahbana 1971: 1,093)

The educationist lobby in the East Indies strongly supported this view and one of its more outspoken members, Nieuwenhuis, argued:

If we want to promote Indonesian unity, let us begin first with the highest social classes, with the elite; and then, as the British did in India and the French in Annam, we must institute a language which can represent international culture fully as the general medium for social intercourse. In Indonesia this language will have to be Dutch.

(Nieuwenhuis 1925: 12, translation by Alisjahbana)

The ultimate failure to impose Dutch as the language of wider communication was due to a number of factors:

1 Non-cooperation by colonists and officials who regarded it as a threat to their privileges.
2 The emergence of Indonesian nationalists who promoted Bahasa Indonesia as the language of independence and national identity.
3 The occupation of the Dutch East Indies by Japan in 1942 and the Japanese support for Bahasa Indonesia.

The net effect of the Dutch language policies, as indeed the policies of the other imperial powers surveyed here, is a weakening and marginalization of the vast majority of smaller languages. The more 'liberal' and 'enlightened' attitudes that prevailed from the late nineteenth century strengthened the idea that civilization and development required a modern unitary means of communication.

The Germans

Germany was a latecomer on the colonial scene and its presence in the Pacific came to an end in 1914 when its colonies were occupied by the Allied Forces. Whilst in Samoa and Micronesia English and Pidgin English were firmly established, New Guinea was virgin territory for language policies. The official view throughout their period was that the use of English was a major threat to continued German colonization and that it should be replaced by German whenever possible.

Before this goal could be reached the promotion of a small number of indigenous languages (Tolai in New Guinea and Samoan in Samoa) was seen to be the more acceptable solution. Again, the reduction of the great linguistic diversity in parts of the German Pacific occupied a prominent place in many official statements.

In contrast with such official policies, the day-to-day reality could be very different. In fact by 1914 German was widely used only in Kiautschou (German China) and German Micronesia, having successfully pushed back the use of English and Pidgin English. Solenberger (1962) reports from the Marianas:

> In the short period from 1899 to 1914 a small staff of Germans so impressed those inhabitants of the Northern Marianas who were educated within that period that they will show a marked preference for German speech, literature, music, and dances. Use of German by both islanders and some of the recent American administrators carries the prestige of a somewhat authoritarian efficiency which the islanders are fond of ascribing to the Germans. In 1952 most Chamorro and Carolinian leaders were products of the German Volksschule, and the handwritten German alphabet remained in use for personal correspondence in Carolinian – which is rarely written otherwise.
>
> (Solenberger 1962: 59–60)

In contrast to this success story, the German efforts in Samoa were ineffective. When Germany took over Samoa in 1899, both English and Pidgin English were fairly well established, the former as the normal means of communication in the small multinational white community, the latter among the imported black plantation labourers (see Mühlhäusler 1978a). In fact, Samoa remained the 'least German colony of the German Reich' (*Samoanische Zeitung* 26 July 1913, my translation) until the end of German control.

Official attempts to promote German in Samoa date from the beginning of colonial control, when attempts were made to exclude other European languages from the school system. The *Deutsches Kolonialblatt* (1901: 599) reports that the following instructions were sent to missions operating in Samoa:

> Shortly after the German flag was raised in March last year, I made it clear to the missions operating in the protectorate that it must be the aim of the Government to take steps against the undesirable state of affairs that in a German colony European languages other than German were preferred by the natives.
>
> Having given the missions a year's grace to adapt to the changing

circumstances, I now proclaim that, as of July of this year, the medium of education in the schools for natives will be Samoan and that no European languages other than German can be permitted in the syllabus of these schools.

(my translation)

Samoan and German were also the official languages outside the schools. However, as pointed out by the *Samoanische Zeitung* (8 July 1911) in an editorial on '*Die Deutsche Sprache in Samoa*', English was widely used in official transactions. The *Zeitung* deplores the fact

that there are a considerable number of Government employees who unnecessarily prefer the English to the German language in their official dealings with the white, half-caste, and Samoan populations. In Samoa, it can even happen that a German who does not speak English cannot communicate with a colonial official of the Reich, as there are some who do not speak a word of German.

(my translation)

An attempt to spread German to a wider section of the population was made in 1909 when a government school for Samoans (mainly members of aristocratic families) was set up in 1909. Out of twenty-three weekly hours of tuition, nine were devoted to the study of German. In 1911, sixty Samoans attended this government school. There was also a government school for white and mixed-race children with 14 white and 127 mixed-race children:

The pupils exhibit particular interest for military exercises which take place under the guidance of a former noncommissioned officer of the Samoan police force. The school has been quite successful, and it constitutes the best way to promote German ways and education for a working life.

(V. Koenig in *Koloniale Rundschau* 1912: 731, my translation)

Despite such measures, however, the wish for German to become 'koloniale Einheitsprache' was far from being fulfilled when Germany's colonial control came to an end.

German language policies in New Guinea were hampered by problems, prominent among these being that between 1884 and 1899 it was administrated by a private commercial company. Those in charge of the areas controlled by the company adopted a *laissez-faire* attitude, thereby encouraging the spread of Tok Pisin in the Bismarck Archipelago and Coastal Malay on the New Guinea mainland. Apparently no efforts were made to spread the German language in the first years of German control. Friederici's (1911) attack on the New Guinea

Company on account of its failure to implement effective German language policies sums up the official attitude:

> When the New Guinea Company assumed sovereignty, it encountered Pidgin English and, as the representative of the German Empire, faced a task which, at the time, would probably not have been difficult to solve in the national interest. Yet nothing, or virtually nothing, happened in this respect.
>
> (Friederici 1911: 94, my translation)

In contrast, the years between 1900 and 1914 were characterized by the attempts of the German colonial government, and in particular the governor, Dr Hahl, to eradicate Pidgin English and replace it with German. The administration recognized that the replacement of Pidgin English with German would be a very gradual process. The implementation of such a policy had to rely on two factors: first, the gradual relexification of Tok Pisin with lexical items of German origin and its eventual replacement by Pidgin German; and second, formal schooling of large numbers of New Guineans in German.

Regarding the introduction of German by means of education, little progress was made in establishing state schools, their total enrolment in 1912 being about 400 compared with more than 22,000 students enrolled in mission schools. This state of affairs was felt to be quite unsatisfactory:

> From the very structure of mission organization it follows that the guiding thoughts for the nation's schooling cannot be formed from unitary plans. The diversity of mission staff with regard to nationality and denomination increases this existing lack of uniformity. For the teaching to be effective it must be based on a uniform rationale.
>
> (Governor Hahl in a circular of 2 December 1913, my translation)

An education ordinance intended to restructure and expand teaching facilities, in particular those for teaching German, was to become law in January 1915. One of the central aims of this new ordinance was to eradicate Pidgin English and was outlined by Hahl in the above-mentioned circular of 2 December 1913:

> Education is important to us for another reason which we must assert in the schools and institutions, namely, to bring our language to dominance among the natives in place of Pidgin English. The successful introduction of our language in our dealings with the people also means the predominance of our way of life as far as it can be adopted by the natives. Without German in our dealings

with the native, on the other hand, we will have to forget about his conversion to our point of view and ways of thinking in all areas of life. . . . According to my proposals, therefore, teaching should be based upon the living conditions of the native but also open up an understanding of our culture. The immediate aims are the improvement of the original native culture and the spread of German as the lingua franca.

(my translation)

Hahl's policies were shared by the colonial lobby at home. The writer of a letter to the *Kolonialabteilung* of the *Auswaertiges Amt* in Berlin (10 August 1903, *Reichskolonialamt* records, vol. 3,133, Postdam) argued that 'The fight against the English language is a task of self-preservation' (my translation). He echoes frequent warnings by the home lobby, such as:

the spread of Pidgin English politically involves great dangers, especially if, in addition, English is preponderant in communication among the whites as, for example, in German New Guinea, but above all in the Bismarck Archipelago. Is it not risky to raise English to the status of a lingua franca there when Australia is in the vicinity, looking greedily towards this German colony?

(*Deutsche Kolonialzeitung* 1913: 30.21.344, my translation)

Unlike in the older Dutch colonies, no indigenous opinion on language matters (or indeed any aspect of modern administration) had emerged and, as the First World War resulted in the loss of all German colonies, Germany's ability to exercise linguistic imperialism overseas disappeared. The present role of German in its former Pacific colonies is negligible. (For further details see Mühlhäusler 1980.)

Spanish

The impact of Spanish colonial presence on the smaller islands of Micronesia has already been described with special reference to Guam. Spain's presence in the much larger Philippines, in contrast, illustrates the relative powerlessness of the Spanish colonizers in matters of language. Spain officially took possession of the Philippines in 1565 but contacts with this distant colony were made via Mexico only for almost two centuries and in 1898 the Philippines became an American possession. Spanish language policies were such that all official and legal proceedings were carried out in Spanish only. The education system was run by Spanish priests and Spanish has remained the lingua franca of most convents (Lipski 1987). Education remained the privilege of a very small proportion of the population. According to the census of 1870 only 2.5 per cent of the population could speak Spanish, and they tended to belong to a small elite of Spaniards or Christianized Filipinos. Spanish was the language of the administration, education and low Spanish was kept as an official language side by side with English, with Tagalog added as a third official language in 1939. Whilst the presence of Spanish-speaking Filipinos has declined to about 1 per cent, such has been the status of this language that it has remained an official language. According to Lipski (1987):

> A small number of older non mestizos Filipinos learnt Spanish through contact with the previous generations of Spanish speakers. . . . They are directly descended from Spanish settlers and have at least one grand-parent who was born in Spain. They are land-owning and business/commercial families who have retained the use of Spanish at home and even in public life. Socio-economically, they are at the top of the scale. They represent the last wave of Spanish emigration to the Philippines. Most of them are proficient in English and they regard Tagalog with scorn and resentment, whereas speaking Spanish is a source of pride and a mark of aristocratic authenticity. According to Whinnom (1954) the Spanish speakers belonged exclusively to the upper class of Manila and all held responsible positions. Contemporary Philippine Spanish is an aristocratic language, maintained artificially by those who feel nostalgia for earlier privileges and by Filipinos who have studied in Spain or whose immediate ancestors came from Spain.
>
> (Lipski 1987: 39)

The official status of Spanish is maintained at some considerable cost. Spanish remains a compulsory subject in high schools and universities but few students can attain a level of fluency that would enable them to put the language to practical use. The case of Spanish in the Philippines shows how difficult it is to shake off the linguistic heritage of imperialism.

The French

Wardhaugh (1987) characterizes French colonial language policies in general terms:

> French was the language of a high culture and an advanced civilization. An élite had to be educated in French and civilized through that education. Local languages were. almost beneath contempt. In fact, the French adopted the same language policies

in their colonies as they had adopted at home. Just as Breton and Basque were despised in the hexagon itself, all the indigenous languages of the colonies were treated with the same contempt.

(Wardhaugh 1987: 158)

The imposition of French in a fairly monolingual territory (Tahiti) has been documented by Lavondès (1971) and a very similar case, that of Wallisian, has been described in much detail by Rensch (1990). Rensch draws attention to the longstanding conflict between the missions who taught in and were generally supporters of the vernacular and the government for whom the spread of the French language is a primary concern. The outcome of the continued official promotion of French is the transition from an originally monolingual Wallisian to a Wallisian/French and subsequently French/Wallisian bilingualism, with monolingualism in French being on the horizon. One needs to remind oneself that only a hundred years ago the majority of the inhabitants of metropolitan France were not native speakers of French.

The situation in New Caledonia combines the features of a settler colony or Neo-Europe (about 50 per cent of the population are of French extraction) with those of a Melanesian third-world country. It is possible that it will gain political independence from France and develop along the lines of Papua New Guinea or Vanuatu, though this possibility appears to have receded in the 1990s.

The principal impact of French policy on the linguistic ecology of New Caledonia was that it institutionalized a large-scale habitat destruction, forcing many speakers of the twenty-four or more indigenous languages (referred to as dialects by French officials) to seek refuge in the inhospitable interior of the island. Not only did this lead to a decimation of the population (from 50,000 in 1853 to 23,000 by 1900) (see Lyons 1986: 83) and the weakening of the smaller vernaculars but, more importantly, the pre-existing highly structured language chains and language networks were badly affected. As regards official attitudes to language, it would seem interesting to approach this topic from the perspective of the Melanesians, who, in a matter of about three generations, experienced totally conflicting policies and practices including the following:

1 An initial period of vernacular literacy promoted by a number of missions, particularly in the Loyalties from the 1840s to 1863. In the neighbouring Loyalties, vernacular literacy was often supplemented by literacy in English.
2 In 1863 the French Government decreed the closure of all vernacu-

lar mission schools. They were allowed to reopen in 1866 provided they all teach in French. Bible translation and vernacular literacy nevertheless continued on a smaller scale until after the First World War.

3 In 1921 the French government banned all publications in indigenous languages and in 1923 the use of vernaculars in the school grounds was forbidden.

4 From the early 1970s, under pressure from kanak independence groups, the French government relaxed its language policies and began to tolerate the use of vernacular literacy in the mission school and in the cultural life of the indigenous population.

5 With the setting up of an Institut Melanesien in 1981, pedagogical materials of mother tongue instruction in a number of indigenous languages have appeared and there has been a switch to a policy of teaching French as a second language. Observers such as Schooling (1990) seem confident that such measures will strengthen the local languages.

The story of New Caledonia is reminiscent of the treatment of Aboriginal languages in Australia. Again, we have a brief period of tolerance and promotion (the thirty or so years after initial control: 1788 to about 1820), followed by policies of assimilation, and from 1977 onward, policies of maintenance and bilingual education. Each generation of policy makers developed their approach in the 'best interest of the indigenous', whose views, until the mid-1980s, were seldom heard by such policy makers.

Language policies in a condominium

The New Hebrides, as they were called, were under European influence in the early nineteenth century. British and French missionaries, 'settlers' and government representatives competed for superiority; eventually, it was agreed in 1906 that both powers should administer the territory as a condominium, or 'pandemonium' as it was also referred to. The presence of two rival colonial powers in the same territory affords a unique opportunity to compare their respective language policies. For the indigenous people the rivalry between two policies offered a choice which other colonized peoples elsewhere seldom enjoyed.

For reasons which are not clear to me, languages did not figure prominently as an index of metropolitan control in the first fifty years of the condominium, whilst in many other areas of life, a strict division of influence was maintained. Thus, Crowley (1990c) reports that:

There were two currencies in free exchange, the franc des Nouvelles-Hebrides, 'New Hebrides franc', and the Australian dollar. Some stores would post prices in one currency, some in the other; employees of some firms would be paid in one currency and employees of other firms in the other. The post office used its own artificial currency of gold francs and centimes, which had to be converted to dollars or francs depending on what day of the week it was, because on different days proceeds from the sales of stamps went alternately to the British and French treasuries. There were two base hospitals in Vila, one British and one French, while the outer islands cried out for decent health care. Melanesian policemen in different uniforms, one French-educated, the other English-educated, patrolled in pairs (but spoke to each other in Bislama). There were two education systems, each operating with its own language of instruction and its own educational philosophy. There were even two prisons in Vila, one staffed by French-educated warders, the other by warders who had been to school in English-medium schools.

(Crowley 1990c: 4)

As regards language and education, up to the mid-1960s:

Since before the middle 1960s neither the British nor the French government was responsible for education in these islands, the role of educator being left to the various missions. At the pregovernment education stage, there were numerically quite significantly more English-oriented than French-oriented Christians in the New Hebrides, the only French-speaking missions being those run by the Roman Catholic Church, staffed by French-speaking priests and nuns. The English-speaking missions, on the other hand, were represented by the Melanesian Mission, the Presbyterian Church, the Church of Christ, Seventh Day Adventists, and the Assembly of God Church. Numerically, this would indicate roughly a three to one distribution of influence and education, in favour of English. Until the mid-1960s, too, there were a number of areas which subscribed to no church in particular, often preferring the traditional religion to that introduced by the Europeans.

(Tryon 1979: 21)

Since then, a very considerable change has occurred:

Since education was officially taken over by the two metropolitan governments, the picture has changed, in that the French have built a large number of schools, while the British have largely been content to use existing mission school buildings. The net result, apart from the occasionally strange existence of both an English and a French school in the same small village, is that most New Hebrideans under the age of twenty to twenty-five have some knowledge of either English or French. The chief education officers of both residences have assured the author, however, that they consider the passive grasp of the metropolitan languages to be adequate, while an adequate active mastery of either spoken French or English is the exception rather than the rule. This situation is not surprising when one considers that metropolitan languages have no place in the home, where either the local vernacular or Bichelamar are used for everyday purposes. Among younger people, then, roughly fifty percent could be considered 'French-speaking' and fifty percent 'English-speaking'. Among older people, the knowledge of a metropolitan language, be it either French or English, depends much on how closely the individual has been associated with missions or even large trading firms, the main educators until recent times. People closely associated with such organizations are often found to have a reasonable command of a metropolitan language; others have little or none, the proportions being roughly as implied by the discussion of the pregovernmental education scene. As time passes, and more and more people pass through the school systems, the proportion of New Hebrideans with a knowledge of a metropolitan language will obviously increase.

(Tryon 1979: 21)

In 1979, just before independence, the French resident announced that 51 per cent of all children attended French-speaking schools against 49 per cent attending English-speaking schools (see Charpentier nd). After independence, when schools became fee paying, the French percentage dropped. In 1991 only 37.6 per cent of children attended French-speaking schools. According to Charpentier (nd) and Mühlhäusler and Charpentier (1995) there is no chance at present that French will be ousted by English or Bislama. The national government of Vanuatu still fully exploits the competition between France and Anglo-Saxon countries (including Britain and Australia) and is in a position to attract considerable amounts of development aid and political goodwill. Whilst the day-to-day relations of the condominium were full of absurdities, dual control prevented some of the excesses found in other colonies.

Whilst much has been written about the promotion of French and English in Europe and North America (e.g. Wardhaugh 1987), a comparative study of their colonial language policies remains a task properly to be addressed. Countries such as Vanuatu, the Cameroons (amalgamated from a French and British/German colony), or others with a history of both French and British colonial control (Mauritius, Trinidad, Louisiana) can provide interesting insights into the effects of colonial policies.

English

The story of English language policies in the Pacific area is a complex one which cannot be dealt with exhaustively here. I refer the reader to accounts such as Phillipson (1992) and Tollefson (1991) for a discussion of the ideological background to the spread of English, to Baldauf and Luke (1990) for detailed bibliographical references and to Chapter 9 on education in this book where many aspects of English language policies are discussed. Finally, the continuation of English language policies in the independent countries of the Pacific area has been documented in a special issue of *World Englishes* edited by Watson-Gegeo (1989a).

A rather rough generalization about official attitudes to English is that the colonizers tended to take its use in the administrative, legal and educational systems very much for granted, relying on the prestige of English as a language rather than official formulated policies.

The assumption that English was superior tended to be combined with blissful ignorance of the local language ecology. The study of the indigenous languages was considerably more advanced in the Dutch and German parts of New Guinea than in British or later Australian Papua, and serious attempts to understand and use Pidgin English were found mainly in non-English controlled territories. Unlike in the case of the French, however, the view that the British had a civilizing mission and that perfect knowledge of English needed to be spread to all corners of the Empire may have been expressed by individuals but was not official policy and the financial resources to educate significant numbers in English were rarely made available. For a long time there was also a strong feeling that widespread knowledge of English was undesirable as it created 'cheeky natives' with expectations of being regarded as 'equals'. One perceives in the study of British views on language a dominance of racism, which is much less in evidence among Romance speaking colonial powers. However, as Phillipson (1992: 110 ff.) has pointed out, such generalizations are not without danger and British practices differed from territory to territory. Let us briefly examine a small number of Pacific territories.

Fiji

Before the arrival of the British administration in 1874 the Fijian language ecology had already been transformed from a network of interrelated varieties to a diglossic society where 'mission' supported standard varieties of Fijian dominated. This evolving monolingualism was disrupted by the importation of sugar plantation workers from British India and other parts of the British empire. With great tensions between indigenous Fijian and immigrant Hindi speakers, English gradually emerged as a neutral medium. Initially, however, there was a widespread semi-official opinion that English should remain the language of the whites (an early concession being that mixed race children were to be educated in English) commented on in detail by Siegel (1989a: 50). Thus, all important administrative business was carried out in English, the government supported the teaching of vernaculars, and in 1930 the Assistant Colonial Secretary of Fiji, A. A. Wright, argued that the spread of English would 'tend to woo those people away from agriculture' (Siegel 1989a: 50). Siegel further reports:

> Governor Fletcher himself stated: 'The indiscriminate teaching of English will lead people away from their present contentment', and said that he wanted to avoid the urbanization and unemployment which resulted from mass education in other colonies. The following quotation from the memorandum reveals more about the motives behind the administration's policy with regard to the limiting of English teaching:
>
>> A further argument in favour of the teaching of English was the supposed desirability of bringing the three races, Fijian, Indian and European into as close relations and co-operation as possible by enabling them to converse with one another in the English language. Although it has not been the calculated policy of the Fijian government to keep the three races apart on the principle of divide et impera, I believe that the government has deliberately refrained, chiefly in the interest of the Fijian race ... from hastening in any degree the process of forming close ties between the Fijian and the Indian.
>
> Thus, the administration in Fiji at that time was in favour of education in vernacular languages rather than in English.
>
> (Siegel 1989a: 52)

During the Second World War government attitudes shifted to the promotion of English as a universal language of Fiji, a shift which was realized by a massive infusion of funds into the education system. After the granting of independence Fiji has tended to perpetuate these practices. English is the designated language of parliament, the most important language of public broadcasting, the most exclusive language of education and its importance is growing. Some of the negative effects of its use for the indigenous Fijian language have been discussed by Milner (1984).

The British Solomon Islands

The British Solomon Islands were very much a colonial backwater and very little development had occurred by the time the island group got its political independence in 1978. The involvement of the government in education matters occurred only after the Second World War when plans were implemented to educate an indigenous English-speaking elite.

One of the main functions of this elite was seen as that of arresting the spread of Solomon Pidgin English and helping establish English as the general medium of communication. Keesing (1990) comments:

> It was assumed that these first élite students were the vanguards of a new linguistic order in the Solomons, whereby Pijin progressively gave way to English, as adequately trained teachers and successful role models emerged. They, the élite speakers of 'pure' English, were to lead and oversee the metamorphosis of the Solomons from a Pijin-speaking country into an English-speaking country. At first, the English the less advantaged would manage would be 'simple'. 'Simple English', widely used in Government publications and news media, was to supersede Pijin. Indeed, it was imagined by many of the British community that through progressive anglicization, Pijin would progressively turn into 'simple English'; if Pijin had originally developed through Melanesians attempting clumsily to speak the vulgar English to which they were exposed, what they needed was more exposure to better English. Eventually, 'simple' English would be transformed into 'proper' English, once primary education was broadened and teachers were properly educated.
>
> (Keesing 1990: 158–9)

As regards the administration of the territory there were two factions:

> From fairly early in the history of the Protectorate, a division emerged between experienced field officers who used Pijin regularly in everyday administration (and hence tended to speak it relatively well, though virtually never with a grammaticality, semantic and

lexical command, phonology and fluency approaching that of the Islanders) and senior officers based in Tulagi (and after World War II, Honiara), more preoccupied with the rituals, hierarchy and paper-shuffling of Empire than the pragmatics of using a lingua franca for everyday communication. There was thus a contradiction whereby for many years field officers had to pass oral texts of Pijin competence after an initial period of service; yet Pijin was never given a standard orthography, committed to writing, or codified with published dictionary or grammar. It was just something you 'picked up' and spoke, if your job required you to.

(Keesing 1990: 154–5)

The government practice of the colonial period and the colonial ideologies continued to reign supreme in the independent Solomons.

The status of English as the official language of the Solomons is not likely to change because islanders see English as the language of the outside world, of the educated, and as a means to the wealth and power of Europeans. Nevertheless, English is spoken by perhaps only 10–15% of Solomon Islanders and in varying degrees of fluency. Virtually all Solomon Islanders, however, have had some exposure to English, through schooling, church liturgy and hymns, shopping in urban and peri-urban areas, and/or the mass media (especially radio). All middle to higher echelon jobs in the private and public sectors require not only spoken English but also literacy skills in English.

(Watson-Gegeo 1989a: 27)

Watson-Gegeo, like Keesing or Milner for Fiji, deploys the uncritical continuation of colonial ideologies regarding language and recommends that the government should begin systematically to evaluate the social meaning, economic usefulness and educational consequences of practices favouring an introduced metropolitan language.

Malaya

The colonial history of South East Asia differs from the territories so far discussed in that:

1 the area is much larger and more populous
2 the colonizers encountered literate and monotheistic cultures
3 a substantial number of British settlers were attracted.

British language policies in Malaya, however, differed very little from those found elsewhere in the Pacific region. As in Fiji, we can observe the promotion of an indigenous Malay culture by the setting up of Malay medium schools, whilst immigrants, Chinese and other non-Malays were educated in an English medium system. The arguments against a universal knowledge of English again were put forward powerfully by the colonial administration, particularly in its early years. Thus, Ozog quotes the colonial administrator Sir Frank Swetten-ham as having said in 1890:

> I do not think that it is advisable to attempt to give the children of an agricultural population an indifferent knowledge of a language that to all but the very few would only unfit them for the duties of life and make them discontent [*sic*] with anything like manual labour.
>
> (Ozog 1990: 306)

The policy of differentiating between Malay and non-Malay speakers in the school system can be seen as one of the causes for the economic and racial problems that have plagued post-indigenous Malaya/Malaysia.

After independence English and Malay were made official languages. The fate of English has fluctuated over the years, the language having from time to time become the target of Malaysian nationalists, but it appears to have reasserted itself in the 1990s. More importantly, the principle of having two powerful languages established by the colonial administration has remained untouched. Minority languages in Malaysia, on the other hand, enjoy none of the protection and promotion that would be needed to maintain their continued well-being.

POST-COLONIAL LANGUAGE POLICIES

Introduction

Much of what has been said about the arbitrariness of the political boundaries drawn by the colonizing powers can be extended to language boundaries. Again, traditional patterns of communication were largely ignored and such patterns as were put in their place were justified by the needs of the external colonizer. These needs differed from period to period, with shifting views in the mother country. The aims of social control, economic exploitation, civilizing the uncivilized and extending the number of speakers of a metropolitan language are difficult to reconcile, with the consequence that policies could change abruptly. If there is a discernible trend it is that towards monolingualism in a standard language or bilingualism in a privileged indigenous and an expatriate standard language. These trends derive from the prevailing views on indigenous languages of the vast majority of colonial administrators, settlers and missionaries, i.e. that the local languages were inferior to the introduced one and consequently either had to be replaced or developed into a full language. Of the many accounts to this effect, let me quote an example from Vanuatu (New Hebrides):

> During the sixty-six years of joint French and British administration in Vanuatu, official colonial policy was almost totally oblivious to the existence of the 105 indigenous languages of the country. Given the essentially monocultural and monolingual national ethos of the French and British administrators, this is hardly surprising. Not only was it mightily inconvenient that ni-Vanuatu spoke little French or English, it was doubly inconvenient that they spoke such a large number of their own languages.
>
> The assumption was, of course, that Melanesian languages were inherently less worthy as languages than the so-called 'civilising' languages of Europe. The attitude of colonial scorn towards Melanesian languages is reflected in the story of the former French District Agent on Tanna, who could not understand why one university researcher was interested in studying one of the 'rubbish' languages of Tanna, when he could be studying a 'proper' language like French. Also, at a public forum in Vila in 1984, a former French ambassador to Vanuatu asked if it would ever be possible to turn a Vanuatu language into a 'real language'. The underlying assumption behind this question, of course, is that Vanuatu languages are not real languages at all, but something less than that.
>
> (Crowley 1987: 6)

The overall effect of colonial language policies, in ecological terms, was the destruction of the habitat of languages traditionally spoken and the imposition of a linguistic monoculture. At the same time, the colonial system created a sufficiently large population of educated Westernized people to perpetuate these practices after the nominal end of colonialism. Their views on language in many instances were far removed from those of traditional modes of communication and characterized by European ideas above both the structure and functions of language. Planning language meant planning for uniformity, modernization, national identity and the like. This desire for such ends in many instances, however, was not matched by technical expertise.

Language planning in the newly independent nations

In a programmatic statement about the linguistic needs of new nations, Alisjahbana (1965) deplores the inadequacy of the structuralist approach to language, accusing it of being fixated on the description of static grammar rather than the development of new languages. Instead, he urges, we need a more highly developed science of language engineering and planning. To accuse descriptive linguistics of irrelevance of course makes little sense if it is kept in mind that this discipline, with all its faults, was developed to document the largest possible number of rapidly disappearing languages without making cultural value judgements and to overcome some of the prejudices about differences between languages that had led to neglect and contempt for so called 'primitive' languages.[4]

Alisjahbana also fails to do justice to the highly developed knowledge resulting from the creation of artificial and standard languages that emerged during the European enlightenment and the principles that had been successfully applied to the creation of European national languages such as French, Modern Greek, Norwegian, Icelandic or Afrikaans as well as the existence of powerful instruments such as language academies, bodies concerned with terminology, spelling reforms and so on. Kloss's work on New Germanic languages (1978, but originally published in 1962) bears witness to the extent of knowledge and activity in prescriptive linguistics.

Together with most indigenous language planners and European colonizers before and after him, Alisjahbana accepts such objectives as date back to the French revolution, namely the necessity of having a single national language through which a nation could be unified, modernized and find a new national identity, and therefore fails to consider alternative models allowing the maintenance of diversity.

The reader at this point needs to be reminded of the two principal approaches to language planning. For the sake of simplicity I have labelled them the 'streamlining approach', aiming at maximum uniformity, and the 'ecological approach', aiming for functional and structured diversity. When the new nations came into being, only the streamlining approach was on offer and its ideology and practices were eagerly transferred to the new countries of the region.

The idea of linguistic unification of course was a theme that was established in some countries already, for instance, China. I shall now comment on a number of studies of modernization through unified national languages, policies that in most instances are no less imperialistic than those of earlier colonial governments.

Chinese

The policies of language unification in mainland Chinese had a significant effect in most of the Chinese overseas communities. It appears that there is a growing perception among the Chinese of Taiwan, Singapore or Indonesia that their various dialects are not suited to education, commerce and cultural survival into the twenty-first century and that Mandarin should be the language of the educated. The effects of the Mandarin campaign were first felt in Taiwan, which until 1948 was administered as part of the Chinese mainland, and have subsequently reached many other parts of the Pacific, a particularly spectacular example being Singapore.

Taiwan's population were predominantly speakers of South Fukienese (SF). The 1980 census gives the following figures:

Mandarin (NL)	no population estimate
Southern Fukienese/Taiwanese	15 million
Hakka	1 million
Minority languages	200,000

(Kaplan and Tse 1983: 83)

The fact that these are the main native languages must not conceal the fact that Mandarin at that time had become a second language for most Taiwanese. Kaplan and Tse remark:

> In brief, although Mandarin is not the native language of the majority of the population, as a result of the success of the NLM (National Language Movement) it is de facto a common language for the entire population as well as de jure the national language. And, although it is not useful to try to estimate the number of native speakers of Mandarin, it is possible to provide a sociolinguistic estimate. Except for about one million people in the 40–50+ age group who still cannot speak the NL (National Language) (and except for monolingual speakers of the NL), it would be fair to say that the entire population is bilingual in the NL and a native dialect/language – a diglossic situation in which the NL serves as lingua franca and Southern Fukienese (SF) serves as the major vernacular.

(Kaplan and Tse 1983: 83)

By the mid-1980s the shift to Mandarin had significantly gained momentum. Young's study (1988: 323–8) has noted a significant shift to Mandarin in the public domain by all Taiwanese and a significant shift to Mandarin in all domains (including many intimate family contacts) by younger speakers. At present about 25 per cent of all children speak Mandarin before school-going age and the fact that Mandarin is the only school language and by far the most significant language of radio and television (86 per cent of all programmes) is likely to accelerate this trend.

The negative effect of these pronounced trends towards monoculture and monolingualism in Mandarin has as yet not been addressed by the Taiwanese government, but Young (1988) points out that the outcome is by no means definite. It is true that the small Chinese dialects have almost disappeared but Southern Fukienese and Hakka continue to enjoy widespread support.

> The results of this study indicate that Southern Min and Hakka are losing ground. They are diminishing because of the policy to promote Mandarin without an active recognition of the value of Hakka or Southern Min cultures. There will likely be more and more grassroots efforts to promote Hakka and Southern Min culture in the future. If the authorities in Taiwan choose to ignore or suppress these grassroots efforts for cultural revival, then a negative attitude will develop toward the government. However, if the authorities in Taiwan choose to promote ethnic pride and cultural revival among the Hakka and Southern Min peoples, then mutual respect among the different ethnolinguistic groups will no doubt develop.
>
> (Young 1988: 337)

If the policy of the Taiwanese government has been to promote Mandarin by neglecting the other dialects, in Singapore the suppression of non-Mandarin varieties of Chinese has been much more deliberate. Goh (1980) reported on the language situation in Singapore as follows:

> Singapore society is ethnically heterogeneous, with about 76% Chinese, 15% Malay, 7% Indians, and 2% from other ethnic origins. Its language situation is still more diversified since each of the three major ethnic groups speaks many language varieties. A census report identifies more than 33 specific mother-tongue groups, 20 of which have more than 0.1% of the population as native speakers. Four major languages are designated as official languages: Malay, English, Mandarin Chinese and Tamil. Hokkien, while a major language, is not an official language. In addition, there are three minor languages: Teochew, Cantonese and Hainanese.
>
> (Goh 1980: 1, quoted in Kuo 1980: 1)

This policy of egalitarian multilingualism has since given way to a policy of English/Mandarin bilingualism and deliberate official attempts to get rid of Chinese varieties other than Mandarin. The Speak Mandarin Campaign began in the late 1970s following the Goh report on educational policy in 1978. In this report the then Minister of Education, Goh, pointed out:

> The majority of the pupils are taught in two languages, English and Mandarin. About 85% of these pupils do not speak these languages at home. When they are at home, they speak dialects. As a result, most of what they have learned in school is not reinforced.
>
> (Goh 1980: 4)

As a background to this statement one has to consider that English at the time was gaining considerable prestige and the only way to counteract it was seen as to develop a Chinese prestige language, i.e. Mandarin. Bilingualism in English and Mandarin was seen as a way of maintaining the momentum of economic growth whilst preserving significant aspects of Chinese culture. A second part of the argument was that the existence of mutually unintelligible dialects of Chinese could lead to a fragmented society (compare Newman 1980: 10).

Cobarrubias (1983), in summarizing mainland Chinese language policies, points out that Pekinese Chinese (Mandarin), the language in which state affairs were conducted, enjoyed but little prestige *vis-à-vis* the regional languages of Chinese and that attempts to standardize usage nationwide are very recent:

> North Chinese, putonghua, or Mandarin, has been taught for cross-language communication nationally since 1956. In the south-eastern inland and coastal areas, the first language is a regional variety other than putonghua. Thus a national program is likely to achieve cross-language communication between the two-thirds of the Chinese who speak some form of putonghua as a national language, and the other third who speak a regional variety other than putonghua.
>
> It was in 1956 that the People's Republic of China adopted a policy for nationwide use of North Chinese 'as the medium of education in schools and as the principal medium for communication among speakers of other regional languages'. Two significant documents were issued concerning the national language program: (1) 'The Directions of the State Council Regarding the Promotion of Common Language' of 1956, and (2) 'The Directions of the Ministry of Education of the People's Republic of China Regarding the Promotion of the Common Language in Elementary, Middle and Normal Schools' of 1955. Both of these documents formulate

plans for the incorporation of putonghua in public activities. The language was also to become 'the medium of instruction for Chinese language and literature classes in grades one through seven in the fall of 1956.

(Cobarrubias 1983: 22)

Thus, Lee Kuan Yew, when launching the Speak Mandarin Campaign in 1979 in order 'dramatically to alter the language environment of Singapore', expressed this in the following words:

Children at home speak dialect: in school they learn English and Mandarin. . . . The majority have ended up speaking English and dialect. . . . This is the stark choice – English-Mandarin, or English-dialect. Logically, the decision is obvious. Emotionally, the choice is painful.'
(quoted from an unsigned article on 'The Tongue Surgeons', *Asia Week* 14 November 1980: 36–41)

Korean

The case of Korean provides an interesting supplement to the story of Chinese language policies, as this country from 1392 until 1910 was under Chinese linguistic influence. Park (1989) comments:

With the Chinese shadow so omnipresent for much of her history, the bulk of Korea's traditional literature was rendered and preserved in classical Chinese. So were virtually all major publications and documents, both private and public. Furthermore, all government examinations, including the higher civil and military service examinations, were essentially examinations of competence in classical literary Chinese.

(Park 1989: 114)

In 1910 Korean was annexed by the Japanese who in a very different fashion pursued a policy of suppressing Korea. Park upholds:

In the first years of her rule in Korea, Japan allowed the use of Korean as a medium of instruction in the Korean school system. In a Copernican turn from this policy, however, the Japanese colonial authorities soon banned Korean not just as a medium of education but also as one of official communication.

(Park 1989: 114)

Like the Bahasa Indonesian Movement in the Dutch East Indies, the Korean language movement emerged as a powerful force of resistance against colonial control. After the end of Japanese domination in 1945 Korea was rapidly modernized and adapted as the only official language. However, the separate political system in the North and South has created a new linguistic division, described by Park as follows:

> The division of the Korean peninsula into North and South Korea since 1945 has led to a bifurcation of the Korean language. The two Koreas now have two separate standard 'languages', which are mutually intelligible and yet differ quite noticeably in lexicon. The two Koreas also have two different writing systems with the North using Hangul only and the South a combination of Hangul and Chinese characters.
>
> Should the country be reunified, the two standard languages with the two different writing systems must be reconciled in one way or another. This reconciliation will almost certainly involve a process of language standardization and purification. Some Korean linguists are already beginning to suggest that this process can and should get under way now in preparation for eventual national reunification.
>
> (Park 1989: 114)

The unification of Korea is only one of the scenarios that language planners need to be aware of. A look at the linguistic atlas of China (Wurm 1987) reveals that there are large areas of China in which Korea remains spoken and it is not impossible that a reunited Korea may wish to extend its boundaries. The revival of Korean, its successful modernization and standardization results in very special socio-historical circumstances, including relative linguistic homogeneity, the availability of indigenous writing systems and a strong sense of identity. It could well be a model for other linguistically homogenous countries of the region (Samoa, Kiribati).

Indonesian

The linguistic picture of Indonesia differs dramatically from that of Korea and with the annexation of West Irian and East Timor its linguistic heterogeneity has dramatically increased to more than 400 languages. Indonesia exemplifies the kind of new nation which cannot look back to a history of unity.

That Indonesian has been so successful as a national language has been the source of astonishment for many.

Indonesia now stands distinguished in its single-mindedness over a national language whose choice has never been opposed seriously, let alone by language demonstrations or riots, in almost thirty years of independence. Not only the degree of acceptance has been extraordinary among the former colonies in Asia around the Indian Ocean. The decision itself, made in the 1920s, and adhered to almost unquestioningly since 1945, also appears singular. For the Malay Language, chosen and accepted as Bahasa Indonesia, was spoken at home and on all those other vital occasions which give people a place in society, by only a very small proportion of the population.

(Hoffman 1973: 19)

It is interesting to speculate that the linguistic typology of the language, its origins in a Pidgin Malay, has much to do with its success, as learnability is considerably better than it would have been with Javanese. One is reminded of the success of Sango in the Central African Republic, Swahili in Tanzania and Bislama in Vanuatu and the comparative difficulty experienced with languages such as Hindi in India, Tagalog in the Philippines and Quechua in Peru. Linguistic typology alone can hardly account for Bahasa Indonesia's rise, however. Rather, as has already been mentioned, Dutch language policies which had elevated a form of colloquial Malay to the language of administration and education were reinterpreted, continued and enhanced by a reconstructed history and a powerful ideology of national unification. Of course, Bahasa Indonesia is less than 100 years old, and to pronounce on its success or otherwise may be premature. The tensions and disagreements whose absence Hoffman had admired in 1973 certainly have begun to appear since then.

One of the sources of contemporary tension is the decision to use Indonesian as a tool of development and Westernization. The prime figure in this process is Alisjahbana, who was appointed to the chair of the Committee on Indonesian in 1947 and whose writings have been highly influential. He accepts the colonial view that Asian languages and cultures were inferior to the European ones and that there is a clear need not only for development, but for development along Western lines. He writes on Bahasa Indonesia:

it was clear from the outset that as the language of education from primary school to university, especially as the language of science, economics and technology, it would not match and replace the Dutch language.

(Alisjahbana 1984: 81)

This development meant, above all else, making the language

intertranslatable with modern Western languages and sharing a significant proportion of international vocabulary.

In becoming a modern language Indonesian will gradually accept more and more concepts of modern culture. If we know that the Indonesian language up until now has coined or accepted more than 500,000 modern terms expressing modern international concepts, we realize that it is moving faster and faster in the direction of a modern language, leaving far behind the other unmodernized Indonesian languages. Since the concepts of science, technology, and other aspects of modern culture are the same or nearly the same in all modern languages, it is of great advantage in learning modern languages and in the exchange of ideas if the Indonesian language accepts words which are similar or nearly similar to those of other modern languages, such as atom, politik, radio, television, telephone, valuta, etc. It is obvious that the acceptance of international words by newly standardized languages is of the greatest advantage for the growing world community.

(Alisjahbana 1984: 87)

Language modernization like social reform is seen as a deliberate act of promoting change in a number of explicitly stated areas including:

1 It is to be a language for a culture where 'modern man considers himself a centre of activity. With his effort he is able to change and use nature' (Alisjahbana 1984: 91).
2 It needs to exploit 'the possibilities of a rapprochement between the modern languages and their spellings' (ibid.).
3 It is to be a language to promote egalitarianism rather than the hierarchical nature of traditional society.

The development of Indonesian thus did not aim at achieving translatability with local vernacular nor was it meant to be compatible with traditional social structures; rather it has been seen as an instrument of transformation.

The current director of the Centre for Language Improvement and Development, Moeliono, very much shares these sentiments and has compared the improvement and development of the Indonesian language to family planning policies. Moeliono (1994) argues that in addition national integration is perhaps the most important function of Bahasa Indonesia. He is willing to tolerate the diversity of languages still spoken in Indonesia as long as their status is clearly subordinate to that of the national language:

even recognized language differences need not be divisive if there is a diglossic situation, such as is the case in Indonesia with hundreds of vernaculars, since there is a division of functions between the national language and the regional languages spoken by various ethnic groups. It would surely be impossible to carry on official government administration, education, and business in a very large number of languages.

(Moeliono 1994: 118)

The dominant role of Indonesian is reinforced by its use in education at all levels, the only concession being that the first three years of primary education may also be in one of the designated major regional languages. The fate of the numerous smaller languages in such a context of non-recognition and discouragement is dubious. The number of those who speak Indonesian as a second language has reached 70 per cent and the proportion of first language speakers about 15 per cent. The diglossia or bilingualism appears to be of a transitional kind, leading within the next two generations towards monolingualism in Indonesian.

The role of Indonesian as a 'killer language', as a continuation of colonial ideology, has not been a topic of contention within Indonesia. Rather, the divisive issues that have begun to emerge are

1 the reappearance of Javanese as a dominating force in Indonesian language and culture
2 the failure of Indonesian to be a genuine language of equality.

Whilst some of the leading figures of the early phases of development of Indonesian originated in Sumatra and whilst the form of speech spoken on the Riau Archipelago adjacent to Sumatra served as the basis of modern Indonesian, the nation's capital Jakarta is located in Java and the transmigration programme of the 1970s and 1980s has greatly helped to spread the Javanese influence.

The intention of language planners such as Alisjahbana had been to develop Indonesian in order to counteract Javanese domination and to avoid a reliance on Javanese as a source of lexical innovation. Over the years, however, this practice was considerably relaxed and, moreover, existing expressions, borrowed a long time ago from foreign languages, were replaced by expressions of Javanese origins. On the occasion of the Indonesian Language Month 1986 Alisjahbana attacked this trend, and in this he could rely on the support of language planners in neighbouring Malay-using nations. Anderson (1987) writes:

But the issue of Javanization is in the air, as evident in a recent news item appearing in Singapore in THE STRAITS TIMES which reported on the meeting of the Fifth Nusantara Scholars Meeting held in Ujung Pandang, Indonesia. A major concern was expressed by the Malaysians, and reportedly supported by other participants, to the effect that too many Javanese terms were finding their way into the lexicon of the Indonesian language. This development was seen to constitute a barrier to further efforts on the part of Malaysia, Indonesia, Brunei and the Malays in Singapore to develop a common Malay throughout the entire region.

What is reminiscent of Prof. Alisjahbana's comments is the complaint that was reported to have been expressed at the meeting in Ujung Pandang to the effect that 'the Indonesian language . . . is being bombarded by heavy borrowing from local dialects, from dead languages of Java and even by the random use of acronyms'. But on reviewing Prof. Alisjahbana's writings, concern for a commonness of effort and results with regional implications has been his concern as well, but at least until now under the banner of modernization.

(Anderson 1987: 3)

The agenda includes more than the developing rift between Indonesian and other Malay-based languages and the abandonment of early principles of language planning, however. It also raises the issue of the role of Indonesia in bringing about an egalitarian society. In a detailed examination of the language of the Indonesian elite in Jakarta, Errington (1986) comments on an emerging diglossia between a high, standard Indonesian spoken by the ruling classes and administration and low regional or social varieties. Anderson (1966) has listed these developments as mirroring the classical Javanese distinction between high and low speech styles:

> Just as krama itself originally represented a literary religious glorifying and archaizing of the basic ngoko vocabulary, one finds that the kramanization of Bahasa Indonesia naturally turned in the same direction. . . . Many are true krama words in that there are ordinary or ngoko everyday equivalents. . . . All of them tend to be used on most occasions of high ceremonial importance, to be applied to objects and institutions of the highest political prestige.
>
> (Anderson 1966: 111)

Increasingly, the technocratic and theocratic elite also introduced words from English which Errington (1986: 346) links to 'traditional Javanese conceptions of the relation of esoteric linguistic codes to esoteric knowledge and social power'.

Conspicuously Anglicized Indonesian speech similarly serves to manifest one's (putative) elite status as controller of an elite code.

Foreign knowledge associated with modernization is prestigious, as in the foreign language through which it is acquired and transmitted; English-speaking Indonesians, like their Dutch-speaking predecessors, are perceived to be able to penetrate and control exotic knowledge by virtue of control of an exotic language.

and

Such an enduring Javanese orientation toward privileged language codes may in one sense be the most significant and profound indigenous influence on the development of Indonesian and on patterns of borrowing into Indonesian from 'modern' English. At this general level Anderson's approach to the Javanization of Indonesian is most plausible, and in this sense Indonesian official discourse may function symbolically like the use of older prestigious codes to manifest special, esoteric knowledge, and so to legitimate an elite with access to it.

(Errington 1986: 347)

That such issues can be openly debated in Indonesia (e.g. in a special issue of *Prisma* 1989) demonstrates that language planning in Indonesia has reached maturity, but at the same time shows that the main belief in the powers of planners, social engineers and modernizers is on the decline. Increasingly, the role of Indonesian as an instrument to change and/or obliterate minority groups is coming under scrutiny and the ethnic revival which has become a powerful movement in other centrally run nation-states is unlikely to bypass Indonesia. As yet, there is much talk of the benefits of Indonesian and little talk about its costs. The dyseconomies created by many planners promoting policies of streamlining will not fail to become evident.

In one of the most comprehensive longitudinal accounts of the language, Abas (1987) has made the following prognosis:

Projections for the use of IN [Indonesian] in the year 2001 reveal some interesting points, two of which are highly relevant to language planning: the rapid speed of the development of IN in terms of its standardisation which, in turn, will generate a very progressive dissemination of the language, and the regressive development of the vernaculars of the archipelago as the result of the first situation.

By the year 2001, approximately 60% of the population of Indonesia will be speakers of IN and, by the latest by 2041,

Indonesia will have a 100% IN-speaking population. This projection does not take into consideration the progress achieved by the Indonesian Government in the field of electronic communication. In 1976 Indonesia's first communications satellite, PALAPA, was launched and its use inaugurated on August 17, 1976 when a 'state of the nation address' by President Soeharto was beamed by satellite to all parts of the country. This satellite should, no doubt, accelerate the spread of IN, especially in the island of Java, which is very densely populated.

A possible drawback of the PALAPA communication satellite is that it will hinder the development and spread of the vernaculars. If the Pusat Pembiaan dan Pengembangan Bahasa is not able to implement the policy on national language formulated at the Seminar on National Language Policy in 1975 concerning local languages, there is a possibility that the local languages, especially those whose numbers of speakers are small, will cease to exist. The validity of this opinion requires further investigation.

ML [Malaya Language] (IN in Indonesia and Mal in Malaysia) is now in its intermediary stage, i.e. a language of wider communication. As such ML has the necessary attributes to be made the official language of ASEAN [Association of South East Asian Nations]. Because of the facility of the language it quite possibly will go beyond its present stage and emerge as one of the modern world languages.

(Abas 1987: 178–9)

Other Malay-based languages

Malay, like Hindustani and Korean, through political developments in the post-colonial phase, has become a pluricentric language, with the two principal varieties shaped by the differential language policies of Malaysia and Indonesia. Tensions between the two countries in the 1960s widened the rift. However, as Abas (1987) points out, there is agreement in both countries that Bahasa Malaysia and Bahasa Indonesian should become a unified regional super language, a desire which was formalized in the first language agreement between the two countries in 1972. Standard Malay is also one of the official languages of Brunei (English being the other) but, as pointed out by Purnama (1991), its use is restricted to formal situations. In essence, the majority of the population of Brunei uses colloquial Brunei-Malay which is in a diglossic situation with high Malay.

Whilst the role of English in Brunei and Malaysia is very different, what is shared by both societies (and increasingly Indonesia, with a growing English-medium educated elite) is that the function of Malay as a language of liberation for colonial rule and medium of egalitarianism is shifting towards becoming the medium of internal colonization and a support system for social stratification.[5] Moreover, just as English in the past was used to spread Christianity and Western civilization, Malay is being used to spread Islam and Islamic civilization. One is struck by the absence of any programme to recognize, maintain or learn from the hundreds of indigenous 'tribal' languages and is left with the impression that they are seen as an embarrassment and an obstruction to development and modernization.

De Terra's (1982) microstudy of the effects of the National Language Plan of Malaysia on a working-class non-Malay community illustrates the general theme, found throughout the emerging nation-states of the region, that

> the goals of language planning are several, and assurance that these goals will be attained derives from the planners' not the speakers' ideas about what language can do, what can be done to language, and what can be done in the name of language.
>
> (De Terra 1982: 530)

As a consequence, large numbers of minority language speakers fail to achieve their official (and often their own) goal of being fluent in the national language and are blamed for their failure. De Terra concludes:

> If language is considered inherently social and not an abstract, objectified process, then planned language change cannot be separated from social change. The issue is not simply what kind of language is being planned but what kind of society. To restructure society, Bahasa Malaysia was implemented in order to promote national integration and unity, development and modernization. But for some, inadequate implementation has restricted not only language choice but also social and economic choice. Communication has become difficult or impossible for them. In such cases, rather than wider communication, unity, and integration, the result is isolation and division; rather than modernization and development, marginality and decline.
>
> (De Terra 1982: 540)

Such examples can be multiplied and some additional ones are discussed in Chapter 9 on foreign language teaching. One might wish to conclude that the streamlining of policies of language planning has failed because of the failure to consider sociohistorical factors, as Tollefson (1991) has argued, concluding that a planning process inspired by the ideas of Marxism-Leninism provides a more humane and sustained approach. However, a look at the language policies of Marxist societies (e.g. mainland China, former Soviet Union in Siberia) demonstrates that the failure of planning in the linguistic sphere is also very much in evidence in communist approaches and that the solution needs to be sought elsewhere. The new paradigm that is beginning to emerge transcends the nineteenth-century ideologies of human systems, by abandoning the selective privileging of particular cultures or linguistic modes of existence, the streamlining approach of the political right and the political left, and putting in its place a different more equitable view of language.

LANGUAGE MAINTENANCE AS THE THEME IN LANGUAGE PLANNING

That there was something wrong with the massive assimilation campaigns that were carried out in the Pacific both by the first world countries such as Australia, New Zealand and the United States of America and by the developing countries of the region was a notion which began to be mooted at, first very tentatively, in the late 1960s. Gradually the idea that languages other than the dominant languages deserved to be maintained began to take root, particularly in Australia. Much has been written about the history of this idea in Australia, such as Ozolins (1992) or contributors to Romaine (1991), and I shall not pursue details here. Ironically, the idea of language maintenance and multiculturalism was developed first and foremost for introduced migrant languages rather than those of Aborigines and Torres Strait Islanders (or languages introduced by non-white groups such as the Pacific Islanders in Queensland). The guiding principle which emerged, and was strongly supported by the incoming Labour Government in 1972, was that of social justice, particularly for inner city immigrant ethnic groups.

Over subsequent years Australia has developed a National Policy on Languages with considerable emphasis on languages other than English, a policy which has been hailed as a model and praised for its integrity and its sophistication (for a sympathetic but critical review see Fishman 1991). During this period, the national language planners did much to reverse over 100 years of linguistic assimilation policies towards indigenous languages. Over the years, there have been considerable fluctuations and the present-day outcome is very much a solution which perpetuates the dominance of English, whilst making some concessions to languages other than English (LOTE).[6] The present requirement that every Australian should be able to speak English and know (at least) one other language includes, for instance, traditional Aboriginal multilingualism. Of concern is the shift to an implicit policy of English and one economically useful (mainly Japanese, Chinese, Indonesian) language. Economic arguments, in the long term, appear to be considerably more powerful than social justice arguments. What role the maintenance of economically non-powerful languages will play in Australia in coming years is anybody's guess, but the statistics on the loss of LOTE are not encouraging.

Attempts to preserve linguistic diversity and strengthen indigenous linguistic traditions have merged, in the 1990s, in a number of other countries of the region, notably in Papua New Guinea where a decentralized education system and a strong vernacular literacy movement are being put in place; in New Zealand the Maori have been given a considerable amount of official recognition as have the indigenous peoples of Vanuatu, where the survival of the local 100 and more languages is promoted by shielding them from external influence. In Chapter 12 I shall explore the different approaches to language maintenance and assess their potential contribution to maintaining linguistic diversity in the Pacific area.

8 The impact of literacy

> While the creation of a writing system has helped to preserve the Hawaiian language, it may have helped kill it as a spoken language.
>
> (Day 1985: 170)

INTRODUCTION

Literacy, more than virtually any other phenomenon, illustrates the impact of an introduced mode of behaviour on the linguistic ecology of the Pacific. It has led over the years to an almost total transformation of most Pacific societies and most languages spoken in the area. Whereas the use of literacy as an instrument of social change was often deliberate and whilst much has been written on the social effects of the 'literary revolution', its linguistic consequences remain much less well charted. In the popular view, which is also widely shared by the linguistic profession, writing is a form of representing spoken language rather than a mode of behaviour that can radically affect the linguistic structures and practices of language use in a community.

One main reason for the lack of awareness of the full impact of literacy is the virtual absence of in-depth longitudinal studies, illustrating the processes of linguistic and conceptual restructuring and the attrition of traditional modes of communication; the other reason is the well-known trend within modern linguistics to regard writing as a epiphenomenon: as a form of representing speech, not as a force affecting all linguistic practices.

As one begins to consider the vast body of scattered evidence, a different picture begins to emerge, one that puts literacy and derived technology at the centre of an ongoing restructuring in the linguistic ecology of the Pacific.

The changeover from orality to literacy can be characterized as follows:

1 promoting the transition from low-information to high-information societies
2 offering the possibility of storing information over long periods of time
3 supplementing face-to-face interaction with written communication over long distances.

The effect of this changeover on the languages of the area was dramatic and twofold:

1 It led to a conceptual restructuring as evidenced, for instance, in societal views of time. Instead of cyclical concepts of time, the metaphor of time as an arrow and the associated notions of progress began to emerge. Human actions, consequently, were not determined by seeking harmony with natural cycles but by emulating artificial, human-made goals or utopias.
2 As literacy was provided for metropolitan languages and specific privileged dialects of local languages only, it also greatly contributed to the creation of communicative inequalities and decreasing heterogeneity.

The various media that were introduced subsequent to writing (radio, television, video, computers) crucially depended on the cultural changes created by literacy, but promoted five main additional changes.

First, there was a change from time-biased to space-biased communication. Melody, Salter and Heyer (1981), commenting on the work of the Canadian communication scholar, Innis, characterize this transition as follows:

> He argued that media used in ancient civilizations such as parchment, clay and stone were durable and difficult to transport. These characteristics are conducive to control over time, but not over space. These media are time-biased. Paper is light, less durable, and easily transportable with reasonable speed. It is spatially biased; it permitted administration over great distances, and therefore, the geographical extension of empires.
>
> In cultural terms, time-biased communication media are associated with traditional societies that emphasize custom, continuity, community, the historical, the sacred and the moral. They are characterized by stable, hierarchical social orders that tend to stifle individualism as a dynamic for change, but permit individualism in the rich oral traditions or with sophisticated writing technologies where access is limited to a privileged few.

Space-biased communication media have an orientation toward the present and the future, the expansion of empires, an increase in political authority, the creation of secular institutions, the growth of science and technical knowledge. They are characterized by the establishment of systems of information exchange and mass communication that are extremely efficient, but which cannot convey the richness, diversity and elasticity of the oral tradition. The modern media of print, telephone, radio, and television are all space-biased.

(Melody, Salter and Heyer 1981: 6)

A spatial bias crucially depends on the wide spatial distribution of a single language. The spread of English in the Pacific through education and administrative measures is a consequence of this trend. At the same time, population movements in space are encouraged.

In the second change, the possibility to store and retrieve large amounts of information through the print media is accelerated by the introduction of computer storage facilities that surpass the capacity of human memory. The impact of information storage capacity on low-information societies can be far reaching. It is now possible for individuals to have access to vastly differing amounts of information, whereas in traditional societies, secret languages and other restrictions notwithstanding, a great deal of information was shared by all other members of a society. At the same time, it is becoming clear that access to such stored knowledge cannot be via traditional languages.

Differential access to information, together with differential status for different languages and dialects, are the reasons for a third change, that is, from a more egalitarian to a non-egalitarian pattern of communication. Colonialism, imperialism and nationalism have all tended to promote greater inequality in the distribution of material and non-material commodities, and, once created, inequality has tended to grow, following the principle that those that have shall be given. Thus, imported metropolitan languages and a few larger national languages have attracted most of the technological changes, with the smaller local vernaculars losing out.

Fourth, there is an inverse relationship between media and codes. The more new media are introduced, the fewer codes can be maintained at a reasonable cost. The theoretical capacity of high-information technology to store any amount of information in any code is offset by the economics of the enterprise. As oral societies can tolerate any amount of dialectal variation, literacy requires the standardization of 'languages' with preferably above 1,000 speakers. Radio broadcasts are economical only for a much larger number of speakers, with television, video and computers requiring increasingly larger speech communities to support them. As the diversity of media grows, the diversity of languages, particularly small languages, disappears.

Finally, modern media are the promoters and consolidators of the transition from traditional to modern and post-modern societies.

Literacy has tended to be regarded in a mechanistic fashion, that is, as a system where it seems possible to add or take away components, and interchange components without affecting the whole system. It has been argued that literacy and the enjoyment of literature would simply fill the vacuum left by the removal of unsavoury heathen practices and that by giving people literacy one simply added another useful skill to their repertoire of skills. As we shall see in a number of case studies in the next section, literacy in all instances has been an agent of social and linguistic transformation, whose linguistic outcome interestingly is not a strengthening of the local languages but the acceleration of their decline. A widely held view that 'an accepted written form greatly enhances the utility of a language and, indeed, its chances of survival' (Coulmas 1994: 162) does not appear to be universally applicable.

In taking an ecological stance one has to avoid the error of regarding literacy as an entity that can become an inhabitant of a linguistic ecology, rather it is a mode of behaviour adopted by the inhabitants to satisfy a wide range of traditional and non-traditional needs. As Kulick and Stroud (1989: 286) have pointed out, humans, not literacy, are the active force in the transformational process accompanying the introduction of literacy.

I shall begin by illustrating the alleged impact of literacy with a number of case studies.

SOME LONGITUDINAL STUDIES

Maori

The first area affected by the literary revolution in the Pacific was Polynesia, where writing systems for the major languages (Hawaiian, Tahitian and Maori) were developed only a few years after European discovery in the late eighteenth century. The general aspects of this revolution have been discussed in some detail by Parsonson (1967). The case of Maori is particularly instructive, since the debate about Maori literacy is a continuing one.

New Zealand was first 'discovered' by the Dutch navigator Tasman in 1612 and explored in greater depth by Captain Cook in 1770, in which year possession of the colony was taken by Britain. Cook's visits initiated a transformation which, in the first instance, manifested itself in the spread of European plants and weapons and later numerous diseases. Cook was followed by other European explorers and whalers and by 1814 the first *pakeha* ('white') settlers arrived in the Bay of Islands. They were Church of England missionaries who offered protection in exchange for European goods and power. Around the mission station a community of whalers and beachcombers grew up and intensive trade relations developed between the Maori and pakeha, the most desired European commodity being firearms. Mission influence was initially very slow and their eventual success is seen by some not as the result of their teachings but of the realization that missions provided a way of becoming literate.

> The Pacific Islanders had long grasped the fact that the real difference between their culture and the European was that theirs was non-literate, the other literate. The key to the new world with all its evident power was the written word. Indeed, the missionaries had often told them so and every fresh contact with the foreigner emphasized the point. The sheer magic of the written word in primitive eyes needs to be stressed. Quiros notes how the Taumakoans 'were much astonished at seeing one reading a paper, and taking it in their hands, they looked at it in front and behind'. Henry Williams, speaking of the Maori, mentions how on one occasion he spent some time in reading, writing and drawing: 'This last greatly astonished the natives, to see the effect of a few pencil marks on paper.'
>
> (Parsonson 1967: 44)

Crosby (1986) offers the following picture of the rapid spread of literacy among the Maori:

> The missionaries, all but a few of them Protestants who viewed literacy as a major virtue, flung themselves at the problem of Maori illiteracy as if it were the boulder to be rolled away from Christ's tomb. They learned the Maori tongue, devised an alphabet for it, and in 1837 published the entire New Testament in Maori. By 1845 there was at least one copy of that publication for every two Maori in the country.
>
> The missionaries offered the Maori a new religion, a new skills, new tools, and the magic of the alphabet, but it was the Maori themselves who accepted (no, seized) the opportunities offered. The most effective transmitters of Christianity and literacy were the prisoners taken by the Ngapuhi and allies – the lowest of the low, the slaves – who embraced the new religion with the greatest fervor, and then, as the wars waned and they were freed, returned

home bearing the Word with them. When the missionaries penetrated the southern central districts of the North Island, they found the Maori there already clamoring for instruction and books, and often village schools under Maori teachers already in operation.

There were no Maori conversions up to 1825 and only a few – usually of the moribund – between 1825 and 1830. Ten years later, the Anglicans alone claimed 2,000 communicants and thousands more, adults and children, under instruction in Christianity and the basic skills of literacy.

(Crosby 1986: 246)

Crosby also comments on the cargo-cult aspect of literacy:

The Reverend J. Watkins recorded that some Maori believed that the missionaries had a book called *Puka Kakari* that would render the possessor invulnerable to club or bullet. Others had it that the pakeha possessed a book that would restore the dead to life if placed on the chest of the deceased. Watkins found one of these books at Waikouaite; it turned out to be a publication called *Norie's Epitome*. But we are carping if we make much of Maori superstition. Whatever their confusion about the nature of the new religion and books, the fact remains that they did not succumb to barren cultism or alcoholism or apathy, but took hold of Christianity and literacy with the same enthusiasm with which they had picked up the musket.

(Crosby 1986: 247)

Similarly vigorous illustrations of the spread of literacy are given by Parr (1963). According to Hohepa (1984: 1), by 1856 'some 90% of the Maori population were able to read and write in their own language; in that year, the numbers of white settlers equalled the total Maori population'. With the ever increasing numerical dominance of the pakehas, Maori literacy began to decline, for two principal reasons: first, disenchantment with literacy and the mission school system, combined with growing suspicion of literacy. It was considered by 'some of the Hohianga chiefs that the Europeans taught the Maoris to figure and write only to encourage them to go to England where they would be killed for their land' (Parr 1963: 213). The second reason was the growing importance of the state in Maori education, reflected in a changeover to English-medium education from the 1850s onward.

As early as 1852 it was considered by the Auckland school inspectors that it was 'doubtless desirable that the English language should be made a vehicle of instruction exclusively, in cases where it is fully understood, and, as far as can usefully be done, in all cases' (quoted from Parr 1963: 231). An increasing number of Maoris shared this view and by 1867 the government had instituted an English-medium education for all races. English had become both the medium and the message and for generations to come Maoris were discouraged and even punished for using their language at school.

The subsequent history of Maori teaching and the recent changes in attitudes and policies are documented in detail by Benton (1981: 15ff.). Of the many points raised by this author only a few can be mentioned here:

1 There are no signs whatsoever of a return to a Maori-only literacy; bilingualism and biculturalism in Maori and English (with the latter being the dominant language) represents as much recognition as Maori is likely to gain.
2 Maori is the weak language in a diglossic situation dominated by English and a growing number of Maoris speak English only and/ or encourage their children to do so.
3 The language of the media favoured by the Maori population, video, television and printed materials (in that order) is almost exclusively English.

With regard to the last observation, Benton notes that the lack of Maori literature is often used as an argument against formal teaching of this language. He goes on to comment on the familiar issue of 'oral literature':

Some writers have tried to counter the 'no literature' argument by classifying the rich diversity of orally transmitted material to which Maori-speakers still have access as 'oral literature'. Mr Karetu remarks, for example, that 'the language is rich in oral literature and the fact that it is mainly oral does not make it less than literature'. The main point of this assertion, that what has been transmitted by the spoken word is no less worthy of study than that which has been written down, in the case of Maori, most certainly true. But labelling what has not yet been written 'literature' is likely to confuse the real issue. This is undoubtedly a case where an application of the Confucian principle of the 'rectification of names' is badly needed. The word 'literature' in normal English has until very recently referred exclusively to written materials. The extension of the term to other kinds of verbal compositions (an aberration perpetrated originally perhaps by certain anthropologists appreciative of the value of oral tradition) does violence to the

Latin root of the word – litteratura meaning 'alphabet writing', and used in the modern sense of 'that which is written' by Cicero – as well as to the conventional English meaning which was taken directly from Cicero's usage. Those who claim that Maori has no literature clearly mean that there is nothing of any worth written down in the language – so to redefine 'literature' as anything worth reading or hearing is to evade rather than to refute the argument.

(Benton 1981: 26)

What Benton fails to emphasize is the fundamental difference between the pre-contact oral society and the English-dominated literate society. The role of traditional oratory and other forms of oral expression is changed once and for all by the introduction of literacy, and once written down this oral heritage may provide museum exhibits and objects of scholarly study rather than a living tradition. As Benton (1981: 44) observes: 'The future of Maori as a living language is far from assured, although there is now no doubt that it would be greatly honoured as a dead one'.

The story of Maori literacy is mirrored by the other two large Polynesian languages, Hawaiian and Tahitian. In Hawaii, missionary efforts in promoting vernacular literacy had achieved virtually universal literacy in Hawaiian by 1850. In 1853 the first English-language schools for Hawaiians were set up and by 1892 English had replaced Hawaiian as the language of instruction and literacy, a situation which was made official policy of the Republic of Hawaii in 1896. The vast majority of present-day Hawaiians are monolingual English speakers and Hawaiian is likely to become the first Polynesian language to become extinct in 'historical' times.

Lavondès (1971: 1,100ff.) gives a similar account for Tahitian. By 1829 the majority of Tahitians were literate in their language. However, as early as 1860 the transition to literacy in French had been made by many Tahitians, though literacy in Tahitian continues to be of some importance as a result of mission policies to teach religious subjects in the vernacular.

The principal lesson to be learnt from the Polynesian languages is that vernacular literacy typically is transitional literacy, a transition often promoted by the existence of writing systems that incorporate orthographic conventions of the metropolitan languages. One also sees the strong link between literacy and cultural transition: vernacular literacy is typically associated with missionization, whilst metropolitan literacy reflects attempts by colonial and post-colonial governments to bring about social and economic change.

Whilst the developments in Polynesia are now largely history, very similar processes can still be observed with the smaller languages of Melanesia. This is the topic of the next section.

Tolai

Literacy for the Melanesian and Papuan languages of Papua New Guinea would seem to be different from Polynesian literacy for three reasons:

1 The languages concerned have fewer speakers and are more localized.
2 Intermediate between the local vernacular and the metropolitan language of English we have two widely used and highly developed pidgin languages: Tok Pisin and Hiri Motu.
3 Literacy in the majority of instances began rather later and thus had the opportunity to draw on the experience of Polynesia.

One of the earliest local languages that was reduced to writing was Tolai (Kuanua), one of the larger languages spoken in the Gazelle Peninsula and surrounding areas of New Britain and New Ireland. This language was used in its written forms by Methodist and Catholic missions as well as the German government. As was the case with other languages used by competing mission societies, orthographic standards which were developed differed sufficiently to make it difficult to read publications of a competing mission.

Early literacy in Tolai concentrated almost entirely on non-indigenous issues: transactions with the German colonial administration and religious instruction. Mosel (1982) reports:

> The churches take the credit for having made the people literate. The Imperial judge Schnee published a collection of letters he had received from tribal chiefs. To what extent writing was practised for private purposes is unknown, but a small collection of letters written to Rev. H. Fellmann suggests that at least some people were able to write and practised it not only in their dealings with officials. Natives also wrote articles for the Church papers Nilai Ra Dorol (Methodist) and Talaigu (Catholic), but one can hardly speak of indigenous creative writing in these cases, as the articles followed the pattern of European Christian literature. The only book that has been written by a native in Tolai seems to be the autobiography by Hosea Linge, which was translated into English and published in Australia in 1932. It does not seem to have been printed in Tolai, since Threlfall certainly would have mentioned it. Thus the only literature offered to the people was Christian litera-

ture. It is hard to believe that there were no attempts to have people commit their traditional oral literature to writing. If the Catholic missionaries had not published the old myths in Germany for anthropological reasons, they would be completely lost today. In 1976 and 1978 I tried to collect old stories, but it was almost impossible to find people who could remember any.

(Mosel 1982: 162–3)

The extent to which Tolai speakers became literate in Tolai is not known. However, what seems to have happened is very much what happened in Polynesia. After an initial peak in Tolai literacy, government education policies subsequently advocated the exclusive use of English and literacy skills in Tolai began to decline. The growth of Tok Pisin literacy, though on a modest scale among the Tolai, further undermined literacy in Tolai.

The writing skills of young Tolai people in their native language are on the decline. Thus, for instance, some of my informants did not know whether to write subject markers and tense–aspect markers separately or in one word, or separated them at the wrong point, e.g. diata or dia ta instead of diat a 'they will' (such cases are nevertheless interesting for the linguist, as they give some information on the psychological reality of word boundaries).

One can easily imagine what will happen if people lose interest in going to the church services, where they at least have to read passages from the Bible in Tolai, so that they become familiar with its spelling. The writing skills in English of those who have left school after 'standard six' are – naturally – even worse than their writing skills in Tolai. If nothing is done in the very near future, the English based education will result in two kinds of social classes: a privileged class of those who could go to high school and are literate in English and an underprivileged class of illiterates or semi-illiterates. Two things could be done to prevent illiteracy: either reading and writing in Tolai must be reintroduced as a subject in primary schools, or the children must be taught to read and write in Pidgin, so that they become literate in a language they speak.

(Mosel 1982: 164)

Literacy for the smaller languages of Papua New Guinea

From the early 1970s, as has been pointed in the surveys by Joice Franklin (1977) and Tryon (1988), there have been considerable efforts to promote literacy for the speakers of small vernaculars spoken in Papua New Guinea. Next to such 'neutral' reports, there are other more critical analyses asking questions as to the social and linguistic impact of literacy. Summing up literacy before the Second World War, Neuendorf and Taylor (1977) state:

> There were, in fact, extremely active literacy programmes in many areas. However, most majored on the mechanics of reading and paid little attention to comprehension. Practically nothing was done with regard to the production of literature for new literates to read other than Bible passages, catechisms and hymn books. Also there was often too big a jump in reading difficulty between school primers and the Christian literature, a problem which has continued in many languages even up to the present. There was little co-ordination in literacy work. Each area was left on its own to develop its own course with little assistance from outside. As missionaries moved – either transferred to another posting or leaving the country – programmes suffered. In many cases the success or failure of a programme depended very largely on the efforts of one person.
>
> (Neuendorf and Taylor 1977: 417)

Lynch (1979), in his inaugural lecture (as Professor of Language at the University of Papua New Guinea) which analysed Franklin's findings, found that little had changed by 1979.

> Only eighteen languages in Papua New Guinea may be considered as having a body of secular literature of any kind. And when one considers that included in this literature are titles such as 'How the Jews Lived', 'Houses of the World', 'Stone Age Men in Britain' (Rule 1977: 397–398) and 'Flies are Your Enemy', one wonders whether one could really refer to a 'body of literature'. On the other hand, a goodly number of the languages of Papua New Guinea have a considerable body of religious literature, including in many cases the whole of the New Testament, and in some cases virtually the whole of the Bible.
>
> (Lynch 1979: 12)

Lynch (1979) identifies four major effects of literacy as imposed by the churches:

> Denigration of traditional cultures. Capell's statements . . . contain many references to the fact that 'no vernacular literature has been collected', or 'no vernacular literature has been published'. The churches have generally ignored the very great wealth of oral

literature when they are denying children in rapidly-changing cultures access to information on what their own culture was like.

(Lynch 1979: 14)

Reversion to illiteracy. It has been clearly shown that, unless literacy is functional, new literates frequently, and very rapidly revert to illiteracy. By functional literacy I mean, very simply, that the new skills of reading and writing must be useful, and used, and used often in a variety of contexts. As Phillips (1970: 14–15) has put it:

> The illiterate can be led to the fountain of knowledge but he cannot be forced to drink if he does not want to. Equally the fountain must in fact slake his thirst if he is to return to it frequently.

My contention is that, by providing only one kind of reading material, people's thirst is not slaked. They do not see literacy as leading to the fountain of knowledge, because there is no material for them to read except religious material. In many cases, they all too soon lose the skill of reading.

(Lynch 1979: 14)

Failure to develop critical reading skills. One of our problems in tertiary institutions in Melanesia is that many students are not critical readers: they believe everything they read, because 'if it says so in the book, or the newspaper, then it must be true'. I suggest that this attitude derives from the policy of the Christian missions, who provide only certain kinds of reading materials and who tell new literates that they must believe what is written, in the Bible or elsewhere. The written word itself becomes sacred, leading to extreme difficulties in trying to develop a state of critical awareness.

(Lynch 1979: 14)

The fourth major effect is restricted access to information: Lynch (1979: 16) sums up the content of literature used by the missions as *baibel, baibel, singsing, nomo* – 'bible, bible, hymns and nothing else' and consequently concludes that such a restrictive use of writing does not provide people with a knowledge of the various options open to them.

Whereas it could be, indeed has been, argued by some that at least some of these effects were deliberately planned, there have been a range of other effects not anticipated by the missions, notably the upsurge of cargo cults in the wake of literacy campaigns. Meggitt

(1967) describes the different agendas of the missionaries and their converts for promoting literacy. The former regarded literacy as a powerful tool in spreading Christianity, whilst the latter saw it as the key to open the door to European wealth (cargo). Meggitt postulated four stages in indigenous literacy:

1 The Europeans arrive to find an indigenous religious system that stresses the acquisition of wealth and ritualized communication with the supernatural.
2 There is an initial native acceptance of Christianity as another road to the Cargo and of writing as an additional form of ritualized communication.
3 The failure of Christianity to deliver the Cargo is followed by its rejection in favour of some variety of cargo cult in which writing continues to be but one of several ritualized modes of communication.
4 The failure of the cargo cult to provide the Cargo leads some far-seeing men to devise a political and economic Movement for change, in which writing regains its typically European secular status as a means of communication.

(Meggitt 1967: 76–7)

Stage 3 is the consequence of the belief that the missionaries were cheating, that they kept back crucial knowledge (secret names or certain Bible passages) which could provide access to Western goods. In the secular arena, it was the role of letters (*pas*) in obtaining cargo that became the focus of the Papua New Guineans' attention. Burridge (1960) reports:

in everyday life, Tangu (people) associate the acquisition of European goods with a pas. Those who have served under Europeans have often been sent to the trade store with a *pas*, and on presentation of the *pas* goods are handed over the counter. Administration officers, missionaries and planters or traders who require replenishment of stores send letters and in due course the cargo arrives. No money is seen to change hands, no apparent exchange seems to take place, no goods are returned to the store; the cargo comes, is distributed, consumed, and more comes. . . . Each transaction is accompanied by a letter. Letters set the whole process in motion.

(Burridge 1960: 193–4)

Meggitt's stages have been criticized by Kulick and Stroud (1989) on empirical grounds, particularly 'the belief that ritualized literacy eventually gives way to a typically "European secular" use of the written word' (1989: 294). Instead, they argue that the people embracing literacy

> have their own ideas about reading and writing, generated from their own cultural concerns. These ideas, rather than ones externally generated and culturally foreign, have been and continue to be applied to the written word in the village. The villagers have not been 'transformed' by literacy. If anything, they themselves have 'transformed' it.
>
> (Kulick and Stroud 1989: 295)

Whereas it has been maintained throughout this book that human agency and language use are to be preferred as focuses of attention to metaphors of language as a code and literacy as an agent, one perhaps has to acknowledge a more complex relationship between human actions and the technology of literacy and derived technologies than that postulated by Kulick and Stroud. Whilst European modes of using literacy are still not being encountered in the more remote villages contacted for the first time in the 1960s and 1970s there would seem to be grounds for recognizing the fourth stage of Meggitt's cycle among the educated members of the urban society.

An important side-effect of literacy, rarely commented on, was encountered, for example, in shifts of bilingualism from vernacular Tok Pisin to Tok Pisin English; in essence, that a small set of cheap-looking and makeshift publications in the vernacular contrasts with a more sophisticated literature published in Tok Pisin and a vast range of glossy, professionally produced materials in English. Vernacular literacy thus can be regarded as a stepping stone to perceived more desirable forms of literacy. The transitional role of vernacular literacy is also seen in its use in modernizing the linguistic structures and cognitive inventories of traditional vernaculars.

The writing systems devised for most small languages of Papua New Guinea were based either on an arbitrary criterion that did little to make reading an easy task (e.g. the tradition of following Fijian spelling conventions by Wesleyan missionaries or German spelling conventions by German missionaries or by people trained in a narrow atemporal phonemics). Phonemic writing systems, as they are incompatible in principle with the accommodation of variation and change, promote fossilization and reduction of stylistic and regional variants. Doubtful spelling systems combined with insufficient attention to indigenous grammatical norms are a recipe for problems. The story of the Gedaged language, once widely used in the Madang area as a lingua franca (Freyberg 1977), is an example.

Much of the literature, produced in haste, was therefore flawed by an excessive degree of 'literal translation' resulting in European thought patterns and constructions that were unidiomatic to the native reader and seriously impeded comprehension. Reading without easy comprehension and enjoyment contributed little to the development of literacy and the urge to read – or to write for publication.

Similar problems caused by bad translation practicing are documented in numerous other cases.

(Freyberg 1977: 862)

The story of literacy for small languages bears out the general trends identified in this chapter. Promoting vernacular literacy does little to arrest their decline and tends to accelerate structural breaks rather than follow the traditional drift of the languages. As a long-term strategy for preserving languages and cultures, literacy does not appear to be a particularly viable approach in the case of small languages.

Fijian

What goes for small languages is repeated in a very large one (for the Pacific area) – Fijian. We are fortunate in being able to draw on a detailed study of literacy and social change by Clammer (1976) as well as an extensive range of other sources. This study appeared after Parsonson's seminal article (1967) which was based on Maori and Tahitian data. Parsonson took a position that is often taken up by defenders of missionization, i.e. that 'the Polynesians had at length explored and exhausted all avenues open to a non-literate society and sought an ampler world' (1967: 39). Parsonson also subscribed to the view that the missionaries used literacy as a convenient tool rather than an intregral part of the intended outcome of having a literate missionized society. Clammer, on the other hand, argues that in the Fijian and most other Pacific societies:

The key to his conversion was indeed literacy as I have argued; but it was literacy backed by economic and other powerful factors. Most important is the recognition that the missionaries from the outset in Fiji (and in Tonga before) saw the way to religion to lie through literacy. This was not a contingency as Parsonson suggests, but the vital principle of Wesleyan missionary endeavour. In the light of this we must reject any suggestion that the missionaries merely 'associated' themselves with the 'literate revolution'. They created it, directed it, controlled access to its availability, and for a

long time dictated the quality, quantity, and content of the information it could give. Similarly it is impossible to claim that the 'real'
revolution was literacy not Christianity.

(Clammer 1976: 200)

Thus control in Fiji as elsewhere, is manifested in the linguistic arena
in

1 the addition and removal of lexical material
2 the setting up of language external norms
3 the control of speech acts and events.

The transformation of Fiji from a 'flourishing native empire to a
colonial theocracy' (Clammer 1976: 1) began with the arrival from
Tonga of the first Methodist missionaries in 1835. The study of the
Fijian language occupied a prominent place in the first phase of
missionization, as they

regarded literacy as an essential element in their struggle for converts, both so that religion among the people could be self sustain-
ing and not for ever dependent on the word and presence of the
missionary, and so that the training of native pastors could proceed
beyond the most rudimentary level.

(Clammer 1976: 13)

It was soon realized that there were a multitude of closely related
languages and dialects in Fiji, which made communication via a single
variety impossible. However, initial attempts to translate the scriptures
into several important varieties soon gave way to the adoption of a
single common mission language, that of Mbauan. It is worth noting
that the prohibitive cost of printing fifteen or more versions of the
Bible was a main consideration in this decision. Subsequent rationaliza-
tions included that the variety of Mbauan was 'evidently the purest'
(Clammer 1976: 21) and that it was a 'diplomatic lingua franca', a
claim which according to Schütz (1985: 66) has some substance; it
might have been a pre-European (trade Koiné), i.e. a variety that had
already undergone some levelling and that was favoured by Fijians in
their dealings with outgroups.

The principal linguistic effect of this linguistic decision was the
rapid spread of Mbauan Fijian as a written standard language throughout the archipelago, followed by the spread of spoken standard
Fijian. In the 1990s, all members of the younger generation are
competent in spoken standard Fijian, competence in other varieties of
Fijian being on the decline. As comparatively little work has been
done on the use and structure of the other varieties, the extent of the

damage remains unknown. Standard Fijian meanwhile has also come under considerable stress as higher education and higher forms of literacy involve English rather than Fijian, as does most printed and video entertainment.

Milner (1984) reports on the overwhelming role of English in the Fijian education system:

> Three years ago I was told that the teaching of English in Fiji begins with six year old children in Class 1, by the direct method: 'Stand up; sit down; go there; come back,' and so on. They receive two hours a week of English. The amount is gradually increased until they reach Class 6, when they are given 38 hours a week of instruction in English, out of a total of 40. This applies to both Indian and Fijian children, in rural as well as urban areas. If the teachers are conscientious, they may also teach two hours of Fijian or Hindustani, but these are said to be low priority subjects. Even they may be taught in English, as if the mother tongue was a second and not a first language. Let me give a few examples of what this policy has already led to. I was told that today, many Fijian and Indian children can read and write in English, but not in their mother tongue. Many of the Fijian speakers no longer even know the names of some of the common animals and plants of their country. If they know them at all, they only know the English equivalents. It is not a kind of affectation or showing off: it has the approval of parents and teachers. If in doubt, use an English word.
>
> (Milner 1984: 18)

Yet again, the initial development of literacy in an indigenous language and the almost universal competence in written Fijian in the nineteenth century were only a transitional stage to literacy in English.

The path of this transition was paved by gradually creating a type of Fijian that looked like an inferior version of English rather than a means of asserting Fijian identity. Some aspects of this increasing dependency of the Fijian language on outside values are the following:

1 That written Fijian was used either as a vehicle of the new religion or as a way of establishing a class of low-ranking indigenous officials who acted as intermediaries between their people and the colonial masters. It was writing rather than the traditional selection criteria that determined who could rise to positions of power and responsibility within the colonial order.

2 The amount of traditional religion and traditional knowledge that was written down in Fijian for the use by Fijians was negligible, as

information about the new order was paramount. Clammer (1976: 178) refers to this and similar aspects as 'the manipulation of knowledge'.

3 The written standard language allowed control over the introduction of new religious and political concepts, thereby creating and reinforcing the new world view.

As Clammer points out:

> As I have maintained, the great flaw in Fijian social structure was the failure to provide alternative orientation systems within itself which would otherwise be destructive. This success of the European order lay in its ability to control the network of communications and thereby control the power of indigenous pressure groups (e.g. the Tuka), to expand the power of European interest groups (e.g. the planters), to restrict the possibility of the local population dictating the disposal of goods and services, to control the flow and content of information (by way of control of newspapers, printing press etc.), to direct the social organisation of specialised knowledge through management of the educational system and by preventing pressure groups (e.g. trade unions) from forming, to define the conditions under which trade and social intercourse were possible and, through the manipulation of the belief system and the control of its material correlates, to influence ideological development, hence the principles which legitimate authority. These are all aspects of the manipulation of knowledge.
>
> (Clammer 1986: 199)

Next to the ubiquitous new words for religious concepts such as sin, baptism, guilt and crucifix and new material culture such as cabbage, mustard, brass, gold, onion or helicopter (full lists are given by Clammer 1976: 48ff.), particularly important change was the restructuring of time. The year was split up into twelve months, the week into seven days, the days into hours and so on. Some of the effects are described by Clammer:

> Little work had been done in Fijian notions of time and similar categories, but from comparative material one might surmise that time was divided according to ecological principles; e.g. seasons, height of the sun, phases of the moon, and by activities associated with such features. How seriously such new divisions as days and hours were taken by the Fijians is difficult to estimate, for as an agrarian people life would still continue to revolve around the ecological cycle. The longer term effects of such new notions are

more significant, for just as European dress has become the stand-ard dress so as [*sic*] 'European time' has become the 'standard' time. Certain immediate effects would become apparent. The setting aside of Sundays as a day of rest was a constant source of conflict between converts and pagans, and similarly the Sunday would be broken up into specific periods, calculated on the basis of hours when services took place, just as the schoolday became divided up by a timetable, based on European time calculations.

(Clammer 1976: 50)

At present, Fijian continues to be one of the more viable Pacific languages, but after 200 years of contacts with the outside world:

1 a very significant part of the population (Indian and Europeans in particular) do not speak Fijian
2 the only language shared by all inhabitants of Fiji is English
3 the number of Fijian publications is insignificant in comparison to those in other languages
4 English and not Fijian is used predominantly in the modern media
5 the structure of the Fijian language has been significantly influenced by English.

With further urbanization and social and technological developments Fijian may well become a threatened language in the not too distant future.

Diyari

Australian Aboriginal languages, like Maori over the last 200 years, became minority languages in a Neo-Europe dominated by the English language and culture. Unlike Maori, which was spoken throughout New Zealand, the linguistic picture of Australia is one of great diversity and the speaker numbers for any Aboriginal language prob-ably never exceeded 5,000 in the past. Now languages with more than 1,000 speakers are regarded as strong. The history of literacy for these languages can be divided into three main periods:

1 a period of early contacts (lasting about twenty years: 1800–20) in which Europeans regarded them as viable and made efforts to learn them and set up schools and literacy programmes
2 a period (approximately 1820–1970) in which Aboriginal languages were deemed to be dying and during which their decline was accelerated by assimilation policies
3 the most recent post-1972 period in which literacy came to be

regarded as a means of strengthening and maintaining the surviving Aboriginal languages.

The case of the Diyari belongs to the first period. A thumbnail sketch of the fate of this language is given by Ferguson (1987).

In the 1860's, some three thousand to five thousand people lived in the Lake Eyre region of south-central Australia, the northeast corner of the present state of South Australia. Among these people about a dozen languages were spoken, of which the principal one was a cluster of language varieties referred to as Diyari (Austin 1981). A hundred years later, these languages were almost completely extinct, and only a handful of the descendants of the earlier inhabitants remained. During that period of rapid human and linguistic decline, however, an unusual episode of the introduction of literacy took place as a direct result of the activity of Lutheran missionaries, who for fifty years (1867–1917) operated a mission settlement on Lake Killalpaninna in the Cooper's Creek district.

(Ferguson 1987: 223)

Ferguson observed that we are dealing with one of the 'rare instances of some form of vernacular literary taking hold in a hunting, gathering society' (1987: 224). 'Taking hold' in his interpretation means 'literacy becomes a part of the shared cultural resources of the society and is not merely a marginal phenomenon activated only by direct involvement with an impinging alien culture'. The graphization of Diyari began when two German pastors, J. S. Gössling and E. Homam, were instructed to become missionaries in the Diyari area and a mission station was set up at Hermannsburg (later Bethesda). As with other Lutheran missions operating in South Australia (e.g. the Kaurna of the Adelaide area), the study of the language, the development of a written form and the preparation of Bible translation were central concerns of the Hermannsburg missionaries. By 1896, the first part of this goal had been achieved: a school was set up and school primers printed. With the arrival of further missionary linguists, in particular J. Flierl, the efforts to turn the Diyari speakers into a literate community were increased. By 1885, a catechism and Bible history had been published. In 1897, the New Testament translation was printed and larger amounts of other written materials were produced. Whilst fostering literacy in Diyari, the German missionaries and their large families set themselves up as a model of a lifestyle which combined many aspects of their home culture:

The use of handwritten and printed material was part of a whole complex of values which included: fixed places of living, working, teaching, and worshipping; cleanliness and order, full clothing, and working for one's living; and truthfulness, public expression of faith in God, and fixed times for prayer and divine services. The missionaries regularly wrote letters and other communications to relatives, church officials, and others with whom they had friendly or business relations. They followed their printed Bible and church Agenda of liturgy and hymns; they often wrote out sermons, and many kept a daily journal.

(Ferguson 1987: 225)

As regards the Diyari:

The peculiar phenomenon of literacy in the mission community must have been a relatively insignificant part of the whole way of life that clashed with their own at almost every point. Only gradually must they have come to understand what it was and what it might do for them, with their very different customs and needs.

(Ferguson 1987: 227)

Whilst for most of the local Aborigines 'the teaching of reading and writing in the classroom must have seemed a useless exercise' (Ferguson 1987: 229), one function of literacy, that of sending messages and writing letters, began to become more widely accepted after the turn of the century and a nucleus of native catechists and evangelists not only regularly read the Bible, but also began to produce their own written materials.

The presence of literacy did little, however, to protect the Diyari community from a number of external threats, above all, the gradual destruction and reduction of their habitat. Ferguson describes this process as follows:

During the years 1885–1908, the Bethesda Mission was a thriving institution, largely because of fairly good rainfalls, a substantial sheep-raising operation, and the availability of government rations for the Aborigines. Even during this period, however, the Diyari faced several obstacles to the viability of their language community. European ranchers and settlers occupied traditional Diyari areas, Diyari men moved from traditional Diyari areas to tribally mixed locations, some took up positions with ranches and other operations in the region, and European diseases made serious inroads into the Diyari population. The mission also was almost constantly in debt, and these debts began to rise alarmingly.

In subsequent years, severe drought conditions, the toll of epidemics of introduced diseases, Aboriginal mobility, personnel problems of the mission, changes in the local scene, and the spread of English all contributed to a rapid decrease in the numbers of Diyari speakers and decreasing use of Diyari by those who could speak it (on the population decline, see Jones and Sutton 1986: 42–43). It is not clear whether there was any reinforcing communal use of literacy in the sense of group literacy events apart from church services, but the use of literacy remained an individual practice that could serve communicative and social functions with others who had attended the mission school and interacted intensively within the mission community. Even as the number of speakers declined and the range of uses became more restricted, the individual competences endured as a shared mark of membership in the mission-influenced Diyari-speaking population.

(Ferguson 1987: 230–1)

Not mentioned by Ferguson are a number of other factors which might have aided this development, for instance, the fact that the dozen or so other languages spoken around Hermannsburg lost their status as equal in a structured language ecology and with their decline became unavailable as sources for borrowing. The effects of grammar standardization and the influence of the missionaries' background language also remain to be investigated.

I would like to share Ferguson's scepticism against simple formulas for the successful introduction of vernacular literacy, in particular his view that support of the maintenance of vernacular literacy by a powerful educational system under local control cannot replace 'a culturally anchored mechanism of intergenerational transmission' (1987: 234).

That an over-reliance on the concentration on the educational system of literacy and language maintenance is a dangerous practice has also been suggested for instances of graphization in the present phase 3 of literacy for Aboriginal languages, and the insight found in studies such as that by Christie (1989) can help explain the fate of Diyari.

SOME GENERALIZATIONS

Case studies such as the one just considered, together with numerous others I have studied, suggest a number of salient responses to and outcomes of the adoption of literacy by speakers of Pacific languages. Similar consequences, no doubt, also occur in other parts of the developing world. In the discussion that follows, literacy should not be understood in the restricted sense of the availability of a writing system or as delivered in the technical administrative census described by Tryon (1988: 41) (able to read and write simple statements in any language or able to read, with understanding, a newspaper, etc.), but as communicative practices widely adopted by language users becoming familiar with the new medium. Johnston's (1979) remarks on the development of a literary mode in the languages of non-literary communities are particularly pertinent in this connection.

In such case studies the following more general findings have been identified:

1 Linguistic diversity is lost.
2 Vernacular literacy is transitional.
3 Literacy brings about conceptual change.
4 Literacy leads to social restructuring.
5 Literacy is seen to reflect truth.

Linguistic diversity is lost

This phenomenon has already been briefly mentioned in connection with Fijian. There appears to be a direct relationship between the medium selected and the amount of linguistic variability tolerated. Thus, in oral communication a wide range of dialectal variation can be maintained, whereas literacy tends to favour single-standard languages whilst computers favour a small number of large international languages. The loss of dialectal variation that goes hand in hand with the introduction of literacy is documented 'between the lines' of many reports.

Thus, in the case of the Suau dialect continuum (Cooper 1975), the dialect of Suau Island was singled out as the basis for literacy.

> Within the speech community, Suau Island speech is generally regarded as being the 'pure' or 'correct' Suau and all extant mission publications are based on Suau Island speech. Standard Suau or Suau Island speech shall designate this form of Suau where such precision is necessary. The term Suau will sometimes be used as a general term for any of the above terms when no ambiguities would result.
>
> (Cooper 1975: 231)

The same process, whereby a formerly egalitarian situation among language varieties is reduced to a non-egalitarian one where one variety is regarded as more correct or better, can also be observed in the case of Kâte, the main mission lingua franca used among speakers of non-Melanesian languages by the Lutheran Mission on the New

Guinea mainland. Of the five principal dialects of Kâte, the Wemo dialect was chosen as the standard variety by the first missionaries in 1892.

In the 1990s, the four other main dialects have all but disappeared. An immediate linguistic consequence is that other dialects are no longer available for internal borrowing or as a source of stylistic effects. Such reduction in variability has made Kâte more dependent on other languages such as Tok Pisin and English. There are indicators that the use of Kâte as a literary language has diminished considerably since the 1970s, partly as a consequence of changed government education policies, partly as a consequence of the speakers' realization that literacy in Kâte did not enable them to participate fully in modern Papua New Guinea society. Very much the same has happened with Yabem, the lingua franca chosen by the Lutheran Church for speakers of Melanesian languages (see J. E. Reinecke 1987).

As observed by Ong (1982: 8): 'Writing gives a grapholect power far exceeding that of any purely oral dialect.' Linguistic diversity in social and topological space was not the only victim. Literacy also reduced developmental diversity (diversity in time):

> By the first of [these events, i.e. literacy] the native language took a permanent form, and was no longer subject, without due sanction, to those changes incidental to all living tongues; the accumulated knowledge of one generation could be passed on to the next in a medium secure from interference.
>
> (*Handbook of Western Samoa* 1925: 9,
> quoted in Baldauf and Luke 1990: 269)

Vernacular literacy is transitional

As has been mentioned in connection with bilingualism in a vernacular and a metropolitan language, most linguistic practices that involve a power differential are unstable once language becomes a tool of social mobility. Vernacular literacy in a situation where access to metropolitan languages and society was barred to speakers of the vernaculars could be stabilized and maintained, given enough outside support and dedication. In a situation where the vernacular is no longer perceived as a means of achieving individual and social goals, this is not possible. In such a situation vernacular literacy is simply a stepping stone for literacy in a more useful language. This, of course, is freely acknowledged by some missionary linguists, for instance Gudschinksy (1968):

Fortunately, the process of reading need be taught only once. When a person has learned how to read, he adds new languages and dialects to his reading repertory by extending the inventory of symbols to which he can respond automatically. Time spent teaching someone to read a minority language is not time lost; he will come to the reading – and speaking – of the second language with enormously greater facility if he already knows what reading is, and is prepared to use it as a tool for learning.

(Gudschinksy 1968: 150)

In societies where literacy in the vernacular came relatively early, the transition to literacy in a metropolitan language has more or less been completed, as in the cases of Maori and Hawaiian.

Literacy brings about conceptual change

Of the many conceptual changes that can be brought about by literacy none seems more fundamental than that in concepts of time. Time, far from being a culture-neutral object that can be discovered, is approached by different cultures by means of elaborate culture-specific metaphors. Of these, the following two best characterize the difference between traditional Pacific societies and modern Western ones:

1 time is a cycle
2 time is an arrow.

Arrow time has been characterized by Gould (1988: 10–11) in that it 'regards history as an irreversible sequence of unrepeatable events. Each moment occupies its own distinct position in a temporal series.' Moreover, events move in a direction. Arrow time is the primary metaphor of literate cultures, cultures that have a means of recording what they regard as a long series of unrepeatable events.

Cyclical time, on the other hand, is the primary time metaphor of oral or preliterate cultures. Under the cyclical view (Gould 1988: 11), 'events have no meaning as distinct episodes with causal impact on a contingent history. Fundamental states are immanent in time, always present and never changing. Apparent motions are part of repeating cycles.' Time, in this view, has no direction.

There are many consequences associated with whether one lives with a cyclical or arrow metaphor of time. Culture in the former case is geared towards understanding seasons, lifecycles and the inherent nature of being, whilst the arrow view emphasizes progress, change and evolution. The latter is the standard view of literate Western societies today.

The role of literacy in the transition from a cyclical to an arrow conception of time is a relatively straightforward one; being able to write down events makes it possible to store accounts of them and retrieve information about past events. It makes it possible also to portray history as a sequence of events reaching back into the past far beyond the memory of individuals. The arrow metaphor of time, in the case of those Australian and Pacific languages that have been reduced to writing, received very considerable support from Bible translation. In most if not all cases, the primary aim of literacy has been to make available the Bible to the indigenous population. As Gould points out (1988: 11), 'Time's arrow is the primary metaphor of biblical history.' He calls it 'the most important and distinctive contribution of Jewish thought, for most other systems, both before and after, favoured the immanence of time's cycle over the chain of linear history.' Such changes in the metaphors of time have been documented in the already mentioned Fijian case (Clammer 1976) and for the New Guinea Highland language Yagaria. Renck (1990) writes:

> As the arrow metaphor of time became dominant, the cycle metaphor receded, as indeed it did in virtually all cultures invaded by literacy. The advantages of this changeover, and there are undoubtedly advantages, did not reach the entire population at an even rate. Rather, it provided selective advantages to semi-literate and literate in a new colonial and post-colonial society.
>
> (Renck 1990: 71–7)

Whilst most of the inhabitants of outlying and rural districts continue to live by the cycle metaphor, a Westernized group of islanders have adopted ideas of linear time, particularly that of progress, a concept that is not found in any of the languages of the Pacific with which I am familiar. The effects of literacy on concepts of time are compounded by effects of a similar order of magnitude on concepts of place, in particular the locatedness of human beings in their natural and cultural environments.

Literacy leads to social restructuring

Authority in traditional societies was either hereditary (e.g. in Polynesia) or, as in Melanesia, based on the oratory and physical skills of individuals. The introduction of both colonial lingue franche and writing triggered off some far-reaching changes by replacing traditional power structure with other structures based on skills needed in dealing with outside authority, the distinctions based on traditional criteria in preliterate societies gave way to a distinction between literate and illiterate. In a carefully documented study of the social restructuring in Fiji, Clammer relates this change to the introduction of a new source of knowledge, written text which made traditional sources of knowledge seem insignificant. Commenting on knowledge of new economic activities, urban living and administrative tasks he concludes:

> In the case of Fiji each of these is related to literacy, as functional literacy is a prerequisite of many of these functions, or is responsible for their appearance. Access to knowledge, opinion leadership, achievement motivations, and cosmopolitanness are all likely to be positively related to literacy, in that a literate person unlike his non-literate counterpart has access to, and can make use of, the sources of information which make all these functions viable. Conflict with the traditional social structure is likely to arise when an individual transcends it by virtue of these functions, and ... such mobility is often related to literacy and its corresponding ability to obtain, retain and use information.
>
> (Clammer 1976: 78)

The advantages that literacy brought in the past have long since been overtaken by demands that literacy should be in the metropolitan language. It is literacy in English and not literacy *per se* that is the way to social advancements.

A second major conceptual change, one that should be of particular interest to linguists, is in notions of language. In Western semantics the same metaphorical processes that have given rise to the reification of literacy have also turned communicative activities into an object called 'language'. In those Pacific languages that I have surveyed there is no equivalent of the abstract noun 'language' and consequently a lack of language names. The reification of language is basically a result of literacy. Following the arbitrary isolation of a small subset of linguistic activities as the basis for developing a literate language, objects such as dictionaries and grammars are created. As literacy and sedentary habits tend to go hand in hand, the impression that these objects were located in space was created. Pacific linguistics, as has been argued elsewhere in this book, has generally gone astray when taking such metaphorical reified actions for describable objects.

Literacy is seen to reflect truth

Related to what has been said just now is the question of differential practices in oral and literate societies for the establishment of 'truth'. In oral societies this is related to the authority of the speaker, to the fact that a statement is made over and over again or, as in the case of Meriam Mir of the Torres Straits, to grammatical correctness:

> My focus, therefore, is on a particular way of speaking, the ways of speaking which is the 'bar kak mir' of my title. Bar kak mir means, literally, 'curves-without talk'. The man who speaks bar kak – who speaks 'without curves' – is the man whose words are true. The man who is educated in the ways of dugong, and in the making of spears, will throw his spear only once, for the spear of educated man flies true and will strike its target. His spear is said to fly bar kak. The man who knows good formal language, and who is educated in the making of speech, need speak only once, for his speech is true. It is these few men who are said to command bar kak mir.
>
> (Cromwell 1980: 26)

Ong (1982) reports the absence of certain types of logical truths from oral societies:

> We know that formal logic is the invention of Greek culture after it had interiorized the technology of alphabetic writing, and so made a permanent part of its noetic resources the kind of thinking that alphabetic writing made possible. In light of this knowledge, Luaria's experiments with illiterates' reactions to formally syllogistic and inferential reasoning is particularly revealing. In brief, his illiterate subjects seemed not to operate with formal deductive procedures at all – which is not the same as to say that they could not think or that their thinking was not governed by logic, but only that they would not fit their thinking into pure logical forms, which they seem to have found uninteresting. Why should they be interesting? Syllogisms relate to thought, but in practical matters no one operates in formally stated syllogisms.
>
> (Ong 1982: 52)

Numerous writers have reported that printed messages are regarded as inherently true by the first few generations of literates. The editor of the Papua New Guinea newspaper *Wantok* (in Tok Pisin), Mihalic, observes: 'Our readers tend to take as gospel truth whatever is printed' (1977: 1,122ff.). The fact that most printed materials are of a religious nature and that incipient literates are directed towards taking them as true reinforces this. The power of the printed word thus is considerably greater than in older literate societies.

Taken together, the five points discussed here would seem to indicate that vernacular literacy is potentially as powerful an agent of social change and decline of traditional modes of expression and life as literacy in a metropolitan language. Contrary to what has been claimed by the supporters of literacy programmes, literacy has seldom emerged as a response to needs inherent in traditional societies but has in virtually all instances been used by outsiders to achieve certain objectives.

9 The impact of foreign language teaching

In these circumstances it may seem doubtful that schools can
have any positive role in ensuring the continued viability of
Oceanic languages.

(Benton 1981: 171)

INTRODUCTION

Education has been only one of the many new parameters recently
introduced into the Pacific language ecology in the last 100 years.[1]
Like other developments, its effects on the languages of the area have
been largely uncontrolled and the debate as to what contribution
education could make goes on unabated. The principal task of education has always been that of promoting certain social and economic
developments rather than either preserving or supplanting the languages of an area, although the latter motive has been a powerful one
from time to time and place to place.

Education in the Pacific area, as in most colonial and post-colonial
settings in the third and fourth world, has been based on the premise
that there exist major deficits, these having been variously identified
as spiritual, economic, cultural and so forth at different periods. It
was regarded as virtually axiomatic that the direction of knowledge
flow had to be from the Western 'developed' world to the Pacific
region. However, as this is not the place to survey the issue of
colonization through education as a whole. I shall instead comment on
the more restricted topics of language as a medium and language as a
subject of educational programmes. The two cannot always be neatly
separated, since Western languages, such as English, are increasingly
becoming both the medium and the message. I am dealing with a vast
area and I shall have to both be selective and resort to simplification
and generalization.

SOME PHASES IN THE HISTORY OF EDUCATION

Speaking very generally, one can distinguish the following phases:

1 use of vernaculars
2 attempts to impose monolingualism in a metropolitan language
3 transitional bilingualism
4 monolingualism in a powerful language
5 equitable bilingualism.

These phases are associated with the following sociopolitical situations:

1 colonization and separate development
2 assimilation policies in early nationalism
3 late nationalism and multiculturalism
4 technocratic post-modern societies
5 societies dominated by ecological thought.

Most countries of the area belong to category 2 with few late developers still being in category 1 which some richer more advanced countries are moving towards 3 and 5. The functions of education in the Pacific area varied greatly from period to period, as did the degree to which education was centralized. The differences that can be encountered are due to the degree of indigenous multilingualism, the pressure of pidgin languages, the colonial powers and various other factors. As this book aims at giving a top-down approach, many of the local features will have to be ignored. In Chapter 5 some more detailed analyses were given, however.

The earliest period, beginning shortly after the first contacts were made in the late eighteenth century, was one where education went hand in hand with missionization. Most missions initially operated on the assumption that the best way to penetrate and change traditional cultures was to employ traditional languages. In the large monolingual islands of Polynesia, where missionization began, this was not a major problem and the use of indigenous languages such as Tahitian, Samoan, Maori and Tongan soon became established in the educational process. However, with the smaller languages of Polynesia, this practice put considerable strain on manpower and resources and the practice of missionizing and educating their speakers in related larger languages soon became the common practice. Tahitian was employed in educating Easter Islanders and Tokelauans, and Samoan was made the mission and education language of the Ellice Islands (Tuvalu and Tokelau). As observed by Atoni (1975) at the Regional Bilingual Education Conference in Pago Pago:

The Tokelau Islands for many decades have been administered from West Samoa ... and because of this close association, most of the materials used for teaching and so forth have come from the Samoan education service. The Bible has not been written in Tokelauan and the Samoan Bible is used, so the effect has been that the Samoan language in written form has been in use in the Tokelau Islands. When Samoa became independent in 1962, the education material was developed locally or with the New Zealand Department of Education, and consequently the Tokelauan people are left with a very distorted knowledge of their own language.

(Atoni 1975: 129)

The implicit message to the speakers of Tokelauan and other small languages was that their languages were not worthy to be vehicles for obtaining new, non-traditional information and their speakers often reacted by abandoning them.

Foreign language teaching in this period occurred almost as a by-product and it comprised the teaching of related more powerful, indigenous languages that were conceived as future first languages. The teaching of metropolitan languages by the missions, on the other hand, was much less widely promoted initially, as it was seen as both unnecessary and potentially dangerous. However, following the colonization of the area, some missions were eager to promote the colonizer's language, e.g. the Catholic Church in parts of German New Guinea. Its prelate, Limbrock, is reported (*Deutsches Kolonialblatt* 1901: 523) to have advocated education in German only and to have said:

Nobody should expect that all the tribes of New Guinea will give up their language and become perfect speakers of our language. This, by its very nature, is a task for several generations.

A similar argument was made much more recently by Renck (1990):

That one side effect of education in English would be the mass-unemployment of more or less 'educated' people, and as a consequence, disappointment and lawlessness, was seen already by some in the early 1960's. The violence in the towns of Papua New Guinea, and the organized bands of 'rascals' all over the country are its most obvious consequences today.

(Renck 1990: 159)

As missions entered the more multilingual areas of Micronesia and Melanesia, the policy of promoting large mission lingue franche as media of all education missionization became more pronounced, with languages such as Kâte (Papua New Guinea) or Mota (Solomons, Vanuatu, New Hebrides) becoming widely used.

The policy of promoting genuine vernaculars, no matter how small, in education was adopted by only a few missions, most prominent amongst them the Summer Institute of Linguistics (SIL). However, as Litteral (1985) made it clear, the use of the vernacular as a medium in education is transitional. In his proposal for a national education plan for Papua New Guinea he conceives of an initial transition to Tok Pisin followed by a shift to English as a medium of instruction at higher levels of education.

Changes in mission language policies occurred mainly in the wake of the colonial carving up of the Pacific area and, as providers of religion as well as education, the mission was often seen to be promoting the national language of the colonizers among their flock.

Renck (1990: 152ff.) and the authors of numerous articles in Wurm (1977) offer detailed accounts of the situation in North East New Guinea. New Guinea is of particular interest for three reasons:

1 It was controlled first by Germany and subsequently as a mandate of Australia.
2 During the mandate one can observe the interplay between specific Australian policies and world opinion on educational matters.
3 It was administered jointly with Papua which had been first British and subsequently an Australian colony.

Before North East New Guinea was taken out of private company control by the German government at the turn of the century, education was in the hands of the missions. Some of these operated from English-speaking countries and continued to teach English or through English, others operated from Germany and tended to promote larger local languages as well as teaching some German (see Mühlhäusler 1979). It was only towards the very end of German control that an ambitious educational programme was formulated whose main aim was the teaching of German and through German in government-controlled schools. This programme, as pointed out in Chapter 7, was never implemented.

The role of government continued to be weak in the first twenty years of Australian administration (1914–34), and German-run missions continued to implement their own policies, including that of teaching German and through German in some schools.

Still, although some mission groups taught English in their schools between the two World Wars, the teaching media which were much more frequently used were vernaculars, church lingue franche, and

Pidgin; and the administration, having hardly any schools of its own, could not have enforced any language policy with regard to English. Besides this, people in the administration too realized the value of vernaculars in education, and tried to promote them. W. C. Groves, who had been in the country as an anthropologist since 1922, and who became the first Director of Education after the Second World War, had written in 1936: 'When English is widespread in New Guinea villages, they will no longer be New Guinea villages. And a sorry day that indeed will be'.

(Renck 1990: 152)

Although such policies were intended to preserve a relatively conservative status quo, in actual fact they laid foundations for a radical restructuring of Papua New Guinea's linguistic ecology. Most important, they put into place and strengthened a hierarchical order of the languages spoken in the area of the type:

Language of colonial power
Pidgin English
Mission lingua franca
Local vernaculars.

At the same time, mission education prepared the indigenous population for becoming part of the colonial workforce, where languages of wider communication such as Pidgin English dominated. Finally, missions also contributed to the expansion of infrastructures (roads, mission shipping lines, etc.) that enhanced those lingue franche.

There was an implicit or explicit policy on the part of many missions to restrict access to English, arguing that English language and culture would lead to the destruction of indigenous cultures. What the missionaries did not realize is that the least powerful languages are not threatened by the most powerful ones but rather by those which are just a little more powerful. Enhancing the status of a small number of local languages had from this perspective severe consequences for many smaller languages.

The use of a vernacular in education in numerous instances involved the teaching of a foreign language (or at least a foreign dialect). The number of children that were educated in their real mother tongue was very small in many parts of the Pacific, but even those who were in this lucky position were hardly sheltered from cultural and linguistic change. The language used in the schools was in part engineered and changed to suit the aims of cultural change. Such policies of cultural and religious change through vernacular education in many instances were replaced by policies of assimilation with the metropolitan languages. Teleni (1990) summarizes studies by Ochs, Schieffelin and Duranti in the mid-1980s as follows:

> In the past, the relationship of language and identity has been neglected by language planners. Duranti and Ochs present ethnographic data on Samoan society to support their contention that a global effect of literacy instruction is a change in the social identity of the child. Traditional Samoan caregiver speech and socialisation through child–adult relationships are juxtaposed with literacy instruction in the school. The different behaviours, expectations, attitudes, values and instructional methods in the two processes provide persuasive evidence for their hypothesis. This paper points to possible unanticipated outcomes and concomitants to language and literacy education programs. Such insights, yielded by ethnographic fieldwork, are of value to language planners.
>
> (Teleni 1990: 288)

TOWARDS MONOLINGUALISM IN THE METROPOLITAN LANGUAGE

The imposition of the metropolitan languages and outspoken assimilation policies took different forms in different countries and occurred at different times, though it tended to occur after the abolition of vernacular education policies. In the words of Topping:

> although the shift from mission to government schools did not occur simultaneously throughout the Pacific, when it did, the pattern was essentially the same.
>
> (Topping 1991: 12)

The most notorious and radical example of assimilation is found in Australia in the form of the dormitory system which began in 1883 and ended only in the early 1970s (see Read 1981). Under this system

> children were taken from their parents, placed in separate girls' and boys' dormitories, and permitted to see their parents for only a few hours a week.
>
> (Schmidt 1991a: 12)

Annette Schmidt continues to spell out some of the linguistic consequences of this assimilation policy:

> The dormitory system had devastating consequences for Aboriginal language vitality. For many languages, it effectively destroyed the vital intergenerational language transmission link by severely disrupting family structure and parent–child relationships. Children

were forcibly removed from the social structure and the set of primary role-relationships which enabled the acquisition of Aboriginal language, sociocultural values, knowledge and skills. In effect, they were denied the link with their cultural and linguistic heritage. Moreover, any opportunity to use an Aboriginal language in the dormitory system was scarce – children in a single dormitory often came from radically different language groups and so could not understand each other's Aboriginal language. For example, Roger Hart, a Barrow Point language speaker from North Queensland, recalls that he arrived at Hope Valley dormitory speaking only the Barrow Point language. He knew neither English or Guugu Yimithirr, the languages of the mission: 'I couldn't understand them. I couldn't speak to anyone because they didn't know my language. The only one I had to talk to was the hospital cat. He was my friend. I talked language to him.'

Furthermore, speaking an Aboriginal language in the dormitory lifestyle was frequently actively discouraged on many missions by punishment and rebuke. As one woman brought up in a Queensland dormitory system explained: 'So I never picked up language. We used to get cane if we talked language there [in the dormitory]. No language. It was all English then.' Thus, through the dormitory system, Aboriginal individuals were involuntarily subject to rapid and radical social and linguistic upheaval, triggered by the white population's determination that the indigenous inhabitants of the continent abandon their linguistic and cultural heritage and social organisation in favour of the English language and associated values.

(Schmidt 1991a: 12)

The imposition of English as the sole medium of education is also found in many other parts of the Pacific. Particularly hard hit were smaller islands, where education in a local language would have added significantly to the cost of education. During the 1974 Pago Pago Meeting (South Pacific Commission 1975) a large number of delegates reported very similar consequences. Examples include Niue, American Samoa and Western Samoa. Other areas discussed below include Papua New Guinea, Chatham Islands, Nauru, Fiji and Hawaii.

Niue

Niue (Hafe Vilitama reporting). Mr Vilitama attributed much of the present confusion about Niuean goals and identity to the long-time colonial association of the island with New Zealand. Earlier mission schools operating in the Niuean language were gradually replaced by government schools emphasizing English and an academic curriculum. This has favoured migration by many Niueans to New Zealand in search of material betterment through employment in that country. More than half of all Niueans now reside in New Zealand. At home, Niuean culture has lost respect and the language is infused with English borrowings. Social cleavage exists between older and younger generations and between those with experience in New Zealand and those without it.

(South Pacific Commission 1975: 9)

American Samoa

American Samoa (Mere T. Betham reporting). Mrs Betham noted that the earlier U.S. Naval Administration sought to Americanize Samoans. Interior Department policy, since 1951, continues to emphasize school use of English. In practice, the vernacular is used by many Samoan teachers to explain concepts not readily understood in English. Formal recognition of the need to teach Samoan language and culture began about a decade ago, when educational television was instituted. Education Department objectives were redefined in 1971 to promote greater respect for Samoan culture and fluency and literacy in both Samoan and English.

(South Pacific Commission 1975: 11)

Details of these policies have been given by Baldauf (1990).

Western Samoa

1 In the early fifties, the New Zealand Administrator in Western Samoa reported annually to his Government that the language of the people of Samoa is taught in the primary schools and is in fact the vehicle of instruction at that level. However, there was a big difference between the official report and what actually took place in the classroom. The Samoan parents and teachers believed that 'being educated' is learning to speak English, therefore, every school subject was taught in English. The quality and accuracy of the English used depended on the individual teacher's command of the English language and there was no attempt to introduce a 'uniform approach'. The students were more at home in Samoan and had very few opportunities for using the English language outside the classroom.

2 The practice of using a foreign language as the vehicle of instruction by teachers who were not fluent or confident in the language, added to the unrelatedness of formal schooling to the reality of life lived by both the teachers and students.

(South Pacific Commission 1975: 76)

Many educators subscribed to the atomistic view that the introduction of English had no great effects on other aspects of the indigenous cultures. Thus, Benton (1981: 100) quotes the Superintendent of Education in the Cook Islands as having said: 'it is important to preserve native institutions but not the language'.

Papua New Guinea

Extensive documentation of educational policies in Papua New Guinea can be found in Wurm (1977). In spite of the widespread use of Tok Pisin as a lingua franca, post-war administrations have invested much time and energy to replace it with English, particularly in the area of education and public life.

Gunther, in 1958, in the capacity of Assistant Administrator of Papua New Guinea, is reported by Renck (1990: 153) to have stated:

There is no education until people have a knowledge of English. Teach them English, English and more English, this is what they want. . . . Only Christianity can replace the original philosophies, legends, pagan practices and supernatural fears that 510 tongues have engendered. It is only by removal of these 510 tongues and the acceptance of a common language that the end of many unnatural behaviours can be achieved.

Chatham Islands

In other areas not represented at the South Pacific Commission the early commencement of English-only policies had effectively eliminated the indigenous languages. One such example is the Chatham Islands where the indigenous Moriori languages were first weakened by introduced Maori and English, and where subsequently Maori also came under attack. Smythe (1984) writes:

In 1879, the Education Department took control of the native schools from the Department of Native Affairs. The Maoris of the time wanted a chance to compete in the English speaking dominated society. The Education Department with the same end in view directed that the use of Maori be forbidden in the schools. In the native schools Maori crafts were included in the curriculum and in return for extra curricular activities, such as cleaning the school, the pupils received free exercise books and other stationery.

(Smythe 1984: 4)

Nauru

Another small island where a foreign education programme was imposed was Nauru. Jupp (1988) points out that

Australia had direct responsibility for the island of Nauru after its seizure from Germany in 1914, until it became independent in 1968. During this period it was administered as a territory, constituting a United Nations trusteeship after the Second World War, during which time it had been occupied by Japan. Indigenous Nauruans were Australian protected persons and were eligible to apply for naturalization. They were educated in English, with a curriculum based on that used in Victorian schools.

(Jupp 1988: 727)

The English educational policy, as is well known, also had a detrimental effect on larger Pacific languages in formerly monolingual areas such as Aotearoa (New Zealand), Fiji and Hawaii. I shall not repeat Benton's excellent and detailed accounts of the effect on the Maori language (Benton 1981), but will comment briefly on the other two countries.

Fiji

Fiji was one of the British colonies where an English-only policy in education was seen as an instrument of reducing friction between population groups (in this case indigenous Fijians and the descendants of and introduced Indian labourers). At the 1974 South Pacific Commission meeting the Fijian delegate reported, however,

that the requirement that curriculum content be British-oriented contributed to the depreciation of Fijian language and custom. Following independence in 1970, steps were taken toward the great utilization of Fijian-oriented materials in the primary grades. He noted some resistance by the people to this trend because of their continuing higher respect for the English language as a means towards better job opportunities and higher education.

(South Pacific Commission 1975: 9)

As we have seen, Milner (1984) reported that such lip-service to Fijian has had little concrete effect (see p. 228).

Hawaii

Hawaii, like other American-controlled parts of the Pacific (Samoa, Guam, Philippines and Micronesia), was subjected to an English-only policy in education for a long time.

Over a brief period of twenty years (1870 to 1890) the (mainly Protestant) missionaries operating in Hawaii had built up an impressive elementary school system which attracted large proportions of the population. School attendance increased from 21,000 in 1824 to 37,000 in 1831 and 52,000 or two-fifths of the population by 1831 (Kuykendall 1968: 106). In 1835 school attendance was made compulsory for children above four years of age. In the 1830s new religious groups began to appear on the scene, a direct result being that by 1840 the universal schooling in the Hawaiian language was not sufficient to strengthen either the cultural or the political aspects of the native Hawaiian. Ever since the first contacts with the Europeans, the numbers of Hawaiians had fallen, a fact that is reflected in school attendance.

1847	19,644
1850	15,308
1853	12,705
1854	10,241

(Data adapted from Kuykendall 1968: 357)

With the decline in the numbers, the belief in the traditional language and culture also declined.

The Minister of Public Instruction, the American, Armstrong, who had previously praised the common Hawaiian schools, began to lend support to a change in the medium of instruction.

> Armstrong discussed the subject of English schools for native Hawaiians in his reports to the legislature in 1850, 1851, 1852, 1853, and 1854. He held it to be a certainty that English 'must, eventually, become the language of the natives.' In 1853 he wrote:

> On my tours around the Islands, I have found parents everywhere, even on the remote island of Niihau, most anxious to have their children taught the English language; and the reason they generally gave was a most sound and intelligent one, that without it – they will, by-and-by be nothing, and the white man everything.

He said that the people were willing to do what they could to aid in supporting such schools, but they were poor and the cost of English schools would be very great. 'The burden of English schools is too heavy to be sustained by natives generally, without aid from government.' He therefore recommended an appropriation by the legislature to aid in the support of such schools.

The legislature of 1853 appropriated $1,500 for the support of English schools for Hawaiians and this was used in promoting the study of English in select schools already established. In 1854 a law was enacted 'for the encouragement and support of English schools for Hawaiian youth;' it provided for the appointment of a board of directors for English schools in each district of the kingdom and authorized the establishment of such schools, to be supported in part by government funds and in part by contributions from the people.

(Kuykendall 1968: 361)

The missionaries, too, had begun to change their views and in 1854 the American Protestant missionaries voted that

in the opinion of this meeting it is expedient that the Hawaiian Government and the friends of education make immediate and strenuous efforts to impart a knowledge of the English language to the natives of these islands.

(Kuykendall 1968: 361)

The result was a rapid increase in official school teaching through the English medium and small temporary and often inefficient schools, 'whose only principal object was to teach the English language to native Hawaiians' (Kuykendall 1968: 365).

Hawaiian was further weakened by the rapid influx of foreign plantation workers from 1876 onwards, and 'the native population was submerged under a polyglot flood of imported labourers' (Reinecke 1938: 779). This increased multilingualism, a common consequence of colonization in the Pacific, helped accelerate the movement towards instruction in English only. In 1876

English was the medium of instruction of 31.3 per cent of the school children, in 1886, of 77.6 per cent, in 1895, of 99.5 per cent, in 1902, of all.

(Reinecke 1938: 780)

Education in Hawaii, like elsewhere in the Pacific, appears to have done little permanently to strengthen the indigenous languages. It is the change in educational policy which helped accelerate the demise of Hawaiian from 1850 onwards. Subsequent policies were aimed at reducing the varieties of introduced languages and, in particular, were attracted by the emergence of Pidgin English which had become the language of intercultural communication. More on this language has been said in Chapter 4 on pidgins and creoles. There exists a vast body of educational literature (summarized in J. E. Reinecke 1969) on the desirability of introducing the 'clear, intelligent speaking of English' (Wilson 1937: 106) and this sentiment became particularly strong during the Second World War in the face of threats from Japan (Okura 1943):

> Many of us think of the 'Speak English' campaign as something new. Let me point out that it is as old as the schools, for the schools and other educational agencies have been working on this for years.
>
> Speaking good English is particularly important in Hawaii. There is no doubt that Hawaii is one of our nation's main lines of offence against our ruthless enemies. It is essential that we in Hawaii unite in order to maintain and even improve that position. One way of becoming united is through one common language – the American language. We need to think American, and since we think with words, we must try to use only American speech. Everyone must try his best to speak American, and he must avoid using any foreign language, especially Japanese language, since that is the language of the key enemy in the Pacific.
>
> (Okura 1943: 268)

Seen from the perspective of someone who is not an American (Nayar 1991), the linguistic outcome of such policies in Hawaii and in other American possessions in the Pacific

> reflects attempts by administrative bigotry and jingoism systematically to discount and denigrate local languages and to 'civilize' and 'emancipate' the natives by forcing the wonderful gift of the English language down their throats.
>
> (Nayar 1991: 322)

These policies continue. Sato (1990: 3) quotes the following extract from the Hawai'i Board of Education Memorandum on proposed language policy:

> Standard English will be the mode of oral communication for students and staff in the classroom setting and all other school related settings except when the objectives cover native Hawaiian or foreign language instruction and practice.
>
> (excerpted from Hawai'i Board of Education Memorandum on proposed language policy, 1987)

The English language continues to be the most influential introduced language of the region. Assimilation to languages other than English has, on the whole, been much less widespread and much less successful in its long-term effects. By the time Spain initiated the Hispanization process in the Philippines (Bernabe 1986) in 1865, time was running out for it as a colonial power in the Pacific and at the end of its control in 1898 only about 2.5 per cent of the population could speak Spanish. German policies, as already mentioned, came too late to have any significant impact (Mühlhäusler 1980). The case of Dutch is more complex. After many years of reluctance to spread the language in the Dutch East Indies, more vigorous efforts to do so began in the 1920s and only two decades before the end of Dutch colonial control, Moeliono (1994) reports:

> the estimated total number of four hundred thousand people, who in 1940 had a knowledge of Dutch, may be indicative of the relatively minor role of the language *vis-à-vis* the total native population of about seventy million.
>
> (Moeliono 1994: 119)

What Moeliono ignores are the indirect effects of Dutch, helped by the fact that both the transformation of Indonesian society and the creation of Bahasa Indonesia almost exclusively involved the Dutch-educated elite and that this very far-reaching restructuring was mediated by this elite.

Among the dramatic changes brought about by Dutch educational policies, discussed in the Indonesian journal *Prisma* (September 1990) we find the following:

1 A Western notion of language as a tool of communication replaced the indigenous notion of bahasa which unlike Western languages,

> was neither simply a tool of communication nor a system of codes or symbols that arbitrarily signified something else (a reality). It was a social activity. It was socially bound, constructed and reconstructed in specific settings, rather than scientifically and universally rule-governed.
>
> (Heryanto 1990: 43)

2 Western notions of grammar and discussing grammar were adopted almost wholesale, a consequence of subscribing to the Western notion of language as pointed out by Heryanto (1990: 50).

3 A vast number of new Western concepts were either borrowed or introduced via loan translations, resulting in the intertranslatability

of Indonesian with the languages of Western industrialized societies but much less translatability with vernacular languages of the area.

4 The Roman script replaced other scripts that had been used before the arrival of the Dutch.

In sum, Bahasa Indonesia exhibits very strong Dutch influence at all levels as do the methods employed for teaching it in the schools of Indonesia.

Portuguese, in spite of its having been the first European language in many parts of the Pacific rim and the Indonesian archipelago and in spite of its widespread use as a lingua franca throughout the region from the seventeenth to nineteenth centuries, has all but disappeared. Even in Portugal's last remaining overseas province, Macau, English, in spite of having no official status, is making significant inroads. Harrison (1984) reports:

> Four large schools have English language sections where the medium of instruction for most subjects is English. They are in the Yuet Wah, Santa Rosa de Lima, Perpetual Help and Sacred Heart Schools, which are all Roman Catholic foundations, though their pupils are from a range of religious backgrounds. It is possible for a Macau child to be enrolled in an English medium kindergarten and to proceed through primary and secondary education with the same principal medium – Chinese being taught in Chinese, naturally ... at the University of East Asia, Macau and graduate after completing a degree course taught entirely in English. The number of parents wishing their children to attend English sections of Macau schools is enough to put an element of competition into initial enrolments and advertisements for kindergarten and primary enrolments stress requirements and times and places rather than facilities and educational or even examination successes.
>
> (Harrison 1984: 479)

It is particularly interesting to note that

> English language books are quite widely available and take up sizeable runs of shelf space in both new and second-hand book shops.
>
> (Harrison 1984: 480)

The only European language other than English which has achieved some lasting success has been French, particularly in the large territories of New Caledonia and Tahiti.

New Caledonia

New Caledonia is the major French settlers' colony in the Pacific with more than 50 per cent of the population being either French or inhabitants of a number of former French colonies. The indigenous Melanesian population speaks a larger number of languages and communalects. Early missionary attempts to educate the indigenous population in their own languages (and a small minority of advanced students in English) date from the 1840s but in 1863 the French administration prohibited the use of local languages in the schools and made French the obligatory language of education (see Rivierre 1985: 1,693ff.). In 1921 all publications in indigenous languages were banned and their oral use in school playgrounds was forbidden. A rigorous policy of French-only education persisted until the mid-1970s.[2] Programmes for bilingual education on a smaller scale were developed in the 1980s but unofficially French continues to dominate the education system.

The outcome of 100 years of French colonization may be summarized thus:

1 the clear dominance of French as both the language of education and the language of intergroup communication
2 the emergence of a group of urban Melanesians who have lost their mother tongue
3 widespread bilingualism among the Melanesians but not among other groups.

According to Schooling (1990) the success of French teaching policies has been less than spectacular and much knowledge of the indigenous language and culture has been retained. However, with the impact of new media such as television and video becoming only now felt among the Melanesians, and with the French attempts to make higher education available to more Melanesians, the decline of the remaining local languages could accelerate in the near future. The survival of most Melanesian languages, it should also be pointed out, is not the outcome of any deliberate policy to protect them, but probably more due to the neglect of French education and policy makers of the indigenous languages and cultures.

If the highly multilingual nature of New Caledonia has, until the mid-1970s, served as an excuse for using French at all levels of education, the same argument cannot be convincingly applied to Wallis, Fortune and Tahiti, which before the arrival of the colonizers were virtually monolingual. The French on Wallis took the superiority of their own language and culture for granted and what little education they provided was in French. As Rensch observed:

although there is no overt French policy to suppress the language, a long term educational goal of integration through gallicization is endangering the status of the native language and will in the near future affect its viability.

(Rensch 1990: 231)

Tahiti

Tahitian, like Maori, was used as a medium of education and literacy before French colonization began and, at one point, literature in this language was both widespread and prestigious (see Mühlhäusler 1987a). However, after this initial period of recognition of Tahitian came about 100 years of neglect and suppression by a French-only policy. Lavondès (1971) reports:

French language policy should be studied not merely on the level of Polynesia, but in relation to the overall community formed by France and all those territories that once comprised the French Union. Such a study would unquestionably be of interest, but would surely exceed the compass of this article.

It is education on all levels (primary and secondary) and in all forms (public and private) that is the chief instrument of the policy of gallicization. From the most elementary level, all education is dispensed in French. At no stage in public education is Tahitian taught. Use of the vernacular is forbidden in the schools, not only to the teachers, but to the pupils, who may not speak it in class or even during recreation. The object of these measures is to help the children to acquire a practical knowledge of French and keep them from considering it a dead language that they cannot use in daily life.

(Lavondès 1971: 1,118)

At the time Lavondès was writing, Tahitian was still growing in importance, having become the lingua franca of immigrants from various outlying island groups (Marquesas, Tuamotu, etc.) Furthermore, because of low school attendance there was a significant number of Tahitian monolinguals.

From the 1970s onward due to many new motives (television, a growing number of metropolitan migrants, tourism, employment) and many more opportunities – a significantly larger number of high schools were learning French (see Corne 1979) and the introduction of bilingual programmes teaching French as a foreign language in the first years of school in 1982 – the number of Tahitians proficient in French and educated in French has increased significantly. Corne

(1979: 658) speaks of a progressive qualitative and quantitative expansion of French.

Whether further urbanization, new media and greater mobility of the population will lead to a gradual decline of Tahitian cannot be predicted at present, but it seems a distinct possibility. Equally likely is that English will again play a more important role in Tahiti. The relative strength of English and weakness of French can be illustrated with data from Vanuatu, the former French-British condominium of the New Hebrides, where one can observe a significant decline in the popularity of French as the medium of instruction in spite of very considerable French support for this type of education. The data in Table 9.1 were given by Charpentier and Tryon (1982).

Table 9.1 Students enrolled in government schools (Vanuatu)

	French-medium	*English-medium*	*Proportion in English-medium* (%)
1980	12,266	11,303	47.9
1982	10,674	11,024	50.8
1983	10,496	11,748	52.8
1984	10,687	12,671	54.3
1987	9,282	15,543	62.6

The 1992 change in government favouring French-educated politicians may reverse this trend, however.

A similar switch to English has already been commented on for Macau and a future Independent New Caledonia may also revise its linguistic dependence on French in favour of English, which is more widely spoken elsewhere in Melanesia.

Attempts to impose monolingualism in the colonial language came under attack from educationists from the 1950s onwards, and spurred on by (albeit somewhat inconclusive) 1953 UNESCO findings that education in a child's mother tongue provided better learning and reduced behaviour problems. These findings were implemented in one form or other in several new nation-states and also found their way into colonial language policies in the form of transitional bilingual education. I shall now comment on these two developments.

TRANSITIONAL BILINGUALISM: INTRODUCTION

If the motto of education from the turn of the century to about 1960 was one of assimilation, the new key words are bilingualism and multiculturalism, particularly in those countries where the dominance of one language is no longer in doubt. Thus, whilst the newly emerged nations of Indonesia, Taiwan and Malaysia pursue a policy of imposing a powerful language, other countries such as Australia, New Zealand and the United States (in Hawaii and other dependencies) act differently.

Before beginning to look at latter-day bilingual education it should be noted that the sort of bilingualism that is promoted and institutionalized in the 1990s differs quite significantly from pre-existing indigenous patterns of bi, dual- and multilingualism. Most notably traditional patterns

1 tended to be relatively long-lasting and stable
2 were embedded in a sophisticated cultural support system
3 tended to be egalitarian and reciprocal
4 had clear social functions
5 occurred in a largely oral context with little formal teaching or learning
6 developed as a response to local needs rather than national policies.

The principal motive in all contemporary bilingual education surveyed is it that it should involve minimally one modern international or national language and, in a few countries (e.g. Singapore, Philippines, Malaysia), a modern national plus modern international language. A similarly strong fact in bilingual education is that it tends to be a response to circumstances newly created by colonial powers, not a traditional problem. Thus, bilingual education in Australia primarily means education in English and another migrant language. In Hawaii it involves catering for the Japanese and other immigrant groups, the Chinese in Tahiti or Hindi in Fiji.

The practices and problems of national bilingual education are best illustrated with some case studies.

THE SOUTHERN PHILIPPINES

In discussing the situation, Randall (1983) begins by pointing out that bilingual programmes are not a response to particular local needs:

> For the Philippines, however, the 'bilingualism' debate is not about the provision of minority-language services to national minorities

but about whether it is desirable and feasible to counter American colonial influence by making education, media, and government services bilingual in English and in Tagalog-based Filipino. The attempt is to lessen the grip English has on the nation by instituting a dual-language policy. At the same time, however, the bilingualism policy achieves an effect quite opposite to similarly named policies in North America, for Philippine bilingualism policies deliberately restrict access to education, information, and government among those who, for whatever reason, do not know English and Filipino.

(Randall 1983: 57)

Neither English or Filipino feature prominently in the everyday lives of the majority of inhabitants of the Southern Philippines such as those of Zamboanga City, whose linguistic situation is characterized as follows:

To sum up then, there are at least ten languages spoken either as a first language or as an auxiliary language by significant numbers of people in Zamboanga: Arabic, Bisaya, 'Chinese', English, Filipino, Sinama, Subanun, Tausug, Yakan, and Zamboangueño. Arabic, Chinese, and English are completely unrelated to Philippine languages and to each other, and Zamboangueño is only remotely related to English and the Philippine languages.

(Randall 1983: 62)

Randall discusses some of the recurring communication problems in this multilingual and multicultural environment and suggests:

One would hope, of course, that language education policies could somehow be designed to provide Zamboanga people with the language skills needed to live in Zamboanga. In this respect it is instructive to look at policies Manila is attempting to implement in the area. In general, they were formulated as national policies with apparently little informed knowledge about whether they were feasible or desirable in the Zamboanga area. Given the recent date of relevant research, this is hardly surprising.

(Randall 1983: 65)

In his view, educational policies that promote fluency in Zamboanga, Simano, Tansug and Subanun combined with promoting literacy and media coverage in these languages would go a great length to resolving communication problems in the area. As it is, only a small elite profit from education whilst the majority will continue to remain marginalized.

The case of the Southern Philippines should alert us to the problem of identifying the linguistic resources most likely to be useful in later life to those students educated. A simplistic notion of mother tongue education is certainly of little help, as will be shown in the next section.

BILINGUAL MIGRANT EDUCATION IN AUSTRALIA

That there are numerous problems with the bilingual programmes that grew out of the policy of multiculturalism of the 1970s has been observed, among others, by Foster and Stockley (1988). Of the many problems let me single out just one: which language other than English should be taught? Most educationists have selected one of the better known national languages such as Italian, Modern Greek (Dimotiki Katarevousa), Castillian Spanish, or Standard High German, ignoring the fact that a large proportion of migrant children were not native speakers of the ethnic language but rather spoke local dialects or non-recognized languages such as Galician, Macedonian, Sardinian, or Catalan, etc. The actual practice of bilingual education thus was not very different from that of the Southern Philippines and certainly far removed from the ideal of mother tongue education which inspired bilingual education in the first place.

Again, costly mistakes could have been avoided by proper socio-linguistic research.

Smolicz (e.g. 1982) has carried out detailed sociolinguistic research, mainly in South Australia. His writings illustrate, on the one hand, the very considerable group-specific differences in attitudes to language maintenance and teaching of migrant languages, and on the other, the lack of clear government educational policies that could create or maintain the ecological conditions needed for the long-term survival of such languages. He is particularly outspoken in his attack on policies of 'residual multiculturalism' which are aimed at 'preserving' only fragments of the migrant culture (1982: 30).[3]

Bilingual education involving Aboriginal languages ran into similar problems for very much the same reasons. It was inspired by Gough Whitlam, the Prime Minister of Australia, who stated on 14 December 1972:

The Federal Government will launch a campaign to have Aboriginal children living in distinctive Aboriginal communities given their primary education in Aboriginal languages.

The Government will also supplement education for Aboriginal children with the teaching of traditional Aboriginal arts, crafts and skills mostly by Aborigines themselves.

(Whitlam, quoted in McGrath 1983: 51)

By 1973 the scholarly basis for a bilingual programme was created (Watts, McGrath and Tandy 1973) and the first five schools were set up. There are two types of programmes, both of them leading to dominance in English in the upper grades. McGrath (1983) reports:

Type A Based on initial literacy in the Aboriginal language, followed by literacy in English. This type of program depends on the availability of a practical orthography in the Aboriginal language, and on the availability of teaching materials in that language.
Type B Based on early oral instruction in the Aboriginal language together with oral instruction in English where appropriate. Literacy is attained in English only, but oral instruction continues in the Aboriginal language where this is feasible. This type of program is used where a particular orthography of the Aboriginal language has not been established, where materials are not available for teaching initial literacy in that language, or where a Creole-pidgin dialect has largely replaced the Aboriginal language.

(McGrath 1983: 52–3)

The programme as conceived, however, ignored a number of important aspects of Aboriginal languages and language use. Thus, in a study of one of the first Northern Territory bilingual schools, Milingimbi (established in 1973) (reported in Christie 1984), it was found that there were a number of fundamental problems that had not been sufficiently addressed, in particular, the myth of the 'universal child':

Many writers assume that, underneath, all children are alike. The reason why we find difficulties communicating with Aboriginal children, they are saying, is that they are linguistically and sociolinguistically different from us; if they could understand what we are saying they would learn. (Much of the less informed enthusiasm for bilingual education is based on this assumption.) In this view, Aboriginal children are not considered to be different, in any fundamental way, from their white counterparts. Little mention is made of the pervasive Aboriginal world view, which gives rise to both the semantic and sociolinguistic structures of the children's language and to their interpretations of the language they hear. Aboriginal differences in world view, in classroom perspectives, personal goals or preferred modes of interpretation are seldom considered to be inhibitors of classroom communication.

(Christie and Harris 1985: 81)

When examining the learning culture dominant among the children of the Milingimbian school, it emerged that

> these children believe that the means whereby they will attain their education are threefold. Firstly, their mere presence in school ritually endows them with education. Secondly, the careful performance of ritualised classroom activities (copying from the blackboard, reading loudly in chorus, etc.) is efficacious. Thirdly, the status of educated individuals is marked by their successful progression through the age grade stages as they move up through school (rather than by any particular school-learned skill like the ability to read and write). The individual creative and self-directed effort which is crucial to academic learning, is de-emphasised and, in fact, considered irrelevant.
>
> Naturally, these Aboriginal student perceptions are attended by expectations of appropriate teacher behaviour. Teachers, say the Milingimbi children, must be firm and provide their pupils with plenty of work. (Work, that is, which conforms to their ritualised conception of appropriate classroom tasks.) Teachers who give work which is not ritualised, who make their pupils think or talk about what they are learning, and teachers who provide regular feedback concerning errors, are resisted as pushy, hostile and irrelevant. Using the words of a Milingimbi teacher,
>
> *'The children seem to think that addition should be enough and it's unfair to have to do harder ones. Any teacher that gives them maths that require problem solving is, so far as they are concerned, just being ornery . . . Teachers who badger children into using their brains all the time are just being flies in the ointment'. (Christie, 1984)*
>
> Christie also found that, while a few teachers had some appreciation of this situation, they failed to identify the children's perspectives as a reflection of traditional culture. Rather, they were mystified by much of the children's behaviour, some of them labelling it as lazy or uninterested, and generally attributed their pupils' failure to the irrelevance of formal education, or to the lack of support from parents.

(Christie and Harris 1985: 83)

Awareness, among education policy makers and white teachers, of such sociolinguistic factors is on the increase and the search for better bilingual programmes continues.[4] One of the more radical departures will be discussed in the next section.

The principal aim of the bilingual programme surveyed appears to be to smooth the transition from an indigenous vernacular to proficiency in the dominant language. The preservation and strengthening of the indigenous language in many instances is only a secondary goal and in those cases where it has been a primary consideration the relationship between bilingual education and language preservation has remained ill understood.

There have also been voices arguing that bilingual education could speed up the assimilation into the majority culture and the loss of indigenous languages. A particularly cynical approach discussed at length in Benton (1981) is that of Kloss (1977), who suggests that

1 languages with fewer than 50,000 speakers have no future anyway
2 their disappearance can be sped up by means of bilingual programmes that make small languages compulsory school subjects.

The problems experienced with most bilingual programmes have come under intense scrutiny. As LePage (1964, 1992) has pointed out, many of the assumptions of the 1953 UNESCO Document on teaching in the vernaculars now seem highly problematic. Apart from the fact that the notion of mother tongue is highly variable, and, as has been shown in this chapter, liable to be exploited for all kinds of political objectives, there is growing evidence that speakers of many smaller traditional languages do not wish to see their languages used for education literacy. As pointed out by Charpentier (1992) for Vanuatu, where more than 100 Melanesian vernaculars are spoken besides the official languages of English, French and Bislama, for the Melanesians the proper role of the vernaculars is regarded as that of serving as an oral means of communication about traditional matters, whilst the official languages are for teaching new and extended ideas and literacy. The only ones trying to change this *ordre naturel* are white linguists and educators. Underlying such white views is the ill-founded belief that by elevating vernaculars to school languages one might 'empower' those speakers and help preserve such vernaculars. However, the very notion of empowerment is one that is absent from the traditional Melanesian language ecology and there are neither the resources nor the political will to empower 105 Melanesian languages and their speakers.

Preservation of traditional languages and access of their speakers to political and economic power thus must rely on solutions other than bilingual education.

SOME NEW DEPARTURES: EQUITABLE BILINGUALISM

Dissatisfaction with conventional approaches to bilingual education has given way, in some areas, to more radical experiments outside the

educational mainstream. Of the various alternatives to institutionalized bilingual education, let me single out two:

1 the two-way schools in Aboriginal Australia
2 the Language Nests of New Zealand Aotearoa.

The former approach (discussed by McConvell 1981) developed out
of the realization that (as has been commented on in many sections of
the present book) white-indigenous relations were one way: 'the
system was "one-way" – *kartiya* way – in terms of power relations as
well as teaching content' (McConvell 1981: 62). The 'two-way alternative is based on the concept of a two-way flow in reciprocity and
exchange between groups. This is basic to Aboriginal social life, but is
present in most human social relations to some degree. A programme
developed at the Shelly School (Western Australia) for Manjiljarra
and Nyangumarta children was established after intensive consulta-
tions with the Aboriginal community, along lines that differed significantly from government-sponsored programmes (McConvell 1981:
65):

1 The school programme was preceded by an extensive adult vernacular literacy programme.
2 The Nyangumarta programme was first introduced in the upper
grades of the school and only later came into the earlier grades.
3 Programmes in two Aboriginal languages were started in the one
community.

Whilst decisions such as the second one would be seen to run counter
to the aims of Western educationists, there are excellent cultural
reasons for it:

> In many communities young children may use a different form of
> language ('child language' or 'baby talk') even up to seven or eight
> years old. Later introduction of vernacular literacy might then be
> chosen so that this can coincide with the consolidation of adult
> speech. Introduction of more than one language program in a
> community might be thought necessary to satisfy all groups that they
> are getting a fair deal, and to avoid repeating the original problem of
> teaching literacy to children in a foreign language, this time another
> Aboriginal language rather than English. If the two programs co-
> operate and share resources there is no reason why this solution in
> mixed communities should be very costly or troublesome.
>
> (McConvell 1981: 65)

McConvell, who has had the opportunity to observe the operations of
this two-way programme, expresses the view that it presents a viable

alternative to the 'current bilingual school framework [which] could be seen as playing into the hands of those who would undermine or destroy bilingual education' (McConvell 1981: 66).

The solutions that have emerged in New Zealand differ in that they involve postponing contact with English for the first years of the Maori child's education. In an update of earlier accounts by Benton and others, Peddie (1991) writes (following the proclamation of a new Education Act):

> Other recent developments strengthen the claim that Maori language has nevertheless become a critical factor in education and in other areas of government policy. As noted earlier, several Maori schools have now opened, modelled along the lines of the language nests, as Maori people increasingly turn to their own cultural strength to provide education for their children (Smith, forthcoming). At government level, an event of key importance was the Maori Language Commission. The Act gives Maori official status with English in arenas like the courts and parliament, while the Commission is to be involved in both promoting and preserving the Maori language. It must be added, however, that the total budget for the Commission is minute and that English remains the normal language of courts and parliament.
>
> (Peddie 1991: 29)

At present, limited budgetary resources and the very considerable degree to which urban Maoris have been acculturated into the English-speaking community remain major obstacles. However, positive policy and attitude changes would seem to provide some basis for an equitable long-term Maori–English bilingualism in Aotearoa-New Zealand. Very much the same can also be said for the much more limited attempts to reverse the decline of Hawaiian by means of 'Immersion Education' (Hawkins 1991).

There are a number of factors common to the 'new departures' discussed here. First, they all were developed in the region's Neo-Europe rather than the new indigenous nation-states. Second, they were introduced after English-only policies had dramatically reduced the viability of the indigenous vernaculars and thirdly, they were developed in a reaction against prevailing patterns of bilingual education and only subsequently given some official recognition. A great deal of rethinking will need to be done before such more equitable educational models have a chance of becoming widely adopted. One would like to think it possible that similar models of education will be imitated by small languages of the region which have not as yet lost most of their speakers and linguistic viability.

The metaphor of ecology for languages promoted in this book may be a useful one here. Ecological questions to be asked would have to include:

1 What role can educational measures play in preserving existing language ecologies?
2 How can education programmes fit into a language ecology?

Only once these major questions have been addressed can one turn to the details of classroom applications such as:

3 What ecological factors promoted the use and learning of languages *x, y*, etc. in a classroom?
4 What ecological factors are needed for languages used in education to thrive outside the classroom?

The ecological support system will differ from language to language, as will the role of language in maintaining other cultural values of a group. Unless such questions are addressed, educational measures will do little to check the trend towards more inequality among languages of the Pacific region.

CONCLUSIONS

It is probably not difficult to agree with Benton that education and school language policies have done little to ensure the continued viability of the languages of the Pacific area. Like other linguistic developments, educational language policies were devised with little or no understanding and/or respect for the complexities of the linguistic ecology of the area and, in many instances, education has been seen as an instrument of radically altering the linguistic situation.

Education, in this chapter, has referred not to indigenous patterns of socialization and imparting knowledge to a new generation, but rather education introduced into the area with a view to missionization, modernization or otherwise changing its inhabitants. Such education is the primary vehicle for the knowledge flow from Western 'developed' countries to the rest of the world.

Over the last 200 years one can observe a number of different fashions in educational practices but few substantial differences and at the same time a trend towards an all-embracing mass education. Mass education like mass literacy can be administered economically only if it is given in the smallest number of languages possible, particularly at levels above the first couple of years in primary school. Thus, we can presume that an almost relentless shrinking in the number of languages used for educational purposes, with a few powerful languages, notably, English, Mandarin, French or national languages such as Filipino, Thai and Bahasa Indonesia. The advance of these few languages appears to be crucially related to educational policies. French- or English-only policies have again and again led to uninhibited and undesirable outcomes, such as the development of creoles, and well-meant bilingual programmes of the 1980s have at times weakened rather than strengthened the indigenous languages. The mismatch between objective and outcomes is mostly due to educational policies concentrating on what goes on in the classroom rather than taking into account the wider language ecology. Consequently, the social and cultural transformation of the area has occurred only in part as an answer to the many needs of its inhabitants. Indeed, the perceived need, such as that for a symbol of national identity, smooth administration, a vehicle for modern thought, inexpensive media services and so on, often conflicts with the real needs of a large proportion of the indigenous population.

How differently the recipients of language education and language planning perceive their own needs and how differently they would plan their own education was illustrated with examples from New Zealand and Aboriginal Australia. Alternative proposals of any language teaching need to be sensitive to a complex cultural environment, and that, moreover, learning should be a two-way process would seem to provide a basis for developing more humane language teaching programmes in harmony with the linguistic ecology in which they are implemented.

The arguments for a radical rethinking of language education are primarily ecological ones. Educationists have to address the question of the inherent value of linguistic and cultural diversity and adopt practices which promote a balanced and sustainable linguistic ecology rather than a blind modernization and streamlining with its high human and economic cost and doubtful chance of long-term survival.

10 The sociolinguistics of language shift, decay and death

In order for a language to die, injustice and oppression must be mediated precisely by the culturally appropriate practices that oppressed people adopt in order to defend threatened identities.

(Hill 1993: 90)

INTRODUCTION

This and the following chapter focus on the effects of the disruptive processes discussed in Chapters 3 to 9. The identification of these effects is by no means a simple matter, partly because linguists have as yet to come to grips with the difference between normal and pathological language change and partly because the prevailing emphasis on synchronic states offers few insights which could be of use to a theory of language attrition.

This chapter has as its principal domain the sociolinguistic aspects of this process. I have refrained from recounting McConvell's (1991) valuable survey of theories of language attrition, mainly because I feel that the more fundamental issue of problem recognition needs to be addressed before progress can be made on the theoretical and indeed the applied front. It would seem essential to spell out what precisely the problem is which is in need of remedy.

1 Is it the loss of a particular group of speakers together with their language?
2 Is it the loss of languages?
3 Is it the fact that languages lose prestige?
4 Is it the shrinking of functions and domains?
5 Is it the fact that languages change?
6 Is it the fact that language ecologies collapse?
7 Or is there nothing really to worry about, as seems to be suggested by Matisoff (1991):

All in all, however, I do not find reason to be overly gloomy about
the possible loss of linguistic diversity in Southeast Asia. Though
some languages are dying, others are just being discovered! New
forms of speech are being spawned all the time, or at least are just
coming to the attention of linguists. We can only trust that the
forces of renewal are in the long run just as powerful as the forces
of decline.

(Matisoff 1991: 221–2)

That there really is no problem has also been argued by Ladefoged
(1992):

So now let me challenge directly the assumption of these papers
that different languages, and even different cultures, always ought
to be preserved. It is paternalistic of linguists to assume that they
know what is best for the community. One can be a responsible
linguist and yet regard the loss of a particular language, or even a
whole group of languages, as far from a 'catastrophic destruction'
[Kraus 1992: 7]. Statements such as 'just as the extinction of any
animal species diminishes our world, so does the extinction of any
language' [Kraus 1992: 8] are appeals to our emotions, not to our
reason. The case for studying endangered languages is very strong
on linguistic grounds. It is often enormously strong on humanitar-
ian grounds as well. But it would be self-serving of linguists to
pretend that this is always the case.

(Ladefoged 1992: 810)

DIVERSITY

In my view, the problem is in essence one of understanding the role of
linguistic diversity. Towards an understanding of the problem, it
would seem that both of the writers just quoted ignore the crucial
difference between genuine diversity, which reflects thousands of
years of human accommodation to complex environmental conditions,
and what Toffler (1970: 240ff.) has labelled 'overchoice', a surfeit of
industrial products, subcults and lifestyles. However, whereas former
diversity was timeful in the compound sense of each species being a
repository of past knowledge and shaped by long-range goals,
present-day variation is non-evolutionary, *ad hoc* and intolerant of
'grown' diversity. This sentiment is summed up in Gauguin's famous
painting portraying the disappearance of the traditional lifestyle of
Tahiti in the face of a profusion of introduced and imposed new ones,
entitled:

Qui sommes nous, d'où venons nous, où allons nous?

We are dealing with the opposition between the quality of timeful diversity and the quality of temporary shallow variation. What the function of such diversity might be remains ill understood. However, it might be profitable briefly to explore a couple of metaphors employed by biologists investigating the functions of biological diversity. Briefly, the competing metaphors are that the diversity of species are the passengers and crew of an aeroplane or else that these same species are the rivets that hold the aeroplane together. Under the former metaphor, the loss of quite a few species other than 'pilot' species is of no great impact, whilst under the latter metaphor, the loss of only a few species can have very dire consequences. Ontological experiments on controlled ecologies appear to favour the rivet metaphor in the domain of natural ecologies.

Sociolinguists at this point in time have no clear idea as to how much diversity can disappear before more drastic consequences occur, nor do they have a clear idea what the consequences might be. It seems clear that existing labels such as 'language death' are insufficient as a characterization of such a wide range of phenomena. If we are to adopt, as many practitioners have done, a medical metaphor in talking about language decline then it seems essential to know what the disease is, and what its consequences are before the cure can be proposed. Let us consider some diagnoses.

First, the loss of languages through the extermination of their speakers is (as shown elsewhere in this book) by no means unique to the European imperialistic expansion. However, ever since the disappearance of the Guanche and the languages of the Canaries this process appears to have become accelerated. Next to notorious cases such as the extermination of the Tasmanians, there are many other less frequently discussed ones. Diamond (1991: 255–9) presents detailed information about genocides since 1492, emphasizing that the number of victims from genocides has increased significantly since the Second World War, an observation borne out by information produced by the London-based organization Survival International.

The linguistic consequences of two examples of genocides in highly multilingual areas are as yet unknown. Matisoff (1991: 219) speculates that of the 2 million plus victims of the Pol Pot regime in Cambodia (1975–8), 'whilst most of these were undoubtedly Khmer speakers several minority groups must also have suffered grievous losses'. Similarly undocumented are the effects of the Indonesian invasion of East Timor in 1975 and the consequent death of a large proportion of the population of this country. Many little-known Papuan languages may also have disappeared for good together with their speakers. The losses of people from direct genocide are augmented by genocide through economic or habitat destruction, a process which has been particularly vigorous in mining and logging areas such as Borneo, the Amazon, the Malay peninsula and the Philippines. Linguists have rarely been at the forefront of attacking contemporary forms of genocide, but in this we have not been any less ready to acknowledge the reality of this process than other groups.

That genocide is an utterly undesirable phenomenon is a view virtually all linguists would support and there have been over the years quite a few outspoken statements by linguists on the brutal invasion of East Timor and other deplorable instances of genocide, but on the whole their writings have tended to down-play or ignore this phenomenon. It does not appear to˙be the case as Wurm (1991a: 2) states that genocide prevailed more 'in days gone by than in recent years and at present'. Australian Aboriginal languages were described, classified and catalogued whilst their speakers were slaughtered or poisoned and in the objective descriptions of American Indian languages one rarely finds any outraged statements about genocidal policies of the white settlers and their leaders.[1] Outspokenly racist and intolerant statements about linguistic minority groups continue to be made by the ruling classes in Bangladesh, Brazil, China, Malaysia and other newly developing states. It is high time linguists sat down and addressed the moral issue of genocide and took a stand on this matter. The absence of any concerted effort on the part of linguists to stop genocide contrasts with the prolificity of activity in the next section.

The second diagnosis is that the loss of languages without genocide involves their speakers shifting to other typically more powerful ones. The number of languages currently spoken is estimated to be around 6,000 (see Kraus 1992: 5; Pörksen 1988: 15). However, the strength of these languages varies widely, as pointed out by Coulmas (1985) and Fishman (1991). Of the world's population, 95 per cent speak 100 languages, with 5 per cent speaking the remaining thousands of languages. As pointed out by Kraus (1992) the proportion of moribund languages in this last group is high; in some instances, very high:

Thus in Alaska and the Soviet North together, about 45 of the 50 indigenous languages, 90%, are moribund. For the whole of the USA and Canada together, a similar count is only a little less alarming: of 187 languages, I calculate that 149 are no longer being learned by children; that is, of the Native North American languages still spoken, 80% are moribund. These North American numbers are relatively well known to us. The situation in Central and South America, though less well known, is apparently much better. It would seem, so far, that only about 50 of 300, or 17%, of Meso-American indigenous languages (including Mexico) and 110 of 400, or 27%, of South American languages are likely to be moribund. So for all the Americas the total is 300 of 900, or one third.

For the rest of the world, the worst continent by far is Australia, with 90% of 250 aboriginal languages that are still spoken now moribund, most of those VERY near extinction.

(Kraus 1992: 5)

An interesting observation is that the sickness of languages is greatest in areas where English is the official language:

It would seem that English-language dominance in the 'English-speaking world' has achieved and continues to achieve the highest documented rate of destruction, approaching now 90%. In comparison, Russian domination has reached 90% only among the small peoples of the North; in the Russian Republic itself, 45 of 65 indigenous languages, or 70%, are moribund, while for the entire USSR the total is more like 50%.

(Kraus 1992: 5)

This observation should give cause for thought as English is rapidly becoming established in the most highly multilingual parts of the world such as Melanesia.

There is widespread ignorance among linguists as to how many languages currently spoken are moribund and estimates as to how many will die during the next century vary widely. Kraus comments on estimates by Grimes and Grimes (1988):

Allowing that a good majority of the unknown 40% may still be viable, the Grimeses themselves might agree that as many as 20% of the world's languages are already moribund. However, two other linguists with wide experience have both independently guessed, along with me, that the total may be more like 50%, or at least that the number of languages which, at the rate things are going, will become extinct during the coming century is 3,000 of 6,000.

(Kraus 1992: 6)

The loss of absolute numbers, as has been repeatedly pointed out in this book, can only be seen as a problem if the functions of linguistic diversity are understood.

In the third diagnosis, a symptom which a number of writers have drawn attention to is the ever increasing inequality among the world's languages, the development of a clear pecking order with a single or very few world languages at the top and a large number of barely viable 'vernacular', minority languages, or whatever, at the bottom, a development that has accelerated subsequent to the end of official colonization, as is documented profusely by Phillipson (1992: 27ff.). Languages which were fairly important sources of knowledge, cultural practices and political prestige such as Javanese, Fijian or Tibetan are being displaced and disempowered by a very small number of world languages. In the mid-1930s, Reinecke (1937b) coined the term 'marginal languages' to characterize pidgins and creoles. The marginalization of most of these languages has continued and very few pidgins and creoles are likely to survive into the middle of the twenty-first century. What is more disturbing is that the class of marginal languages and the processes of marginalization have extended to a large number of non-pidgins and creoles, that is, the bulk of indigenous languages, which are becoming increasingly irrelevant to the social, economic and political processes around them and whose speakers are treated as if they were suffering from a major deficit.

Fourth, one of the main processes by which traditional languages lose their power is through the loss of functions and domains. Most noticeable among these is the function of education where a few metropolitan languages have displaced the majority of the world's languages as sources of knowledge. How subversive educational language policies have been to traditional languages and cultures has been illustrated in much detail by Phillipson (1992), who summarizes his findings as follows:

What the French and British empires had in common was:

- the low status of dominated languages, whether these were ignored or used in education
- a very small proportion of the population in formal education, especially after the lowest classes
- local traditions and educational practice being ignored
- unsuitable education being given to Africans
- an explicit policy of 'civilizing the natives'
- the master language being attributed civilizing properties.

The continued dominance of French and English in independent African countries indicates that these countries have inherited the same type of legacy. This is a legacy of linguicism in which the colonized people have internalized the language and many of the attitudes of their masters, in particular their attitude to the dominant language and the dominated languages. This linguistic legacy was the foundation on which French and English linguistic imperialism were to build in the neo-colonial phase of imperialism.

(Phillipson 1992: 128)

There have been recommendations and attempts to reclaim part of the territory lost by indigenous languages by promoting teaching by the speakers of indigenous languages. However, this has often meant the translation of an exo-cultural syllabus from a metropolitan language into the indigenous one. This is typically (as has been pointed out in Chapter 9 on education) seen as the first step in a transition phase leading to education in the dominant language.

The fifth diagnosis is that language change is unavoidable and the view that traditional languages were either stable or changing very slowly has little to recommend it. There are, however, at least four features which render doubtful the view that present-day developments are of a kind and order of magnitude comparable to the past:

1 The past balance between divergent and convergent changes appears to have been replaced by a linguistically unidirectional convergence of the many small languages in the direction of the dominant ones.
2 Whereas past changes were complexity-preserving, many of the changes in small indigenous languages are of a complexity-reducing type, a kind of pidginization in reverse, as Trudgill (1983b) has called it. The loss of lexical and grammatical complexity is a consequence of functional dislocation and narrowing.
3 The size of a viable speech community needs to be greater in the 1990s than in the past. Whilst small and very small languages with fewer than 500 speakers could survive for long periods of time in places like Papua New Guinea (Laycock 1979a) or Charlotte Bay in Australia (Rigsby and Sutton 1982) the fate of quite large languages is now in doubt. Kraus (1992: 7) reminds us of 'the case of Breton with perhaps a million speakers in living memory but now with very few children speakers, or Navajo, with well over 100,000 speakers a generation ago but now also with an uncertain future'.
4 The lifespan of many larger indigenous lingue franche and koines which have developed at the cost of smaller vernaculars is quite short. The medium-size fish, having eaten the small fish, in turn get eaten by the remaining large fish.

Finally, it is a central argument of this book that the decline and loss of small languages, illustrated with examples from Australia and the

Pacific, is not a self-contained phenomenon, but embedded in and related to a much larger range of ecological factors (see Coulmas 1994). Languages weaken and disappear because of a large-scale habitat destruction. Each language needs for its sustained well-being a complex ecological support system which includes factors such as other languages from which they can borrow, internal dialect variation, territory, language-centred cultural practices, natural boundaries, optimum size of a population of speakers, metalinguistic belief systems and many more. Different languages of course require different ecological support systems (e.g. Aboriginal languages of Australia are bound to land, Romany is not). What the ecological support system for a language or group of languages might be is usually not known but unless this question is addressed, the reversal of language shift would seem to be based on very shaky foundations.

COURSES FOR ACTION

The following section is concerned with a small number of received ideas within the linguistic profession which have influenced both the assessment of the problem and the course of action taken to remedy it. My discussion of such 'common-sense' interpretations will be supplemented in Chapter 12, with a discussion of theory-based approaches to language maintenance.

Shared by the principal common-sense approaches is that they perpetuate the view of the linguist as a detached outsider and observer of a natural process rather than someone capable of intervention, as would be a shop steward who takes up the cause of small cultures and languages.

They perceive their function as that of an archival or museum curator, though in fairness to them, little else can be undertaken in some countries, given the political and economic pressures under which linguists have to operate. Thus, the UNESCO Red Book on Endangered Languages (Wurm 1994) is oriented to 'the actual study or collection of materials in, etc. of endangered languages hitherto not or little studied' (Wurm 1994: 2), though Unesco also has begun to emphasize that 'there is considerable scope for self-help in cases in which a speech community whose language is endangered, wishes to safeguard, protect and maintain its language' (Wurm 1994: 2). This, of course, presupposes that speakers are aware of the language marketplace.

Whilst not wishing to deny that 'it is a task of the utmost importance to provide documentation of as many languages as possible before they disappear' (Dixon 1991: 230) it is at best a partial view and it appears to perpetuate a number of questionable assumptions, including four discussed here.

The first assumption mistakenly believes that diversity is a disease rather than a balanced state of health, that technical progress and successful development require a reduction in diversity and that the benefit from such a reduction is greater than its cost.

The second assumption is that one can 'preserve' languages by writing them down in a book. What professional linguists have documented (and can document) is only a small portion of real language. Their descriptions were constrained by a narrow range of research questions and by unsophisticated research tools. Thus, virtually nothing is known about the semantic and pragmatic aspects of most languages for which structural descriptions exist. The status of bi- and multilinguals in areas such as Australia or New Guinea remains largely undescribed and virtually nothing is known about metalinguistic resources, metaphors or special registers for the vast majority of languages in this area. The preserving of languages by describing their putative grammatical core structures may turn out to be a very dubious policy, as Norah England (1992) has pointed out in connection with Maya linguistics:

Many of us have been used to thinking that our work is pure science, that the most compelling reasons for doing linguistics are to know how specific languages work and what language is. The widely accepted Western idea that knowledge in and of itself is valuable for society is often the only justification we need to do what we do. And if the people we work with do not or cannot understand that it is because they are poor and do not have the luxury of being able to think about the universal benefits of science, or it is because they are uneducated or unsophisticated. The Mayas who spoke at the XI Workshop may be poor, but they are not uneducated nor unsophisticated. What they are saying is that the conduct of social science research, in which category they definitely place linguistics, can have negative or positive consequences for the group where that research is carried out, and that an evaluation of the possible consequences must start with a consideration of the political status of the group in question. . . .

We have been taught to be true to our data, to report it as accurately as we possibly can, and to be as exhaustive as possible in descriptive linguistics and as honest as possible in using descriptive data in theoretical work. We have not been as well drilled in sociolinguistic sensitivity; to be honest and accurate requires taking the broad social situation into account. Every time we write an article about a language we do several things: we make an analysis of some body of linguistic data, we discuss that analysis in the light of the current pertinent theory, we select examples of speech to illustrate our points, and we bring that language into at least momentary prominence according to the analysis, the theory, and the selection of data. Language prominence resulting from linguistic research has many non-linguistic consequences, and selection of data is guided by a multiplicity of nonlinguistic as well as linguistic factors.

Having said all this, there is merit in recording disappearing languages, if only, in order to revive them at a future point. However, such records should be guided by theories other than narrowly structural descriptive ones.

(England 1992: 32–3)

Third, a very problematic area is that of selecting languages for preservation of various sorts. Dixon (1991), when addressing the need for descriptive work, comments on the situation in the Pacific:

Every language is important and interesting, and worthy of study and description. But we must be realistic – there is no way that good materials can be gathered for all of these languages before they cease to be spoken. Priorities have to be set. It seems to me that we should aim to gather some information on languages from every language family and from every branch of each family. Good descriptions are already available for languages from all major branches of the large Austronesian family. While more work is required on some Austronesian languages, by far the greatest need concerns languages from the fifty to sixty 'Papuan' families, from Papua New Guinea, Irian Jaya and neighbouring parts of Indonesia, and from the Solomon Islands.

(Dixon 1991: 230)

This recommendation, of course, is based on the assumption that diversity within a language family is less important than diversity between a language family. That this is not necessarily so has been illustrated by Hale (1992) with the example of the Damin register of the Australian Aboriginal Language Lardil. In this subvariety a number of unique abstractions occur:

It is clear from what little we know of Damin that it involves a sophisticated semantic analysis of the lexical resources of Lardil. The system of abstractions lays bare aspects of lexical semantic structure to a degree which, quite possibly, is not achieved by any other system of analysis that attempts to accommodate an ENTIRE vocabulary.

(Hale 1992: 40)

In the same subvariety some highly unusual phonetic phenomena can be observed:

> The feature of Damin that first caught my attention was its phonology. It departs drastically from the phonology of Lardil, and it has sounds in it which do not exist in any other Australian language. For example, it has click consonants, otherwise found only in Africa – in the Khoisan languages, for example, and in the Nguni languages of the Bantu family, languages with no historical connection to Lardil. The use of clicks in Damin developed locally. Damin has the appearance of an invented language, and it is attributed, in fact, to a legendary figure named Kalthad (Yellow Trevally). If it was invented, then it is a clever invention, indeed, because it is almost unheard of for an invented language to depart radically from the phonological constraints of the ordinary language of the inventor. The impression that Damin is an invention is strengthened by the fact that it not only has sounds absent elsewhere in Australia, but it also has sounds found nowhere else in the world – as true phonological segments, that is. These include an ingressive voiceless lateral and a labio-velar lingual ejective.

(Hale 1992: 36–7)

There is no saying, in principle, whether similarly unique phenomena might not be found in a number of the smaller languages of the Austronesian language family.

Privileging of a different sort occurs when decisions need to be made as to which languages need to be singled out for revival or other special support. There is a widespread view in Australia, for instance, that numerically larger languages offer the best conditions for support. A modified form of this view is Schmidt's (1991a) distinction of languages in different states of health (healthy – weakening – dying – extinct) and her implicit suggestion that preferential treatment should be given to the healthy languages (which incidentally all have about 200 speakers). In practice, it is the stronger languages that tend to get the largest support systems in many parts of the Pacific, for example, languages with more than a million speakers in Indonesia, Tahitian in French Polynesia, or Wallisian in Wallis and Futuna.

The problem with the privileging of species is that no one has a clear idea to what extent strong languages depend for their continued survival on weak ones. The problem is somewhat analogous to Diamond's (1991) problem of selectively preserving natural species:

> Then could we not preserve only those particular species that we need, and let other species become extinct? Of course not, because the species we need also depend on other species. Just as Panama's antbirds could not have anticipated their need for jaguars, the ecological chain of dominoes is much too complex for us to have figured out which dominoes we can dispense with. For instance, could anyone please answer these three questions. Which ten tree species produce most of the world's paper pulp? For each of those ten tree species, which are the ten bird species that eat most of its insect pests, the ten insect species that pollinate most of its flowers, and the ten animal species that spread most of its seeds? Which other species do these ten birds, insects, and animals depend on? You would have to be able to answer those three impossible questions if you were the president of a timber company trying to figure out which species you could afford to allow to become extinct.
>
> (Diamond 1991: 324)

In the absence of clear ideas of the interdependency of languages, privileging the strongest ones may not be a viable policy. More on this will be said in Chapter 12 of this book.

Finally, there is an often expressed view that the source of diversity is isolation (e.g. in Dixon 1991: 232) and that isolation is a main element in language survival. On the latter point Kibrik (1991) has observed:

> The more contact there is with other cultures, especially in another language, the worse it is for the viability of the given ethnic language.
>
> (Kibrik 1991: 260)

This view has little to recommend itself. Physical isolation did not result in a multiplicity of Eskimo languages any more than close contacts led to the large-scale disappearance of languages in the Bismarck-Archipelago or Charlotte Bay of Australia in pre-colonial days.

We have very good information about the prolific language contacts, bi- and multilingualism in the entire Pacific region and numerous examples (e.g. in Laycock 1979a) of languages surviving with very few speakers in highly multilingual areas of Papua New Guinea. Isolation in itself thus does not seem to be a recipe for survival any more than apartheid was a recipe for racial harmony.

CONCLUSIONS

In this chapter, I have tried to argue that sociolinguists and linguists have proposed solutions and expressed views before properly recognizing what the problem might be. As a discipline concerned with the description of idealized language states and correlating such states to equally idealized social parameters, linguistics would seem insufficiently prepared to tackle language attrition. In the studies of the phenomenon surveyed mostly superficial symptoms are observed and *ad hoc* explanations are given but few of them can be accommodated within the theoretical frames that continue to exist in this discipline.

Around the turn of the century, a situation comparable to what is happening in the Pacific region in the 1990s arose in North America: the near-cataclysmic decline of Amerindian cultures and languages. Linguistic descriptivism was developed as an answer to the problem, and, beginning with Boas' (1911) *Handbook of American Indian Languages*, a large body of structural descriptions was compiled. In spite of the many advances in documentation, there has been very little success in arresting the decline of these languages, nor has there been much change in the direction of knowledge flow from the dominant to the dominated cultures.

A view put forward in this book is that by reframing the question of language loss as an ecological question, we gain not only new perspectives, but also the possibility of new courses of action. An ecological perspective would ask two questions that have been conspicuous by their absence in most of the linguistic and sociolinguistic writings surveyed:

1 What is the ecological support system that sustains the continued well-being of languages and their speakers?
2 What are the meaningful links between the linguistic and non-linguistic inhabitants of a language ecology?

These two themes will be further developed in Chapter 12, whilst some recommendations for a different linguistics are given in the appendix.

11 Assessing the damage: structural and lexical effects

> Only through massive effort can linguistic groups keep themselves distinct from neighbouring groups, and only by emphasising their uniqueness can they slow down the loss of traditional knowledge and retain a degree of respect for older generations while they acquire, piecemeal, the knowledge of foreigners that is integrating them into the global community.
>
> (Thurston 1992: 136)

INTRODUCTION

One of the recurrent themes of this book has been that the very notion of separate languages is an imported one and that the process which has led to the emergence of Pacific and Australian 'languages' has at the same time accelerated their decline. We can appeal to an ecological metaphor and liken the selective breeding of languages to that of a small number of indigenous biological species. Such breeding not only requires a very considerable effort if the chosen species is to survive over longer periods of time, but also results in new varieties that are dependent on factors other than those encountered in the traditional ecology.

The term 'natural language' consequently is quite inappropriate as a description of languages such as Fijian, Chamorro or Kâte. We have also seen that the naming of languages in many cases is a very recent phenomenon, introduced by Europeans over the last 100 years or so. It is often not remembered that the existence of a name over time is not a guarantee of structural identity over time. What is called Fijian in the 1990s significantly differs from Fijian 100 years ago as much and more than present-day Common Market Golden Delicious apples differ from apple varieties current 100 years ago.

This chapter is not so much concerned with the ecological changes that have led to these developments but with some of the lexical and grammatical consequences thereof. It tries to answer the question of how present-day Australian and Pacific languages differ from those spoken prior to contact with Europeans.

It is difficult to generalize for a wide range of cases, including such questions as

1 different types of language obsolescence
2 newly emerged stable bi- and multilingualism
3 modernization of traditional languages

and the researcher has to be reminded that 'every case is special' (Dorian 1989a: 7). Nevertheless, one should also remember that the outcome of both language death and radical modernization of indigenous languages is the same: speakers will employ the grammatical and semantic categories of Standard Average European (SAE) languages and deeper-level differences between human languages will have been replaced by superficial variation.

It is my view that the often appealed to principle of effability – that everything can be expressed in any language – is an unproven assumption and not an established fact and that at the semantic level languages differ in a number of important ways.

First, languages differ in what choices or distinctions have to be made obligatorily: whilst a language such as English does not force users to signal deference, social status or attitude by means of pronouns, other languages do. Next to the fairly simple tu/vous distinction of many continental European languages we find highly developed systems of choice such as that in Japanese or the Loyalty language Iai. There are no proper translation equivalents in SAE languages for the deictic words of Japanese that index the position of the person referred to *vis-à-vis* the other, the situation, formality, etc., nor are there adequate translation equivalents for Iai pronouns that inflect for time and thus are not predicated on the SAE assumption of the 'self' as maintaining its identity over time. Many examples and a detailed discussion can be found in Mühlhäusler and Harré (1990). Nor is it possible to express in English the triangular kinship terms of several Australian Aboriginal languages, where a single lexical item encodes simultaneously, in for example the term 'her mother's brother', the relationship of the person referred to as brother and the speaker's kinship status *vis-à-vis* the same person.

Second, languages differ in their boundaries between concepts (expressed by lexical means) and percepts (expressed by grammatical means). There appear to be no principled semantic criteria for a universal boundary between grammar and lexicon.

Third, one can note considerable differences in the linguistic conventions underlying communicative activities such as information seeking, learning, ambiguity or metalinguistic activities. Many of the components of speech events and speech acts found in the small languages of Australia and the Pacific have no equivalents in SAE languages (for Aboriginal languages, see Malcolm 1982).

The relationship between lexicon and grammar on the one hand, and semantics/meaningful communication on the other is not likely to be direct. The loss of a lexical item need not imply the loss of a concept nor need the addition of a new concept require new lexical material.

In pre-colonial days the languages of the area were dynamic and changing, not static as Western stereotype has it. However, where, in the past, semantic change led to both convergence and diversity in the present (particularly since the mid-1970s) change has tended to result in

1 massive loss of lexical and structural resources
2 typological change from esoteric to exoteric
3 convergence with English, Pidgin English or an SAE language.

Changes that have occurred thus are both qualitatively and quantitatively different from changes in the more distant past in many instances and these recent changes have put languages under such strain that structural collapse occurs. The relationship between linguistic collapse and cultural collapse is complex and not necessarily a causal one. It is not unreasonable, however, to portray such linguistic decline as an index of a more general cultural transformation, as have many of the contributors to a research project addressing this question (Dutton 1992). As yet, the mechanisms involved remain ill understood. As Hill (1993) has pointed out:

> No matter how powerful the agents of oppression, we have no evidence that they can enforce practices like 'freeze derivation in the fifth position of verbal prefixation' or 'shift from ergative to nominative – accusative marking of arguments' or 'use honorific marking only in direct address'.
>
> (Hill 1993: 68)

An ecological perspective on such losses will focus on the effects of social and cultural changes on the links between languages which, in the past, may have helped maintain morphological complexities. Thus linguistic and cultural transformation is not restricted to individual languages, for the simple reason that traditional languages have tended to borrow from one another.[1] 'Westernization' is bound to be transmitted to all the other members of a linguistic ecology once one of its 'inhabitants' is affected, which sooner or later they will be. This chapter examines some of the structural indices of language decline in the Pacific area, classified in a pragmatic and pre-theoretical fashion in terms of the well-known classes of morphological, syntactical, lexical and other changes.

MORPHOLOGICAL CHANGES

Morphology performs a number of functions in human languages including, among others:

1 signalling relationships between words
2 signalling word-class membership
3 signalling indexical information about speakers
4 creating new words from existing ones.

Seen from the perspective of universal grammar, many morphological categories are 'accidents', for example information not central to the foregrounded meaning of lexical items and consequently dispensable. Many a linguist (including the author of this book) have agreed that languages might be better off without such morphological trappings as gender. Others have emphasized that the uniqueness of languages derives, to a significant extent, from what their speakers have to say, rather than what they can say. An Oceanic language with obligatory nominal number distinctions such as singular, dual, trial, paucal and plural compels its speakers to focus on quantity in a manner that Melanesian Pidgin English with no obligatory number marking does not, and a language such as Huli (see Laycock 1970) which compels the users of statements simultaneously to encode in the verbal morphology whether such statements are based on direct observation, hearsay or deduction would seem to promote attention to truth values in a way that a morphologically neutral language such as English does not. Such links between morphology and speakers' world view or social indexicality have been down-played in Western linguistics where linguists have tended to concentrate on the grammatical aspects of morphology (how it is used to signal case, same or different subject, number, etc.) rather than social or indexical functions. We shall return to this point shortly.

First of all, however, I would like to comment on a general typological matter. Languages differ morphologically along at least two parameters:

1 synthesis
2 fusion.

The former means that in more highly synthetic languages words are

Synthesis

	more	less
Fusion more	–	inflectional
less	polysynthetic	isolating

Figure 11.1   Language types defined morphologically

composed of more 'morphemes', the latter that in fusional languages the formal boundaries between morphemes within a word become blurred (see Figure 11.1).

The trend in most languages surveyed is threefold:

1 from more to less synthesis
2 from more to less fusion
3 towards the loss of grammatical concordance.

In sum, this means that languages are becoming morphologically less complex, very complex features such as polysynthesis being the first to disappear. The disappearance of polysynthesis in Northern Australian Tiwi is an example (Pilling 1970).

> Capell's notes on Tiwi grammar (1942: 26) document the nature of the highly polysynthetic verbs which were still used by the oldest generation in 1953. In this usage such words as tinawatipikupuwa-miniyamarnipa (freely translated as 'she got up from her camp') were common and, in large part, have defied complete translation by either anthropologists or the younger native speakers who have an adequate command of English. Such younger speakers rarely, if ever, use exceptionally complex verbs; they employ simpler forms preceded by free forms indicating the type of action undertaken. Thus, in 1953 an eighteen-year-old said:
>
> ninani kutupa   ma-ri-mi
> today jump   dual inclusive-past tense-do
> That is: 'Today we jumped.'
>
> (Pilling 1970: 267)

Pilling suggests that this loss is the result of a massive influx of loan words from English:

It is clear when hearing English loan words in use that they fit more easily with the less polysynthetic verb structure.

```
kiyiti-ni      tatapi      a-witi-na-mi
young boy   stand up    he-go-with feet-do
```
That is: 'That young boy is getting to his feet.'
```
naki    mila-ta-ma-ni    rayiki    ti-kari-mi
that    shoe    rag you              (past tense)-manual-do
```
That is: 'You tied up that shoe with a rag.'

(Pilling 1970: 267)

One might add that had this grammatical change not been under way, loan words might not have been accepted as free forms, but would have become incorporated within the verbs (Pilling 1970: 268). Similar loss of polysynthesis is also reported in the dying languages of other parts of the world, for instance North American Indian languages such as Cayuga (Mithun 1989).

I would like to single out a morphological phenomenon that appears particularly important when trying to understand the conceptual framework of uses of other languages: nominal classification systems. Such systems, in as much as they are semantically based, provide valuable insight into the way speakers of other languages categorize their experiences, establish samenesses, similarities and differences and foreground information. Among the languages of the Pacific area one finds numerous complex noun-class systems, the best known one being that of Kiriwina (studied first by Malinowski 1935, and subsequently by Senft 1992) and Aÿiwo (described by Wurm in numerous papers, particularly 1981, 1991b). Both languages have undergone a radical simplification of their noun-class systems since the mid-1980s (see Wurm 1992) and the same is true for a large number of classifying languages in parts of the Sepik in Papua New Guinea. Wurm (1983) reports:

> Another striking example of such grammatical decay in a Papuan language is provided by the Buna language of the East Sepik Province of Papua New Guinea. This language, for which Kirschbaum (1926) reported the presence of a complex noun-class system comprising 12 classes, has been found by Laycock (1975b) to have no noun-class system at all today. The same situation appears to be present with Murik of the same province for which Schmidt (1953) reports the presence of a noun-class system, but during his fieldwork in 1970–71, Laycock (1973) was unable to find any trace of it. Similarly, Laycock (1975b) reports the tendency towards a breakdown of the elaborate noun-class system in Mountain Arapesh. . . .

A situation in which the breakdown and decay of an elaborate noun-class system is at present in progress and is in direct proportion with the descending age of the speakers, is observable in the Aÿiwo language of the Reef Islands of the Santa Cruz Archipelago at the extreme eastern end of the Solomon Islands chain.

(Wurm 1983: 5–6)

In both the typological change towards isolation and in the disappearance of noun classes we are dealing with semantic impoverishment rather than simplification in the technical sense (meaning more regular expression of content). Distinctions that could be made in earlier stages of the language, no longer have to be made by younger speakers and in many instances can no longer be made by younger speakers. Very much the same can also be said about tense, aspect and mood morphology with verbs, as numerous studies have demonstrated. The end point again is a radically reduced number of conceptual distinctions in the affected languages. Instead of giving examples of the rather well-documented process (Schmidt 1991a; Wurm 1983), I shall turn to one of the social functions of morphology and the reason for its loss.

Apart from providing a finely calibrated tool for its speakers to categorize the world around them, complex morphology also serves the indexical function of signifying insiders within a group, full membership of a group and relationships between members of groups.

Learning the morphological complexities of certain Pacific languages was not a matter of simple acquisition but involved careful training of youngsters by initiated adults. Complex morphology was one of the attributes of esoteric languages (see Markey 1986; Thurston 1992). The effort needed to learn such complexities was considerable and for many languages full mastery was not acquired until speakers were well into middle age. This dependence on a social learning context has made these languages very vulnerable in an age where children are expected to attend school from the age of 6 or 7 and join the workforce by the age of 16 or earlier.

Complex morphology also served another social function, that of reinforcing existing social structures by encoding relationships grammatically. A good example is the sensitivity of grammatical structures in Australian languages to kin relationships (Dench 1988). As traditional kinship structures are replaced by Western models, such grammatical reflexes also disappear.

One might wish to ask what this loss of inflectional morphology does to the language. We have to remind ourselves that the language can be used to talk about concepts (generalities) and to talk about percepts (singularities).

Whereas the lexicon tends to be the repository of the concepts that are prominent in a given language, syntax and inflectional morphology can be thought of as providing a conceptual grid that directs language users to focus on particular aspects of singularities, such as simultaneous or sequential occurrence of two actions, the relative social status or gender of speaker and addressee, shape, size, or usefulness of an object, and many more which can be ascertained by anyone prepared to study existing morphological descriptions of the languages of the area.[2]

Such distinctions are rarely found necessary in English, nor is the compulsory mention of control in possessive pronouns (such as in many Polynesian languages) which focuses speakers' attention to who controls or what controls or is controlled. Put differently, inflectional morphology provides constraints on the ways that singularities can be described.

This may be the point at which I should comment on a phenomenon which is often mentioned anecdotally, but whose real importance is seldom fully understood: the principle that there is a direct relationship between the degree to which a lexical item has been established in a language and its susceptibility to morphological rules. For instance, Bradshaw (1978: 91) observes that Tok Pisin verbs used in Numbami do not take Numbami subject prefixes, and Pilling (1970: 268) comments on the change of morphological typology in Tiwi as follows: 'It is clear when hearing English loan words in use that they fit more easily with the less polysynthetic verb structure.'

Similar examples can be found in many of the region's languages. The effect of borrowing thus is twofold:

1 It makes existing grammatical regularities less general.
2 It accelerates the transition from inflectional morphology to syntactical ways of expressing grammatical 'accidents'.

It is not clear to me whether this also has conceptual consequences but the following seem plausible:

1 The lack of compulsory 'accidental' information accompanying lexical items can promote greater abstractedness.
2 The loss of uniform signalling of such 'accidents' means that the samenesses and similarities suggested by the traditional forms of language are different from those suggested by the recently introduced borrowed words.

One suspects that different formal grammatical means are more than just neutral encoding devices and that there are significant links between typological properties and the emphasising and de-emphasizing of different types of meaning. The evidence from indigenous American languages is of interest here. Moore (1988: 466) has suggested that the loss of morphological complexity turns words into unanalysable name-like entities, a process of lexicalization that is also encountered in incipient pidgin languages.

Thus far, our remarks have been focused on inflectional morphology. Similar erosion of morphological complexity can also be observed in the domain of derivational morphology. The main functions of derivational morphology are

1 to enable speakers to create new words on the basis of an existing lexicon
2 to signal overtly semantic relationships between words
3 to make available stylistic alternatives to existing words.

As traditional languages came under the influence of modern lingue franche and metropolitan languages, all the above functions came under attack.

Hans Fischer (1962) believes that he has identified some general principles in the attrition of derivational morphology. Traditional languages in contact with modern culture tend to resort to circumlocution for new concepts initially, followed by semantic extension and new derivational coinings. Such internally motivated creations tend to be replaced later by direct loans and replacement of existing forms by loans.

The main problem with loans replacing existing items is that they are outside the existing system of lexical organization and that borrowing in this case leads to suppletion and eventual dissolution of productive word formation devices. My own studies of the English loan words in Tok Pisin confirms that within a relatively short time established patterns can disappear. In some instances heavy borrowing results in paradigm splicing rather than suppletion and consequently – at least for a shorter period – increases stylistic flexibility. Thus for a while, Tok Pisin admitted nominal compounds following both the Melanesian and English pattern, as in:

botol glas	glas botol	(glass bottle)
haus simen	simen haus	(concrete building/prison)
kot ren	ren kot	(rain coat)

For younger speakers, the productivity of the first paradigm has gradually disappeared whilst membership of words in the second paradigm is on the increase. How the relationship between words and cultural context is expressed by compound forms is illustrated with the following examples from Hua, a language spoken in the Highlands of Papua New Guinea:

> Consider, for example, a word like *bade* 'boy', which we have just translated, successfully it would seem, into English. In fact this word is composed of two words, *ba* 'woman' and *de* 'man'; etymologically, a boy is half woman, half man. Etymology reflects a cultural belief: people are not born male and female in Hua thinking, but achieve masculinity and femininity through a series of initiation rites. At their initiation boys are subjected to a number of trials, including nose-bleeding and induced vomiting to 'purge themselves of the woman within them.' The word *bade* resonates with these beliefs and is quite literally untranslatable into English, Pidgin, or any other language.
>
> (Haiman 1979: 40)

As more and more Hua speakers borrow core lexical items from Tok Pisin or switch to this language, the cultural content of *bade* is bound to disappear. The way new words are formed in traditional languages remains ill understood, since linguists, for reasons best known to themselves, have tended to pay more attention to syntax, basic lexicon and inflectional morphology than derivational morphology. As derivational morphology typically signals the distinctions between primary and secondary concepts within a culture, this lack of attention is particularly deplorable.

SYNTACTIC CHANGES

To begin with we have to remind ourselves of the already mentioned typological change away from synthesis and fusion. The main consequence of this is greater reliance on syntactic means for signalling relations between words. A second often mentioned characteristic is that speakers of threatened languages avoid grammatically complex constructions. Thus, Donaldson (1985) reports for the Ngiyampaa language of New South Wales:

> The second way in which the Carowra Tank generation's Ngiyampaa differs grammatically from the Ngurrampaa generation's is of a piece with the first, in that it involves simplifying the business of speaking the language, but less spectacular in that it does not involve changes to frequently necessary forms like verb- and noun-endings. Anyone who has spent time amongst people whose language they do not know well will have realised what a lot of

mileage they can get out of the few constructions they do know. Imagine travelling in France on a little school French for instance. If you need to say the equivalent of 'I don't know whether the train has gone' but do not feel up to it, you can perhaps say the equivalent of 'Has the train gone? I don't know', or failing that of 'The train has gone?' with a questioning intonation. Variable amounts of this sort of thing go on in the Ngiyampaa of the Carowra Tank generation. If one of them records a story, it will be likely to have fewer subordinate constructions in it than an older speaker's, though when they do occur they are formally just the same. . . . The fact that Ngiyampaa is in competition with English sometimes affords other ways of avoiding the grammatically complex. There is one Ngiyampaa construction which is complicated because there is no other at all like it. There is no verb in Ngiyampaa meaning 'to want' or 'to need'. Saying that you want something is achieved by adding a special suffix -nginta, which means roughly 'in-need-of' to the word for the thing you want, and using the verb 'to be', saying something like, for instance: 'Water-in-need-of I am' or 'To dance-in-need-of I am'. What the Carowra Tank generation have done is to form a regular Ngiyampaa verb 'to want' on the basis of the English one, so that they can say: 'Ngathu wantitmara kali' 'I want water' or 'Ngathu wantitmara wakakirri' 'I want to dance'. Older speakers too were using this stratagem in the early seventies. When I asked some of them how you would talk about 'wanting' without putting any English in they revived the -nginta construction, and have stuck with it since. But it has not caught on with the Carowra Tank generation.

(Donaldson 1985: 136–7)

Two main sources of syntactic restructuring are translations and literacy (often combined). We have already noted that the translation of the Scriptures and other religious materials has led to an influx of foreign syntactic conventions and we may add that this new syntax often becomes the model of future literary products. Thus, the revival of the Kaurna language of South Australia relies heavily on missionary writings in which this language might have been changed extensively, for the German missionaries who developed grammars and a writing system for Kaurna carried out a considerable amount of prescription and normalization; moreover, they were influenced by their training in the classical languages (see Teichelmann and Schurmann 1840).

As speakers become bilingual in the traditional language and a lingua franca or metropolitan language, traditional structures begin to be replaced, a process which has been documented in much detail. To consider briefly what such syntactic changes may mean:

1 Perhaps foremost is the loss of syntactic flexibility, a feature which allows speakers to express subtle differences, to emphasize or de-emphasize observations and to signal syntactically indexical information such as degrees of formality, or types of speech events.
2 One of the main functions of syntax is to enable speakers to talk about new information, new percepts. As the syntactical resources shrink, so does the ability to talk about new matters. In the most extreme cases, syntax is reduced to recitation of memorized texts.
3 Syntactic structures are suggestive, as Benjamin Lee Whorf (1956) has demonstrated, of samenesses and differences. Replacing traditional systems with an imported version thereof or with an SAE language will evoke a different view of what constitutes similarities between percepts.

GRAMMATICAL CATEGORIES

It has already been observed that the differences between languages are greatest not in what they can express but in what they must express. The functioning of so-called word classes (categories) is a good example. In most SAE languages, word classes divide the lexicon up into entities, processes, qualities and a number of smaller categories. Once a member of a certain category (e.g. noun) has been chosen, accidental information (number, case or diminutive) is added whether or not this is relevant to a speaker's message. The choice of a noun in a Western language evokes ideas of countability, self-contained object, being capable of decontextualization, and so on. This metaphorical process of reification significantly influences the ways that Westerners deal with topics such as language, emotions and behaviour.

Contact between the traditional languages of the area and international ones has affected the word-class system of the former in a number of ways:

1 new word classes have been added
2 the introduced lexicon inflates the size of existing word classes
3 introduced accidental information replaces indigenous requirements.

The addition of new word classes can be illustrated with the example of Warlpiri. According to Bavin (1989):

In Warlpiri there is no justification for a syntactic category adjective. Any 'adjective' is a nominal in that it can form a noun phrase on its own. It can also function as a modifier to another nominal (as can other nominals). So in sentence (6), wiri is translated as 'the big one', but in (7) as 'big':

(6) Nyangu-rna wiri.
    saw-1SG   big
    'I saw the big one'
(7) Nyangu-rna marlu wiri
    saw-1SG   kangaroo big
    'I saw the big kangaroo'

The addition of -*wani* to borrowed English adjectives marks them as nominals.

(Bavin 1989: 273)

Leaving aside the problem of what it means for a language to have or not to have adjectives, I would like to consider the observation that all adjectives borrowed from English are overtly signalled by the addition of -*wani* (as observed by Bavin):

In Warlpiri, any borrowed adjective has wani attached, regardless of its position in the sentence, so it is assimilated into the system, which distinguishes nouns and verbs but not adjectives. Warlpiri nominals (such as wiri 'big' and wita 'small') do not have wani attached. A wani-suffixed word can have other Warlpiri affixes attached (case and number markers).

(Bavin 1989: 274)

The splitting up of a present class into two formally different ones would seem to suggest that a new class is being added. With English becoming the important language of the Warlpiri community it may not be long before forms such as *wiriwan* 'big one' may make an appearance.

A class of words that is rarely found in Pacific languages is that of abstract nouns derived from verbs or adjectives such as *talk, idea, independent, virtue* or *love*. Such abstract nouns suggest that what they refer to can exist independently of those who exhibit the characteristic referred to. They promote a shift from a transitive to an intransitive view of the world, thereby reducing agency or involvement of speakers. Abstract nouns such as *independence, self-government, freedom, self-sufficiency, development, progress* and numerous others that have been added to the lexicon of the languages of the area would also seem to flood those speakers with conceptual clutter of the type that is difficult to accommodate into their traditional mode of thought, thus increasing for example irrational behaviour, word magic and misunderstandings. It may not be accidental that the term 'cargo movement' was understood by the practitioners of Melanesian cargo cults as referring to physical population 'movement' from the interior to the coast.

The few existing attempts to classify the language of the area according to the word class that is most important to them (Capell 1966 for Papuan languages) distinguish between verb- or action-centred and noun- or object-centred languages. It is not known to what extent borrowing from outside sources and missionary language engineering have affected this typology.

In fact, it appears that the greatest changes have not occurred with the main word classes but with subclasses, for example changes in, or abolition of, the various subdivisions of alienable and inalienable nouns. Traditionally, these subdivisions signal either control over a noun or control of the relationship that obtains between two nouns. It is well known that the subtleties of the A- and O- noun classes in the Polynesian languages have escaped Western analysts for a very long time and that misunderstandings as to what precisely was signalled by this distinction have led translators and missionaries and other language makers greatly to distort the system (for data refer to Mühlhäusler and Harré 1990).

In an important paper contrasting syntactic change in a number of New Britain languages, Thurston (1992) compares conservative esoteric languages such as Anêm where some lexical borrowing but no syntactive calquing occurs, with the neighbouring Lusi, which is riddled with Tok Pisin lexicon:

> In 1981, we found that young people failed to understand fairly basic Lusi words and constructions, as, for example, 'I like it':

(1) Lusi syntax and lexicon	*mana-gu*	like-my
(2) Tok Pisin syntax, Lusi lexicon	*na-mana*	I-like
(3) Tok Pisin syntax and lexicon	*na-laikim*	I-like

> (Thurston 1992: 134)

Thurston's study implies that the prime function of syntax is an indexical rather than communicative one and that the belief among Anêm speakers that an orderly traditional language is an index as well as cause of the well-being of their society constitutes a powerful reason for not letting its syntax decline. Thurston's empirical study would also seem to render problematic Markey's (1986) assertion that esoteric small languages are particularly vulnerable.

CHANGES IN PRONOMINAL SYSTEMS

Pronouns are usually regarded as being primarily anaphoric devices, creating cohesion within grammatical structures and their behaviour is believed to be governed by rules that specify which pronouns can 'replace' which other nominal constructions. As Mühlhäusler and Harré (1990) have shown, however, the more important feature of pronouns is deixis, the dividing up of people space and the indexing of participant relations to one another and the world. Pronoun systems thus reflect the culture-specific organization of people space and the limits within which speakers can create speech situations. The availability of honorific pronouns, for instance, forces speakers to code social rank, distance and solidarity, whilst pronominal systems distinguishing between harmonic and dysharmonic relations provide an important reinforcement for a certain type of kinship system. By contrast, the pronouns of English are relatively neutral, or, at least, make provision for personal deixis (speaker, hearer, addressee) that does not have to signal other information (such as gender, class, social relationships, etc.). When considering the pronominal system of the language of the Australian and Pacific areas, one is struck by their enormous diversity and the wide range of social information which is expressed in many of them.

Because pronoun systems are typically dependent on an existing social order and cultural beliefs, cultural changes can have dramatical consequences in this area of grammar. These consequences include

1 formal simplification
2 large-scale loss of pronouns indexing culturally rather than situationally relevant information
3 the addition of new pronouns signalling the social asymmetries between colonizers and colonized
4 typological convergence with SAE six-pronoun systems
5 inconsistent usage.

These changes, of course, should not be taken as a direct reflection of changes in group-specific conventions as to the use of pronouns (e.g. 'we' to address the hearer in English or to signal diminished responsibility of speakers), however unfortunately, very little information about pronoun use (as against abstract grammatical systems) in traditional languages is available.

By formal simplification we mean the reduction of pronominal variation signalling grammatical categories such as case and tense. Such reductions tend to be accompanied by a typological shift from clitic pronouns (attached to verbs) to independent pronoun forms, a process well known from pidgin studies.

An example is provided by Bavin (1989) from Warlpiri:

> One of the domains in which we have noted most variation in the speech community is the pronominal system. Warlpiri has independent pronouns for 1st and 2nd persons singular, dual, and plural. For the 1st person, there is also a distinction between inclusive (of hearer) and exclusive (of hearer) for the dual and plural forms. In addition, there is a series of cross-reference clitics which appear in second position in the clause, either attached to an auxiliary base (marking imperfective aspect or future tense) or attached to the end of the first element in the clause, whatever that element may be. There are distinct forms for subject and object with the dative object taking precedence over the absolutive. There are 21 clitic forms in the traditional system. . . . Note that it is not easy to segment these forms into distinct morphemes for person, number, and inclusion.
>
> From the data we have collected we see that some of the traditional distinctions are being lost, and some of the forms being used show innovation. . . . It is clear that the complex system is changing. The results of a survey of Warlpiri speakers ranging in age from 9 to 60 indicate that for the 1st person pronominal forms, all speakers interviewed over the age of 37 retained five distinct forms for independent pronouns, five distinct forms for subject clitics, and five distinct forms for object clitics. No person younger than 17 did.
>
> (Bavin 1989: 280–1)

She sums up the findings of the survey as follows:

> There is a great deal of variation in the forms used but this variation does not have social correlates. Rather it reflects a move towards more semantic transparency in the pronominal forms as well as a move towards reducing the number of oppositions in the system. As the young people receive so much language input from peers as well as from people a few generations older, it is likely that the changes will continue.
>
> (Bavin 1989: 283–4)

Similar changes have been reported for other languages (see contributions to Dorian 1989a) all of them signalling a gradual collapse of traditional distinctions in form and a leaner, meaner SAE-type pronoun system. The traditional view that pronominal systems are the most stable area of a language is not confirmed by such evidence.

CONCEPTUAL CHANGES

Bechert (1991: 9) noticed that 'the assumption of universal semantic structures, abstracted with European methods from mostly European language data, is a self-fulfilling prophecy insofar as the expansion of European culture is bound to lead to ever increasing conformity of the languages and cultures of the world with these universals'. He also comments that 'the semantic system of colonised languages become hollow once the culture is dead'. The prevailing dogma of effability has, of course, hampered the investigation of this matter. We have reasons to believe, however, that next to SAE languages there have been a wide range of linguistically encoded conceptual systems of a very different kind. The difference between Western SAE systems and other conceptual systems lies

1 in their lexically and grammatically coded knowledge of semantic distinctions
2 in the culture-specific metaphors that are used to obtain new knowledge.

Knowledge relates to the number of 'realities':

1 the natural environment
2 states of the mind
3 philosophies and religious frameworks.

Such knowledge is transmitted socially from generation to generation. The natural environment of Australia and the Pacific, as anywhere, is complex and not open to simple direct observation. It took many generations to build up knowledge of the places, climatic patterns, plants and animals that shared this environment with its human inhabitants. Such knowledge enabled the majority of the region's inhabitants to adapt their language to the natural resources provided to enable them to survive over long periods of time. It is true, of course, that the relationship between human beings and the natural environment has been a dynamic and changing one, and it is also true that misjudgement and lack of knowledge has resulted in local ecological disasters and led to a significant transformation of the ecology. Nevertheless, it is also true that Australian Aborigines, for instance, have been able to survive for more than 50,000 years whilst 200 years of European colonization of the continent has caused changes of an order of magnitude (e.g. to the top soil, forests and waterways) that threaten the survival of Australia's inhabitants in only a few generations.

Knowledge of the natural environment is encoded twofold:

1 in the lexicon
2 in grammatical devices such as classification systems and possessive pronominals.

As regards the former, numerous writers have commented on the loss of vocabulary for indigenous flora and fauna (e.g. Milner 1984):

> Many of the Fijian speakers no longer even know the names of important parts of their bodies, such as the fingers. They do not know the names of some of the common animals and plants of their country. If they know them at all, they only know the English equivalents. It is not a kind of affectation or showing off: it has the approval of parents and teachers. If in doubt, use an English word.
>
> One day, three years ago, as I scanned my Fijian newspaper, I came across the word ELIKOPUTA. Five syllables, so it sounds like, and it is, a loan-word from English. It seemed to me that one could do a little better than that. It was the time of year when there are a lot of dragon-flies in Suva. Could one not use the Fijian name for them, *cecewai*, for a helicopter? After all, the resemblance is striking. Full of my ingenuity, I went to see the Fijian editor, who listened to me gravely and politely. He said that he would consider my suggestion. Full of a sense of achievement, I mentioned this idea to Dr Paul Geraghty of the Fijian Dictionary Project. He smiled. 'What you don't realize', he said to me, 'is that like you, Fijian boys have also seen the resemblance between a dragon-fly and a helicopter. But you're too late. They call dragon-flies *elikoputa*.'
>
> (Milner 1984: 18)

I have explored the relationship between syntax and semantics on the one hand and societal perceptions of the environment on the other in much detail elsewhere (Brockmeier, Harré and Mühlhäusler 1996; Mühlhäusler 1995), where I have summarized the existing literature. A major finding is that parallel to syntactic changes that increase the transitivity of human beings, there is a cultural transformation from a holistic world view to one emphasizing human control over nature.

Whilst natural space continues to exist, the languages and the cultures interpreting such space in quite diverse ways rapidly disappear. It would be rash to expect that Western biology, physics or geology have come even remotely close to replacing such traditional knowledge as is now being lost. The reasons for this include that the learning context in which the knowledge was acquired was interaction involving the participation of young people and their socialization into the older cultural conventions of dealing with the natural environment. This context of learning has largely been replaced by Western-type schools that teach Western-type knowledge. Thus, for example, the special pandanus-gathering languages of Imbonga and other New Guinea Highlands languages, with their own modified syntax, disappear because people feel that 'they do not need to use it because they are no longer afraid when they go to the forest areas where the bush spirits reside' (Franklin 1992: 4).

THE LEXICON

Conceptual changes are most closely associated with the lexicon, both the inventory of lexical bases and its derived items. These changes manifest themselves in

1 obsolescence of traditional concepts
2 addition of new concepts
3 transformations.

Much has been written about obsolescence of the lexicon and some fairly comprehensive studies are available, such as in-depth studies of certain lexical fields. Generally speaking, the loss of lexical items encoding traditional concepts reflects the change in sources of knowledge. Whereas in the past the older members of the society tended to be the guardians of most knowledge, new external sources have become more powerful; missionaries, government officials, teachers and the printed word all are sources of authoritative knowledge. As these new sources tend to be ignorant of most traditional knowledge, this is no longer passed on. In saying this I am referring to not only formal teaching but also informal transmission of knowledge, such as story-telling. In a study of language change in central Australian Warlpiri, Bavin (1989) reports that she has

> been told that the young children do not sit around the camp fires at night to listen to stories as much as they used to. After an overnight camping trip for two of the school grades, one of the Warlpiri ladies was pleased that the children had a chance to hear the old people telling stories. There seems to be some pride when a young adult tells us that his/her father (or someone else) was the source of a particular story. In addition, people in the community are aware of who the good story-tellers are, so story-telling is a valued skill. Now, however, there is a place where children can go in the evenings to listen to music, and the adults are often busy with cardgames so, according to our helpers, the children no longer

have the same exposure to traditional stories. When we have more details, it will be of interest to see if there is a strong correlation between the linguistic skills of the children and their exposure to story-telling. Our impressions are that there may be.

(Bavin 1989: 284–5)

As a consequence we find that 'children of this age are not familiar with traditional words for hunting weapons, words such as *pikirri* "spear thrower", and *kurdije* "shield", although *kurlada* "spear" is still well known' (Bavin 1989: 277). Knowledge of traditional botanical names is another area of loss, as are words expressing the distinctions of traditional medicine, religion, transport and legal systems.

Borrowing from European sources has not been restricted to the smaller, less powerful languages. Even important regional languages such as Bahasa Indonesia are affected: 'Approximately 10% of the items entered under -*s* for example are Dutch borrowings, which penetrated deeply into all levels of the vocabulary' (Laycock 1971: 881).

The term 'loss' fails to draw attention to the fact that many of the traditional concepts and their lexical forms were not, in fact, lost but taken away and/or destroyed. Thus, the 'loss' of the Maori concept 'hahunga' (the digging up of a dead person after two or three years for the cleaning of the bones and final interment) was caused by the missions who discouraged the notion that death was gradual and by the government who did not wish to encourage what they regarded as an unhygienic practice. The Samoan concept of public defloration of young girls suffered a similar fate as did numerous other concepts that violated the sensitivities of missions, traders or administrators. One can refer to numerous instances of the deliberate destruction of traditional crafts (such as carving craven images), social practices (polygamy, cannibalism, male menstruation, tree burials) in almost any society one cares to consider.

It is difficult to quantify such losses as comprehensive data reflecting the traditional state of the Australian and Pacific vernaculars are very few and few detailed studies of the process of lexical loss exist. However, such studies as are available suggest that the losses have been extensive. An excellent quantitative study of the lexicon of a number of Milne Bay (Papua New Guinea) languages between 1960 and 1990 is given by Lithgow (1992).

Traditional concepts are not always lost when traditional lexical forms are lost, as in some cases we are dealing simply with the replacement of word shape. Bavin (1989: 275) gives a list of such formal replacements in Warlpiri:

boomerang	for karli
kangaroo	for malu and wawirri
dingo	for warnapari
tea	for nalija
horse	for nantuwu
no	for lawa
and	for manu
night	for munga

This list demonstrates that even the closed set of grammatical words is affected, as are words such as *boomerang* that clearly belong to the local and not English culture. The power to name things and to change existing names obviously lies with the speakers of the metropolitan languages.

There is a fine dividing line between replacements and additions but it is generally not the case, as is believed by many investigators, that languages are capable of simply absorbing any new lexical material without effect on the existing the lexicon. Such a view would seem to be based on a very simplistic notion of the lexicon as an unstructured list of arbitrary signs, rather than one exhibiting complex semantic field properties, with redundancy rules governing the distinction of lexical information and other non-lexical information. Whilst keeping in mind reservations about the atomistic and mechanistic approach to lexical changes, we shall nevertheless concentrate in the next section on additions *per se* and disregard their effect on other non-local lexical properties.

Additions are clearly associated with modernization of traditional societies through the introduction of new technologies, social and educational practices and the dividing up of the social and temporal space. Of the many studies concerned with the massive introduction of English items 'by bible and by bottle' (K. J. Hollyman 1962: 313) let me consider first those of Samoan. As early as 1852, Pratt's dictionary of the language listed 142 foreign borrowings, mainly dealing with introduced religion, 73 of which were of English, 28 of Greek and 9 of Hebrew origin. In a survey carried out in the 1950s Milner (1957) reports a significant increase in this number with new words added to the domains of religion, but also transport, sports, politics, administration and industry. The Samoan case also illustrates how early the division of time was rearranged, with the names of days of the week and months of the year firmly established by 1862.

Milner, in his 1957 article, is of the view that the number of foreign words in Samoan is too small to be capable of destroying the nature of the Samoan lexicon, but it would appear that in more recent writings Milner has changed this view.

Additions to the lexicon of many other languages have been documented in great detail, in studies ranging from anecdotal to quantitative studies. Anecdotal evidence, for instance, is given by Hollyman (1962) on lexical changes in Melanesia.

> In the Loyalty Islands, one finds a number of English words. In Lifu, for example, altar has replaced the indigenous tepen, and we find ngerog in wene ngerog 'grog fruit', mani 'money', paip 'pipe', tepek 'tobacco'; mbolok, kau, hos; mbaket 'bucket', mbalaiket 'blanket', mbot 'boat', imbut 'boot', jam, janua, julit, sileva 'silver'. In New Caledonia itself, in the Wailu language, there appears from Leenhardt's dictionary to be a fairly even distribution of English and French words: from English, mbangä 'bag', mbokesi 'box', ngalasi 'glass', ki, kofi, lasi 'rice', maci 'matches', paipi 'pipe', sopo 'soap', waki 'work'; and from French, ndisu 'metal coin' (Fr. dix sous), faraki 'franc', ngavana 'Gouverneur', ngerenu 'frog' (Fr. grenouille; Hula aurea (Less.) has been introduced from Australia), ngeresi 'fat, oil' (Fr. graisse), jarapu 'flag' from drapeau, as well as pavion from pavillon, koniake 'cognac', laloa 'law' (Fr. la loi), mandai from mÇdaille, monä from mannaie, sovari 'horse' (Fr. cheval).
>
> Some of the Biblical borrowings have been thoroughly integrated and their usage extended; for example, in Nengone, basileia, of Greek origin, is now applied to local tribes and chieftainships. Shifts of meaning can also be noted in non-religious borrowings: in ArhÉ, a New Caledonian language for example, sevÇrä from French chèvre 'goat' means 'deer'.
>
> (Hollyman 1962: 318)

Whilst most descriptions of traditional languages contain lists of words of non-native origin, we do not have information about the actual occurrence of new words in everyday discourse. The fact that words are listed in a dictionary does not say much about their use and, as informed observers suggest, if 'loans' are becoming more extensively used, their impact on the rest of the lexicon may be much more considerable than that suggested by mere inventories. I believe that former everyday domains of traditional languages are increasingly becoming special domains, used only in the context of story-telling, discussion of the past and traditional religion. It is hoped that studies of lexical use and discourse will become available to further illustrate this point.

More thorough analyses of lexical additions are available for instance for Hua (Haiman 1979) and Numbami (Bradshaw 1978). The differential outcome of borrowing in these two New Guinea languages deserves a brief comment, as the evidence points to two types of multilingualism or diglossia. In my view the main difference between the two cases is that, in the Hua case, the languages that make up the repertoire of Hua speakers are distinguished in terms of functions and domains, rather than in terms of social status. Stable bi- and multilingualism involving traditional languages appears to have been a widespread phenomenon in the area of the New Guinea Highlands (see Salisbury 1972), whereas other forms of intercultural communication prevailed in many coastal areas, including the use of simplified versions of the language of the most powerful people in trade. In that situation, an asymmetry developed between high and low languages, with the high languages encroaching on the lexicon and grammar of the low ones. This trend was reinforced when prestige mission and trade pidgins were introduced by the colonizers. We also have to consider the time depth involved in the two case studies. The coastal areas and Lae came under intensive contact with the outside world before 1900 whereas the Westernization of the New Guinea Highlands began only after 1950.

At the time when Haiman was writing about Hua (1979), Tok Pisin had been in the country for about twenty-five years and had become the medium which Hua people used to communicate with outsiders (administrators, Europeans, police officers). It had also been adopted as the language of most mixed marriages, replacing traditional bi- or dual-lingualism as well as being the language in which the modern world was discussed. Thus, the present-day language of card games is Tok Pisin as is that for discussion of local government affairs. As is to be expected, many modern Hua words were borrowed from Tok Pisin.

> Hua borrowed Pidgin words like pasindia ka 'passenger car,' rendio 'radio,' makit or pakit 'market,' haussik 'hospital,' kiap 'patrol officer' (in Hua, generalized to mean 'official') and bia 'beer.' There is nothing in the least surprising or uncommon about borrowing of this sort.
>
> (Haiman 1979: 84)

Such borrowings arguably are peripheral and unlikely to affect the structure of the lexicon dramatically. Another type of borrowing identified by Haiman (1979) would seem to be more serious, that is, the borrowing of superordinate terms when Hua has only basic and subordinate expressions.

> The same mystery attends the borrowing of bihainim(hu) 'follow' when Hua already has words meaning both 'to follow in line' and

'to obey precepts'; opim(hu) 'open,' when Hua has no less than a half-dozen verbs signifying various kinds of opening (as by lifting a cover, peeling skin or bark, removing slats, parting a curtain, etc.); save(hu) 'know,' when Hua has go 'know by seeing' and havi 'know by hearing'; pasim(hu) 'fasten,' 'shut,' when Hua has as many verbs for shutting as it does for opening; and there are many others of this sort.

Heavy Pidgin-borrowing of this sort, which seems both indiscriminate and unmotivated, is probably one of the reasons why some of the older Hua are able to predict the complete disappearance of their language within the lifetime of their children.

(Haiman 1979: 84)

Haiman admits that such borrowing is frequently followed by the loss of the traditional terms.

If borrowing from Pidgin has been heavy in a quarter-century, it is impossible to guess how extensive and deep borrowing has been from Gimi, Siane, and Chimbu, with which Hua has been in contact for hundreds (or perhaps thousands) of years. The fact that Hua has maintained its integrity and autonomy for so long despite such prolonged and intimate contact is an augur for its continued life today.

(Haiman 1979: 85)

His conclusion that the lexicon of Hua has not been affected very deeply is difficult to understand in the light of such evidence. Lexical losses and additions may turn out to be relatively unimportant but here we are dealing with transformation, the conversion of traditional conceptual organization into a modern Western type. Words often no longer mean what they used to mean and have changed their value as introduced words bring into being new systems of semantic contrast. A brief look at some such transformations in another language, Maori, illustrates this point. These remarks are based on Schwimmer's (1965) study of cognitive changes between traditional and modern Mormon Maori. Some of the terms considered by Schwimmer are *tangi, tangi ganga* – 'funeral wake'; terms for 'human kindness'; terms for 'authority'; and terms for the sources of healing power.

With regard to the terms for 'funeral wake', one can contrast two concepts of death, a traditional one and a Mormon one. In the former view, death is a gradual process embracing the disintegration of the body on a physical level and it is caused by ritual pollution or black magic. In the Mormon model death is an instantaneous and natural phenomenon. In Maori culture it is of fundamental importance that the dead person's immortal soul (*wairue*) is separated successfully from the body. Thus, it is essential closely to monitor putrefaction and to find the right moment for the soul to depart and stop troubling the community of the living.

Thus, in contrast to Mormon practice, the Maori *wairue* is a ghost who continues communicating with people of its former home and who needs to be reassured that all the right practices have been observed to allow its departure. The power of the *wairue* is contradicted by practical devices such as charms, language formulae and speeches. Traditional Maori had a large inventory of terms dealing with the objects and practices accompanying the successful wake and related discussion.

The term *tangi* 'wake' is also applied to a wake in present-day Mormon religion, but the meaning of this term has been transformed entirely (Schwimmer 1965).

> I intend to discuss only those aspects of the Mormon conception of death which contradict the traditional Maori conception and were understood in Whangaruru and led either to changes in ritual or at least to significant discussions.
>
> According to Mormon doctrine, before men are born into this world, they live as spirits awaiting the joyful moment when they may take on flesh and bone. At birth, they enter 'the school of mortal experience, meeting, contending with and overcoming evil'. At death the spirit sheds its earthly tabernacle and, if adjudged righteous, ascends to heaven at the moment of death. The sacral significance of the body, after death, is that the righteous will be physically resurrected at the Last Judgment.
>
> (Schwimmer 1965: 156–7)

One of the main differences between the traditional and Mormon *tangi* does not concern the actual ritual but the meaning attached to it. For instance, there is no notion that bodies are polluted by death and need to be purified over a period of time; the spirit cannot be helped by kinsmen in its ascent to heaven; there is no justification for collective wailing, in fact the Mormon reinterpretation is that wailing may trouble the spirit in its ascent to heaven and those engaged in the wailing are seen to be in breach of religious dogma.

A more formal difference is that smoking, which played an important role in the old wake, is forbidden. Schwimmer reports an incident:

> At the third tangi, a notice was posted on the marae forbidding smoking, a measure which outside visitors considered so insulting

that some left almost at once. Those who posted the notice admitted to me afterwards that they did not care if it drove off visitors; the fewer there were, the better.

(Schwimmer 1965: 158)

This incident highlights another semantic transformation discussed by Schwimmer, the meaning of the expression 'human kindness':

> One example was the opposition to the posting of the 'no smoking' notices. The Whangaruru Mormons objected to these because the kinsmen from other districts, who were not Mormons and who were attending the tangi, had the right to say that Whangaruru was 'their marae' and therefore, they had a right to smoke on it. Others said that the prohibition was inconsistent with 'human kindness', which was also a value the Mormons preached frequently. A third argument was that the notice would scare away potential converts.

(Schwimmer 1965: 164)

Regarding the meaning of this term, it has

> its place both in Maori and in the Mormon cognitive universe, and in each system it has a special meaning. In the Maori system it designates virtues emphasised in a kinship network in which security depends on the fulfilment of reciprocal obligations of the most intimate kind. In the Mormon system it designates toleration and benevolence. Both of these are considered important virtues but toleration is not acceptance and benevolence, according to Mormon teaching, is displayed preeminently in missionary labour and imparting substance to the needy. Clearly, in the Maori meaning of 'human kindness', both the 'no smoking' notices and the forcible removal of the old lady were wrong, but in the Mormon meaning of the term, 'human kindness' has no bearing on the permitting of actions which are categorised as pollutions or desecrations.

(Schwimmer 1965: 164)

Similar transformations of semantic content, again resulting from missionization, have been documented by Renck (1992: 63–4).

A particularly powerful example of missionary reinterpretation of an indigenous expression is the use of the key Pitjantjatjara concept *tjukurpa* 'dreaming, nature, humans, universe, myth, environment', descriptive of their holistic world view in the expression *tjukurpa palya* 'good dreaming' as the word for 'gospel'.

The cumulative evidence presented in this section suggests that most traditional languages of the area have begun to undergo a massive restructuring in the direction of intertranslatability with SAE languages and that this process is unlikely to stop before it has run its full course. When asking the question 'what is lost?' we can expect two answers:

1 A simple answer which lists lexical items, grammatical and pragmatic devices that have disappeared from most languages of the area in the last 200 years. There is mounting evidence that a great deal of linguistic material has indeed been lost.

2 A more complex answer involving the meaning of such losses which, of course, is a much more difficult task and one which, in the absence of more comprehensive theory, cannot have clear answers at this point.

The nature of this chapter is pre-theoretical as a consequence, taking as its point of departure the recognition of losses, preceding the systematization of available observations and the classification of such phenomena into pre-theoretical classes. The implicit theory is that what is lost is neither superficial variants of a universal language capacity, nor material that is unrelated to other aspects of culture. In other words both the belief in total effability (translatability) and the independence of language from other phenomena are rejected.

A crucial consideration for rejecting such views (which are common enough among hard-core linguists) is that they derived from the dubious practice of labelling human languages 'natural'. I feel that we have excellent reasons for regarding many aspects of existing languages as a reflection of a long history of cultural development. The lexicon and structures of language, apart from reflecting universal constraint, contain a very considerable amount of codified cultural knowledge. It is widely held by those working on traditional languages (e.g. Sapir 1949a, 1949b) that

> Vocabulary is a very sensitive index of the culture of a people and changes of the meaning, loss of old words, the creation and borrowing of new ones are all dependent on the history of culture itself. Languages differ widely in the nature of their vocabularies. Distinctions which seem inevitable to us may be utterly ignored in languages which reflect an entirely different type of culture, while these in turn insist on distinctions which are all but unintelligible to us.
>
> (Sapir 1949a: 27)

Whilst such lexical characteristics significantly shape the conceptual resources of a group of speakers, there would appear to be mounting evidence that certain grammatical characteristics are equally important in structuring the perceptions of new entities, as languages differ very significantly in what they have to express when describing singularities.

The availability of grammatical embedding or inflections would seem to be important for highlighting or backgrounding information, compulsory tense distinctions tend to draw attention to the temporal embeddiness of what is talked about, and compulsory encoding of truth values would appear to lead to increased monitoring of the reasons why certain pronouncements are made. Grammatical categories, like lexical distinctions, contribute to the establishment of samenesses, similarities and differences and the possibility of concepts being talked about together in conjuncts.

One of the main obstacles to recognizing such losses has been the inability of linguists to distinguish between simplification, impoverishment, modernization and, above all, their misleading use of the same language name to refer to a language before and after massive lexical and grammatical changes. The belief that all languages at all times are fully capable of catering for all their speakers' needs has not helped either. Linguists share the very human trait of not realizing that something is being lost until it is gone. I hope that they will grasp the last opportunities to learn from traditional languages and cultures before these are irretrievably lost.

CONCLUSIONS

In this chapter our main task has been to survey the grammatical and lexical changes brought about by contact between traditional Pacific and Australian languages and introduced, more powerful metropolitan languages. I have argued that such contacts have drastically changed the character of these languages, a fact that cannot be concealed simply by using traditional labels referring to 'modernized' languages. My main concern has been to document traditional language decline and restructuring and to demonstrate just how missionization and modernization of languages can have effects far beyond those intended by language planners. Much less has been said about more sudden instances of language murder and language shift, though it is not difficult to see that such catastrophic changes can lead to an even greater loss of lexical structural resources. In the absence of any clear documented cases one can only guess at the loss of lexically encoded concepts and of the grammatical resources that have influenced the perception of the users in those languages that have already disappeared. We simply do not have any analysis of the lexicon, cryptogrammar, metaphorical devices and conventions of use of the vast majority of Pacific languages. Two summaries of Papuan languages (Foley 1986b; Wurm 1971b), for instance, have almost nothing to say about these matters. Whatever could have been learnt from a study of such languages has disappeared for good and a vast body of additional knowledge will also disappear without trace.

I do not claim that what has disappeared was necessarily better, purer or more conducive to the long-term survival of humans than SAE languages but I would maintain that it was different and that it represented knowledge of the type that might well be needed in our own languages. My argument is one about the intrinsic value of diversity rather than about rating the merits of different languages. As Arthur (1990: 16) has argued, we should be aware of 'the potential which language has to create maps which can seriously mislead about the nature of the landscape that they purport to represent'.

And it is one of the reasons why it is useful to have a number of different maps, a number of conceptual systems to serve as a corrective against particular assumptions about the world. To express it in the words of Benjamin Lee Whorf (1956):

> Western culture has made, through language, a provisional analysis of reality and, without correctives, holds resolutely to that analysis as final; the only correctives lie in all those other tongues which by aeons of independent revolution have arrived at different, but equally logical provisional analyses.
>
> (Whorf 1956: 244)

Two hundred years of Western industrialized culture constitute a short period in the history of humankind, and to assume that the provisional assumptions, interpretations and metaphors that have dominated this period are indeed the supreme answer, and that no alternative view should be considered, seems quite shortsighted. The loss of lexical and structural resources in traditional languages seems catastrophic in a technical sense, but it is also possible that it will turn out to be catastrophic in its consequences. The often-heard beliefs that the loss of languages need not lead to a loss of cultural diversity or that traditional semantics continue as substrate in the modernized, new languages have little to recommend them. Once the distinctions that used to be culturally relevant have been replaced by other distinctions; they cease to have an important effect on people's perception and conceptualization of the world around them. As Ferguson (1968) observes:

> Modernisation of a language may be thought of as the process of its becoming the equal of other developed languages as a medium of communication. It is in a sense a process of joining the world community of increasingly intertranslatable languages as appropriate vehicles of modern forms of discourse.
>
> (Ferguson 1968: 33)

12 Preserving linguistic diversity: outlook and prospects

The real question for modern life and reversing language shift is
... how one can build a home that one can still call one's own
and, by cultivating it, find community, comfort, companionship
and meaning in a world whose mainstreams are increasingly
unable to provide the basic ingredients for their own members.

(Fishman 1989: 16)

INTRODUCTION

This book has addressed questions concerning the rapid decline of
linguistic diversity in the Pacific area, and has brought together a
rather amorphous body of evidence, much of it quite depressing. We
have established that the principal reason for this mass loss of diversity
was European colonization, whose agents set in motion a number of
processes that have changed the region almost beyond recognition.
We have tried to refrain from putting too much emphasis on motifs
such as exploitation, selfishness, intolerance and ill will, though all of
these were present. Much more importantly, in our opinion, is the
sheer ignorance with which the newcomers approached the area and
the numerous instances where good intention had unexpected and
unwanted long-term effects.

Ignorance of the linguistic situation of the area has been profound
and continues to be so. In many areas of life (economic, political,
educational and linguistic) expatriate problems and solutions have
been imported, distorting local reality and leading to rather costly
patch-up jobs when things go wrong. Just as the population and
environmental crises have begun to force radical rethinking, the
growing realization that there is a cultural and linguistic crisis of
equal proportion will no doubt necessitate similar readjustments in
this area.

Language planning until the 1980s was based on the premise

that linguistic diversity is a problem which can be overcome only by streamlining and central planning. The major conceptual shift that is now occurring is that linguistic diversity may in fact be an asset as well as a solution to former problems, and language maintenance has become the new area of focus.

Understanding and promoting language maintenance would seem to involve the following elements:

1 the framing of the problem and aims
2 themes of causes
3 themes of maintenance
4 means adopted for finding solutions
5 spreading awareness.

There are two distinct views on the question of language maintenance. The first and most widespread is that one is dealing with a problem of social justice, since it is not right that society after society should lose language and that those who continue to speak a non-mainstream language are educationally and economically disadvantaged. This view continues to see diversity as a problem but one that can be attenuated with the infusion of money and goodwill. Current Australian language policies are an example of this view.

A second radical view is that the trend toward monolingualism and monoculturalism is the problem: that diversity itself is a necessary precondition of economic and social well-being and that the cost of preserving such diversity is small compared to its benefits. This view, advocated in this book, does not as yet have the moral high ground that mainstream development ideology has enjoyed and, in particular, is not widely found among the speakers of many small languages themselves.

Fishman (1989) lists some of the criticisms that the mainstream have tended to direct against language maintenance movements, including those of irrationality, backward attitudes and oppressiveness. It is for these reasons that a comprehensive theory of language maintenance is needed.

THEORIES

A theory, to me, is an explicit, structured and falsifiable bunch of prejudices. Theories are tools for investigating complex subject matter, not mirror images of reality and their *raison d'être* is that prejudice-free observation is not a property of human beings.

Much of this book has been concerned with the causes of the loss of linguistic diversity. In proposing an ecological approach which investigates the support system for a structural ecology of language rather than individual languages and in proposing causal factors additional to the stereotypically given factors of population decline, change of lifestyle and modern technology, I hope to have added to the knowledge of the causes of catastrophic change in the life of languages. A particularly strong claim of the ecological approach is that the focus of inquiry should be upon the functional relationship between the factors that affect the general interrelationship between languages rather than individual factors impacting on individual languages.

Because of this wider focus I would suggest that a realistic approach to language maintenance also needs to be ecological. Before returning to this point, I would like to present a brief commentary on a range of other explicit and implicit theories of language maintenance. Not all of these have been fully articulated but it would nevertheless seem useful to list the numerous approaches to language maintenance that have emerged in recent years. The theories I would like to consider here are the following: all but the first and second have emerged since the mid-1980s.

1 'classical theory' of language planning
2 historical-structural theory (Tollefson)
3 language and identity (accommodation theories) (LePage and Giles)
4 reversing language shift (RLS) theory (Fishman)
5 deficit reduction/empowerment theories
6 empowerment theories
7 domain separation/diglossia theories
8 ecological theory.

'Classical theory' of language planning

This theory (discussed in great detail in Tollefson 1991) is based on the assumption that language loss and maintenance reflect the free and rational choices that speakers make. Speakers will abandon languages that are of no use to them in their search for economic and social advancement. The large-scale abandonment or 'language suicide' witnessed in Aboriginal Australia would be interpreted as a 'natural' process and attempts to slow it down or to maintain linguistic diversity are interpreted as interfering with progress. Ladefoged's (1992) criticism of language maintenance is a good example of the linguistic counterpart of economic rationalism.

The classical theory illustrates the tendency of many advocates and silent supporters to convert the historical process into the myth of a natural development. In debunking this myth, Tollefson has done the field of language maintenance a good service. However, what he has put in its place also suffers from a number of inadequacies.

Historical-structural theory

This theory derives from Marxist sociology and is represented in Tollefson's (1991) writings as well as in work on critical language awareness (e.g. Fairclough 1992). The principal argument in this theory is that minority speakers do not have a free choice but are controlled by the social, economic and ideological forces that obtain in capitalism.

Tollefson's inclusion of social class, gender and preceding history increases the number of explanations for language loss and maintenance but his argument that language maintenance in Marxist societies, such as the former Soviet Union, is a significant improvement over maintenance in societies where the classical theory prevails has little empirical support, as can be readily seen from studies of the minority languages of Siberia in Collis (1990).

In Australia, the contributors to J. Bell (1981) have put forward a range of suggestions on language maintenance from a non-Marxist historical-structural perspective, emphasizing the need for cultural democracy and solutions initiated by the speakers of minority languages rather than by 'benevolent' central planning agencies.

Language and identity (accommodation theories)

The principal reasons why language comes into being and continues to be maintained is seen in the speakers' wish to mark their separate identity by means of a shared language and by accommodating their speech to that of perceived role models (e.g. political and cultural leaders). LePage and Tabouret-Keller (1985) illustrate how low-status languages can become high-status viable languages in a relatively short lifespan if a communal act of identity occurs and if languages can be reinstated as core values of a community. The factors that lead to such an act of identity can be more numerous and diverse than the factors considered in the historical-structural theory and would seem to have applications to the situation of many Australian indigenous and Pacific languages.

In an important interview, LePage (1993) spells out a number of the implications of a 'language and identity' approach to language maintenance, particularly for the role of the education system.

LePage's first observation is that language maintenance is hampered by prevailing mainstream attitudes, which are supported by the dominant language:

> there is a good deal of arrogance built into our language and that is a symptom of the relationships we have with the rest of the world. And when I first went to Jamaica I thought I was a liberal sort of person and I had not realized until I had been there for about three years how arrogant in fact I was in many ways towards our societies, how many stereotypes were built into the kind of language I use. I think the French and the English have been particularly guilty in this way but we are not the only ones. True, I think also of the Northern Chinese, of the Mandarin speakers who have a similar attitude towards many Southern Chinese and certainly to people like the Tibetans and so on. I think, awareness of this built-in arrogance ought to be part of the task of education.
>
> (LePage 1993: 7)

This implies the need to extract the role of education to

1 promote critical language awareness in all schools, particularly those for the mainstream
2 promote critical language awareness among all educators.

He concludes:

> If we are going to do any planning, then generally the instrument for putting planning into effect is the education system, whatever that may be. And we have to try to educate the educators and to get to understand the nature of all the variants, passions and motives that are at work, and to understand the nature of the stereotypes which they themselves cling to. This is a very very uphill task. The subject of language is one on which a great many people have strong opinions and they do not very easily change those opinions. There is no point in attempting to present programs for language planning unless you can have some prospect of putting them into effect effectively. That means a great deal of preparative work has to be done and one has to recognize that although it sounds a terribly arrogant thing to say, it is nevertheless true that most of the things that most people believe about language are not true.
>
> University courses designed to 'educate the educators', such as the ones developed by LePage at York University (United Kingdom), in his opinion will need to supplement and/or replace current programs in applied and theoretical linguistics, and in-service

language awareness courses need to be put in hand to speed up the process of reorienting mainstream attitudes to language and language maintenance.

(LePage 1993: 20)

Given that in Australia and the Pacific many educators and policy makers were brought up in a period when ideas of assimilation and monoculturalism prevailed, LePage's recommendation would seem to be highly relevant to this context.

Reversing language shift (RLS) theory

One of the most elaborate and coherent attempts to construct a theoretical base for language maintenance is that of Fishman (summarized in Fishman 1989 and detailed in Fishman 1991). The latter contains numerous case studies, including one of Australia's attempts to maintain indigenous and migrant languages.

Fishman, like other theoreticians, sees prevailing mainstream ideologies as fundamentally incapable of dealing with the problem:

> The ability of universality and particularism to develop and co-exist simultaneously within the very same populations was a rude awakening for both Marxist and non-Marxist theorists who had assumed that industrialisation, urbanisation, modernisation and the spread of education would inevitably reduce ethnic consciousness and lead to the demise of narrow loyalties in favour of broader ones.

(Fishman 1989: 15)

RLS theory is an attempt to explain the rationality of ethnocultural behaviour and language and identity movements, a task ignored by modern social science.

Fishman (1991) expresses the view that Australian language policies, in spite of the good intentions of many politicians and educators, are likely to fail, as political will and financial commitment are neither sufficient nor necessary reasons for a language to be maintained:

> However, when all is said and done, the RLS outlook in Australia is far bleaker than the sheer. amount of RLS activity currently ongoing might seem to imply. Aboriginal languages are dying at the rate of one or more a year and language shift continues unabated in the immigrant-based 'community languages' fold. This is a tremendous attrition for a country that recognizes, as few others do, its own dire need for languages other than English and

that has shown as much admiration, recognition and support as Australia has for the languages still spoken within its borders. Unfortunately, as we have noted so many times before, good intentions are not enough and the steps taken or about to be taken are either largely unrelated, non-productive or even counter-productive as far as intergenerational RLS-payoff is concerned. . . .

Australian policies and processes constitute a positive but ineffective approach to RLS on behalf of recent immigrant languages and a negative but potentially effective approach to RLS on behalf of Aboriginal languages. Because of its relative proximity to and ultimate commercial connectedness with South and Southeast Asia Australia may well be the first anglo-establishment country to break out of the prison of English mono-lingualism. However, few of its immigrant language communities and none of its Aboriginal language communities will benefit directly from this self-liberation. Indeed, over the long run (during the next fifty years or so), a few Aboriginal languages associated with 'outstations' and genuine community schools may be far more successful on the RSL scene than any of the recently proliferated immigrant languages currently marked by social mobility and urban demographic dispersion, on the one hand, and by a luxuriant growth of language courses, radio programs and television broadcasts, on the other hand. This will come about because a very few, fortunate (i.e. governmentally benignly neglected) Aboriginal languages are genuinely linked to the intergenerational mother tongue transmission process rooted as it is in home-family-neighbourhood and community, whereas no such linkage generally exists in connection with the highly publicized efforts on behalf of immigrant languages.

(Fishman 1991: 277–8)

Like LePage, Fishman advocated (1989: 17) far-reaching 'conscience heightening and reformation'. At the same time, and in common with an ecological theory, he favours solutions that do not isolate indigenous communities from the mainstream but that 'safeguard their aspirations for that they will be in touch with but not inundated by the world at large' (p. 16).

As regards schools, he maintains:

For RLS success the school must be an integral part of the family–neighbourhood axis of child socialisation and identity–commitment formation. Schools cannot succeed, whether their goal be RLS or merely history or mathematics instruction, if the relationship between teachers, parents and students is such that they are estranged from each other and from the curriculum. 'Schools are the children of the community'. . . .

Childcare/playgroup arrangements that involve contact with adult specialists in tutoring, computers, dance, drama, writing, library research, athletics, scouting and after-school jobs contribute to an amazing widening of perspective and learning experiences, as well as to a diversification of interests and interactive competence, that have great significance not only for academic success but for success in the larger society thereafter.

(Fishman 1989: 30–1)

Finally, Fishman is sceptical of academic attempts to solve the problem of RLS as a logical problem and advocates greater understanding for those minority groups that have begun to put in place local practical solutions, such as the 'language nests' in Aotearoa (New Zealand) and Hawaii.

Fishman's theory is complex and it is impossible to do justice to it here. His writings will take a central place in any programme designed to educate or re-educate educators, administrators and the public at large.

Deficit reduction/empowerment theories

As in many areas debated by technocrats, the idea that the language to be maintained or planned suffers from inherent deficits is very widespread. These deficits are usually framed in terms of those criteria which in the past were used to distinguish languages from dialects or patois. The latter often lacked a proper name, a writing system, standardization, were incapable of expressing modern ideas, and lacked political power and/or official recognition. To maintain languages, it is argued, one needs to equip them with all the paraphernalia that 'real' languages have. This approach, apart from its conceptual problems, runs into very considerable economic difficulties. A multilingual nation such as Papua New Guinea could not afford fully to 'develop' its 800 plus languages and it would quite simply be beyond the powers even of an affluent country with a much smaller number of languages, such as Australia, to afford a programme of this type. There are more favourable conditions in formerly monolingual countries such as Fiji or Aotearoa (New Zealand). That Maori could become a language for all domains of communication in New Zealand is at least not economically impossible.

Deficit theoreticians are faced with a stark choice: either selectively to privilege a few strong languages or else employ the 'watering can' approach and add a bit of what is perceived as missing to many languages.

Clearly related to this view are empowerment theories.

Empowerment theories

Most empowerment theories are based on the technocratic argument that languages are best maintained through the use of up-to-date media and communication technology. In the past literacy and print have often been identified as major resources for language preservation and more recently radio, television, videos and computers have been given the same role. An interesting new departure in the area of literacy is the development of shell books, which contain

> everything found in a book except words. The illustrations, pictures and page numbers are printed on uncut, unbound pages. After translation, any local language text may be added and good quality books printed right in the village, inexpensively, using a simple silkscreen printer.
>
> (Trainum 1993)

They are widely used in the campaign to promote vernacular literacy in Papua New Guinea and as one of its most active promoters, Trainum has opined that:

> Books for Literacy and Awareness, Adult Education for Development, Village Elementary Schools – all these and more can be produced locally by the people themselves. These information and communication materials will come from outside their cultures. But the people will control the process of adapting the new information so that it is integrative – in harmony with their traditional values – and not disruptive.
>
> This is true Integral Human Development, controlled by the communities themselves. You and I cannot know the best way to communicate in 869 different languages which represent unique cultures in Papua New Guinea. But by offering communication and information opportunities in a form that respects the dignity of the receptor communities – by looking upon the task of communicating with them as a partnership – you have the opportunity to communicate in a way that will strengthen Integral Human Development in this nation.
>
> As you develop a National Communication Policy, I urge you to take this opportunity. Communicate with the people – not to them – in languages which they speak.
>
> (Trainum 1993)

A similarly strong claim has been made about the potential role of the computer as the resource of endangered languages. The magical powers of the computer are evoked, for instance, in a news item in the *Australian* (26/6/84) subtitled 'Technology rescues Eskimo language' which informs its readers that 'thanks to the silicon chip, the survival of Canada's beleaguered native languages may now be safe!'

A more critical view of the role of the electronic media in language maintenance is given by Mühlhäusler, Philpott and Trew (1996).

Domain separation/diglossia theories

Domain separation is a fashionable theory in contemporary Australia and in some nearby Pacific countries. In essence it is the assumption that traditional languages can be contained in a restricted range of contexts (family affairs, traditional law or knowledge, primary education, religion) whilst other domains (public domains, secondary and tertiary education, modern culture) are reserved for English (or another dominant language). Domain separation, it needs to be remembered, once helped small traditional languages to survive side by side with other languages.

On the other hand, domain separation has also been associated with unequal distribution of power. The language and educational practices of former apartheid in South Africa are an example of how domain separation of language can be used to underpin racial and cultural segregation. Even in the absence of colonialist or racist policies, domain separation tends to come at a cost.

The greatest problem appears to be that domain separation in present-day Pacific and Australia leads to diglossia, a situation where power domains are associated with the dominant language and non-power domains with the indigenous languages. In an important study, Topping (1992) has drawn attention to the diglossic situation, with its powerful and powerless domains, that characterizes development in many Pacific territories:

> The shift in language use described has established a newly stratified social order throughout the Pacific Islands. There are new lines separating the illiterate from the literate, the traditional from the modern, and the old from the young. A new elite has risen to displace the old, just as new rituals (e.g. high school graduation) have become the accepted rites of passage. Storytellers, navigators, healers and diviners have all been shunted aside in favour of movies, scheduled airlines, allopathic physicians and theologians –

all of them products of the literate societies of the western world. Although there are still some areas in the Pacific – usually rural – where the old social hierarchies and practices still prevail, they are relatively insignificant. If the dominant pattern prevails, these pockets of the traditional Pacific way will follow the path that has been set in the urban centres.

Perhaps the most lamentable consequence of the encroachment of the western languages in the Pacific is the resulting language loss and concomitant cultural erosion. Following the pattern of the Polynesians of Hawaii and New Zealand, and the Chamorros of Guam, the island people from one side of the Pacific to the other run the serious risk of losing their languages. The danger signs are already present.

In the schools, playgrounds, and even in the offices, it is more and more common to hear English or French spoken by one Islander to another, even when both are speakers of the same Pacific language. More and more frequently, town-dwelling teen-agers speak to each other in the school language.

(Topping 1992: 10)

Diglossic situations are noticeably unstable and liable to promote the shift to the power language over a few generations. Domain separation theories tend to promote the view that the preservation of indigenous languages in its traditional form should go hand in hand with the promotion of skills in a dominant standard language. It does not take into account the role of modern koines, young people's varieties, pidgins and other languages of a domain-bridging type which are found in many parts of Australia. A particularly clear-cut example is Tiwi, discussed by Dorian (1992), a Northern Australian language which has experienced rapid structural changes since the early 1970s (see J. Lee 1987). The older and influential members of the Tiwi community have successfully blocked attempts to promote a modern young people's version of the language, thereby reinforcing a costly state of diglossia:

For the present, the gap between fully traditional Tiwi and the young people's everyday Tiwi complicates the language-support efforts of educators and community leaders. It may be that realistic hopes for the vigorous survival of Tiwi among a literate younger population lie with a standardization of one of the more accessible forms of Modern Tiwi and with its determined support in educa-tional programs, especially as the elderly mother-tongue speakers of fully traditional Tiwi are lost to the community by the natural attrition of age. Yet if, as seems to have been the case among the Tiwi, community support for bilingual education requires the use of a more conservative form of language, and any use in print of a restructured (and sharply simplified) form of the language seems to community leaders a debasement of their tongue, the route to an effective support program for more accessible forms of the language may be effectively blocked.

(Dorian 1992: 147)

Let me now return to the theory introduced at the start of this chapter.

Ecological theory

Ecological theory, as developed by Mühlhäusler (1990b, 1991b, 1992) and in Fill (1993), addresses the question:

> What is the support system that sustains a language ecology over time?

It reframes the question of language maintenance to highlight:

1 the fact that the aim of maintenance is to enable the survival of a structured diversity rather than individual languages
2 the fact that the functional links between languages are regarded as central.

Many of its concepts are borrowed from studies of natural ecologies (e.g. 'species crush' – the loss of a 'keystone species' may trigger the loss of many others or that of 'habitat destruction'). Languages are not so much lost as a result of speakers' or planners' intentions, but as a result of the loss of their non-linguistic support system.

I should point out again that theories and metaphors are tools to explain a very complex state of affairs – not descriptions of a pre-existing reality. The test is whether they lead to improved language maintenance practices. The fact that ecological theory is far from simple, that it forces its practitioners to consider a very large number of parameters and interrelationships would seem to be compatible with other sophisticated theories of language maintenance which stress the limitations of single or few-cause approaches.

The decline of Pacific and Australian languages, according to this view, is due primarily to the loss of their ecological support system (language ownership, cultural practices, speakers' lifestyles, settlement patterns, speakers' physical and spiritual well-being) and their functional relationship with other languages (language chains, bi-, dual- and multilingualism, sign languages, pidgins, etc.). Whilst much of the traditional support has been lost for good, it might well be possible to reconstitute different ecologies in which such languages can coexist with other introduced languages. The analogy of permaculture suggests that new self-sustaining ecological systems can be created, combining indigenous and introduced species.

To apply the ecological theory of language maintenance in the area, the following requirements must be met:

1 The long-term goal of maintenance needs to be identified (e.g. equitable coexistence of a number of indigenous languages, pidgins, creoles, and koines together with English or another 'economically useful' language).
2 Knowledge has to be obtained as to what sustained traditional multilingualism and how much of the traditional support system is still in place.
3 The first and second requirements will have to rely primarily on indigenous wishes and knowledge: solutions that worked elsewhere may not be applicable.
4 An understanding of the factors that have caused language decline in the past needs to be obtained as well as an understanding of which forces continue to operate.
5 Critical awareness of the factors that promote or negatively affect language ecology need to be generated among outside decision-makers and the outside public.

As in permaculture, the guiding idea is

1 high knowledge – low cost
2 emphasis not on quantity of languages but a functional relationship between them.

Ecological maintenance is incompatible with

1 solutions that are not intelligible or acceptable to the inhabitants of a linguistic ecology
2 monoculturalism or diglossia
3 views that advocate isolation (physical or domain) as a permanent solution, though temporary isolation, as in Maori 'language nests', is compatible with this theory
4 high-tech and quick-fix solutions driven by the wish to have results within the life of a government.

Having surveyed a number of approaches to language maintenance, the question is not so much 'Will all 1200 survive?' (Crocombe's question about the Oceanic subgroup of languages, 1989: 41), but rather 'How many languages will survive?' or even 'Will any languages survive?'

Appendix: Linguistics in the Pacific[1]

Traditionally most languages have been studied and described as if they were standard languages.

(Coulmas 1994: 175)

INTRODUCTION

The phrase 'linguistic imperialism' can be understood to mean, as it has for most of this book, 'imperialism of languages' and, as I am about to discuss in this appendix, imperialism of linguistics. My discussion will make special reference to Pacific linguists but it would be quite unreasonable to make a fine distinction between Pacific linguistics and other kinds of linguistics, for Pacific linguistics is entirely derivative of the large Western creation called linguistics and not an approach to language confined to the Pacific or developed by scholars indigenous to the area. Its discourse, by and large, has remained that of other English-speaking centres of learning. The story of Pacific linguistics thus is yet another example of the unidirectionality of the flow of knowledge from its European and Western sources to the more peripheral countries of the new and third world.

The ways in which human language is investigated by linguistics is of course only a small subpart of this phenomenon and, many would argue, a rather innocuous one. There is a long-standing ambition of linguistics to be seen as a science, or more precisely a natural science, concerned with the objective description of natural languages, laws of linguistic change and so forth (see Crowley 1990). This objective discipline prides itself on having overcome the subjective and frequently openly racist message of nineteenth-century linguistics inspired by social Darwinism and its implicit views of the inequalities of human languages. It is indeed a lasting achievement of modern descriptivists, beginning with Boas and Sapir, to have exorcized unconfirmed theories of superiority from Western linguistics. However, the step from the realization that there was a diversity of equal languages to the realization that there was inherent value in this very diversity was made by only a few scholars, most prominent among them Benjamin Lee Whorf (1956):

> Western culture has made, through language, a provisional analysis of reality and, without correctives, holds resolutely to that analysis as final. The only correctives lie in all those other tongues which by aeons of independent evolution have arrived at different, but equally logical, provisional analyses.

(Whorf 1956: 244)

Many other twentieth-century scholars have exchanged ideologically laden theories for theory-free (and putatively value-free observation) and the search for methods that would enable them to discover the patterns inherent in directly observable data, ended up bringing to the subject of linguistics a highly suspect assortment of implicit theories, ethnocentric prejudices and practices. They also propagated the idea of theory-free notational systems, an idea which still haunts linguistics.

Thus, ever since the turn of the century the linguistic profession has built up an impressive array of instruments, techniques and recording procedures. Terms such as 'phonetics laboratory', 'minimal pair test', 'A-over-A principle', 'sound law' and 'formal universal', enhance the status of the discipline as a precise and objective one. The intellectual crisis that has shaken disciplines such as chemistry or physics since the mid-1970s and forced them to rethink the nature of their objectivity has barely reached linguistics. A cynic might say that this is small wonder with a discipline that subscribed to mechanical discovery procedures a long time after such procedures were abandoned by other disciplines and where even today discredited metaphors of human communication such as the conduit metaphor (dismissed by Reddy 1979) continue to be part of the foundation of the discipline.

Linguists, not unlike practitioners of other disciplines, can be accused of having spent a great deal of energy on the erection of disciplinary fences and rather less on critically reflecting on the practices that occur within such fences. As has been observed from time to time by more articulate members of the discipline, there is a widespread reluctance to ditch notions that have been shown to be of no use, such as the 'phoneme', or seriously to question the universality of concepts such as the 'sentence', 'word' or 'subject' or the metaphor of 'related' languages.

Linguistics, and this is the particular point I wish to make here, is the arbitrary outcome of an array of sociohistorical processes rather than a logical progression from more to less biased views on human language. This chapter is also an attempt to show that many of the explicit principles of the discipline as well as its implicit assumptions, far from being neutral, objective or merely descriptive stand in an important feedback relationship with the languages of Australia and the Pacific. Their welfare and their future are intimately linked to the practices of professional linguists. Making linguists aware of their role in the linguistic ecology of the area, it is hoped, can lead to developments in the discipline which could enable it to make a contribution to preserving, restoring and learning from the languages of the area.

Given the limitations of time and space I shall not attempt to present a detailed historiography of Australian and Pacific linguistics, nor can I do justice to the many topics suggested by the title of my book. This chapter will focus on the question 'What use has linguistics been. . .

1 in solving certain intellectual puzzles
2 in speeding up the process of ecological change in the Pacific
3 in preserving existing linguistic patterns
4 in making available plans for the linguistic future of languages of the area
5 to speakers of these languages
6 to human knowledge in general?

My wider topic is the role of linguistic studies in changing the linguistic picture of Australia and the Pacific. A question which has been addressed several times before, for instance in Meinhof's (1905) address to the German Colonial Congress. In presenting my arguments I shall proceed in three stages by concentrating on the instruments, the purposes and the outcomes of Western linguistic concerns about the languages of the Pacific area. Similar concerns have been voiced by others for other parts of the world, e.g. by Calvet (1974) for Africa.

THE INSTRUMENTS

Apart from numerous *ad hoc* studies by laypersons, the languages of Australia and the Pacific have been studied with the conceptual apparatus of

1 historical linguistics (philology)
2 structuralism
3 transformationalism

and, since the late 1980s, and as yet rarely applied to the languages of the area:

4 post-structuralist and post-transformationalist approaches to language.

Many of the fundamental assumptions of the practitioners of these approaches have remained unquestioned by the various intellectual revolutions in the discipline. Thus, throughout the history of linguistics we find

1 the belief in distinct word classes
2 the belief in the possibility of using the same descriptive labels for all languages
3 the belief in the separability of language and other non-linguistic phenomena
4 the belief in the existence of separate languages.

None of the above beliefs, in my view, has been particularly helpful in the study of the traditional languages of the Pacific area.

In exemplifying the relationship between existing conceptual approaches and the linguistic picture of the area, let me first briefly examine some consequences of adopting a comparative historical view. The bread and butter of comparative linguistics is the comparison of languages. This of course can be done only when one has identified separate languages, just as a jugged hare can be cooked only once you catch your hare, as Mrs Beeton has allegedly pointed out. In the modern nation-states of Europe to catch a language is no longer a problem. In many traditional oral societies on the other hand distinct languages did not exist. Rather, communication took place along dialect and language continua. Splitting up such a continuum into discrete languages is an arbitrary act, as the widely different figures that have been given for the number of languages in Australia, and Papua New Guinea or Vanuatu demonstrate. Grace (1991), in a paper re-examining aberrant languages, that is, those that do not fit the comparativist model, gives the following charitable interpretation:

> But, it also appears that comparative-historical linguistics has been assuming a relation between language and people which is much simpler than the reality. In some cases the reality has come close enough to the assumptions to permit the comparative methods to have quite impressive success. But in other cases, it has not, and therefore, we have 'aberrant languages'.
>
> (Grace 1991: 28–9)

There is more to this, however, than the inability of certain approaches to 'languages' to solve a certain intellectual puzzle. The view that languages are countable entities has many consequences, including some that are potentially dangerous for the users of traditional forms of communication:

1 It is suggestive of obstacles to communication (language boundaries) where in fact no such obstacles exist.
2 It can lead to qualitative distinctions between dialect and languages, with a resulting power differential of the speakers.

Another requirement of comparative linguistics is that the forms to be compared be invariant, a requirement similar to that implicit in much dictionary making when constancy of form and meaning are characteristic of most entries. Ignoring the wide range of pronunciation variants and their social functions thus led to standardized kinds of languages unheard of in the traditional context. Fixing meaning led to even more serious results: the process of negotiating meaning in face-to-face interaction has been replaced by one where objective meanings can be looked up in a printed dictionary. A further problem with historical linguistics is the dominant role assigned to linguistic divergence (diversification by splitting up), suggesting that break-ups and splits were common in both language and society. More than a few observers have commented on the intolerance, jealousy and lack of co-operation that must have been endemic among people who have become linguistically divided. I have already suggested that a good deal of this division is a mere fabrication. If we add to this that the Pacific and Australia have been areas of intensive language contacts and that convergence rather than divergence may have been the main reason for the development of new languages, a very different interpretation begins to emerge.

This even goes for an area which in the past has been regarded as a canonical example of language development through parthenogenesis: Polynesia. When examining the history of the Polynesian languages in greater detail, one finds a very considerable body of evidence for continued, long-standing contacts of many islands with other islands near and far for warfare, trade, visits, multiple settlements and so forth, which make a mockery of a historical-comparative linguistics centred around divergence. I do not stand alone in my conclusions, that 'There are methodological difficulties of applying the family tree model to Polynesia' (Rensch 1987: 578). A detailed account of language contacts in Polynesia is in Wurm, Mühlhäusler and Tryon (1996).

In all this debate about language family trees, the important question of the social functions of diversity has been virtually ignored. That it might be a deliberate choice, enabling indigenous peoples to maintain a complex network of interdependent egalitarian societies was first mooted by the late Don Laycock (1981) and then developed by Grace (1991).

A final problem with comparative linguistics is its concern for reconstructed earlier historical stages. In carrying out such reconstruction linguists imposed an arrow metaphor of time (Gould 1988) which portrays linguistic history as an irreversible sequence of unrepeatable events as a kind of arrow-like progression from A to B. They are incapable of dealing with the numerous known and even more numerous unknown discontinuities in the development of the languages of the area and moreover they fail to account for change which is merely a part of a repeating cycle. Applied to linguistic data this latter possibility means that many of the apparent changes over time identified by historical linguists are in fact not changes at all, but merely a reflection of the constant variability of human communication systems. If we combine this argument with the previous one we should add that such historical changes as have occurred are typically a reflection of convergence and contact rather than the workings of some natural sound laws under conditions of split.

The tendency to view language and communication in traditional societies through the glasses of nation-state, monolingual, literate educated speakers is continued and reinforced in structuralism. Put concisely, its negative contribution to an understanding of the languages of the Pacific has been:

1 the removal of considerations of meaning and function
2 the reduction of variation to a common core
3 the exclusion of linguistics from the wider intellectual debate still possible in the days of philologists such as Max Müller and Meinhof
4 the view that one can and must study single languages at one point in time
5 the exclusion of all qualitative issues.

How little is known about meaning in some of the areas' languages is evidenced in the fact that neither of the scholarly books on Papuan Languages (Foley 1986a; Wurm 1971a) contain a chapter on their semantics.

On the positive side, structuralists were not obsessed with the reduction of all languages to a universal set of rules, principles and constraints. However, the descriptive apparatus they applied to the description of linguistic diversity was superior to the blundering efforts of amateurs to describe, for instance, the languages of Tasmania (Plomley 1987: 37ff.) and was often such that their grammars looked remarkably like those of standard average European languages, an unintended consequence of the structuralists' belief in immaculate perception. It is perhaps the most significant contribution of transformational generative grammar (TGG) that its founder, Chomsky, insisted on the necessity of coming up with an explicit theory (though even here a lot of Western intellectual baggage has been smuggled on board as implicit rather than explicit assumptions). On the debit side their search for universals, the dogma of effability (that all languages are totally intertranslatable) and the practice of taking English as the point of departure or even the only point of reference for establishing universals has led to an implied denigration of linguistic diversity. Such studies of traditional languages that have occurred have been in the manner of selective ransacking for confirmation of general principles rather than anything else. Further on the debit side (from the point of view of small languages) is the construction of an ideal speaker/hearer, the exclusion of bilingualism, pidginization and linguistic accommodation as well as the adoption of computer metaphors such as input and output.

The existence of indigenous pidgins was pretty well unknown until Foley's (1986a) discovery of a pidgin language used in the Sepik area; a survey of language use in the Pacific Ocean (Watson-Gegeo 1986) reveals that the number of languages in the area greatly outnumbers the studies of their use. For the majority of languages sociolinguistic and pragmatic information is nonexistent: it is even absent in the writings of people who have lived with the informants for years at a time. Malinowski's promising beginnings in the 1920s to understand Melanesian languages in their situational context appears to have been overtaken by an obsession for formal calculi and sterile analyses.

In as much as linguistic diversity is a surface phenomenon, it is seen to muddy the view on deeper universals, and the reduction of diversity seen from a transformational perspective must seem a rather attractive proposition. Transformational grammarians can also be accused of promoting a particularly dangerous metaphor; that of the speaker/ hearer as a kind of rule-governed machine engaged in exchanging messages that can be converted into signals and back into messages by the decoder. In doing this they not only fail to obtain their desired goal of psychological reality, but also positively prevent investigators from paying attention to important phenomena such as accommodation. Moreover, in transformational, as in previous structuralists' views the arbitrary signs rather than the icon and the index is the centre of all linguistic communications. This has the consequence of excluding any consideration of speech markers (Scherer and Giles 1979) that provide information about individual attitudes or states of mind and body. A parameter uniting all the above models is that they are concerned with full languages, not with languages that develop from less to more complex systems such as child language or pidgins. Further, they are concerned with dividing up, classifying, regularizing and analysing a small subcomponent of the human ability to communicate only rather than synthesizing the multiplicity of human communicative abilities into a consistent whole. As such, the available views of philological, structuralist and transformational linguistics are unsuited to understanding the special needs of small languages and their speakers.

If the instruments used have led to analyses that are of little use to the speakers of the numerous languages of the area one might ask: what use have they been to the analyst?

There is a growing body of evidence that the tools of the trade have led to quite serious distortions in the area of description of core grammatical structures. An interesting illustration is given in Duranti's (1981) analysis of Samoan. Insufficient attention to contextual factors in language use paired with overreliance on elicited forms has meant that

> In the Samoan case, by limiting the analysis to elicited linguistic form, one risks to be describing only a single variety of speech, one which is in fact of very limited use. In the case of Samoan, the variety elicited through interviews does not closely correspond to either informal or formal varieties of most spontaneous interaction in traditional settings.
>
> (Duranti 1981: 165)

Failure to take such discrepancies into account has resulted in linguists' misinterpretation of Samoan phonology, their postulating a basic VSO (verb–subject–object) instead of SVO (subject–verb–object) word order and in the elicitation of a whole bunch of grammatical phenomena which do not occur in either everyday or formal speech. Put differently, a substantial number of linguists have taken the foreigner talk register to represent the everyday language.

Samoan, it needs to be added, is one of the best-described Pacific languages, with a long-standing tradition of literacy and grammar making. If such blatant misanalysis could go undetected in this case, one wonders whether many more serious errors have occurred in the account of less intensely studied languages. As a basis for comparative work or linguistic typology, existing descriptions are frequently useless, particularly when using non-comparative descriptive devices such as the phoneme or the morpheme.

Whereas it is possible within limits to refer to the three linguistic approaches discussed thus far as paradigms, such a label would be quite inappropriate for the multitude of perspectives that have emerged since the 1970s, partly in reaction against transformational grammar, partly as an addition and partly as a totally new departure from earlier practice. This intellectual diversity in itself gives one grounds to hope that there is also greater regard for diversity of languages.

Some of the more important 'tools' that have been made available by the mixed group of sociolinguists, variationists, pragmaticists, ethnographers of speaking and integrationalists include

1 ways of dealing with variation and qualitative change
2 a framework for the description of the ethnic factors in the analysis of a wide range of communicative events
3 suggestions as to how to deal with the correlation or integration of linguistic and non-linguistic factors
4 ways of dealing with iconicity, indexicality, accommodation and other hitherto largely neglected aspects of language.

It is not possible to go into great detail here. What can be said is that there seems to be a growing body of intellectual tools that could be meaningfully applied to the question of small and dying languages, and that, moreover, concern over these matters has grown significantly among linguists (see Robins and Uhlenbeck 1991). It is probably fair to say that there is considerable uncertainty

1 as to whether or not linguists should go beyond their traditional business of documenting disappearing languages
2 as to how linguistics needs to be developed to be of use in preserving endangered languages.

That linguistics can and should go beyond description has been stated by none other than Chomsky (1970):

> I like to believe that the intensive study of one aspect of human psychology – human language – may contribute to a humanistic social science that will serve, as well, as an instrument for social action.
>
> (Chomsky 1970: 155)

However, I would also like to argue that the very metaphors by which Chomsky's linguistics lives (language as a natural object, rule-governed behaviour, universal properties) makes this approach an inappropriate basis for questions of preserving culturally embedded linguistic diversity. Rather, it is non- and anti-TGG approaches to language that would seem to offer the best basis for a socially useful linguistics. Among the more promising departures from conventional linguistics must be counted a number of attempts to understand the social forces that bring languages and notions of language into being (acts of identity, acts of power, cultural practices), such as in the work of Harris (1979) and LePage and Tabouret-Keller (1985). In such a constructivist approach, one can begin to account for problems such as the one outlined by Grace (1991):

> One of the things which I found puzzling was that in some areas the people seem to have no conception of what their language is and no sense of belonging to a linguistic community. Another Westerner in Melanesia at that time reported similar experiences and similar reactions to them.
>
> (Grace 1991: 15)

As Heryanto (1990: 41) points out: 'Language is not a universal category or cultural activity though it may sound odd, not all people have a language in a sense of which this term is currently used in English.'

Heryanto's discussion of how the term *'Bahasa'* came to mean 'language' in a Western sense is one of the most informed sources for the understanding of non-Western metalinguistics. Another important development initiated by Haugen (1972) and developed subsequently by a number of scholars is the idea of ecological linguistics. The nature and merit of the ecological approach to language have been emphasized in a number of places in this book.

Whereas most structural approaches to linguistics were based on the assumption that observation was a straightforward matter, ever since Labov's first sociolinguistic studies the question of the observers' role in distorting the very data they wish to observe has come to be seen as a problem. Interestingly, however, it is regarded as a problem for linguists who are afraid of contaminated data, rather than a problem for the speakers of languages which will never be the same after they have been subjected to an intensive study by outsiders or stronger measures such as dictionary making and graphization.

Studies on languages and politics in Australia and the Pacific are rare and what has been written has tended to be concerned with micro-aspects. Sankoff (1980b: 6) has criticized observers for this and suggested that sociolinguists should concentrate on 'the larger social and political forces that shape and constrain the place language comes to occupy in people's everyday life.'

Much work remains to be done before linguistics can claim to be in a position to offer answers to the problems of language decline in the Pacific and Australian area.

THE PURPOSES

Instruments tend to be designed for particular purposes and those designed by professional linguists are no exception. Having discussed the instruments thus already tells us a lot about the purposes of the designers. In retrospect the principal task of linguistics has always been seen as that of description (a more recent explanation of a very restricted range of phenomena). It has been believed that this description is neutral and not an act of social engineering. It is only in the late 1970s in the writings of Harris (1979, 1980) that the role of linguists as language makers has been seriously discussed. There are of course exceptions, such as the investigation of the relationship of colonial languages with a view to selecting one of them as the basis of a colonial lingua franca, or, during the Second World War the preparation of grammars and lexicons of a structuralist type as the basis of audiovisual language courses for soldiers. Mention should also be made of the branch of American structuralism of tagmemics, the school which was devoted to the translation of the Bible into all of the world's languages. In this school, the role of linguistics is ancillary to that of producing translations of the scriptures and that of reducing languages to writing, as has been shown elsewhere in this book.

In some instances, linguists have been genuinely concerned with improving the lot of those with whose languages they worked, whereas in other cases they preferred to remain 'neutral observers'. Few linguists have considered the possibility that they could improve themselves by studying other languages. Indeed, when surveying the purposes of linguistic study one can conclude that by and large it has never been the intention of the practitioners of linguistics to learn from the cultures where these languages are spoken. Rather it was presumed that either the languages were at a more primitive stage of development or else that they were essentially the same as any other language, both good reasons for not paying too much attention to them. Semantics under the latter view has become the study of finding out how the same information is packaged in different languages, rather than an explanation of different world views. What is known about the semantics of the Papuan and Australian Aboriginal languages therefore remains minimal.

THE OUTCOMES

The outcomes of many years of linguistic studies of Australian Pacific linguistics cannot be characterized easily, nor do I wish to simply dismiss them totally negatively. Given the enormous linguistic complexity of the area, some of the historical classificatory and descriptive studies were certainly necessary. What we know in the 1990s about the linguistics of the area is a great deal more than what we knew at the turn of the century. Still, compared with what we know about languages such as English, French or German, what is known about the languages of the Pacific area is minimal.

What is known, moreover, to a large extent reflects what theoretical linguists elsewhere wanted to know, for example

1 that there appeared to be no structurally primitive first languages
2 that family trees can be established for languages with no written tradition
3 that the same linguistic universals are found in the Pacific as elsewhere
4 that the languages of the area can be characterized by the same typological features that can be used to characterize languages elsewhere.

To what extent such findings result from the experimental effect, that is, the tendency of experiments to confirm the experimenter's expectations, is difficult to quantify, but it is certainly true that Pacific and Australian linguists have been highly selective in their use of linguistic evidence.

The prevailing intellectual climate has been one that has suppressed many of the most promising areas of study and has led fieldworkers to miss valuable opportunities. I shall mention just four examples.

First, prior to the advent of the Europeans in Papua New Guinea, indigenous pidgins and indigenous bilingualism fulfilled a major role in intercommunication across linguistic boundaries of this multilingual area. Records of these two phenomena by linguists are exceedingly rare. Concern for coming to grips with the grammar of a single language prevented them from asking the simple question about communication across linguistic boundaries.

Second, semantics has been another victim, as has the study of language in its social context (very few have tried to emulate the work of Malinowski on the social embedding of the language of Kiriwina).

Third, virtually nothing is known about the ways that speakers of small languages talk about language; their terminology solutions and metaphors may well provide a way out of the terminological crisis that linguistics currently finds itself in.

Fourth, an important area for the study of conceptual differences is that of metaphor. However, thousands of papers on metaphors of Indo-European languages since the mid-1970s contrast with only a handful of papers on metaphors in Papuan languages for the same period. The study of English, French and German in Queensland, Western Australia and South Australia attracts many times more personnel, funding and publicity than the study of the Aboriginal languages of these states. Pacific and Australian linguistics (and this is probably a most undesirable outcome) are seen as being of very marginal intellectual interest and as having little applicability. It is certainly easier to ignore evidence from a little-known Papuan language than similar evidence from English or French.

The view of the wider public, reflected by funding bodies such as states and universities, of the study of minor languages as a non-essential luxury, may at first sight seem justified. However, intellectual inquiry cannot be measured in terms of short-term outcomes. What a relatively small body of workers has accumulated over the last hundred years in terms of knowledge of the languages of Australia and the Pacific is impressive considering their restricted resources. Researchers who have worked in the field have also exhibited a fair and healthy amount of scepticism against armchair theories. It is not an accident that many of the revolutionary changes in the study of human language since the mid-1970s can be traced back to people who have dirtied their hands with field data, though data from the Pacific region remain widely unknown in Europe and North America.

Given the number of languages in the area, their structural and historical diversity and their geographical spread, too little is known and research priorities too often have been determined by external agendas. It is not surprising that the outcome is not necessarily one that is of great use to the inhabitants of the region.

CONCLUSIONS

As I am writing this, indigenous languages of the Pacific and Australian area are declining and dying at an alarming rate. Others, under the influence of video, mission and near universal schooling in English or French, are being progressively Westernized, particularly in their semantics. The forceful assimilation of minority groups in Indonesia and its colonies and other parts of South East Asia continues unabated and the international linguistic community shows little inclination to condemn the deplorable genocide of thousands of speakers of Papuan languages in East Timor following its invasion by Indonesian forces in 1975. Linguists hide behind the shield of scholarly objectivity whilst the linguistic diversity that has been in existence for tens of thousands of years is being eroded at an alarming rate. Little is done to preserve the languages of the area. Economic pressures, central governments, military actions and the decline of the natural environment have not been counteracted by any genuine progress in the area of language preservation. The chance that most, or even a substantial number, of the smaller languages of the area will survive seems remote.

Apart from the moral considerations that would seem to force linguists to speak up for the preservation of linguistic and conceptual diversity we should also realize that this is the last chance for Western linguists to learn from the numerous alternative philosophical and conceptual systems that may be hidden in the small languages of the Pacific area. They should be seen as a reservoir of human knowledge, as examples of the ability of humans to create rules, create explanations and accommodate a wide range of circumstances. So long as we cannot be certain that the progress we are experiencing is progress in the right direction, to discard diversity for seemingly progressive uniformity seems a very dangerous gamble.

Scientific inquiry can be attacked in a number of ways, either by judging it by its own rules, by pointing out the misfit between theory and observable data, by pointing out internal contradictions or by attacking the lack of explicitness. Pacific and Australian linguists again and again have fallen short of the high standard one expects of a developed social science, though this is quite common for linguists elsewhere (for details see Labov 1975) and perhaps a reflection of the inevitability of gross oversimplification and misjudgements when faced with a huge body of complex evidence. A second way of attacking theories is to point out their irrelevance. In the case of much of linguistics, the range of questions that have been addressed have been unduly narrow, ethnocentric and insensitive to the plight of the languages and their speakers. Moral questions and questions of the consequences of linguistic activity have been notoriously avoided in the mistaken belief that it is possible to engage in an ideologically free linguistics.

The chance to learn from the disappearing small languages of the Pacific area has rarely been helped by the prevailing practices. What is needed now is a new reformed linguistics that addresses some of the fundamental issues of the place of language in human life, of the uses of intellectual and linguistic diversity and of the responsibility linguistics has in helping to maintain and rescue a very fragile linguistic ecology. These issues have barely begun to be addressed.

One hopes that they will move towards the centre of the discipline before it is too late and that the new generation of linguists will overcome the limitations of early approaches. As Labov (1975: 56) has observed:

If there is a moral issue in the business of doing linguistics, it is that we will struggle to avoid making our students the victims of our personal histories and limitations.

Notes

1 THE CHANGING LINGUISTIC ECOLOGY OF THE PACIFIC REGION

1 An early example of applying an ecological perspective to language decline is C. H. Williams's (1979) study of Welsh.
2 The metaphor of 'shop steward' is better known in contemporary discourse on environmental issues, i.e. in Lovelock's remark (1992: 121): 'We are not managers or masters of the earth, we are just shop stewards, workers chosen, because of our intelligence, as representatives for the others, the rest of the life forms of our planet'.
3 This has been done, for instance, by Grace (1975).
4 Exoteric languages are used for wider communication between groups whilst esoteric languages are owned and cultivated by groups who tend to guard them jealously against outsiders.
5 Toffler (1975: 107) has characterized the outcome of this type of imperialism, as the work of 'hard-headed realists' rather thant 'utopians or impractical idealists', thus emphasizing the unintended nature of our current economic predicament.

2 LANGUAGE ECOLOGY IN PRE-EUROPEAN DAYS

1 This creation of dependency has been documented, in much detail, for Australia, for instance by Fesl (1993).
2 Prevailing methodology does not appear to be suited to questions such as the linguistic relationship between Australian and Papuan languages or whether Aboriginal languages reflect different waves of immigration to Australia.
3 Consider the contrasting practices of European and Papuan observers, as described by Laycock and Voorhoeve (1971):

> A word must be said on nomenclature. Names of languages are cited in the form considered by the authors to be most appropriate, or – in some cases – in the form used in the literature cited; but it must not be assumed that these names have any more validity than as convenient labelling devices. It is rare for speakers of Papuan languages to have a name for themselves, in their own language, as a linguistic unit; rather, they will use a word which simply means 'the people', in an ethnocentric

sense, and this term may frequently be much narrower in its extent than the linguistic group. This deficiency of nomenclature has been overcome by European observers in a number of ways:

(1) by using a locality name, which may be the indigenous name of a village, island, mountain, valley or other geographical feature; or it may be an introduced topographical name ('Western Highlands language', 'Big Sepik language', etc.);
(2) by using the name given to the people by another tribal group;
(3) by using a group name: clan, totem, dialect designation;
(4) by using an arbitrary name based on the language's form for some common word. Those that have been frequently chosen are words for 'man' (Tuo, Moando, Nor, Pondo); 'water' (Ok); 'language' (Kam, Pay, Pila); 'no' (Olo, Elkei, Au); 'what' (Ngaing); and 'my child' (Natik, Barok).

4 A comparison of the prevailing Western view with indigenous metalinguistic beliefs about samenesses and differences suggests that our views are highly culture-specific. Cooper (1975) in discussing coastal Suau (spoken in the Milne Bay Province of Papua New Guinea) remarks:

> COASTAL SUAU shall be defined to include those varieties of Suau generally spoken within the Suau Administrative Area of the Milne Bay District.
>
> Coastal Suau, thus defined, is a somewhat arbitrary label for a major part of the Suau speech continuum. Its western boundary is fairly distinct, for the neighbouring languages, Mailu and Oima, are non-Austronesian; its southern boundary is the sea itself, but across the mountains to the north and into the islands to the east there appear no sudden breaks. Kwato and Fife Bay circuits of the United Church have made Suau a lingua franca in some areas along Milne Bay and inland. Bearing these indeterminate factors in mind, it is probable that between eight and ten thousand persons use some form of Suau as a first or second language.
>
> To designate these other forms of the Suau speech continuum whose boundaries are still indeterminate and provide a label for the entire domain of Suau communities, the terms SUAUIC and SOUTHERN MASSIM have been applied. E.g. the Logea and Sariba communities are clearly Suauaic though published data includes little more than short word lists. Wari and TubeTube speech also seem to be Suauic, but again data is limited.

(Cooper 1975: 230)

The expatriate classification and labelling suggested by Cooper differs from indigenous practice in significant ways:

> The term *alina* is generally used to designate language, dialect, or speech in general. Any degree of difference, from a small bundle of lexical and phonological distinctions to mutual unintelligibility, may be designated by this term followed by a name, most often a place name.

(Cooper 1975: 231)

The distinction between language and dialect (in the social sense of dialect as an unwritten, less prestigious form of speech) has come to the awareness of Suau speakers only after the development of a writing system based on the 'correct' speech of Suau Island. Not only is the identification of dialects of Suau a foreign practice, it also fails, as is readily admitted by Cooper, to account for the ways in which Suau speakers communicated across a wide range of structurally different linguistic systems:

> The description does not explain the ability of Coastal Suau speakers to intercommunicate as easily as they are observed to do – this despite great differences in 'basic' vocabulary, and considerable differences in the shapes of many lexical items; indeed, it may be that 'none of the present techniques are really adequate to describe the facts about any speech continuum'.

(Cooper 1975: 235)

5 In some instances, information is restricted to subgroups such as initiated males. How much communication presupposes shared knowledge was brought home to me when, during fieldwork in the Torricelli Mountains of New Guinea I failed, for a long time, to understand why some people were greeted 'apinun' and others 'gutnait' at the same time of day. It turned out that the former greeting was for people who had not completed their day's work and the latter for people who had.

6 Note the abbreviations: AN = Austronesian; NAN = Non-Austronesian

4 PIDGINS AND CREOLES

1 It must be emphasized that the term 'weed' is used as a metaphor rather than a descriptive label. The weed metaphor, like other metaphors, highlights certain properties of pidgins whilst de-emphasizing others. Any conclusion that Mühlhäusler regards pidgins as weeds is quite illegitimate.

A second point is that 'weed' is used in the technical sense of a plant which outcompetes others in disturbed soil, rather than in the more emotive everyday meaning. Note also that the weed metaphor is not applicable to all pidgins but only to a subclass, namely the ones I focus on in this chapter. Finally, note the dynamic use of the term 'weed' in what follows. My use differs from the numerous nineteenth- and twentieth-century evaluations of organisms such as that of this chapter in Von Pferdekämper (1906):

> The languages resemble plants; one encounters fruit bearing and flowering plants and those that are insignificant, shabby or diminutive; the former one cultivated and looked after, the latter vegetate without being noticed.

(Von Pferdekämper 1906: 933, my translation)

2 Note the analogy in the biological sphere. The habitat of the indigenous species is destroyed to make room for. a range of new introduced plants catering for the needs of different immigrant groups (e.g. Chinese or English vegetables, German flowers, Italian fruit or decorative shrubs, etc.).

3 In a few instances in monolingual settings, pidgins based on indigenous languages could develop, for instance, Pidgin Hawaiian. However, symptomatically, this Pidgin Hawaiian was replaced by Pidgin English as soon as a large-scale influx of plantation workers from different regions outside Hawaii occurred.

4 The use of Pidgin Fijian in the early phase of the Fijian plantation system is a counter-example. For special details see Siegel (1987).

5 A particularly detailed account of this process is given by Ross (1987).

6 'Now' refers to 1883.
7 Note that 'development' has been defined in many different ways by writers on the Pacific area. Literal's use differs dramatically from that of Heryanto (1988) on whose work I have commented elsewhere in this volume.
8 William M. Samarin (1971) comments:

> Chomsky believes, along with Humboldt, that language is primarily a 'means of thought and self-expression' (1966: 21). This being true, 'The purely practical use of language is characteristic of no real human language, but only of invented parasitic systems' (22) adding in a footnote, 'For example, the *lingua franca* of the Mediterranean coast', probably referring to Sabir. A pidgin is therefore a parasitic form of speech whose primary function is not the expression of thought but that of practical interchange. (The paraphrase is my own.) Chomsky is led to this assertion by his commitment to the Cartesian principle, so named by him, that language is a human species-specific endowment that liberates man from contextual restraints and stimuli and permits him to freely encode his own experience. He does not suggest how thought and self-expression are to be measured and he surely could not deprive my Central African assistant of these gifts when he and I discuss cultural relativity and the importance of saying 'Thank you' in Western society! Still, we know what Chomsky is driving at.
>
> (W. M. Samarin 1971: 120)

9 The characteristics of pidgins and creoles as 'illegitimate' offsprings of uncontrolled linguistic miscegenation is a common theme in much of the past literature on these languages.
10 The insufficiency of this view is discussing by Dutton and Mühlhäusler (1979).
11 Slightly more promising is the suggestion made by Eades (1982) that the social conventions for the use of language rather than the grammar or lexicon are the principal locus for the survival of substratum languages.

5 CASE STUDIES

1 Having coined this name myself, I am no longer sure that it is a good label. Most important among the reasons against its use is that very much the same pidgin language was spoken widely in the Torres Strait Island which, until the imposition of international boundaries, was part of the same communication community.
2 A parallel situation exists in West Africa; Cameroon Pidgin English became established as an independent language during the brief era of German control, whilst negative attitudes and policies perpetuated the instability and structural dependence of English of pidgins such as Ghanese or Nigerian Pidgin English.

6 MISSION LANGUAGES AND LANGUAGE POLICIES

1 It is somewhat astonishing, for instance, that in a reader on Language Obsolescence (Dorian 1989a) no reference is made to the role of missions in this process.
2 The haphazard character of missionary language policies is fully admitted

by some insiders. Strauss (1971: 68), for instance, observes: 'One can only guess what would have been possible if the missionaries had agreed on a united one clear strategy in matters of language when Papua was first opened up to Christianity' (my translation).

3 Of those missionaries that used a vernacular at all, a fair proportion found it difficult to achieve proficiency in it. Fesl (1993) reports on the Revd Lancelot Threkeld's ability to communicate in the Lake Macquarie area of New South Wales in the 1830s:

> Despite his own opinions of his linguistic skills, a report of what Koories thought of Threlkeld's abilities is noted in Broome (1982: 66): 'Threlkeld's bumbling efforts to learn the Awakabal language were corrected endlessly by his Aboriginal teachers who often rebuked him with: "What for you so stupid, you very stupid fellow".'

(Fesl 1993: 81)

Similarly, Rensch (1991) discusses missionary misconceptions about the simplicity of Tahitian as manifested in the following example:

> By then, they also knew that they had made fools of themselves in the early days when they used to say to the Tahitian kind, 'Mity po, tuaana'. By putting together mity (maita'i) 'good', po (po:) 'night' and tuaana (tua'ana) 'elder brother' they had produced an interlanguage construct which easily matched in its naiveté any Ormaism. When the Tahitians finally found out what the missionaries wanted to express, they just laughed without making any assumptions about speech defects or inferior mental capacity of the religious envoys. After all, nobody in paradise had ever heard of Rousseau.

(Rensch 1991: 414)

4 This can be illustrated with the well-documented practice of banning the use of languages other than those approved by the missionaries: Abel (1977: 983), in his paper on the missionary lingua franca Suau (Papua New Guinea) writes: All who came to school had to learn two second languages, namely Suau and English. In the early days, speaking Tavara at the Kwato head station was prohibited.
   Fesl (1993) writes:

> Punishments such as beatings or withdrawal of food were meted out by many missionaries on Koories who did not conform with their rules not to speak Australian languages. The following is a story told to the author by Melanie.

Melanie (born 1966)

> At the Carnarvon Mission, I was sometimes beaten when I spoke my language but it wasn't as bad as at other times when I was punished by them not letting me have any food. The food was not very much but when I didn't get any, I used to get pains in the stomach in the middle of the night. That was the way the missionary punished me for speaking my language.

(Fesl 1993: 83)

5 Kir = Kiribati language.

6 Pidgin German was still used on some mission stations in Papua New Guinea when I carried out fieldwork there in the 1970s.

7 Fesl (1993: 84 ff.) describes such practice in some detail:

One of the much-used ploys to 'Christianise' was to concentrate on the children. Many koorie parents were at first persuaded, or coerced, into leaving their children with the missionaries whilst they went out into the bush; in some cases, however, kidnapping took place. 'Reverend Watson of the Lake Wellington mission gained recruits by kidnapping. Aborigines in the area were forced to hide their children when he was near . . .' (Broome 1982, 33). Koories had no recourse to justice for the kidnapping of their children. No doubt, had Koories kidnapped a white child, the English law would have been applied quite differently.

(Fesl 1993: 84)

8 A summary of very severe criticisms of the practices of SIL and other evangelical missions operating in South America is given by Read (1980).
9 Shell books contain, in the words of their principal promoter Trainum:

> everything found in a book except words. The illustrations, pictures and page numbers are printed on uncut, unbound pages. After translation, any local language text may be added and good quality books printed right in the village, inexpensively, using a simple silkscreen printer.

(quoted in Philpott 1993: 4)

10 In a more elaborate model, the message 'is perceived through the cultural filter' (Whiteman 1974: 29) of the indigenous audience.

7 OFFICIAL POLICIES AND LANGUAGE PLANNING

1 On perusing these sources one is struck by the absence of the involvement of the speakers of small languages themselves. It is only in the early 1980s that speakers of Aboriginal languages discussed their concerns at Alice Springs in 1981 (J. Bell 1981) or that representatives of diverse Pacific nations met to discuss their language problems (see Crowley 1984). The number of indigenous voices is growing, but for the majority of speakers of small languages in the area, the basis for an informed discussion is lacking and they continue as in colonial days to be the objects, rather than formulators, of language planning activities in the area.
2 A very similar case is that of Pacific Motu/Hiri Motu. Dutton (1985) shows that the traditional Hiri trade language had little to do with its putative descendant, the lingua franca of the colonial administration of Papua which to a significant extent was an expatriate creation.
3 Very much the same removal of words of Arabic origin was carried out by the German administration in Tanganyika (see Brumfit 1972).
4 Its origins in the USA in the works of Boas and Sapir coincides with the awareness that the linguistic heritage of the country was rapidly disappearing.
5 For some highly illuminating remarks on the continuation of Western ideologies see LePage (1993).
6 Interestingly the policy makers use the term LOTE rather than LOTA (language other than Aboriginal), thereby signalling what is the unmarked case. To use a language other than English is accountable behaviour in Australia.

9 THE IMPACT OF FOREIGN LANGUAGE TEACHING

1 Recently in terms of the total age of language in the area.
2 Many of the developments in the French Pacific are mirrored by educational and language policies in the mother country. For a detailed sociohistorical analysis of these, see Grillo (1989).
3 For a discussion of some of the consequences of this among the Italian community, see Bettoni (1991).
4 A good idea of the current state of the debate can be gained from the many papers in Hartman and Henderson (1994).

10 THE SOCIOLINGUISTICS OF LANGUAGE SHIFT, DECAY AND DEATH

1 A frightening catalogue of quotations is listed in Diamond (1991):

PRESIDENT GEORGE WASHINGTON. 'The immediate objectives are the total destruction and devastation of their settlements. It will be essential to ruin their crops in the ground and prevent their planting more.'
BENJAMIN FRANKLIN. 'If it be the Design of Providence to Extirpate these Savages in order to make room for Cultivators of the Earth, it seems not improbable that Rum may be the appointed means.'
PRESIDENT THOMAS JEFFERSON. 'This unfortunate race, whom we had been taking so much pain to save and to civilize, have by their unexpected desertion and ferocious barbarities justified extermination and now await our decision on their fate.'
PRESIDENT JAMES MUNROE. 'The hunter or savage state requires a greater extent of territory to sustain it, than is compatible with the progress and just claims to civilized life . . . and must yield to it.'
PRESIDENT ANDREW JACKSON. 'They have neither the intelligence, the industry, the moral habits, nor the desire of improvement which are essential to any favourable change in their condition. Established in the midst of another and a superior race, and without appreciating the causes of their inferiority or seeking to control them, they must necessarily yield to the force of circumstances and ere long disappear.'
PRESIDENT THEODORE ROOSEVELT. 'The settler and pioneer have at bottom had justice on their side; this great continent could not have been kept as nothing but a game preserve for squalid savages.'

(Diamond 1991: 272ff.)

11 ASSESSING THE DAMAGE: STRUCTURAL AND LEXICAL EFFECTS

1 Such borrowing could be highly structured and functional and is difficult to reconcile with the prevailing Western view that 'language contact means language conflict' (Nelde 1986).
2 Very occasionally, influence from a dominant language can lead to morphological enrichment: Hooper *et al.* (1992: 361) comment on the influence of Mission Samoan on Tokelauan: 'Tokelauans regard their

language as having a relatively impoverished vocabulary of respect and they are aware that the great majority of the forms which they currently use to mark respect, deference and holiness are direct borrowings from Samoan.'

APPENDIX: LINGUISTICS IN THE PACIFIC

1 I am indebted to Dr W. McGregor for valuable comments on an earlier version of this appendix.

References

Aarsleff, H. (1982) *From Locke to Saussure*, London: Athlone.

Abas, H. (1987) *Indonesian as a Unifying Language of Wider Communication: A Historical and Sociolinguistic Perspective*, Canberra: *Pacific Linguistics* D23.

Abel, C. (1977) 'Missionary Lingue Franche: Suau', in S. A. Wurm (ed.) *New Guinea Area Languages and Language Study 3*, Canberra: *Pacific Linguistics* C40.

Adler, M. K. (1977) *Pidgins, Creoles and Lingua Francas: A Socio-Linguistic Study*, Hamburg: Buske.

Alisjahbana, S. T. (1965) 'New National Languages: A Problem Modern Linguistics has Failed to Solve', *Lingua* 15: 515–30.

Alisjahbana, S. T. (1971) 'Language Policy, Language Engineering and Literacy: Indonesia and Malaysia', in T. A. Sebeok (ed.) *Current Trends in Linguistics 8: Linguistics in Oceania*, The Hague: Mouton.

Alisjahbana, S. T. (1984) 'The Concept of Language Standardization and its Application to the Indonesian Language', in F. Coulmas (ed.) *Linguistic Minorities*, Berlin: Mouton.

Alkire, W. H. (1977) *An Introduction to the Peoples and Cultures of Micronesia*, Cummins.

Anderson, B. R. (1966) 'The Languages of Indonesian Politics', *Indonesia* 1: 89–116.

Anderson, B. R. (1990) 'Language, Fantasy, Revolution in Java, 1900–1945', *Prisma* 50: 25–39.

Anderson, E. A. (1987) 'Indonesian Language Month 1986: Tempest at the Forum', *New Language Planning Newsletter* 1(3): 1–3.

Anti-Slavery Society (1990) *West Papua: Plunder in Paradise*, London: Indigenous Peoples and Development Series Report 6.

Arms, D. G. (1988) 'Some Problems in Fijian Orthography', paper presented at the Fifth International Conference on Austronesian Linguistics, Auckland.

Arthur, C. (1990) 'Here be Monster for the Verbal Unwary', *Times Higher Education Supplement* 19 October: 16.

Atoni, T. (1975) 'Cultural Conversation: Tokelan Island Language', *South Pacific Commission*: 129–30.

Aufinger, A. (1948–9) 'Secret Languages of the Small Islands near Madang', *South Pacific* 3: 90–5, 315; 4: 113–20.

Austin, P. (1981) 'Diyari', MS, La Trobe University, Melbourne.

Babib, A. A. (1989) 'Bahasa Indonesia and Tok Pisin as National Languages', in C. Thirwall and P. J. Hugen (eds) *The Ethics of Development*, Port Moresby: University of Papua New Guinea Press.

Bahnemann, G. (1964) *New Guinea Crocodile Poacher*, London: Jarrolds.

Bain, B. (ed.) (1982) *The Sociogenesis of Language and Human Contact*, New York and London: Plenum.

Baker, P. (1990) 'Off Target?', *Journal of Pidgin and Creole Languages* 5(1): 107–20.

Baker, P. and Mühlhäusler, P. (1990) 'From Business to Pidgin', *Journal of Asian-Pacific Communication* 1(1): 87–115.

Baker, S. J. (1966) *The Australian Language*, Sydney: Currawong.

Baldauf, R. B. (1990) 'Education and Language Planning in the Samoas', in R. B. Baldauf and A. Luke (eds) *Language Planning and Education in Australasia and the South Pacific*, Clevedon, PA: Multilingual Matters.

Baldauf, R. B. and Luke, A. (eds) (1990) *Language Planning and Education in Australia and the South Pacific*, Clevedon, PA: Multilingual Matters.

Bardon, G. (1970) 'Models of Consciousness', MS, Australian Institute of Aboriginal Studies, Canberra.

Bateson, G. (1944) 'Pidgin English and Cross-Cultural Communication', *Transaction of the New York Academy of Science* 2: 137–41.

Bauer, F. H. (1970) 'The Kartans of Kangaroo Island, South Australia: A Puzzle in Extinction', in A. R. Pilling and R. A. Waterman (eds) *Diprotodon to Detribalization*, East Lansing, MI: Michigan University Press.

Baumann, A. (1916) *Das neue, leichte Weltdeutsch*, Munich: Huber.

Bavin, E. L. (1989) 'Some Lexical and Morphological Changes in Warlpiri', in N. C. Dorian (ed.) *Investigating Obsolescence: Studies in Language Contraction and Death*, Cambridge: Cambridge University Press.

Beaver, N. (1920) *Unexplained New Guinea*, London: Seeley Service.

Bechert, J. (1987) 'Universalienforschung und Ethnozentrismus', paper presented at the International Congress of Linguistics, Berlin.

Bechert, J. (1990) 'Universalienforschung und Ethnozentrismus', *Proceedings of the Fourteenth International Congress of Linguistics*, Berlin: Akademie Verlag.

Bechert, J. (1991) 'The Problem of Semantic Incomparability and its "Solution" through Linguistic Colonization', MS, Bremen University.

Bell, A. and Holmes, J. (eds) (1991) *New Zealand Ways of Speaking English*, Clevedon, PA: Multilingual Matters.

Bell, H. L. (1971) 'Language and the Army of Papua-New Guinea', *Australian Army Journal* 264: 31–42.

Bell, J. (ed.) (1981) *Language Planning for Australian Aboriginal Languages*, Alice Springs: Institute for Aboriginal Development.

Bender, B. W. (1971) 'Micronesian Languages', *Current Trends in Linguistics* 8: 426–65.

Bender, B. W. (1982) 'Proto-Micronesian Wordlist', computer printout, Department of Linguistics, University of Hawaii, Honolulu.

Bender, B. W. and Rehg, K. L. (1991) 'Micronesian Languages in Jeopardy?', paper presented at the Sixth International Conference on Austronesian Linguistics, Honolulu.

Benton, R. A. (1980) 'Changes in Language Use in a Rural Maori Community 1963–1978', *Journal of the Polynesian Society* 89(4): 455–78.

Benton, R. A. (1981) *The Flight of the Amokura: Oceanic Language and*

Formal Education in the South Pacific, Wellington: New Zealand Council for Educational Research.

Bernabe, E. F. (1986) *Language Policy Formulation, Programming, Implementation and Evaluation in the Philippines Education (1565–1974)*, Manila: Linguistic Society of the Philippines.

Besnier, N. (1983) 'Diglossia in the Atolls: The Role of the Samoan Language in Tuvalu since 1865', MS, University of Southern California.

Bettoni, C. (1991) 'Language Variety among Italians: Anglicization, Attrition and Attitudes', in S. Romaine (ed.) *Language in Australia*, Cambridge: Cambridge University Press.

Bichakjian, B. H. (1988) *Evolution in Language*, Ann Arbor, MI: Karoma.

Bickerton, D. and Odo, C. (1976–7) *Change and Variation in Hawaiian English*, vols 1 and 2, Final Report of NSF Grant, University of Hawaii, Honolulu.

Bickley, V. (ed.) (1987) *Re-Exploring CELT*, Hong Kong: Institute of Language in Education.

Biggs, B. G. (1971) 'The Languages of Polynesia', *Current Trends in Linguistics* 8: 466–505.

Biggs, B. G. (1972) 'Implications of Linguistic Subgrouping with Special Reference to Polynesia', in R. C. Green and M. Kelly (eds) *Studies in Oceanic Culture History* vol. 3, Honolulu: Bishop Museum.

Bilmes, J. (1975) 'Misinformation and Ambiguity in Verbal Interaction: A Northern Thai Example', *Linguistics* 164: 63–75.

Black, P. (1981) 'Why and How Languages Change', in J. Bell (ed.) *Language Planning for Australian Aboriginal Languages*, Alice Springs: Institute for Aboriginal Development.

Blust, R. (ed.) (1991) *Currents in Pacific Linguistics: Papers on Austronesian Languages and Ethnolinguistics in Honour of George W. Grace*, Canberra: *Pacific Linguistics* C117.

Boas, F. (1911) *Handbook of American Indian Languages*, Washington, DC: Smithsonian Institution.

Boas, F. (1929) 'Classification of American Indian Languages', *American Anthropologist* 12: 367–76.

Borchardt, K. (1926) 'Tok Boi Wörterbuch', MS, Vunapope, Rabaul, Papua New Guinea.

Boretzky, N. (1984) 'The Indo-Europeanist Model of Sound Change and Genetic Affinity and Change in Exotic Languages', *Diachronica* 1(1): 1–51.

Boyce, M. (1991) 'Maori Language Maintenance and Shift in Porirua', paper presented at the Sixth International Conference on Austronesian Linguistics, Honolulu.

Bradley, D. (1981) 'Majority–Minority Linguistic Interfaces in Thailand', *Working Papers in Linguistics, University of Melbourne* 7: 79–86.

Bradley, D. (1987) 'The Disappearance of the Ungong in Thailand', in N. C. Dorian (ed.) *Investigating Obsolescence: Studies in Language Contraction and Death*, Cambridge: Cambridge University Press.

Bradshaw, J. (1978) 'Multilingualism and Language Mixture among the Numbami', *University of Hawaii Working Papers in Linguistics* 10(1): 85–100.

Brenneis, D. L. and Myers, F. R. (eds) (1984) *Dangerous Words: Language and Politics in the Pacific*, New York and London: New York University Press.

Brenninkmeyer, L. (1924) 'Einfuehrung ins Pidgin-Englisch: Ein Versuch', MS, Kanmancham, Papua New Guinea.

Bridge, C. (1885) 'Further Correspondence Respecting the Establishment of the New Guinea Protectorate', *Queensland Parliamentary Papers 1885*: 30–46.

Bridgman, Fr (1849) Untitled notice in *The Missionary Herald* 45: 53.

Bright, W. (ed.) (1966) *Sociolinguistics*, The Hague: Mouton.

Brockmeier, J., Harré, E. M. and Mühlhäusler, P. (1996) *Greenspeak*, MS, Oxford: Oxford University Press.

Bromilow, W. E. (1929) *Twenty Years among Primitive Papuas*, London: Epworth.

Broome, R. (1982) *Aboriginal Australians*, Sydney: Allen & Unwin.

Brosnahan, L. F. (1963) 'Some Historical Cases of Language Imposition', in J. Spencer (ed.) *Language in Africa*, Cambridge: Cambridge University Press.

Brumfit, A. (1972) 'The Development of a Language Policy in German East Africa,' *Journal of the Language Association of Eastern Africa* 2(1): 1–9.

Burke, P. and Porter, R. (eds) (1987) *The Social History of Language*, Cambridge: Cambridge University Press.

Burridge, K. O. L. (1960) *Mambu: A Melanesian Millennium*, London: Methuen.

Byrne, F. and Huebner, T. (eds) (1992) *Development and Structures of Creole Language*, Amsterdam: Benjamins.

Calvet, L.-J. (1974) *Der Sprachenfresser: Ein Versuch über Linguistik und Kolonialismus*, Berlin: Das Arsenal.

Calvet, L.-J. (1985) 'Mehrsprachige Märkte und Vehikularsprachen: Geld und Sprache', *Osnabrücker Beiträge zur Sprachtheorie* 31: 91–101.

Cameron, C. (1923) *Two Years in Southern Seas*, London: Fisher Unwin.

Capell, A. (1942) 'Languages of Arnhemland', *Oceania* 12: 364–92; 13: 24–50.

Capell, A. (1966) *A Survey of New Guinea Languages*, Sydney: Sydney University Press.

Capell, A. (1968) 'What do We Know of Tasmanian Languages?' *Records of the Queen Victoria Museum* 30: 1–7.

Capell, A. (1969) 'The Changing Status of Melanesian Pidgin', *Monda Lingvo-Problemo* 1: 107–15.

Cargill, D. (1836) Letters to the Secretaries of the Wesleyan Missionary Society, London.

Carle, R., Heinschke, M., Pink, P. W., Rost, C. and Stradtlander, K. (eds) (1982) *GAVA: Studies in Austronesian Languages and Cultures* (Festschrift Kahler), Berlin: Reimer.

Cartledge, B. (ed.) (1992) *Monitoring the Environment*, Oxford: Oxford University Press.

Charpentier, J. M. (1992) 'Interaction entre langue parlée et langue ecrite en Vanuatu', paper presented at the Sèvres Workshop of the International Group for the Study of Language Standardization and the Vernacularization of Literacy (IGLSVL), Paris.

Charpentier, J. M. (nd) 'La Francophonie au Vanuatu: Concept juridique ou réalité sociolinguique', MS, Paris: LACITO-CNRS.

Charpentier, J. M. and Tryon, D. T. (1979) *Le Pidgin Bislama*, Paris: SELAF.

Charpentier, J. M. and Tryon, D. T. (1982) 'Functions of Bislama in the New Hebrides and in Independent Vanuatu', *English Worldwide* 3(7): 146–60.

352   *References*

Chomsky, N. (1966) *Cartesian Linguistics*, New York: Harper & Row.
Chomsky, N. (1970) 'Language and Freedom', in J. Peck (ed.) *The Chomsky Reader*, New York: Pantheon.
Christie, M. J. (1984) 'The School World of the Aboriginal Child', PhD thesis, University of Queensland.
Christie, M. J. (1989) 'Literacy, Genocide and the Media', *The Aboriginal Child at School* 17(5): 27–32.
Christie, M. J. and Harris, S. (1985) 'Communication Breakdown in the Aboriginal Classroom', in J. B. Pride (ed.) *Cross-Cultural Encounters*, Melbourne: River Seine.
Churchill, W. (1911) *Beach-La-Mar*, Washington, DC: Carnegie Institution.
Clammer, J. R. (1976) *Literacy and Social Change: A Case Study of Fiji*, Leiden: E. J. Brill.
Clark, R. (1991) 'Pidgin English and Pidgin Maori', in A. Bell and J. Holmes (eds) *New Zealand Ways of Speaking English*, Clevedon, PA: Multilingual Matters.
Clerk, C. (ed.) (1984) *The Effects of Development on Traditional Pacific Island Cultures*, London: Royal Commonwealth Society.
Cobarrubias, J. (1983) 'Language Planning: The State of the Art', in J. Cobarrubias and J. A. Fishman (eds) *Progress in Language Planning*, Berlin: Mouton de Gruyter.
Cobarrubias, J. and Fishman, J. A. (eds) (1983) *Progress in Language Planning*, Berlin: Mouton de Gruyter.
Codrington, R. H. and Palmer, B. D. (1896) *A Dictionary of the Language of Mota*, London: Society for Promoting Christian Knowledge.
Collis, D. R. F. (1990) *Arctic Languages: An Awakening*, Paris: UNESCO.
Cooper, R. E. (1975) 'Coastal Suau: A Preliminary Study of Internal Relationships', in T. E. Dutton (ed.) *Studies in Languages of Central and South-East Papua*, Canberra: *Pacific Linguistics* C29: 227–78.
Corne, C. (1979) 'Le Français à Tahiti', in A. Valdman (ed.) *Le Français hors de France*, Paris: Honoré Champion.
Corne, C. and Hollyman, J. (1996) 'French in the Pacific', in S. A. Wurm, P. Mühlhäusler and T. Tryon (eds) *Atlas of Languages of Intercultural Communication in the Pacific Hemisphere*.
Coulmas, F. (ed.) (1976) *Language Planning for Modernization*, The Hague: Mouton.
Coulmas, F. (ed.) (1984) *Linguistic Minorities*, Berlin: Mouton.
Coulmas, F. (1985) *Sprache und Staat*, Berlin: De Gruyter.
Coulmas, F. (1994) 'Protestant Ethics and Profane Language: Economic Aspects of Language Standardization', in G. Lüdi (ed.) *Sprachstandardisierung*, Freiburg: Swiss Academy of Humanities and Social Science.
Crocombe, R. (1989) *The South Pacific: An Introduction*, Christchurch: Institute of Pacific Studies.
Cromwell, L. G. (1980) 'Bar Kar Mir: To Talk with No Curves', *Anthropological Forum* 5(1): 24–37.
Crosby, A. W. (1986) *Ecological Imperialism: The Biological Expansion of Europe 900–1900*, Cambridge: Cambridge University Press.
Crowley, Terry (1984) 'Pacific Languages: Directions for the Future', *Language Planning Newsletter* 10(4): 1–2.
Crowley, Terry (1987) 'Language Issues and National Development in Vanuatu', MS, Vila University of the South Pacific.

Crowley, Terry (1989) 'Language Issues and National Development in Vanuatu', in I. Fodor and C. Hagège (eds) *Language Reform: History and Future*, Hamburg: Buske.

Crowley, Terry (1990a) 'The Position of Melanesian Pidgin in Vanuatu and Papua New Guinea', in J. W. M. Verhaar (ed.) *Melanesian Pidgin and Tok Pisin*, Amsterdam: Benjamins.

Crowley, Terry (1990b) 'Tasmanian Aboriginal Language: Old and New Dialects', reprinted in M. Walsh and C. Yallop (eds) (1995) *Language in Aboriginal Australia*, Canberra: Aboriginal Studies Press.

Crowley, Terry (1990c) *Beach-La-Mar to Bislama*, Oxford: Oxford University Press.

Crowley, Tony (1990) 'That Obscure Object of Desire: A Science of Language', in J. E. Joseph and T. J. Taylor (eds) *Ideologies of Language*, London: Routledge.

Day, R. (1985) 'The Ultimate Inequality: Linguistic Genocide', in N. Wolfson and J. Manes (eds) *Language of Inequality*, Berlin: Mouton.

Deckert, G. D. (1987) 'Methological Pitfalls in Researching Reading Habits in Less Developed Societies', in V. Bickley (ed.) *Re-Exploring CELT*, Hong Kong: Institute of Language in Education.

Deer, D. S. (1975) 'The Missionary Language Learning Problem', *Missiology* III(I): 85–102.

DeFrancis, J. (1977) *Colonialism and Language Policy in Vietnam*, The Hague: Mouton.

Dench, A. (1988) 'Kinship and Collective Activity in the Ngayarda Languages in Australia', *Language in Society* 16: 321–39.

de Terra, D. (1982) 'The Lingua Genesis of Society: The Implementation of the National Language Plan in West Malaysia', in B. Bain (ed.) *The Sociogenesis of Language and Human Contact*, New York and London: Plenum.

Diamond, J. (1991) *The Rise and Fall of the Third Chimpanzee*, London: Vintage.

Dixon, R. M. W. (1980) *The Languages of Australia*, Cambridge: Cambridge University Press.

Dixon, R. M. W. (1991) 'The Endangered Languages of Australia, Indonesia and Oceania', in R. H. Robins and E. M. Uhlenbeck (eds) *Endangered Languages*, Oxford: Berg.

Donaldson, T. (1985) 'From Speaking Ngiyampaa to Speaking English', *Aboriginal History* 9(2): 126–45.

Dorian, N. C. (ed.) (1989a) *Investigating Obsolescence: Studies in Language Contraction and Death*, Cambridge: Cambridge University Press.

Dorian, N. C. (1989b) 'Small Languages and Small Language Communities: News, Notes and Comments 3', *International Journal of the Sociology of Language* 80: 139–41.

Dorian, N. C. (1992) 'Small Languages and Small Language Communities: News, Notes and Comments 10', *International Journal of the Sociology of Language* 95: 143–8.

Dorian, N. (1993) 'A Response to Ladefoged's Other View of Endangered Languages', *Language* 69: 575–9.

Drost, D. and König, W. (eds) (1961) *Beiträge zur Völkerforschung*, Berlin: Akademie Verlag.

Duranti, A. (1981) *The Samoan Fono: A Sociolinguistic Study*, Canberra: Pacific Linguistics B80.

Duranti, A. and Ochs, E. (1986) 'Literacy Instruction in a Samoan Village', in B. B. Schieffelin and P. Gilmore (eds) *The Acquisition of Literacy: Ethnographic Perspectives*, Norwood, NJ: Ablex.

Dutton, T. E. (1975a) 'Language and National Development – long wanem rot?', inaugural lecture, University of Papua New Guinea.

Dutton, T. E. (ed.) (1975b) *Studies in Languages of Central and South-East Papua*, Canberra: *Pacific Linguistics* C29.

Dutton, T. E. (1978) 'The Melanesian Problem and Language Change and Disappearance in South-Eastern Papua New Guinea', MS, Department of Linguistics, Research Institute of Pacific Studies, Australian National University.

Dutton, T. E. (1982) 'Borrowing in Austronesian and Non-Austronesian Languages of Coastal South-East Mainland Papua New Guinea', Canberra: *Pacific Linguistics* C74: 109–77.

Dutton, T. E. (1985) *Hiri Motu – Iena Sivarai*, Port Moresby: University of Papua New Guinea Press.

Dutton, T. E. (1987) 'Successful Intercourse was had with the Natives', in D. C. Laycock and W. Winter (eds) *A World of Language*, Canberra: *Pacific Linguistics* C1,000: 153–71.

Dutton, T. E. (ed.) (1992) *Culture Change, Language Changes: Case Studies from Melanesia*, Canberra: *Pacific Linguistics* C120.

Dutton, T. E. and Mühlhäusler, P. (1979) 'Papuan Pidgin English and Hiri Motu' in S. A. Wurm (ed.) *New Guinea and Neighbouring Areas: A Sociolinguistic Laboratory*, The Hague: Mouton.

Dutton, T. E. and Mühlhäusler, P. (1989) 'Language Decline in Papua New Guinea', paper presented at the Annual Meeting of the Linguistic Society of Papua New Guinea.

Dutton, T. E., Ross, M. and Tryon, D. T. (eds) (1992) *The Language Game: Papers in Memory of Donald C. Laycock*, Canberra: *Pacific Linguistics* C110.

Eades, D. (1982) 'You Gotta Know How to Talk. . . .: Information Seeking in South East Queensland Aboriginal Society', *Australian Journal of Linguistics* 2(1): 61–82.

Ehrhart, S. (1993) *Le Créole français de Sti-Louis (le tayo) en Nouvelle-Calédonie*, Hamburg: Buske.

Elson, B. F. and Comas, J. (eds) (1961) *A William Cameron Townsend en el Vigesimoquinto Aniversario del Instituto Linguistico de Vereno*, Mexico City: Summer Institute of Linguistics.

England, N. (1992) 'Doing Mayan Linguistics in Guatemala', *Language* 68(1): 29–35.

Enninger, W. and Haynes, L. M. (eds) (1984) *Studies in Language Ecology*, Wiesbaden: Steiner.

Errington, J. T. (1986) 'Continuity and Change in Indonesian Language Development', *Journal of Asian Studies*, 45(2): 329–53.

Fairclough, N. (ed.) (1992) *Critical Language Awareness*, London: Longman.

Farrar, F. W. (1899) *Language and Languages*, London: Longmans, Green.

Fase, W., Jaspaert, K. and Kroon, S. (eds) (1992) *Maintenance and Loss of Minority Languages*, Amsterdam: Benjamins.

Ferguson, C. A. (1962) 'The Language Factor in National Development', *Anthropological Linguistics* 4(1): 22–37.

Ferguson, C. A. (1968) 'Language Development', in J. A. Fishman, O. O. Dasgupta and C. A. Ferguson, *Language Problems of Developing Nations*, New York: Wiley.

Ferguson, C. A. (1987) 'Literacy in a Hunting-Gathering Society: The Case of Diyari', *Journal of Anthropological Research* 43: 223–37.

Fesl, E. M. D. (1993) *Conned*, Brisbane: University of Queensland Press.

Fill, A. (1993) *Ökolinguistik*, Tübingen: Narr.

Fischer, H. (1962) 'Einige Linguistische Indizien des Kulturwandels in Nordost-Neuguinea', *Soziologus* 1: 18–36.

Fischer, J. L. (1966) 'Syntax and Social Structure: Truk and Ponape', in W. Bright (ed.) *Sociolinguistics*, The Hague: Mouton.

Fischer, J. L. (1971) 'Style Contrasts in Pacific Languages', in T. A. Sebeok (ed.) *Current Trends in Linguistics 8: Linguistics in Oceania*, The Hague: Mouton.

Fishman, J. A. (ed.) (1974) *Advances in Language Planning*, The Hague: Mouton.

Fishman, J. A. (1989) 'What is Reversing Language Shift (RSL) and How Can it Succeed?', in D. Garter, J. F. Hoekstra, L. G. Jansma and T. Ytsma (eds) *Fourth International Conference on Minority Languages*, Clevedon, PA: Multilingual Matters.

Fishman, J. A. (1991) *Reversing Language Shift*, Clevedon, PA: Multilingual Matters.

Flierl, W. and Strauss, H. (eds) (1977) *Kâte Dictionary*, Canberra: *Pacific Linguistics* C41.

Fodor, I. and Hagège, C. (eds) (1989) *Language Reform: History and Future*, Hamburg: Buske.

Foley, W. A. (1986a) 'Language Birth: The Process of Pidginization and Creolization', MS, Australian National University.

Foley, W. A. (1986b) *The Papuan Languages of New Guinea*, Cambridge: Cambridge University Press.

Foster, L. and Stockley, D. (1988) *Australian Multiculturalism: A Documentary History and Critique*, Clevedon, PA: Multilingual Matters.

Fox, C. (1967) *The Study of the Solomons*, Tarnaniara: Diocese of Melanesia Press.

Franklin, J. (1977) 'Vernacular Literacy: General Remarks', in S. A. Wurm (ed.) *New Guinea Area Languages and Language Study 3*, Canberra: *Pacific Linguistics* C40.

Franklin, K. J. (1975) 'Vernaculars as Bridges to Cross-Cultural Understanding' in K. A. McElhanon (ed.) *Tok Pisin i Go We?*, Port Moresby: Linguistic Society of Papua New Guinea.

Franklin, K. J. (1977a) 'Institutional Framework of Language Study: S.I.L.', in S. A. Wurm (ed.) *New Guinea Area Languages and Language Study 3*, Canberra: *Pacific Linguistics* C40: 855–64.

Franklin, K. J. (1977b) 'The Kewa Language in Culture and Society', in S. A. Wurm (ed.) *New Guinea Area Languages and Language Study 3*, Canberra: *Pacific Linguistics* C40.

Franklin, K. J. (1992) 'The Pandanus Languages of the Southern Highlands Province', in T. E. Dutton (ed.) *Culture Change, Language Changes: Case Studies from Melanesia*, Canberra: *Pacific Linguistics* C120.

Franklin, K. J. and Stefaniw, R. (1992) 'The Pandanus Languages of the Southern Highlands Province, Papua New Guinea: A Further Report', in

356   *References*

T. E. Dutton (ed.) *Culture Change, Language Changes: Case Studies from Melanesia*, Canberra: *Pacific Linguistics* C120.

Freyberg, P. G. (1977) 'Missionary lingue franche: Bel (Gegaded)' in S. A. Wurm (ed.) *New Guinea Area Languages and Language Study 3*, Canberra: *Pacific Linguistics* C40: 855–64.

Friederici, G. (1911) 'Pidgin-Englisch in Deutsch-Neuguinea', *Koloniale Randschau* 3: 92–106.

Fromkin, V. and Rodman, R. (1988) *An Introduction to Language*, New York: Holt, Rinehart & Winston.

Fugmann, G. (1976) 'Preaching in Melanesia', *Catalyst* 6(4): 259–68.

Garter, D., Hoekstra, J. F., Jansma, L. G. and Ytsma, T. (eds) (1989) *Fourth International Conference on Minority Languages*, Clevedon, PA: Multilingual Matters.

Geertz, C. (1972) 'Linguistic Etiquette', in J. B. Pride and J. Holmes (eds) *Sociolinguistics*, Harmondsworth: Penguin.

Gilbert, G. G. (ed.) (1987) *Pidgin and Creole Languages*, Honolulu: Hawaii University Press.

Giles, H. and Saint-Jacques, B. (eds) (1979) *Language and Ethnic Relations*, Oxford: Pergamon.

Gilliam, A. M. (1984) 'Language and "Development" in Papua New Guinea', *Dialectical Anthropology* 8: 303–18.

Gilliam, A. M. (1986) 'Language, Communication and Power: Some Ethical Considerations', paper presented at the Waigani Seminar on the Ethics of Development, Port Moresby, Papua New Guinea.

Goh, Keng Swee (1980) 'Report on the Ministry of Education 1978', in J. Newman (ed.) *Proceedings of the Symposium on Language Planning*, University of Singapore.

Gonzales, A. and Thomas, D. (eds) (1981) *Linguistics across Continents*, Manila: Linguistic Society of the Philippines.

Gould, S. J. (1988) *Time's Arrow, Time's Cycle*, Harmondsworth: Penguin.

Grace, G. W. (1975) 'Linguistic Diversity in the Pacific: On the Sources of Diversity', paper presented to the Thirteenth Pacific Science Congress, Vancouver.

Grace, G. W. (1981) 'Indirect Inheritance and the Aberrant Melanesian Languages', in J. Hollyman and A. Pawley (eds) *Studies in Pacific Languages and Cultures*, Auckland: Linguistics Society of New Zealand.

Grace, G. W. (1991) 'How do Languages Change? More on "Aberrant" Language', paper presented at the Sixth International Conference on Austronesian Linguistics, Honolulu.

Grace, G. W. (1993a) 'What are Languages?', *Ethnolinguistic Notes* 3(45): 1–17.

Grace, G. W. (1993b) 'Culture in Language and Linguistics: Linguistic's Role in Monocultural Imperialism', MS, University of Hawaii, Honolulu.

Grace, G. W. (1996) *Culture in Language and Linguistics: Linguistics' Role in Monocultural Imperialism,* Honolulu: University of Hawaii Press.

Greenberg, J. H. (1965) 'Urbanism, Migration and Language', in H. Kuper (ed.) *Urbanization and Migration in West Africa*, Berkeley and Los Angeles: University of California Press.

Greenberg, J. H. (1971) *Language, Culture and Communication*, Stanford, CA: Stanford University Press.

Grillo, R. D. (1989) *Dominant Languages*, Cambridge: Cambridge University Press.

Grimes, B. and Grimes, J. (1988) *Ethnologie: Languages of the World*, Dallas: Summer Institute of Linguistics.

Grimshaw, B. (1912) *The New New Guinea*, London: Hutchinson.

Grubner, F. (1967) 'Affective Judgement of the Term "Pidgin" I', *Pacific Speech* 2(2): 67–76.

Grubner, F. (1968) 'Affective Judgement of the Term "Pidgin" II', *Pacific Speech* 2(3): 73–84.

Gudschinksy, S. C. (1968) 'The Relationship of Languages and Linguistics to Reading,' *Kivung* 1(3): 146–52.

Gumperz, J. J. and Wilson, R. (1971) 'Convergence and Creolization: A Case from the Indo-Aryan/Dravidian Border', in D. Hymes (ed.) *Pidginization and Creolization of Languages*, Cambridge: Cambridge University Press.

Gunther, J. T. (1958) 'The People', in J. Wilkes (ed.) *New Guinea and Australia*, Sydney: Angus & Robertson.

Gunther, J. T. (1969) 'More English, More Teachers: Putting a Cat among the Pidgins', *New Guinea* 4(2): 43–53.

Guy, G. R. (1989) 'International Perspectives on Linguistic Diversity and Language Rights', *Language Problems and Language Planning* 13(1): 45–53.

Haiman, J. (1979) 'Hua: Papuan Language of New Guinea', in T. Shopen (ed.) *Languages and their Speakers*, Cambridge, MA: Winthrop.

Hale, K. (1992) 'Language Endangerment and the Human Value of Linguistic Diversity', *Language* 68(1): 35–41.

Halliday, M. A. K. (1975) *Explorations in the Functions of Language*, London: Edward Arnold.

Hanlon, P. (1995) *Upon a Stone Altar: A History of the Island of Pohnpei to 1890*, Honolulu: University of Hawaii Press.

Hanzeli, V. E. (1969) *Missionary Linguistics in New France*, The Hague: Mouton.

Hardman de Bautista, M. (1985) 'The Imperial Languages of the Andes', in N. Wolfson and J. Manes (eds) *Language of Inequality*, Berlin: Mouton.

Harlow, R. (ed.) (1991) *Vical 2 – Western Austronesian and Contact Languages*, Auckland: Linguistic Society of New Zealand.

Harris, R. (1979) *The Language Makers*, London: Duckworth.

Harris, R. (1980) *The Language Myth*, London: Duckworth.

Harris, R. (1990) 'Language as Social Interaction: Integrationalism versus Segregationalism', in N. Love (ed.) *The Foundations of Linguistic Theory: Selected Writings of Roy Harris*, London: Routledge.

Harrison, G. J. (1984) 'The Place of English in Macau and a Theoretical Speculation', *Journal of Multilingual and Multicultural Development* 5(6): 475–89.

Hartman, D. and Henderson, J. (eds) (1994) *Aboriginal Languages in Education*, Alice Springs: Institute for Aboriginal Development (IAD) Press.

Haugen, E. (1972) *The Ecology of Language: Essays by Einar Haugen*, Stanford, CA: Stanford University Press.

Haugen, E. (1985) 'The Language of Imperialism: Unity or Pluralism', in Wolfson and Manes (eds) *Language of Inequality*, Berlin: Mouton.

Hawkins, E. (1991) 'Hawaiian Immersion Education: Where Will it Take the Language?', paper presented at the International Conference on Austronesian Linguistics, Honolulu.

Heeschen, V. and Schievenhövel, W. (1987) *Mensch, Kultur und Umwelt im Zentralen Bergland von West-Neu-Guinea*, Berlin: Reimer.

Hefley, J. and Hefley, M. (1974) *Uncle Cam: The Story of William Cameron Townsend*, Waco, TX: Word Books.

Heidegger, M. (1986) *Unterwegs zur Sprache*, Pfullingen: Neske.

Heine, B. (1970) *Status and Use of African Lingua Francas*, Munich: Weltforum.

Heryanto, A. (1988) 'Language of Development and Development of Language', MS, Universitas Kristen Satya Wacana, Indonesia.

Heryanto, A. (1990) 'The Making of Language: Developmentalism in Indonesia', *Prisma* 50: 40–53.

Herzfeld, A. (1980) 'Creole and Standard Languages: Contact and Conflict', in *Zeitschrift für Dialektologie und Linguistik*, Beiheft 23 (Languages in Contact and Conflict), 83–90.

Hill, J. H. (1993) 'Structure and Practice in Language Shift', in K. Hyltenstam and A. Viberg (eds) *Progression and Regression in Language*, Cambridge: Cambridge University Press.

Hilliard, D. (1978) *God's Gentlemen: A History of the Melanesian Mission 1849–1942*, Brisbane: University of Queensland Press.

Hockett, C. F. (1950) 'Age-Grading and Linguistic Continuity', *Language* 26: 449–57.

Hockett, C. F. (1987) *Refurbishing our Foundations*, Amsterdam: Benjamins.

Hoffman, J. E. (1973) 'The Malay Language as a Force for Unity in the Indonesian Archipelago, 1815–1900', *Nusantara* 4: 19–35.

Hohepa, P. (1984) 'Current Issues in Promoting Maori Language Use', *Language Planning Newsletter* 10(3): 1–4.

Hollyman, J. (1962) 'The Lizard and the Axe', *Journal of the Polynesian Society* 71(3): 310–27.

Hollyman, J. and Pawley, A. (eds) (1981) *Studies in Pacific Languages and Cultures*, Auckland: Linguistic Society of New Zealand.

Höltker, G. (1945) 'Das Pidgin-Englisch als sprachliches Missionsmittel in Neuguinea', *Neue Zeitschrift für Missionswissenschaft* 1: 44–63.

Hooker, V. M. (1990) 'The New Order Standardization of Language', *Prisma* 50: 54–67.

Hooley, B. (1976) Communication Association, Melbourne, *Twenty Years in Papua New Guinea: SIL*, Ukarumpa: Summer Institute of Linguistics.

Hooley, B. A. and McElhanon, K. A. (1970) 'Languages of the Morobe District – New Guinea', Canberra: *Pacific Linguistics* C13: 1,065–94.

Hooper, A., Huntsman, J. and Kalolo, K. (1992) 'The Tokelau Language 1841–1991', *Journal of the Polynesian Society* 101(4): 343–71.

Hughes, R. (1987) *The Fatal Shore*, London: Collins Harvill.

Humphries, W. R. (1923) *Patrolling in Papua*, London: Fisher Unwin.

Hüskes, J. (ed.) (1932) *Pioniere der Südsee: Werden und Wachsen der Herz-Jesu-Mission . . . 1882–1932*, Hiltrup: Herz-Jesu Mission.

Huttar, G. (1992) 'Nduka Organization of Experience: African or Universal', in F. Byrne and T. Huebner (eds) *Development and Structures of Creole Language*, Amsterdam: Benjamins.

Hymes, D. (ed.) (1966) *Language in Culture and Society*, New York: Harper International.

Hymes, D. (ed.) (1971) *Pidginization and Creolization of Languages*, Cambridge: Cambridge University Press.

Hymes, D. (1974) *Foundations of Sociolinguistics*, Philadelphia, PA: University of Pennsylvania Press.

Hyltenstam, K. and Viberg, A. (eds) (1993) *Progression and Regression in Language*, Cambridge: Cambridge University Press.

Jaspaert, K., Fase, W. and Kroon, S. (eds) (1992) *Maintenance and Loss of Minority Languages*, Amsterdam: Benjamins.

Jernudd, B. H. (1981) 'Planning Language Treatment: Linguistics for the Third World', *Language in Society* 10: 43–52.

Jernudd, B. H. and Shapiro, M. J. (eds) (1989) *The Politics of Language Purism*, Berlin: De Gruyter.

Johnston, R. L. (1979) 'Development of a Literary Mode in the Languages of Nonliterary Communities', in S. A. Wurm (ed.) *New Guinea and Neighbouring Areas: A Sociolinguistic Laboratory*, The Hague: Mouton.

Johnston, R. L. (1980) *Nakanai of New Britain*, Canberra: *Pacific Linguistics* B70.

Jones, G. (1990) 'How Bilingualism is Being Integrated in Negaro Brunei Darussalam', in R. B. Baldauf and A. Luke (eds) *Language Planning and Education in Australasia and the South Pacific*, Clevedon, PA: Multilingual Matters.

Jorgenson, J. (1842) 'Aboriginal Languages of Tasmania', *Tasmanian Journal of Natural Science, Agriculture, Statistics, & c*, 1: 308–18.

Joseph, J. E. (1987) *Eloquence and Power: The Rise of Language Standards and Standard Languages*, London: Pinter.

Joseph, J. E. and Taylor, T. J. (eds) (1990) *Ideologies of Language*, London: Routledge.

Jourdan, C. (1985) 'Sapos Iumi Mitim Iumi: Urbanization and Creolization in the Solomon Islands', PhD thesis, Australian National University.

Jourdan, C. (1990) 'Solomons Pijin: An Unrecognized National Language', in R. Baldauf and A. Luke (eds) *Language Planning and Education in Australasia and the South Pacific*, Clevedon, PA: Multilingual Matters.

Jupp, J. (ed.) (1988) *The Australian People: An Encyclopedia of the Nation, its People and their Origins*, Sydney: Angus & Robertson.

Kale, J. (1990a) 'Language Planning and the Language of Education in Papua New Guinea', in R. Baldauf and A. Luke (eds) *Language Planning and Education in Australasia and the South Pacific*, Clevedon, PA: Multilingual Matters.

Kale, J. (1990b) 'Controllers or Victims: Language and Education in the Torres Strait', in R. Baldauf and A. Luke (eds) *Language Planning and Education in Australasia and the South Pacific*, Clevedon, PA: Multilingual Matters.

Kaplan, R. B. and Tse, J. K.-P. (1983) 'The Language Situation in Taiwan (The Republic of China)', *Incorporated Linguist* 22: 82–5.

Karim, N. S. (1981) 'Bahasa Malaysia as a Medium of Instruction in a Modern, Plural Society' in A. H. Omar and N. E. M. Noor (eds) *National Languages as Medium of Instruction*, Kuala Lumpur: Dewan Bahasa Dan Pustaka Kementerian Pelajaran Malaysia.

Kearins, J. (1985) 'Cross-Cultural Misunderstandings in Education,' in J. B. Pride (ed.) *Cross-Cultural Encounters*, Melbourne: River Seine.

Keenan, V. and Keenan, V. (1971) 'On the Universality of Conversational Implications', *Language and Society* 5: 67–80.

Keenan, V. and Keenan, V. (1979) 'Becoming a Competent Speaker of Malagasy', in T. Shopen (ed.) *Languages and their Speakers*, Cambridge, MA: Winthrop.

Keesing, R. M. (1988) *Melanesian Pidgin and the Oceanic Substratum*, Stanford, CA: Stanford University Press.

Keesing, R. M. (1990) 'Solomons Pijin and Colonial Ideologies', in R. Baldauf and A. Luke (eds) *Language Planning and Education in Australasia and the South Pacific*, Clevedon, PA: Multilingual Matters.

Keesing, R. M. and Fifi, J. (1969) 'Kwaio Word Tabooing in its Cultural Context', *Journal of the Polynesian Society* 78(2): 154–77.

Keller, R. (1990) *Sprachwandel*, Tübingen: Francke UTB.

Keysser, C. (1929) *Eine Papuagemeinde*, Kassel (repr. 1950 Neuendettelsau: Freimund Verlag).

Kibrik, A. E. (1991) 'The Problem of Endangered Languages in the USSR', in R. H. Robins and E. M. Uhlenbeck (eds) *Endangered Languages,* Oxford: Berg.

King, J. (1909) *W. L. Lawes of Savage Islands and New Guinea*, London: Religious Tract Society.

Kinkade, M. D., Hale, K. and Werner, W. (eds) (1975) *Linguistics and Anthropology in Honour of C. F. Voegelin*, Lisse: De Ridder.

Kirschbaum, F. J. (1926) 'Miscellanea aus Neuguinea', *Anthropos* 21: 274–7.

Klarentius, Br (1909–10) 'Eine Schulwanderung über See', *Steyler Missionsbote* 37: 110.

Kloss, H. (1977) 'Ten Types of Language Planning', in B. P. Sibayan and A. Gonzales (eds) *Language Planning and the Building of a National Language*, Manila: Linguistic Society of the Philippines.

Kloss, H. (1978) *Die Entwicklung neuer germanischer Kultursprachen seit 1860*, Düsseldorf: Schwann.

Krämer, A. (1919) *Palau*, Hamburg: Friedrichsen.

Kraus, M. (1992) 'The World's Languages in Crisis', *Language* 68(1): 4–10.

Kreckel, M. (1981) *Communicative Acts and Shared Knowledge in Natural Discourse*, London and New York: Academic Press.

Kulick, D. (1991) *Having Head and Showing Knowledge*, Department of Anthropology, University of Stockholm.

Kulick, D. (1992) 'Language Shift as Cultural Reproduction', in T. E. Dutton (ed.) *Culture Change, Language Changes: Case Studies from Melanesia*, Canberra: *Pacific Linguistics* C120: 7–26.

Kulick, D. (1993) 'Growing Up Monolingual in a Multilingual Community', in K. Hyltenstam and A. Viberg (eds) *Progression and Regression in Language*, Cambridge: Cambridge University Press.

Kulick, D. and Stroud, C. (1989) 'Christianity, Cargo and Ideas of Self-Patterns of Literacy in the Papua New Guinea Village', *Man* 25: 286–304.

Kuo, E. C. Y. (1980) 'Language Planning in Singapore', *Language Planning Newsletter* 6(2): 1–4.

Kuo, E. C. Y. and Jernudd, B. H. (1988) 'Language Planning in a Multilingual State: The Case of Planning in Singapore', paper presented at the CAS-Dell Seminar on Language Planning in a Multilingual Setting, Singapore.

Kuykendall, R. S. (1968) *The Hawaiian Kingdom 1778–1854*, Honolulu: University of Hawaii Press.

Labov, W. (1972) *Sociolinguistic Patterns*, Philadelphia, PA: University of Pennsylvania Press.

Labov, W. (1975) *What is a Linguistic Fact?*, Lisse: De Ridder.

Ladefoged, P. (1992) 'Another View of Endangered Languages', *Language* 68: 809–11.

Larkin, F. (1975) 'Bilingual Education in Western Samoa', *South Pacific Commission*: 76–8.

Lavondès, H. (1971) 'Language Policy, Language Engineering and Literacy: French Polynesia,' in T. A. Sebeok (ed.) *Current Trends in Linguistics 8: Linguistics in Oceania*, The Hague: Mouton.

Lawrence, P. (1964) *Road Belong Cargo*, Australia: Melbourne University Press.

Laycock, D. C. (1966) 'Papuans and Pidgin: Aspects of Bilingualism in New Guinea', *Te Reo* 9: 44–51.

Laycock, D. C. (1969) 'Sublanguages in Buin', Canberra: *Pacific Linguistics* A22: 1–23.

Laycock, D. C. (1970) 'Language and Thought in a Polyglot Island', *Hemisphere* 14(8): 11–15.

Laycock, D. C. (1971) 'English and Other Germanic Languages', in T. A. Sebeok (ed.) *Current Trends in Linguistics 8: Linguistics in Oceania*, The Hague: Mouton.

Laycock, D. C. (1972) 'Towards a Typology of Ludlings, or Play Languages', *Linguistic Communications* 6: 61–114.

Laycock, D. C. (1973) *Sepik Languages: Checklist and Preliminary Classification*, Canberra: *Pacific Linguistics* B25.

Laycock, D. (1975a) 'Observations on Number Systems and Semantics', in S. A. Wurm (ed.) *New Guinea Area Languages and Language Study 1*, Canberra: *Pacific Linguistics* C38.

Laycock, D. C. (1975b) 'The Torricelli Phylum', in S. A. Wurm (ed.) *New Guinea Area Languages and Language Study 1*, Canberra: *Pacific Linguistics* C38: 767–80.

Laycock, D. C. (1977) 'Creative Writing in New Guinea Pidgin', in S. A. Wurm (ed.) *New Guinea Area Languages and Language Study 3*, Canberra: *Pacific Linguistics* C40.

Laycock, D. C. (1979a) 'Multilingualism: Linguistic Boundaries and Unsolved Problems in Papua New Guinea', in S. A. Wurm (ed.) *New Guinea and Neighbouring Areas: A Sociolinguistic Laboratory*, The Hague: Mouton.

Laycock, D. C. (1979b) 'Melanesia has a Quarter of the World's Languages', *Pacific Islands Monthly* 40(9): 71–6.

Laycock, D. C. (1981) 'Melanesian Linguistic Diversity: A Melanesian Choice?' in R. J. May and H. Nelson (eds) *Melanesia Beyond Diversity*, Canberra: Research School of Pacific Studies.

Laycock, D. C. (1985) 'The Future of Tok Pisin', in S. A. Wurm and P. Mühlhäusler (eds) *Handbook of Tok Pisin*, Canberra: *Pacific Linguistics* C70: 665–8.

Laycock, D. C. and Voorhoeve, C. L. (1971) 'History of Research in Papuan Languages', *Current Trends in Linguistics* 8: 509–40.

Laycock, D. C. and Winter, W. (eds) (1987) *A World of Language*, Festschrift for S. A. Wurm, Canberra: *Pacific Linguistics* C100.

Lee, J. (1987) *Tiwi Today: A Study of Language Change in a Contact Situation*, Canberra: *Pacific Linguistics* C96.

Lee, Kee-dong (1975) *Kusaiean Reference Grammar*, Honolulu: University of Hawaii Press.

Leeding, V. J. (1976) 'Contrasting Semantic Units in the Teaching of Concepts in a Bilingual Education Programme', paper presented at the Eighth Congress of the Linguistic Society of Australia, Adelaide.

Leibniz, G. W. (1713) Letter to Peter the Great, 26 October, Vienna, in von F. Adelung (1815) *Catherinens der Grossen Verdienste um die Vergleichende Sprachkunde*, St Petersburg.

Lennox, G. (1984) *Oyster Cove Historic Site*, Hobart: National Parks and Wildlife Service.

LePage, R. B. (1964) *The National Language Question*, Oxford: Oxford University Press.

LePage, R. B. (1992) 'Introducing Comment' (draft), paper presented at the Sèvres Workshop of the International Group for the Study of Language Standardization and the Vernacularization of Literacy (IGLSVL), Paris.

LePage, R. B. (1993) 'Language, Economy and Tolerance: An Interview with Benigno Fernandez Salgado', MS, University of Oxford.

LePage, R. B. and Tabouret-Keller, A. (1985) *Acts of Identity: Creole-Based Approaches to Language and Ethnicity*, Cambridge: Cambridge University Press.

Lewis, D. (1972) *We the Navigators*, Canberra: Australian National University Press.

Liberman, K. (1982) 'The Organization of Talk in Aboriginal Decision Making', *Anthropological Forum* 5(1): 38–53.

Lipski, J. M. (1987) 'Contemporary Philippine Spanish: Comments on Vestigial Usage', *Philippine Journal of Linguistics* 18: 37–48.

Lithgow, D. (1992) 'Language Change on Ferguson and Normanby Islands', in T. E. Dutton (ed.) *Culture Change, Language Changes: Case Studies from Melanesia*, Canberra: Pacific Linguistics C120: 27–47.

Litteral, R. (nd) 'Tok Pisin: The Language of Modernization', MS, Ukarumpa, Papua New Guinea: Summer Institute of Linguistics.

Litteral, R. (1975) 'A Proposal for the Use of Pidgin in Papua New Guinea's Education System', in K. A. McElhanon (ed.) *Tok Pisin i Go We?*, Port Moresby: Linguistic Society of Papua New Guinea.

Litteral, R. (1985) 'Vernaculars Education', *Papua New Guinea Journal of Education* 22: 41–8.

Love, N. (ed.) (1990) *The Foundations of Linguistic Theory: Selected Writings of Roy Harris*, London: Routledge.

Lovelock, J. E. (1992) 'The Earth is not Fragile', in B. Cartledge (ed.) *Monitoring the Environment*, Oxford: Oxford University Press.

Lüdi, G. (ed.) (1994) *Sprachstandardisierung*, Freiburg: Swiss Academy of Humanities and Social Sciences.

Lynch, J. D. (1979) 'Church, State and Language in Melanesia', inaugural lecture, Department of Languages, University of Papua New Guinea.

Lyons, M. (1986) *The Totem and the Tricolour*, Kensington: New South Wales University Press.

McConvell, P. (1981) 'Supporting the Two-Way School', in J. Bell (ed.) *Language Planning for Australian Aboriginal Languages*, Alice Springs: Institute for Aboriginal Development.

McConvell, P. (1982) 'Understanding Language Shift: A Step towards Language Maintenance', MS, University of the Northern Territory, Darwin.

McConvell, P. (1991) 'Understanding Language Shift: A Step towards Language Maintenance', in S. Romaine (ed.) *Language in Australia*, Cambridge: Cambridge University Press.

McDonald, B. (ed.) (1976) *Language and National Development: The Public Debate 1976*, Port Moresby: Department of Language, University of Papua New Guinea.

McDonald, B. (1977) 'Georg Friederici's "Pidgin Englisch in Deutsch-Neuguinea"', Department of Language Occasional Paper 14, Waigani: University of Papua in New Guinea.

McElhanon, K. A. (ed.) (1975) *Tok Pisin i Go We?*, Kivung Special Publication 1, Port Moresby: Linguistic Society of Papua New Guinea.

McElhanon, K. A. (1979) 'Some Mission Lingue Franche and their Sociolinguistic Role', in S. A. Wurm (ed.) *New Guinea and Neighboring Areas: A Sociolinguistic Laboratory*, The Hague: Mouton.

Mac Eoin, G., Ahlquist, A. and ÓhAodha, D. (eds) (1986) *Third International Conference on Minority Languages: General Papers*, Clevedon, PA: Multilingual Matters.

McGrath W. J. (1983) 'The Northern Territory Bilingual Program', *Education News*: 51–3.

McKay, G. R. (1982) 'Attitudes of Kunibidji Speakers to Literacy', *International Journal of the Sociology of Language* 36: 105–14.

Mackay, W. F. (1980) 'The Ecology of Language Shift', in *Zeitschrift für Dialektologie und Linguistik*, Beiheft 32–35–41.

McKenzie, D. F. (1987) 'The Sociology of a Text: Oral Culture Literacy and Print in Early New Zealand', in P. Burke and R. Porter (eds) *The Social History of Language*, Cambridge: Cambridge University Press.

Malcolm, I. G. (1982) 'Speech Use in Aboriginal Communities: A Preliminary Survey', *Anthropological Forum* 5(1): 54–104.

Malinowski, B. (1935) *Coral Gardens and their Magic*, London: Allen & Unwin.

Malinowski, C. (1930) 'The Problem of Meaning in Primitive Languages', in C. K. Odgen and I. A. Richards (eds) *The Meaning of Meaning*, London: Routledge & Kegan Paul.

Manchester, W. (1980) *Goodbye, Darkness*, Boston, MA: Little, Brown.

Mandelbaum, D. G. (ed.) (1949) *Selected Writings of Edward Sapir*, London: Cambridge University Press.

Mandelbaum, D. G. (ed.) (1966) *Sapir – Culture, Language and Personality*, Berkeley, CA: University of California Press.

Markey, T. L. (1986) 'When Minor is Minor and Major is Major: Language Expansion, Contraction and Death', in G. Mac Eoin *et al.* (eds) *Third International Conference on Minority Languages: General Papers*, Clevedon, PA: Multilingual Matters.

Markey, T. L. (1987) 'When Minor is Minor and Major is Major: Language Expansion, Contraction and Death', in G. M. Eoin *et al.* (eds) *Third International Conference on Minority Languages: General Papers*, Clevedon, PA: Multilingual Matters.

Markham, C. (ed.) (1904) *The Voyages of Pedro Fernandes de Quiros 1595 to 1605*, London: Hakluyt Society.

Matisoff, J. A. (1991) 'Endangered Languages of Mainland Southeast Asia', in R. H. Robins and E. M. Uhlenbeck (eds) *Endangered Languages*, Oxford: Berg.

May, R. J. and Nelson, H. (eds) (1981) *Melanesia Beyond Diversity*, Canberra: Research School of Pacific Studies.

Mead, M. (1931) 'Talk-Boy', *Asia* 31: 14–157, 191.

Meggitt, M. J. (1967) 'Uses of Literacy in New Guinea and Melanesia', *Bijohagen tot de taal landen en volkenkande (BTLV)* 123: 71–82.

Meinhof, C. (1905) 'Die Bedeutung des Studiums der Eingeborenensprachen für die Kolonialverwaltung', Berlin: *Verhandlungen des Deutschen Kolonial Kongresses*: 344–468.

Melody, W. H., Salter, L. R. and Heyer, P. (eds) (1981) *Culture, Communication and Dependency: The Tradition of H. A. Innis*, Norwood, NJ: Ablex.

Michaels, E. (1986) *Aboriginal Invention of Television*, Canberra: Australian Institute of Aboriginal Studies.

Milligan, J. (1859) 'On the Dialects and Languages of the Aboriginal Tribes of Tasmania, and on their Manners and Customs', *Papers and Proceedings of the Royal Society of Tasmania*, III(II): 275–82.

Milner, G. B. (1957) 'Mots et concepts étrangers dans la langue de Samoa', *Journal de la Société des Océanistes* 13: 51–68.

Milner, G. B. (1984) 'The New Missionaries? Language, Education and the Pacific Way', in C. Clerk (ed.) *The Effects of Development on Traditional Pacific Island Cultures*, London: Royal Commonwealth Society.

Milroy, L. (1980) *Language and Social Networks*, Oxford: Blackwell.

Miracle, A. W. (ed.) (1983) *Bilingualism, Social Issues and Policy Implications*, Athens, GA: University of Georgia Press.

Mithun, M. (1989) 'The Incipient Obsolescence of Polysynthesis: Cayunga in Ontario and Oklahoma', in N. C. Dorian (ed.) *Investigating Obsolescence*, Cambridge: Cambridge University Press.

Moeliono, A. M. (1994) 'Standardization and Modernization in Indonesian Language Planning', in G. Lüdi (ed.) *Sprachstandardisierung*, Freiburg: Swiss Academy of Humanities and Social Sciences.

Moore, R. E. (1988) 'Lexicalisation versus Loss in Wasco-Wishram Language Obsolescence', *International Journal of American Linguistics* 54: 453–68.

Moorehead, A. (1966) *The Fatal Impact*, Harmondsworth: Penguin.

Moresby, J. (1876) *Discoveries and Surveys in New Guinea and the D'Entrecasteaux Islands*, London: Murray.

Morgan, F. (1986) 'New Visions – Old Echoes: Radio and Television Training in South East Asia and the Pacific', paper presented at the First Canberra Conference on International Communication.

Mosel, U. (1980) 'The Influence of the Church Missions on the Development of Tolai', paper presented a the Twenty-First Deutscher Orientalistentag, Berlin.

Mosel, U. (1982) 'The Influence of the Church Missions on the Development of Tolai', in R. Carle *et al.* (eds) *Gava* (Festschrift Kahler), Berlin: Reimer.

Mühlhäusler, P. (1978a) 'Samoan Plantation Pidgin English and the Origin of New Guinea Pidgin', Canberra: *Pacific Linguistics* A54: 67–119.

Mühlhäusler, P. (1978b) 'Papuan Pidgin English Rediscovered', Canberra: *Pacific Linguistics* C61: 1,377–446.

Mühlhäusler, P. (1979) *Growth and Structure of the Lexicon of New Guinea Pidgin*, Canberra: *Pacific Linguistics* C52.

Mühlhäusler, P. (1980) 'German as a Contact Language in the Pacific', *Michigan Germanic Studies* 11(2): 163–89.

Mühlhäusler, P. (1982) 'Language and Communication Efficiency: the Case of Tok Pigin', *Language and Communication* 2(2): 105–22.

Mühlhäusler, P. (1985) 'Good an bad pidgin: nogut yu toktok kranki', in S. A. Wurm and P. Mühlhäusler, *Handbook of Tok Pisin*, Canberra: *Pacific Linguistics* C70: 275–91.

Mühlhäusler, P. (1987a) 'The Politics of Small Languages in Australia and the Pacific', *Language and Communication* 7(1): 1–24.

Mühlhäusler, P. (1987b) 'Evolution des langues pidgin dans le Pacifique', *Diogène* 137: 49–68.

Mühlhäusler, P. (1987c) 'The Identification of Language Mixing, with Special Reference to the Reef-Santa Cruz Situation', Canberra: *Pacific Linguistics* C100: 481–93.

Mühlhäusler, P. (1990a) 'Reducing Pacific Languages to Writing', in J. E. Joseph and T. J. Taylor (eds) *Ideologies of Language*, London: Routledge.

Mühlhäusler, P. (1990b) 'On the Causes of Accelerated Linguistic Change in the Pacific Area', in L. E. Breivik and E. H. Jahr (eds) *Language Change: Contributions to the Study of its Causes*, Berlin: Mouton de Gruyter.

Mühlhäusler, P. (1991a) 'Intercultural Communication in the Pacific Area in Precolonial Days', in R. Harlow (ed.) *Vical 2 – Western Austronesian and Contact Languages*, Auckland: Linguistic Society of New Zealand.

Mühlhäusler, P. (1991b) 'Language Planning and Small Languages: The Case of the Pacific Area', paper presented at the Swiss Academy Symposium on Language Planning, Chur.

Mühlhäusler, P. (1992) 'Preserving Languages of Language Ecologies: A Top-Down Approach to Language Survival', *Oceanic Linguistics* 31(2): 163–80.

Mühlhäusler, P. (1994) 'Language Planning and Small Languages: The Case of the Pacific Area', in G. Lüdi (ed.) *Sprachstandardisierung*, Freiburg: Swiss Academy of Humanities and Social Sciences.

Mühlhäusler, P. (1995) 'On the Relationship between Linguistic and Biological Diversity', in D. Myers (ed.) *The Politics of Multiculturalism in Asia and the Pacific*, Darwin: Northern Territory University Press.

Mühlhäusler, P. (1996) 'On the Effectiveness of Language Maintenance Programs', in R. Baldauf (ed.) *A Review of the Aboriginal and Torres Strait Islander Languages Initiatives Program*, Canberra: National Languages and Literacy Institute of Australia.

Mühlhäusler, P. and Charpentier, J. M. (forthcoming) 'Literacy of Small Languages with Special Reference to Melanesia and its Pidgin Languages'.

Mühlhäusler, P. and Harré, R. (1990) *Pronouns and People*, Oxford: Blackwell.

Mühlhäusler, P., Philpott, M. and Trew, R. (1996) 'Modern Communication Technology', in S. A. Wurm, P. Mühlhäusler and D. T. Tryon, (eds) *Atlas of Languages of Intercultural Communication in the Pacific Hemisphere*, Berlin: DeGruyter.

Müller, H. (1932) 'Mission und Arbeiter', in J. Hüskes (ed.) *Pioniere der Südsee*, Hiltrup: Herz-Jesu Mission.

Müller, M. (1875) *Science of Languages*, London: Longmans.

Murray, H. (1925) *Papua of To-Day*, London: King and Son.

Myers, D. (ed.) (1992) *The Great Literacy Debate*, Melbourne: Australian Scholarly Publishing.

Nayar, B. P. (1991) 'Review of K. A. Watson-Gegeo (ed.) *English in the South Pacific*', *Journal of Pidgin and Creole Languages* 6(2): 322–6.

Neketeli, O. M. (1984) 'Language Planning in Papua New Guinea: A National-ist Viewpoint', *Yagl-Ambu* 11(1): 1–24.

Nelde, P. H. (1986) 'Language Contact Means Language Conflict', in G. Mac Eoin *et al.* (eds) *Third International Conference on Minority Languages: General Papers*, Clevedon, PA: Multilingual Matters.

Neuendorf, A. K. (1977) 'Missionary lingue franche: Gogodala', in S. A.

Wurm (ed.) *New Guinea Area Languages and Language Study 3*, Canberra: *Pacific Linguistics* C40: 875–80.

Neuendorf, A. K. and Taylor, A. J. (1977) 'The Churches and Language Policy', in S. A. Wurm (ed.) *New Guinea Area Languages and Language Study 3*, Canberra: *Pacific Linguistics* C40: 413–19.

Nevermann, H. (1934) *Admiralitätsinseln*, Hamburg: Friederichsen.

Newbury, C. W. (ed.) (1961) *The History of the Tahitian Mission 1799–1830. Written by John Davies*, Cambridge: Cambridge University Press.

Newman, J. (ed.) (1980) *Proceedings of the Symposium on Language Planning*, University of Singapore.

Newman, J. (1986) 'Singapore's Speak Mandarin Campaign: The Educational Argument', *Southeast Asian Journal of Social Science* 14(2): 52–67.

Newman, J. (nd) 'Singapore's Speak Mandarin Campaign: The Educational Argument', MS, Darling Downs Institute of Advanced Education, Toowoomba.

Newton, H. (1914) *In Far New Guinea*, London: Seely Service.

Nieuwenhuis, G. J. (1925) *Het Nederlandsch in Indië*, Groningen: Wolters.

Nolde, E. (1966) *Welt and Heimat*, Cologne: DuMont Schanberg.

Nunes, S. S. (1965) 'Pidgin is Good: A New Attitude, A New Approach', *Hawaii School* 2(6): 4–8.

O'Barr, W. M. and O'Barr, J. F. (1976) *Language and Politics*, The Hague: Mouton.

Odgen, C. K. and Richards, I. A. (eds) (1930) *The Meaning of Meaning*, London: Routledge & Kegan Paul.

Oetomo, D. (1990) 'The Bahasa Indonesia of the Middle Class', *Prisma* 50: 68–79.

Okura, F. (1943) 'Speak American', *Hawaii Educational Review* 31: 268.

Oliver, D. (1951) *The Pacific Islands*, Cambridge, MA: Harvard University Press.

Olson, D. R. (1988) 'Interpreting Texts and Interpreting Nature: The Effects of Literacy on Hermeneutics and Epistemology', in R. Säljö (ed.) *The Written World*, Berlin: Springer.

Omar, A. H. and Noor, N. E. M. (eds) (1981) *National Languages as Medium of Instruction*, Kuala Lumpur: Dewan Bahasa Dan Pustaka Kementerian Pelajaran Malaysia.

Ong, W. J. (1982) *Orality and Literacy*, London and New York: Methuen.

Ortony, A. (ed.) (1979) *Metaphor and Thought*, Cambridge: Cambridge University Press.

Osmers, D. (1981) 'Language and the Lutheran Church on the Papua New Guinea Mainland', Canberra: *Pacific Linguistics* A61: 71–180.

Ozog, C. K. (1990) 'The English Language in Malaysia and its Relationship with the National Language', in R. A. Baldauf and A. Luke (eds) *Language Planning and Education in Australasia and the South Pacific*, Clevedon, PA: Multilingual Matters.

Ozolins, U. (1992) *The Politics of Language in Australia*, Cambridge: Cambridge University Press.

Pakir, A. (1991) Contribution to workshop on endangered languages, International Conference on Austronesian Linguistics, Hawaii.

Park, N.-S. (1989) 'Language Purism in Korea Today', in B. H. Jernudd and M. J. Shapiro (eds) *The Politics of Language Purism*, Berlin: De Gruyter.

Parr, C. S. (1963) 'Maori Literacy 1813–1867', *Journal of the Polynesian Society* 72: 211–34.

Parsonson, G. S. (1967) 'The Literate Revolution in Polynesia', *Journal of Pacific History* 3(2): 39–58.

Pattanayak, D. P. (1988) 'Monolingual Myopia and the Petals of the Indian Lotus', in T. Skutnabb-Kangas and J. Cummins (eds) *Minority Education: Shame to Struggle*, Clevedon, PA: Multilingual Matters.

Paulston, C. B. (1992) 'Linguistic Minorities and Language Policies', in W. Fase, K. Jaspaert and S. Kroon (eds) *Maintenance and Loss of Minority Languages*, Amsterdam: Benjamins.

Pawley, A. (1981) 'Melanesian Diversity and Polynesian Heterogeneity', in J. Hollyman and A. Pawley (eds) *Studies in Pacific Languages and Cultures*, Auckland: Linguistic Society of New Zealand.

Pawley, A. (1993) 'Kalam Pandanus Language: An Old New Guinea Experiment in Language Engineering', in T. E. Dutton, M. Ross and D. T. Tryon (eds) *The Language Game*, Canberra: *Pacific Linguistics* C110: 313–34.

Peddie, R. A. (1991) 'Coming – Ready or Not! Language Policy Development on New Zealand', *Language Problems and Language Planning* 15(1): 25–42.

Perez, A. Q., Santiago, N. O. and Liem, N. G. (eds) (1978) *Papers from the Conference on the Standardization of Asian Languages*, Canberra: *Pacific Linguistics* C47.

Perion (1554) *Dialogorum de Lingua Gallicae Origine ejusque cum Græcâ Cognatione, libri quatuor*, Paris.

Phillips, H. M. (1970) *Literacy and Development*, Paris: UNESCO.

Phillipson, R. (1992) *Linguistic Imperialism*, Oxford: Oxford University Press.

Philpott, M. (1993) 'Village Gutenberg: Papua New Guinea's Quiet Communication Revolution', paper presented at the National Conference of the Australian Communication Association, Melbourne.

Pilhofer, G. (1933) 'Grammatik der Kâte Sprache', *Zeitschrift für Eingeborenensprachen*, Beiheft 14.

Pilling, A. (1970) 'Changes in Tiwi Language', in A. R. Pilling and R. A. Waterman (eds) *Diprotodon to Detribalization*, East Lansing, MI: Michigan State University Press.

Pilling, A. and Waterman, R. A. (eds) (1970) *Diprotodon to Detribalization*, East Lansing, MI: Michigan University Press.

Plomley, N. J. B. (1976) *A Word List of the Tasmanian Aboriginal Languages*, Hobart: Government of Tasmania.

Plomley, N. J. B. (ed.) (1987) *Weep in Silence: A History of the Flinders Island Aboriginal Settlement*, Hobart: Blubber Head Press.

Pörksen, U. (1988) *Plastikwöerter*, Cotta: Klett.

Price, C. A. and Baker, E. (1976) 'Origins of Pacific Island Labourers in Queensland', *Journal of Pacific History* 11(2): 106–21.

Pride, J. B. (ed.) (1985) *Cross-Cultural Encounters*, Melbourne: River Seine.

Pride, J. B. and Holmes, J. (eds) (1972) *Sociolinguistics*, Harmondsworth: Penguin.

Purnama, K. (1991) 'The Sociolinguistic Pattern of Use of Standard Malay in Brunei Darussalam', MS, University of Brunei.

Randall, R. A. (1983) 'Ten Languages or Two? Southern Philippine Multilingualism', in A. W. Miracle (ed.) *Bilingualism, Social Issues and Policy Inplications*, Athens, GA: University of Georgia Press.

Read, E. (1980) 'Hercules or Hydra? Similarities and Differences amongst Evangelical Missions', *Survival International* 4: 9–16.

Read, P. (1981) *The Stolen Generations: The Removal of Aboriginal Children in New South Wales 1883 to 1969*, Occasional Paper 1, Sydney: New South Wales Ministry of Aboriginal Affairs.

Reddy, M. T. (1979) 'The Conduit Metaphor: A Case of Frame Conflict in our Language about Language' in A. Ortony (ed.) *Metaphor and Thought*, Cambridge: Cambridge University Press.

Reed, S. W. (1943) *The Making of Modern New Guinea*,' Philadelphia, PA: American Philosophical Society.

Reesink, G. P. (1990) 'Mother Tongue and Tok Pisin', in J. W. M. Verhaar (ed.) *Melanesian Pidgin and Tok Pisin*, Amsterdam: Benjamins.

Reinecke, J. E. (1937a) 'Trade Jargons and Creole Dialects as Marginal Languages', reprinted in D. Hymes (ed.) (1966) *Language in Culture and Society*, New York: Harper International.

Reinecke, J. E. (1937b) 'Marginal Languages', PhD thesis, Yale University.

Reinecke, J. E. (1938) 'Pidgin English in Hawaii', *American Journal of Sociology* 43: 778–89.

Reinecke, J. E. (1969) *Language and Dialect in Hawaii*, Honolulu: University of Hawaii Press.

Reinecke, J. E. (1987) 'William Greenfield: A Neglected Pioneer Creolist', in G. G. Gilbert (ed.) *Pidgin and Creole Languages*, Honolulu: Hawaii University Press.

Renck, G. (1978) 'Redend spricht sein Dasein aus', in H. Bürkle (ed.) *Theologische Beiträge aus Papua Neuguinea*, Erlangen: Verl der Ev. – Lutherischen Mission.

Renck, G. (1990) *Contextualization of Christianity and Christianization of Language*, Erlangen: Verl der Ev. – Lutherischen Mission.

Renck, G. (1992) 'Values and Semantic Changes in Yagaria', in T. E. Dutton (ed.) *Culture Change, Language Changes: Case Studies from Melanesia*, Canberra: *Pacific Linguistics* C120: 59–66.

Rensch, K. H. (1987) 'East Uvean, Nuclear Polynesia? Reflections on the Methodological Adequacy of the Tree Model in Polynesia', in D. C. Laycock and W. Winter (eds) *A World of Language*, Canberra: *Pacific Linguistics* C100: 565–601.

Rensch, K. H. (1990) 'The Delayed Impact: Postcolonial Language Problems in the French Overseas Territory Wallis and Futuna', *Language Problems and Language Planning* 14(3): 224–36.

Rensch, K. H. (1991) 'The Language of the Noble Savage; Early European Perceptions of Tahitian', in R. Blust (ed.) *Currents in Pacific Linguistics*, Canberra: *Pacific Linguistics* C117: 403–14.

Rhydwen, M. (1991) 'Kriol is the Colour of Thursday', MS, University of Sydney.

Rhydwen, M. (1993) 'Writing on the Backs of the Blacks' PhD thesis, University of Sydney.

Rickford, J. R. (1983) 'Standard and Non-Standard Attitudes in a Creole Continuum', *Society for Caribbean Linguistics Paper 16*, St Augustine: University of the West Indies.

Rickford, J. R. and Traugott, E. C. (nd) 'Symbol of Powerlessness and Degeneracy, or Symbol of Solidarity and Truth? Paradoxical Attitudes towards Pidgins and Creoles', MS, Stanford University, CA.

Rigsby, B. and Sutton, P. (1982) 'Speech Communities in Aboriginal Australia', *Anthropological Forum* 5(1): 8–23.

Riley, G. A. (1977) 'Attitudes toward Language Maintenance and Language Shift in the Guamian Speech Community', *Pacific Asian Studies* 2(1/2): 112–26.

Riley, G. A. (1980) 'Language Loyalty and Ethnocentrism in the Guamian Speech Community: Seven Years Later', *Anthropological Linguistics* 22(8): 326–33.

Rivierre, J.-C. (1985) 'La Colonisation et les langues en Nouvelle-Calédonie', *Les Temps Modernes* 41(464): 1,688–717.

Roberts, J. (1991) 'The Origins of Pidgin in Hawaii', paper presented at the Sixth International Conference on Austronesian Linguistics, Honolulu.

Robins, R. H. and Uhlenbeck, E. M. (eds) (1991) *Endangered Languages*, Oxford: Berg.

Robinson, O. W. (1943) 'The Case against Pidgin', *Hawaii Educational Review* 31: 169–81.

Rogers, D. M. (ed.) (1961) *The Early Journals of Henry Williams 1826–1840*, Christchurch.

Romaine, S. (ed.) (1991) *Language in Australia*, Cambridge: Cambridge University Press.

Romaine, S. (1992) *Language, Education and Development*, Oxford: Oxford University Press.

Rosaldo, M. (1984) 'Words that are Moving: The Social Meanings of Ilongot Verbal Art', in D. L. Brenneis and F. R. Myers (eds) *Dangerous Words: Language and Politics in the Pacific*, New York: New York University Press.

Ross, M. D. (1987) 'A Contact-Induced Morphosyntactic Change in the Bel Languages of Papua New Guinea', Canberra: *Pacific Linguistics* C100: 583–601.

Ross, R. M. (1972) 'Te Tiriti O Waitangi: Texts and Translations', *New Zealand Journal of History* 6(2): 130–57.

Rosser, B. (1990) *Up Rode the Troopers: the Black Police in Queensland*, St Lucia: University of Queensland Press.

Rubin, J. (1977) 'Indonesian Language Planning and Education', in J. Rubin *et al.* (eds) *Language Planning Processes*, The Hague: Mouton.

Rubin, J., Jernudd, B., Das Gupta, I. and Ferguson, C. (eds) (1977) *Language Planning Processes*, The Hague: Mouton.

Rule, J. (1977) 'Vernacular Literacy in the Western and Lower Southern Highlands Provinces: A Case Study of a Mission's Involvement', in S. A. Wurm (ed.) *New Guinea Area Languages and Language Study 3*, Canberra: *Pacific Linguistics* C40: 387–402.

Ryan, J. (1987) 'Te Kohunga Reo: The Language Learning Nests', *Language Maintenance Newsletter* 4: 6–9.

Salisbury, R. F. (1962) 'Notes on Bilingualism and Linguistic Change in New Guinea', *Anthropological Linguistics* 4(7): 1–13.

Salisbury, R. F. (1972) 'Notes on Bilingualism and Linguistic Change in New Guinea', in J. B. Pride and Holmes (eds) *Sociolinguistics*, Harmondsworth: Penguin.

Säljö, R. (ed.) (1988) *The Written World*, Berlin: Springer.

Samarin, W. J. (1971) 'Salient and Substantive Pidginization', in D. Hymes (ed.) *Pidginization and Creolization of Languages*, Cambridge: Cambridge University Press.

Samarin, W. J. (1982) 'Colonization and Pidginization on the Ubangi River', MS, Toronto.

Samarin, W. J. (1986) 'Sango of the Central African Republic', paper presented at the International Group for the Study of Language Standardization, York University, UK.

Sandefur, J. (1981) 'A New Aboriginal Language?', *The Aboriginal Child at School* 9(1): 52–60.

Sankoff, G. (1972) 'Language Use in Multilingual Societies: Some Alternative Approaches', in J. B. Pride and J. Holmes (eds) *Sociolinguistics*, Harmondsworth: Penguin.

Sankoff, G. (1976) 'Political Power and Linguistic Inequality in Papua New Guinea', in W. M. O'Barr and J. F. O'Barr (eds) *Language and Politics*, The Hague: Mouton.

Sankoff, G. (1977) 'Multilingualism in Papua New Guinea', in S. A. Wurm (ed.) *New Guinea Area Languages and Language Study 3*, Canberra: *Pacific Linguistics* C40: 265–307.

Sankoff, G. (1980a) *The Social Life of Language*, Philadelphia, PA: University of Pennsylvania Press.

Sankoff, G. (1980b) 'Political Power and Linguistic Inequality in Papua New Guinea', in G. Sankoff, *The Social Life of Language*, Philadelphia, PA: University of Pennsylvania Press.

Sankoff, G. (1980c) 'Multilingualism in Papua New Guinea', in G. Sankoff, *The Social Life of Language*, Philadelphia, PA: University of Pennsylvania Press.

Sapir, E. (1949a) 'Language', in D. G. Mandelbaum (ed.) *Selected Writings of Edward Sapir*, London: Cambridge University Press.

Sapir, E. (1949b) 'Language and Environment', in D. G. Mandelbaum (ed.) *Selected Writings of Edward Sapir*, London: Cambridge University Press.

Sapir, E. (1966) 'The Status of Linguistics as a Science', in G. Mandelbaum (ed.) *Sapir – Culture, Language and Personality*, Berkeley, CA: University of California Press.

Sato, C. (1990) 'Language Change in a Creole Continuum: Decreolization?', paper presented at the Conference on Progression and Regression in Language, Stockholm.

Scherer, K. R. and Giles, H. (eds) (1979) *Social Markers in Speech*, Cambridge: Cambridge University Press.

Scheurmann, E. (1921) *Der Papalagi*, Buchenbach: Felsen Verlag.

Schlesier, E. (1961) 'Über die Zweisprachigkeit und die Stellung der Zweisprachigen in Melanesien', in D. Drost and W. König (eds) *Beiträge zur Völkerforschung*, Berlin: Akademie Verlag.

Schmidt, A. (1985) *Young People's Dyirbal*, Cambridge: Cambridge University Press.

Schmidt, A. (1991a) *The Loss of Australia's Aboriginal Language Heritage*, Canberra: Aboriginal Studies Press.

Schmidt, A. (1991b) 'Language Attrition in Boumaa Fijian and Dyirbal', in H. W. Seliger and R. M. Vago (eds) *First Language Attrition*, Cambridge: Cambridge University Press.

Schmidt, J. (1953) *Vokabular und Grammatik der Muriksprache*, St Augustin: Microbibliotheia Anthropos.

Schnee, H. (1901) *Bilder aus der Südsee*, Berlin: Reimer.

Schnitzer, M. L. (1982) 'Against Effability', *Language and Communication* 2(2): 183–96.

Schooling, S. (1990) *Language Maintenance in Melanesia: Sociolinguistics and*

Social Networks in New Caledonia, Dallas, TX: Summer Institute of Linguistics.

Schuchardt, H. (1928) *Hugo Schuchardt Brevier* (Leo Spitzer ed.), Halle: Niemeyer.

Schuchardt, H. (1979) *The Ethnography of Variation: Selected Writings on Pidgins and Creoles*, Ann Arbor, MI: Karoma.

Schultze, E. (1933) 'Sklaven – und Dienersprachen', *Sociologus* 9: 378–418.

Schütz, A. J. (1976) 'Take *My* Word For It: Missionary Influence on Borrowings in Hawaiian', *Oceanic Linguistics* 15: 75–91.

Schütz, A. J. (1977) 'English Loanwords in Fijian', MS, Honolulu: University of Hawaii.

Schütz, A. J. (1985) *The Fijian Language*, Honolulu: University of Hawaii Press.

Schwimmer, E. (1965) 'The Cognitive Aspect of Culture Change', *Journal of the Polynesian Society* 74: 149–81.

Schwoerer, E. (1916) *Kolonialdeutsch*, Munich: Hueber.

Scott, R. P. (1977) 'Agricultural Problems and Pidgin', in S. A. Wurm (ed.) *New Guinea Area Languages and Language Study 3*, Canberra: Pacific Linguistics C40: 723–31.

Sebeok, T. A. (ed.) (1971a) *Current Trends in Linguistics 7: Linguistics in Sub-Saharan Africa*, The Hague: Mouton.

Sebeok, T. A. (ed.) (1971b) *Current Trends in Linguistics 8: Linguistics in Oceania*, The Hague: Mouton.

Senft, G. (1992) 'Changes Observed in Trobriand Islanders' Culture and Language', in T. E. Dutton (ed.) *Culture Change, Language Changes: Case Studies from Melanesia*, Canberra: Pacific Linguistics C120: 67–89.

Sharpe, M. C. (1981) 'Aboriginal Education Policies Prior to 1973 with Special Reference to Language', in J. Bell (ed.) *Language Planning for Australian Aboriginal Languages*, Alice Springs: Institute for Aboriginal Development.

Sharpe, M. C. and Sandefur, J. (1976) 'The Creole Language of the Katherine and Papua River Areas', in M. Vyne (ed.) *Australia Talks*, Canberra: Pacific Linguistics D23: 63–78.

Shopen, T. (ed.) (1979) *Languages and their Speakers*, Cambridge, MA: Winthrop.

Sibayan, B. P. and Gonzales, A. (eds) (1977) *Language Planning and the Building of a National Language*, Manila: Linguistic Society of the Philippines.

Siegel, J. (1987) *Language Contact in a Plantation Environment: A Sociolinguistic History of Fiji*, Cambridge: Cambridge University Press.

Siegel, J. (1989a) 'English in Fiji', *World Englishes* 8(1): 47–58.

Siegel, J. (1989b) 'Pidgins and Creoles in Education in Australia and the Southwest Pacific', paper presented at the Society for Pidgin and Creole Linguistics Meeting, Washington, DC.

Skutnabb-Kangas, T. and Cummins, J. (eds) (1988) *Minority Education: Shame to Struggle*, Clevedon, PA: Multilingual Matters.

Smith, G. H. (forthcoming) 'Kura kaupapa Maori: Contesting and Reclaiming Education in Aotearoa', in D. Ray and D. Poonwassie (eds) *Tomorrow Can Be Better*.

Smith, K. D. (1981) 'Bilingual Education in the Austronesian Languages of Vietnam circa 1974', in A. H. Omar and N. E. M. Noor (eds) *National*

Languages as Medium of Instruction, Kuala Lumpur: Dewan Bahasa Dan Pustaka Kementerian Pelajaran Malaysia.

Smolicz, J. J. (1982) 'Minority Languages and the Core Values of Culture: Changing Policies and Ethnic Response in Australia', paper presented at the Tenth Congress of Sociology, Mexico.

Smythe, S. J. (1984) *I Have the Honour to Remain Sir, Your Obedient Servant: 100 Years of Schooling in the Chathams*, Te One: Chatham Islands Education Centennial Committee.

Solenberger, R. R. (1962) 'The Social Meaning of Language Choice in the Marianas', *Anthropological Linguistics* 4(1): 59–64.

South Pacific Commission (1975) *Sub-Regional Conference on Bilingual Education Pago Pago*, Noumea: South Pacific Commission.

Spencer, J. (ed.) (1963) *Language in Africa*, Cambridge: Cambridge University Press.

Spencer, J. (1971) 'Colonial Language Policies and their Legacies', in T. A. Sebeok (ed.) *Current Trends in Linguistics 7: Linguistics in Sub-Saharan Africa*, The Hague: Mouton.

Spencer, J. (1985) 'Language and Development in Africa: The Unequal Equation' in N. Wolfson and J. Manes (eds) *Languages of Inequality*, Berlin: Mouton.

Spitzer, L. (1966) 'Creole Attitudes towards Krio: A Historical Survey', *Sierra Leone Language Review* 5: 39–49.

Spoehr, A. (1952) 'Time Perspective in Micronesia and Polynesia', *Southwestern Journal of Anthropology* 8: 457–65.

Staalsen, P. (1969) 'The Dialects of Iatmul', Canberra: *Pacific Linguistics* A22: 69–84.

Steiner, G. (1975) *After Babel*, Oxford: Oxford University Press.

Strauss, H. (1971) 'Die Sprachenfrage in Neuguinea,' *Evangelische Missionszeitschrift* 28: 65–78.

Strehlow, T. G. H. (1942) *Aranda Traditions*, Melbourne: Melbourne University Press.

Strehlow, T. G. H. (1966) 'On Aranda Traditions', in D. Hymes (ed.) *Language in Culture and Society*, New York: Harper International.

Stross, B. (1975) 'Variation and Natural Selection as Factors in Linguistic and Cultural Change, in M. D. Kinkade, K. Hale and W. Werner (eds) *Linguistics and Anthropology in Honour of C. F. Voegelin*, Lisse: De Ridder.

Sutton, P. (1980) 'Australian Language Names, in S. A. Wurm (ed.) *Australian Linguistic Studies*, Canberra: *Pacific Linguistics* C54: 87–105.

Sutton, P. (1991) 'Language in Aboriginal Australia: Social Dialects in a Geographic Idiom', in S. Romaine (ed.) *Language in Australia*, Cambridge: Cambridge University Press.

Sutton, P. (1992) 'Last Chance Operations: "BIITL" research in Far North Queensland in the 1970's', in T. E. Dutton, M. Ross and D. T. Tryon (eds) *The Language Game*, Canberra: *Pacific Linguistics* C110: 451–7.

Tagupa, W. E. H. (1979) The Tahitian Language: A Historical and Vernacular Controversy', *Pacific Studies* 2: 144–55.

Taylor, A. J. (1968) 'A Note on the Study of Sociolinguistics, with Particular Reference to Papua New Guinea', *Kivung* 1(1): 43–52.

Teichelmann, C. G. and Schurmann, C. U. (1840) *Outlines of a Grammar of the Aboriginal Language of South Australia*, Adelaide: Thomas & Co.

Teleni, V. (1990) 'Language Planning and Education in Melanesia and Polynesia: The Annotated Bibliography', in R. B. Baldauf and A. Luke (eds) *Language Planning and Education in Australasia and the South Pacific*, Clevedon, PA: Multilingual Matters.

Terrell, J. (1986) *Prehistory in the Pacific Islands*, Cambridge: Cambridge University Press.

Thies, K. (1987) *Aboriginal Viewpoints on Education*, Perth: National Centre for Research on Rural Education, University of Western Australia.

Thirwall, C. and Hugen, P. J. (eds) (1989) *The Ethics of Development*, Port Moresby: University of Papua New Guinea Press.

Thomas, A. (1990) 'Language Planning in Vanuatu', in R. Baldauf and A. Luke (eds) *Language Planning and Education in Australasia and the South Pacific*, Clevedon, PA: Multilingual Matters.

Thompson, R. C. (1980) *Australian Imperialism in the Pacific*, Melbourne: Melbourne University Press.

Thurston, W. R. (1982) *A Comparative Study in Anêm and Lusi*, Canberra: *Pacific Linguistics* B85.

Thurston, W. R. (1987) *Processes of Change in the Languages of North-Western New Britain*, Canberra: *Pacific Linguistics* B99.

Thurston, W. R. (1988) 'How Esoteric Languages Build a Lexicon: Esoterogeny in West New Britain', paper presented at the Fifth International Conference on Austronesian Linguistics, Auckland.

Thurston, W. R. (1992) 'Sociolinguistic Typology Effecting Change in North-Western New Britain', in T. E. Dutton (ed.) *Culture Change, Language Changes: Case Studies from Melanesia*, Canberra: *Pacific Linguistics* C120: 123–39.

Toffler, A. (1970) *Future Shock*, London: Pan.

Toffler, A. (1975) *The Eco-Spasm Report*, New York: Bantam.

Tollefson, J. W. (1991) *Planning Language, Planning Inequality*, London: Longman.

Topping, D. M. (1973) *Chamorro Reference Grammar*, Honolulu: University of Hawaii Press.

Topping, D. M. (1991) 'Language and Social Change in the Pacific Islands', MS, Department of Linguistics, University of Hawaii, Honolulu.

Topping, D. M. (1992) 'Language and Social Change in the Pacific Islands', paper presented at the Sixth International Conference on Austronesian Linguistics, Honolulu.

Trainum, M. (1993) 'District Multi-Language Resource Centres: A Community-Based Model for Communication in Papua New Guinea', paper presented at the National Communication Seminar, Port Moresby, Papua New Guinea.

Trudgill, P. (1983a) *On Dialect*, Oxford: Blackwell.

Trudgill, P. (1983b) 'Language Contact, Shift and Identity', in P. Trudgill, *On Dialect*, Oxford: Blackwell.

Tryon, D. T. (1979) 'The Language Situation in the New Hebrides', in S. A. Wurm (ed.) *New Guinea and Neighboring Areas*, The Hague: Mouton.

Tryon, D. T. (1988) *Illiteracy in Melanesia: A Preliminary Report*, Canberra, Australian Advisory Council on Languages and Multiculturalism Education Occasional Paper 2, Canberra.

Turner, G. W. (1966) *The English Language in Australia and New Zealand*, London. Longman.

Underwood, R. (1989) 'English and Chamorro on Guam', in K. A. Watson-Gegeo (ed.) *English in the South Pacific*, Oxford: Pergamon.

UNESCO (1953) 'The Use of Vernacular Languages in Education', *Monographs on Fundamental Education VIII*, Paris: UNESCO.

UNESCO (1989) *Plan of Action to Eradicate Illiteracy by the Year 2000*, Paris: UNESCO.

Valdman, A. (ed.) (1979) *Le Français hors de France*, Paris: Honoré Champion.

Van der Berghe, P. (1968) 'European Languages and Black Mandarins', *Transition* 34(7): 19–23.

Verhaar, J. W. M. (1989) 'Language Problems: In General and in Papua New Guinea,' MS, Divine Word Institute, Madang.

Verhaar, J. W. M. (ed.) (1990) *Melanesian Pidgin and Tok Pisin*, Amsterdam: Benjamins.

von Pferdekämper (1906) 'Etwas über Vergleichung von Sprachen', *Der Ostasiatische Lloyd* 16: 933–4.

Voorhoeve, C. L. (1979) 'Turning the Talk: A Case Study of Chain Interpreting in Papua New Guinea', in S. A. Wurm (ed.) *New Guinea and Neighboring Areas: A Sociolinguistic Laboratory*, The Hague: Mouton.

Walker, J. B. (1898) 'Notes on the Aborigines of Tasmania, Extracted from the Manuscript Journals of George Washington Walker', *Papers and Proceedings of the Royal Society of Tasmania for 1897*: 145–75.

Walsh, D. S. (1984) 'Is "English-Based" an Adequately Accurate Label for Bislama?', paper presented at the Fifty-Fourth ANZAAS Congress, Canberra.

Wardhaugh, R. (1987) *Languages in Competition*, Oxford: Blackwell.

Wassmann, J. (1982) *Der Gesang an den Fliegenden Hund*, Basle: Ethnologisches Seminar der Universität.

Watson-Gegeo, K. A. (1986) 'The Study of Language Use in Oceania', *Annual Review of Anthropology* 15: 149–62.

Watson-Gegeo, K. A. (1989a) 'English in the Solomon Islands', *World Englishes* 8(1): 21–32.

Watson-Gegeo, K. A. (1989b) *English in the South Pacific*, special issue of *World Englishes* 8(1), Oxford: Pergamon.

Watts, B. H., McGrath, W. J. and Tandy, J. C. (1973) *Bilingual Education in Schools in Aboriginal Communities in the Northern Territory*, Canberra: Australian Department of Education.

Weber, G. (1990) 'The End: Scattered Thoughts on the Decline and Fall of Languages', *Language International* 2(5): 5–13.

Whinnom, K. (1954) 'Spanish in the Philippines: Sociolinguistic Survey', *Journal of Oriental Studies* 1(1).

White, G. (1929) *A Pioneer of Papua*, London: Society for Promoting Christian Knowledge.

Whiteman, D. L. (1974) 'The Christian Mission and Culture Change in New Guinea', *Missiology* II(1): 17–33.

Whorf, B. L. (1956) *Language, Thought and Reality*, Cambridge, MA: MIT Press.

Wilkes, J. (ed.) (1958) *New Guinea and Australia*, Sydney: Angus & Robertson.

William, J. (1837) *A Narrative of Missionary Enterprises in the South Sea Islands*, London: John Snow.

Williams, C. H. (1979) 'An Ecological and Behavioural Analysis of Ethnolinguistic Change in Wales', in H. Giles and B. Saint-Jacques (eds) *Language and Ethnic Relations*, Oxford: Pergamon.

Williams, John (1865) *A Narrative of Missionary Enterprises in the South Sea Islands*, London: John Snow.

Williams, J. P. (1990) 'A Preliminary Survey of Papuan-Based Pidgins', paper presented at the Third International Conference on Pidgins and Creoles in Melanesia, Lae.

Williams, R. (1983) *Keywords*, London: Fontana.

Wilson, W. (1937) 'Speech Problems in Hawaii', *Quarterly Journal of Speech* 23(1): 106–18.

Wolfson, N. and Manes, J. (eds) (1985) *Language of Inequality*, Berlin: Mouton.

Wonderley, W. L. and Nida, E. A. (1963) 'Linguistics and Christian Missions', *Anthropological Linguistics* 5(1): 104–44.

Wurm, S. A. (1971a) 'Language Policy, Language Engineering and Literacy. New Guinea and Australia', in T. A. Sebeok (ed.) *Current Trends in Linguistics 8: Linguistics in Oceania*, The Hague: Mouton.

Wurm, S. A. (1971b) *Papuan Languages of Oceania*, Tübingen: Narr.

Wurm, S. A. (ed.) (1975) *New Guinea Area Languages and Language Study 1: Papuan Languages and the New Guinea Linguistic Scene*, Canberra: *Pacific Linguistics* C38.

Wurm, S. A. (ed.) (1977) *New Guinea Area Languages and Language Study 3: Language, Culture, Society and the Modern World*, Canberra: *Pacific Linguistics* C40.

Wurm, S. A. (ed.) (1979) *New Guinea and Neighboring Areas: A Sociolinguistic Laboratory*, The Hague: Mouton.

Wurm, S. A. (ed.) (1980) *Australian Linguistic Studies*, Canberra: *Pacific Linguistics* C54.

Wurm, S. A. (1981) 'Roles on Nominal Classification Systems in Ayiwo', in A. Gonzales and D. Thomas (eds) *Linguistics across Continents*, Manila: Linguistic Society of the Philippines.

Wurm, S. A. (1982) *Northern Part of Borneo, Southern Part of Borneo*, Maps 41 and 42 in S. A. Wurm and S. Hattori (eds) *Language Atlas of the Pacific Area*, Canberra: *Pacific Linguistics* C66.

Wurm, S. A. (1983) 'Grammatical Decay in Papuan Languages', paper presented at the Fifteenth Pacific Science Congress, Dunedin.

Wurm, S. A. (ed.) (1987) *Language Atlas of China*, Hong Kong: Academy of the Humanities and the Chinese Academy of Social Sciences.

Wurm, S. A. (1991a) 'Language Death and Disappearance', in R. H. Robins and E. M. Uhlenbeck (eds) *Endangered Languages*, Oxford: Berg.

Wurm, S. A. (1991b) 'Language Decay and Revivalism: The Ayiwo Language of the Reef Islanders', in R. Blust (ed.) *Currents in Pacific Linguistics*, Canberra: *Pacific Linguistics* C117: 551–60.

Wurm, S. A. (1992) 'Changes of Language Structure and Typology in a Pacific Language', in T. E. Dutton (ed.) *Culture Change, Language Changes: Case Studies from Melanesia*, Canberra: *Pacific Linguistics* C120: 141–57.

Wurm, S. A. (1994) 'The Red Book of Languages in Danger of Disappearing', *New Language Planning Newsletter* 8(4): 1–4; 9(1): 1–3.

Wurm, S. A. and Hattori, S. (eds) (1982) *Language Atlas of the Pacific Area*, Canberra: *Pacific Linguistics* C66.

Wurm, S. A. and Laycock, D. C. (1962) 'The Question of Language and Dialect in New Guinea', *Oceania* 37: 128–43.

Wurm, S. A. and Mühlhäusler, P. (eds) (1985) *Handbook of Tok Pisin*, Canberra: *Pacific Linguistics* C70.

Wurm, S. A., Mühlhäusler, P. and Tryon, D. T. (eds) (1996) *Atlas of Languages of Intercultural Communication in the Pacific Hemisphere*, Berlin: DeGruyter.

Yarupawa, S. (1986) *Milne Bay Informal Variety of English*, Port Moresby: Department of Language and Communication Studies, University of Papua New Guinea.

Young, F. (1926) *Pearls from the Pacific*, Edinburgh: Marshall Bros.

Young, R. L. (1988) 'Language Maintenance and Language Shift in Taiwan', *Journal of Multilingual and Multicultural Development* 9: 323–8.

Yule, V. (1988) 'English Spelling and Pidgin', *English Today* 4(3): 29–35.

Index